THE PRESENTING PAST

THE PRESENTING PAST

THE CORE OF PSYCHODYNAMIC COUNSELLING AND THERAPY

Third edition

MICHAEL JACOBS

OPEN UNIVERSITY PRESS

Open University Press
McGraw-Hill Education
McGraw-Hill House
Shoppenhangers Road
Maidenhead
Berkshire
England
SL6 2QL

email: enquiries@openup.co.uk
world wide web: www.openup.co.uk

and Two Penn Plaza, New York, NY 10121–2289, USA

First published 2006

Reprinted 2006, 2007, 2008, 2009

A catalogue record of this book is available from the British Library

ISBN–10: 0 335 21766 4 (pb) 0335 22017 7 (hb)
ISBN–13: 978 0335 21766 3 (pb) 978 0335 22017 5 (hb)

Library of Congress Cataloging-in-Publication Data
CIP data applied for

Typeset by YHT Ltd, London, UK
Printed in the UK by Bell and Bain Ltd, Glasgow

Mixed Sources
Product group from well-managed
forests and other controlled sources
www.fsc.org Cert no. TT-COC-002769
© 1996 Forest Stewardship Council

FSC

CONTENTS

'It's in vain, Trot, to recall the past,
unless it works some influence upon the present.'
Charles Dickens, *David Copperfield*

Time present and time past
Are both perhaps present in time future,
And time future contained in time past
T. S. Eliot, 'Burnt Norton', in *Four Quartets*

PREFACE TO THE
THIRD EDITION

It never ceases to amaze me how much a book needs to be revised in the course of just a few years. When a new edition is necessary, there are of course references which need updating: the publication of books about psychotherapy and counselling is sometimes like a flood tide, overwhelming in the amount of words and ideas that could be absorbed if only there were time.

But what is surprising is the amount of text that needs to be changed, partly because of fresh thinking, and partly because what has felt more certain in the past needs to be qualified in the light of experience. I am aware of a much wider debate, because since the second edition I have edited what is now an almost complete series, published by Open University Press, under the title *Core Concepts in Therapy*. The authors of those volumes have shown how pervasive psychodynamic ideas are, as well as how they are paralleled in other therapeutic orientations. My thinking has been enlarged in the process of seeing that series through, as has my attitude to my own discipline. Indeed over the 20 years since the first edition of *The Presenting Past* was published there have been great changes in the way I think and act as a therapist, although without ever feeling the need to discard the core concepts of psychodynamic theory. The editions of this text reflect those changes, although few readers will want to put the different editions side by side to monitor my own development.

The principal changes in this edition can be summarized as introducing more attachment theory, and dividing what were formerly three very long chapters into what are now nine chapters. Most of the other changes are of a cosmetic character, tidying up pedantic English, toning down some of the more definite assertions, referring the reader to more recent literature, and occasionally introducing something that is at least new for me. Since my own life has changed since the second edition, with retirement bringing the opportunity to engage with other interests, while at the same time continuing in a small way to offer therapy to a few clients, I have little doubt that I shall not revise this book again. The time has come to let it go, knowing that I will continue to nurture my thinking and practice, and hoping that this book will help the reader do likewise; it has served well for all those years, and probably has some life left in it yet – like its author! But I encourage the reader of a few years hence to consider whether their questions and disagreements with what is written here may then also (hopefully!) be mine. It is the dynamic part of the term 'psychodynamic' that is so important.

Michael Jacobs
Swanage, Dorset
June 2005

PREFACE TO THE
SECOND EDITION

Writing about the past and the present, in the course of a major revision of the first edition of this book, I am very conscious of the significance of time. In the first place, there has been quite a passage of time since I wrote the manuscript for the original edition, and the present – some thirteen years on. I am amazed at how much the world has moved on since then, not only with topical references to the Thatcher years being thankfully obsolete, but also in the changes in attitudes, which is reflected in a comparison of some of the issues referred to in each edition. The way relationships are described has changed ('fiancé' is now an outdated term); and there are welcome shifts in values, which this new text reflects. But even more so I realize how much my own thinking has developed in such a relatively short time. Any text becomes fixed in print when it is published, and I am aware, reading the first edition in detail, how it reflects a particular stage of my own development as a therapist and counsellor. I was less questioning then than I am now of my psycho-analytic roots. Nevertheless I am more in touch with those roots, and the passing of years has seen more thorough application on my own part of the ideas of a wide variety of psychoanalytic writers. I and this book are still steeped in the fertile waters of that particular form of theory and practice, but perhaps more freely floating than I was before.

I am aware too that the term 'psychodynamic' has developed a meaning that has given psychodynamic counsellors and therapists an identity of their own outside the narrower psychoanalytic community. I find, still somewhat to my surprise, that my writing has contributed to the ever-growing interest in and fascination with psychodynamic counselling – much better represented now both in the literature of counselling, and in its practice. This too is a significant change in the counselling world, in a relatively short time, although the psychodynamic has always been better represented amongst psychotherapists.

Time also shows me how in the first edition I hovered on the edge of stage theory and lifelong themes. I could not let Erikson's ages go, and so took them as chapter headings; yet I was already playing seriously with the idea of themes and variations. This new edition takes a decisive leap out of stage theory and developmental models into the timelessness of themes, something which always was recognized in the principle of the past being played out in the present.

As I write I am conscious also of the future. It is doubtful whether I will revise this book so radically again. Since the time of its revision has in its own way become frozen in print, I recognize that in time some parts of this edition will become outdated. If this second edition continues to have the success of the first, the reader in a few years' time must remember that ideas develop, theoretical positions change, values shift, and research throws up new information. I cannot anticipate those changes, however much I wonder what they may be. I have stressed throughout this edition how prone psychological and psychodynamic thinking is to cultural and social construction. By all means let the reader question my assumptions, and challenge my mistakes; but consider too that it is possible that I may also be doing the same, wondering in years to come what can have possessed me to write such-and-such, however much what I write at present is the latest in my own thinking.

It is difficult to believe, given a first edition of over 25,000 copies, that there was some doubt about accepting this book back in 1984, when Harper & Row were first considering it. I have John Skelton and the Open University Press to thank for finding the book amongst a package bought from Harper & Row, and for giving it the promotion that has enabled its success. I was fortunate in writing the right book at the right time. In more recent years Jacinta Evans has encouraged and facilitated my work with the Open University Press, and I thank her and all the staff, with whom I also currently work as an editorial consultant, for their hard work on producing this edition. I also thank my wife Moira, who constantly supports my writing and my other work; and who, like me, will no doubt be pleased that now this major revision is over, we shall have just a little more time for ourselves.

Staying on a family note, a new edition and a new preface gives me the chance to mention a new generation, who were not even a twinkle in an eye in the first preface. In their own way they take my past and that of my forebears into the future. This book is then particularly dedicated to my grandchildren, for the moment Laura and Joshua, and without imposing pressure on my children, perhaps others yet to come. While we hope to change the present by what we learn from the past, only future generations will know whether or not we were successful. Some day, sooner than we think, they will be our keenest critics.

Michael Jacobs
Leicester 1997

PREFACE TO THE
FIRST EDITION

Without two groups of people this book would not have been possible. The first consists of those clients with whom I have worked over twelve years, who have provided confirmation (at times) and the necessity of refinement (at other times) of analytic theory. Should any of them, despite my disguises, recognize themselves, or parts of themselves which today are hopefully less troublesome than once they were, let me reassure them that their identity remains known only to me. And I can only thank them for all they have taught and given me.

The second group consists of the students at Vaughan College, Leicester, who by their questions, their confusions, and their wish for material to be relevant to their helping work, have forced me to clarify what I mean when I use terms used in analytic theory. So often in teaching it is the teacher who learns most. Apart from the lecture material which my colleague Alan Lilley and I have given, our classes have studied Lowe's *Growth of Personality* and Rayner's *Human Development*. The influence of both will be obvious (and I hope acknowledged) in various places in the text. Since Eric Rayner was at one time my own therapist, his influence will no doubt be more extensive than even I have realized. Yet Low lacks illustrations of counselling situations and Rayner's ideas, although thought provoking, are frequently so terse that their relevance to counselling can easily be missed. I hope I have been able to provide a ready-reference for counsellors which draws together, and supplements, longer and more detailed texts recommended in counselling training, and that in doing so I may help establish the relevance of analytic theory for those who are tempted to rely on the here-and-now alone.

Others, past and present, have been important in my own development: different generations of my own family have helped mould me, and present friends, especially Denis Rice, and Simon and Mary Phipps, have positively encouraged my teaching and writing. All these people illustrate for me the significance of my theme, and my hope is that they will share in anything of merit found in these pages.

Michael Jacobs
Leicester 1985

WHAT'S PAST IS PRESENT

The elements of psychodynamic practice

'What's past is past – let it go', some people say. 'It's water under the bridge', say others. 'You can't change the past, but you can live for the future'. These similar expressions convey an attempt to 'move on', 'achieve closure', as some people put it. What they are probably referring to are things that have gone wrong, unpleasant memories, which are best forgotten. They probably would not say the same about past good experiences, happy memories, or about treasuring moments that bring pleasure. The truth is that we are formed through a variety of experiences, some remembered, some forgotten, some that make us who we are now, some of which have left little mark. Most people and most therapies recognize this, and few would only wish to concentrate upon the here-and-now and the future. Past, present and future are linked inseparably in the way we think and act.

It is sometimes thought that psychoanalysis, or psychodynamic counselling and therapy are principally interested in the past, and involve digging around in a person's history for the events or event that have led to what troubles that person now. There is some truth in this picture, but only some. This book aims to demonstrate how awareness of the past, and of perceptions arising from former experiences informs the present, and in some cases even governs present ways of being, acting and thinking. Psychodynamic therapy (I shall use this term to cover counselling and psychotherapy) is actually more about the present than the past, but works on the premise that in understanding something of the past, and its influence upon the present, the path towards change becomes clearer, if often not much easier to negotiate. Yet the relationship between past and present is rather more complex. Not only may a person be influenced in the present by memories of the past, but memories of the past may be influenced by present experience.

Furthermore, although this book concentrates upon the particular relationship between what has been and what is, this is played out not in combing a client's history, or through learning by making intellectual connections. In addition to the importance of basic listening and responding skills (see, for example, Jacobs 2000b), the essence of psychodynamic work lies in the therapeutic relationship where past and present come together in the meeting of therapist and client, sometimes through the phenomenon of transference; or just as often in the complex interplay between clients' relationships to the therapist, to others in their current situations, and to those who figure strongly not just in memories but also currently in what psychodynamic theory calls 'the internal world': any one personality contains the voices – sometimes obvious and sometimes subtle in their influence – of other persons who have left an imprint upon us.

So a psychodynamic approach engages the therapist in three different ways. The first and fundamental way is the practical application of a number of ways of enabling, containing and understanding the therapeutic relationship, such as I have described in Jacobs (2001, 2004b). Many of the features of psychodynamic practice are shared with other therapeutic approaches, but there is a particular stress in psychodynamic work in ensuring regular, time-boundaried sessions, with encouragement for free association and free-floating attention on the part of client and therapist respectively. Added to this a psychodynamic approach is concerned with identifying the reasons for defences and resistance, as well as trying wherever possible to identify transference and countertransference experiences in client and therapist respectively. But these should never become mere techniques. The psycho-dynamic approach demands a real depth of personal engagement between therapist and client, which extends through empathy and what are often known as core conditions in other therapies towards a concentration on how the therapeutic relationship reflects other relationships – past and present – in the client's experience.

Only with concentration upon the relationships that the client describes with others in the present, and which the client demonstrates in different aspects of the therapeutic encounter, does the second part of a psycho-dynamic approach come alive – otherwise it remains pure theory. This second element is the use of a model or models of how human beings might develop from infancy, through childhood and adolescence into adult life, and what this process imparts to them along the way. This chapter in particular looks at the use of models generally, while the key chapters on trust and attachment, on authority and autonomy and on cooperation and competition relate these models to some major themes and demonstrate the relevance of these themes in therapy. These models provide a series of pointers to what may have proved difficult in the past, and similarly proves difficult in the present.

It is not only therapists who wish to understand how a person's past experience influences the present. Clients also ask 'Why do I feel this way?' and because we live in a post-Freudian world they sometimes search for answers in their upbringing, in their childhood as well as in their adult experience. Just as in medicine a doctor has a picture of what is healthy, and therefore what constitutes disease or abnormality, and just as a doctor asks about the history of an illness or injury in order the more appropriately to heal it, so a psychodynamic therapist draws upon either a single model, or a number of models, to understand what may particularly need to be addressed in order to assist a client towards the healing of emotional suffering, difficult relationships, or unwanted behaviours. Since Freud was trained originally in medicine, it is not surprising that he looked at a person's history in order to formulate some sort of diagnosis. He used the examples of uncovering, layer by layer, as if in an archaeological dig (to use his own metaphor), layers of the mind (or of consciousness) until early trauma might be found. From his work with a large number of patients he was able to formulate his own ideas about human development, which he initially situated in the arena of sexuality. Psychoanalytic theory, which informs much psychodynamic work, has moved into many other dimensions of psychological development since Freud, but the principle remains.

Developmental psychology is a wide discipline. Psychologists, who may or may not also be therapists, are interested in many different features of human development, but psychoanalytic and psychodynamic interest in personal development tends to focus on the development of relatedness to self and others, the formation of character, and the place of emotions in the developing person. The different models upon which a psychodynamic therapist may draw suggest ways of understanding different experiences and reactions:

Ann came to see a counsellor in her first year at university. She had deferred her place for 12 months because her father had died two months before she was originally due to go to university. She thought she had worked through her grief, during a year in which she had first nursed her dying father, then had to look after her younger sister and help console her mother (who had left Ann's father and the family some years earlier). She was frightened when, soon after coming away to college, she found herself crying at what felt to her like the slightest provocation. She thought she should have grown through all that.

The understanding of the processes of mourning was significant in Freud's own development of theory, and since then there have been various studies of the grieving process, often linked to one psychodynamic model or another. Mourning is a developmental process, which may be influenced by past experience, but which is a model in its own right, and Ann's counsellor had initially trained as a Cruse bereavement counsellor. She knew that for Ann to experience such grief 15 months after the death of someone so significant to her was not unusual, and that it might have been delayed in its impact because she had had to spend so much time looking after the interests of others in her family. Her own feelings had little space to be expressed when she had to be strong for others. Now she had only herself to look after; combined with coming away from a home that had been one point of stability, this meant she was 'free' to listen to herself. Her counsellor was able to reassure Ann that her feelings were normal and that their late onset was understandable. Early in the first session she said to Ann, 'You've been so preoccupied looking after everyone else that you haven't had the chance to look after yourself'. A little later in that same session, Ann said she thought she could cope on her own now. The little history the counsellor knew of Ann's family suggested to her, as she did to Ann, that when her mother left Ann had to become the capable one, upon whom others depended. It was perhaps difficult for her to consider that someone might now look after her a little. Ann agreed to a second session and went on to meet with her counsellor for six months. This not only provided a space each week for Ann to express feelings that she had up to that point been unable to share; their relationship also provided a balance to a situation where Ann had learned that her role was to care, not to think about being cared for.

By contrast, an older woman, Beth, also nursed her father when he was dying, but could still not bring herself to use a room in her father's house (which she had inherited) for herself, even though her father had died in that room ten years ago. Her mother also had left the home and family years before, and (like Ann) Beth had been deeply attached to her father. But her complete inability to contemplate even entering the room, except for the briefest time, made it obvious that hers was a grieving process that had gone beyond the normal bounds. It was as if the room stood for some part of her thoughts and feelings that were locked away. Therapy in her case was much longer, during which more complex family relationships had to be unravelled and in one sense 'exorcized' (Beth at one stage talked of bringing in a priest), before she was able to contemplate first entering the room, and in the end feeling it was right to use the room as her own.

These two examples show different aspects of the experience of bereavement. There are many good studies of the process of grief that can enrich the counsellor's sensitivity and expertise and that demonstrate the contribution a psychological model can make to such presentations (e.g. Worden 1991; Lendrum and Syme 2004). Lendrum and Syme, for example, set out the phases of adult mourning (2004: 40) which are very similar to the examples given by Collick (1986):

shock:	'I just went cold.'
numbness and unreality:	'This isn't me.'
disbelief:	'It can't be true.'
yearning:	'Come back.'
emptiness:	'An aching void.'
searching:	'He must be somewhere.'
anxiety:	'Must I sell the house?'
anger:	'He had no right to leave me like this.'
guilt:	'If only . . .'
remembering:	'I'm afraid of forgetting.'
depression:	'I'm too tired to bother.'
loss of identity and status:	'Who am I?'
stigma:	'I'm an embarrassment to others.'
sexual deprivation:	'To have someone's arms round me.'

loss of faith:	'Why?'
loneliness:	'I just dread weekends.'
acceptance:	'He'd have laughed about it.'
healing:	'The loved object is not gone, for now I carry it within myself and can never lose it' (Abraham 1927).

Figure 1.1 An example of the stages of bereavement

Freud (1917) was one of the first to identify the similarity between some cases of depression (or melancholia, as he called it) and aspects of the process of mourning. He suggested that in mourning an identification takes place between the person who is in mourning and the person who has been lost. This can result in anger that is experienced towards the person who has 'gone away' being directed at oneself, explaining the irrational quality of self-loathing that can be experienced by a person who is depressed. Developing his ideas on identification later Freud thought that when a person is relinquished, that person is in some sense set up inside the ego, contributing to the build-up of the character of the one who has experienced the loss (1923/2003: 119). These processes of incorporation, internalization, identification or introjection (all these terms can be used almost synonymously) also partially lead, in Freud's view, to the formation of the conscience, or the super-ego: this is formed from internalization of the parent. The critical or warning 'voice' which many people are aware of in themselves is often capable of being identified, upon closer questioning, with one or both parents, at least as they were perceived by the client when a child (for a study of internalization across therapeutic disciplines see Wallis and Poulton (2001)).

Starting with this insight into the process of mourning, psychoanalytic thinking has come to see how all kinds of significant external relationships are internalized in the process of human growth and development. This internalization process starts as early as life itself, when early separations involve both some kind of loss, and the need to replace that which is lost. Many powerful experiences contribute to the way in which we develop, not only in guiding us one way or another, but in building up our inner life and character.

Freud's paper on mourning and melancholia, and his later papers that developed his idea of internalization, provided the spur for a major development in psychoanalytic thinking known now as 'object relations theory'. The term 'object' sounds very impersonal, although it stands generally for human objects, in other words, ordinary persons. It means the object of a person's thoughts or desires, which may sometimes be a thing (Winnicott (1975: 229–42)) uses the term 'transitional object' of something like a teddy bear), but is more usually a person, or one aspect of another person (a 'part-object'). One person may be seen as a 'good object', another as a 'bad object', which certainly are better expressions than a 'good person' or 'bad person', since these imply it is the person who *is* good or bad, rather than what is really meant, that the person is *perceived* as good or bad. Object relations theory is an example of the third element of a psychodynamic approach, a highly speculative area of theory, which is concerned with how a person, or more particularly what we might call their personality, develops through a process of internalization, of relations both to persons in the external world, as well as internalized objects or part-objects in a person's internal world (that is, in a manner of speaking, in their 'mind'). These objects are perhaps better understood as metaphors, ways of trying to portray mental processes, impossible to demonstrate objectively but providing a way of talking about personal development and personality structure.

How the personality might be structured has always been an area of speculation which Freud aptly called 'meta-psychology', since it bears the same relationship to empirical psychology that 'meta-physics' (a type of philosophical reasoning about the spiritual or the immaterial) has to the way empirical science deals with matter. When using the terms 'mind' and 'structure' in this context we need to remember that 'mind' has one meaning to a therapist, which may be unrelated to the way the brain or intellect can be understood by a neurologist or a psychologist, or the one understood by a philosopher.

To describe 'personality' as having a 'structure' is to use a metaphor that appears to give personality a definite form. There are different models of personality structure within psychoanalysis, and therefore in psychodynamic thinking, as well as in other therapeutic schools (see Totton and Jacobs 2001; Brinich and Shelley 2002). The most familiar psychoanalytic model of personality structure is Freud's tri-partite division: id, ego and super-ego (1923/ 2003: 103–49). As Freud himself recognized, this is not a map of actual parts of the human brain. In some ways this simple picture of personality, and of the struggle that sometimes goes on between one side of a person and another ('Shall I?', 'No, I mustn't', 'But I want to', 'What shall I do?') is actually quite useful, without the need to use those Latinate terms which the original English translators coined in place of Freud's much more ordinary personal pronouns. These terms are pointers to the basic conflict that can exist between our desires and our needs (the id) on the one hand, and our internalized sense of what is right and wrong (the super-ego) on the other, in which the ego ('me' or perhaps the central self) often feels to be acting as the arbiter, while trying simultaneously to relate to the demands of the external world. Some psychoanalytic models have become more complex than Freud's original structure, although Melanie Klein presents another relatively simple model of the internal conflict between 'good objects' and 'bad objects', a different type of conflictual model to that between id and super-ego (Segal 1992: 39–40). The good objects provide us with a sense of nurturing and comfort (even when we are on our own), the bad objects are experienced as attacking and persecuting us (even when there is no external threat).

Other analysts suggest different 'divisions' of the personality. Winnicott, for example, refers to the 'true self' and the 'false self' (1965b: 140–52), an apt description for the way we can experience ourselves as acting a part in a compliant way, rather than being in touch with a more genuine expression of ourselves. Jung elaborates a multi-dimensional model of human personality, including a structure consisting of the ego, the persona (a social self rather than the more pervasive false self in Winnicott), the shadow and the self. Jung describes character in terms that have become common parlance: 'extrovert' and 'introvert', and he distinguishes between feeling, sensing, thinking and intuitive character types, as well as describing a male and female principle that exists at least potentially in every woman and man respectively (see Samuels 1985a: 55–83).

A different structure again was put forward by the Scottish analyst Fairbairn – in many ways a difficult writer to grasp – using different terms to identify aspects of the personality. Fairbairn abandons Freud's concept of the id altogether, instead suggesting that a baby is born with a 'unitary ego'. The baby seeks an object (a person) to relate to, rather than an object to provide relief of tension such as hunger. This unitary ego is differentiated in the early weeks after birth, as a result of the experience of both the satisfaction and the frustration of object (or personal) relationships. This fragmentation leads to an unconscious libidinal ego (an ego that seeks the promise of relatedness); an unconscious anti-libidinal ego (that is hostile to such contact or gratification); and a conscious central ego which is 'the self of everyday life' (Guntrip 1961: 330). The relevance of such a theory can be seen in an example quoted by Guntrip, of a man who has relationships with three women: one with his critical and rejecting wife; one with a sexually exciting but inaccessible mistress; and one in his fantasy with an ideal woman (p. 325; Guntrip provides one of the most accessible descriptions of Fairbairn's ideas, as well as a helpful history of the development of psychoanalytic models of personality structure up to the 1950s).

Some of these ways of describing personality structure are referred to later in this book, since the language they use helps to describe (although does not necessarily explain) a client's personal experience or provides the therapist with pointers to possible internalized interactions which are truly dynamic – in other words, there is a real movement and energy between these different parts of the self. It is as well, however, to remember that these are all images and metaphors used in attempts to describe the different dimensions of human experience. Just as the poet Gerard Manley Hopkins could write that 'the mind, the mind has mountains; cliffs of fall/Frightful, sheer no-man-fathomed', so the language used by psychoanalysts to describe the mind has the same symbolic quality, portraying an area of experience which is in many ways unfathomable. The ability to draw upon these different sets of metaphors, without becoming too concerned for their actual veracity, can be advantageous. A therapist does not have to adhere rigidly to one psychodynamic model of personality structure. There are occasions when the simple tripartite model of id, ego and super-ego (and indeed, as we shall see, straightforward Freudian Oedipal theory) appears to fit the picture that a particular client presents. There are other occasions when only Melanie Klein's stark picture of infancy and childhood seems adequately to describe the client's and therapist's experience of each other. Chapter 3 contains examples of how apt her concepts can be, even if at first sight her writing often seems fantastic and 'over the top', with its images of 'biting', 'tearing apart' and 'destroying the good object'. We can therefore think of the extensive library of psychoanalytic literature as providing in its own way as rich a variety of human character and relationships in the reading of the therapist and counsellor as a library of novels, poetry and drama does in our reading at leisure.

These three elements – the therapeutic relationship, theories of development and theories of personality structure – therefore constitute the psychodynamic approach. Just as there is postulated a dynamic movement and relationship between therapist and client, between past and present, between the external world and the internal world, and between different 'parts' of the personality, so in my view the psychodynamic therapist must allow a creative dynamic to exist between these different models – models of personal development, models of personality types and models of personality structure – not only those that emanate from the psychoanalytic tradition, but from other therapeutic traditions as well. This book concentrates upon psychoanalytic theories as they might be seen in clinical work. The reader's attention is drawn, however, to the ground-breaking series *Core Concepts in Therapy*, published by Open University Press, which extends beyond the psychoanalytic to the other major schools of psychotherapy.

Models and stages

It is the models of human development that have been developed within the psychoanalytic tradition that principally inform this book. There is of course more opportunity for research in relation to psychological development than there is in the meta-psychology of personality structure, although within psychoanalysis theories tend to arise out of clinical observation rather than from more rigorously controlled research methods. This makes for a weakness compared to some other branches of psychology, and for more speculation from the observation of particular client groups. Such a weakness is no bad thing, as long as therapists do not take the models as definitive, since, as I argue in Chapter 2, the individual client is more important than the theory and the more apparently objectively proved the theory, the greater the difficulty in allowing clients to speak for themselves, out of their own experience.

It is possible therefore for scientists to measure physical growth and the development of manual and mental skills with sufficient accuracy to be able to demonstrate the range of normal developments: what a child might be expected to weigh, be able to do, be able to say, or to be able to solve, at a certain age. Nevertheless even such maps of physical, locomotor and cognitive development are approximations. Psychological development, at least in respect of emotional responses and relationships, is less easy to map, although the maps that are produced still have value. The stages of grief, for example, can be described with some accuracy, but the order in which those stages appear can vary greatly. Lendrum and Syme point out, immediately following their table of the phases of mourning, that:

> These phases do not occur one after another, but overlap. The feelings often associated with one phase are sometimes associated with another phase as well. We can move from one phase to the next and back again

... The way in which these phases are experienced is different for each individual and relates to the uniqueness of each person and their personal life-history.

(2004: 40)

There are, then, more variables in a life history making for greater variation in the negotiation of phases of grief than would influence physical growth, or, as an example, the vicissitudes of puberty when considered from a physical perspective alone.

Nevertheless, man (and I use the noun deliberately) likes to exercise some sort of control over mysteries, and there are a large number of models of personality development, one of the earliest being Freud's (1905) postulation of psychosexual stages. Other such models employing the concept of stages are referred to later. Yet a key text on developmental psychology emphasizes that 'the term stage, used simply to describe observations, as is often done in everyday language, has no scientific or explanatory value' (Mussen *et al.* 1969: 23). Stages do not explain behaviour, although they do have some value in the sense of making distinctions clearer. They may help us to see the wood for the trees. Stages are generally distinct periods of development, where certain aspects of behaviour, thought or expression (which often occur together and are therefore clustered) are obviously present in a way that was not evident earlier. Although stage theory has this descriptive value (which is why it is helpful to introduce some examples here) it is essentially artificial, a construct of the theorist rather than an endemic feature in human nature. Such theories have their weaknesses, particularly the tendency to put people into boxes, and label them normal or abnormal depending upon whether or not they appear to have successfully negotiated the sequence of stages expected of them by age or life position. This is not necessarily the intention of the theorist, but it is a consequence of such writing, as I caution more fully in Chapter 2. Measuring development by stage or age is something that many parents are aware of as they observe their children's growth; for some it is a natural concern to see their child take new steps; for others it becomes an ambitious anxiety which frequently has a deleterious effect upon the child, who always feels the obligation to achieve. Erikson called this 'a projection on child development of that success ideology which can so dangerously pervade our private and public daydreams' (1965: 265). I shall explain other reservations about using developmental models further in the next chapter.

When Freud put forward his theory of infantile sexuality, he outlined three stages of development, each of which is focused upon one part of the child's body, which becomes for that stage the source of satisfaction or 'pleasure', although is not 'lost' as the next stage is reached. His is therefore what looks like a three-stage theory consisting of oral, anal and phallic phases where first the mouth, then the anus, and then the penis or the lack of a penis are the focus of the child's concern. It is also a very physical, or body-centred, theory, which in that aspect alone has merit, because in the course of time psychoanalytic theory became too divorced from the 'soma' or the body, tending to dwell overmuch on the 'psyche' or mind. The first stage, the oral, centres upon feeding, with the mouth being the means of satisfaction of hunger and of 'incorporation' of the breast (Freud 1905: 117). The second stage, the anal, shifts attention to 'mastery through the agency of somatic musculature' (p. 117). Although the focus of this stage sometimes appears to concentrate upon the relief and pleasure of defecation, there is also anxiety related to the question of bowel and bladder control. It is also important to note that Freud includes the pleasure of muscular exercise generally and wonders whether this has 'any connection with sexuality' (p. 122). The third stage is the phallic or genital, where questions of sexual differences and the origin of babies form a focus of the child's interest and anxiety. Later Freud was to call this the phallic phase, reserving the genital phase for its fuller expression in adolescence.

Yet it is more than a three-stage model, because Freud adds another phase, that of latency, which I shall describe more fully later. By implication there is also the stage of adolescence, making five stages or phases in all. Adulthood is not delineated as having any particular stages, although Freud may imply that much of adult life consists of working through the legacy of the stages of childhood. Despite its weaknesses, particularly around the phallic phase and the question of gender difference, this model (together with the Oedipus complex which is an integral part of it) can throw light on some of the ways in which adult clients present themselves and their relationships in therapy and counselling.

The weaknesses in the model are obvious. It focuses so much upon the erotic pleasure of various parts of the body, and on the satisfaction of the child's needs, that it appears to neglect any real relationships with others, except inasmuch as those people provide or frustrate satisfaction for the child. My own oversimplification of course neglects the vast corpus of Freud's writing in which can be found qualifications to what appears to be a completely egocentric picture of a child's needs or drives. Another difficulty is the way in which the term 'sexual' is used, as if it is to be equated with genital sexuality. Sexuality as we commonly understand it is of course much more the subject of the third stage of development, or, in its full expression, reserved for adolescence onwards.

Nevertheless the prevalence and pleasure of oral and anal foreplay in adult sexual play are recognized by Freud, as they must be by all therapists, as part of a fuller picture of sexual behaviour, so that it is perhaps not far-fetched to suggest the presence of eroticism in the early childhood stages of orality and anality. Thinking about sexual relations and their link to other forms of relating, the model is insufficient when it appears to suggest that relationships are largely about the need to discharge tension (erotic or otherwise). However, this can be true of some situations and of some people. Freud certainly did not suggest freedom of sexual expression. Another part of his model involved the aim-inhibited love between people, where sexuality has been subsumed into a different kind of loving, which does not require sexual satisfaction.

Another model which presents a more complete picture of adult life, but which takes a clear lead from Freud's psychosexual stages, is Erikson's psychosocial theory of the 'Eight Ages of Man'. It is called 'psychosocial' rather than 'psychosexual' because sexuality occupies a less obvious place in

Erikson's scheme, while societal aspects assume a larger dimension. Although Erikson gave a title to his model largely before gender consciousness made the word 'man' less acceptable in intellectual discourse about humankind generally, he does in fact show a male bias in his work, which feminist psychologists and therapists have criticized (see for example Gilligan 1982). Indeed the reader needs to be conscious of this criticism in relation to all developmental studies, since so many are researched and interpreted by male psychologists or psychotherapists.

Nevertheless Erikson's scheme has much to be said for it, especially if it is adapted and applied in a less definitive way than the model is drawn, which is as a series of clear steps. Used more loosely and with less emphasis on consecutive stages, his ideas as described in each of the stages he identifies provide features of personal development which in my opinion run through the different chronological ages of an individual's life.

Erikson extends Freud's three (or five) stages into adult life, making eight in all; and he frames the issues of each age as being much more than erotic pleasure or frustration, and about much more than the satisfaction of bodily desires. The differences can be seen by placing the two sets of stages alongside each other, as in Figure 1.2. Set alongside the Erikson stages are the tasks that he suggests are key issues in each age; in order to illustrate the parallels and difference I add my own summary of what might be considered the aims of each stage or phase in Freud's scheme.

Freud	Aims	Erikson	Task
oral stage	feeding	oral	basic trust vs mistrust
anal stage	muscular pleasure	muscular–anal	autonomy vs shame and doubt
phallic phase	Oedipal resolution	locomotor–genital	initiative vs guilt
latency phase	learning	latency	industry vs inferiority
adolescence	genital expression	adolescence	identity vs role confusion
(adulthood)	love and work	early adulthood	intimacy vs isolation
		mid-adulthood	generativity vs stagnation
		late adulthood	integrity vs despair

Figure 1.2 Erikson's extension of Freud's stage model

There are a number of other stage models used in developmental psychology and in psychoanalytic theories. One such is Piaget's (1950) model of intellectual functioning, with four stages, the final one of which (that of conceptual thinking) begins at around the age of 11. Using Piaget, but building further upon the model in his research of the development of moral thinking, Kohlberg (1981) proposes stages in the way we make moral judgements. This research was questioned in some of its conclusions, and then refined to take account of gender differences by Kohlberg's colleague Carol Gilligan (1982). Taking the stage theories of Piaget, Kohlberg and Erikson together as the main resources for his own research design, Fowler (1981) mapped out the development of stages of faith or belief, which I at one time drew upon in my own study of the psychology of belief (Jacobs 1993), with some criticism of Fowler's final stages. Other developmental studies can be found in the work of Havighurst or in the observations of psychologists who have concentrated upon adulthood, such as Levinson *et al.* (1978) or Golan (1981). These and other theories are well documented by Sugarman (1986). It is interesting to note how many of those referred to in this paragraph were published as major pieces of research at around the same time, as though stage theory had then its greatest popularity.

How might such stage theories be useful in therapy and counselling? They suggest, of course, tasks and attitudes, strengths and weaknesses – whether physical, emotion-related or intellectual – which a therapist might expect to find in clients of different ages, and which generally can be said to contribute towards adult maturity, or be signs of degrees of immature development. Older psychoanalytic models of what happens when people break down suggest that where there is a crisis or a conflict for an individual he or she will tend to regress, seeking a position of relative safety or security. Technically known as 'regression', this psychological defence was likened by Freud, using militaristic terms, to an army needing to retreat to its first secure base before building up strength to face the enemy again. Pursuing this metaphor, people can then regroup, or in psychological terms renegotiate earlier issues which were not favourably dealt with earlier. Another possibility in psychoanalytic terminology is that people can become in some respects 'fixed' or stuck at a particular stage of development, and demonstrate, for example, a dependent, obsessional, or competitive character, depending upon whether their developmental block is located in oral, anal or phallic stages (to use the Freudian psychosexual model). This is similarly a defence, known as 'fixation'.

The Erikson model is a progressive one, and thinking in terms of regression or fixation can be used as a template to locate possible sources of personal difficulty. His eight ages have some resemblance to a staircase, in which one tread rests upon the other; or even to a tower of children's wooden building bricks. As long as each brick is placed squarely upon the one below, and the first one has a firm foundation, the tower remains stable as it grows upward. Using Erikson's terms, where sufficient trust is achieved in the first age, through its foundation in a reliable relationship with a nurturing parent, this forms a strong base upon which to achieve autonomy in the second age. Upon autonomy is then built the capacity for initiative, and so on. Staying with this image, if the bricks are not set squarely upon each other, the tower grows but has inbuilt structural weaknesses. There comes a point at which either the stress of external circumstances (in the analogy, a heavy footstep nearby), or the internal pressures (the structural stresses of its construction) causes the tower to collapse. This especially occurs when one of the lower bricks has not been placed squarely: in other words, where there is some form of developmental 'weakness' or incompleteness, due to the prevailing circumstances of that period of a person's life, this leads to a predisposition to vulnerability in certain situations.

When such a tower falls, it normally falls only as far as the first badly placed brick. It seldom takes the lower, stable bricks with it. So it is in a human crisis. On this theory where the weight of later stresses in adult life, external or internal, impose impossible strain, collapse or breakdown frequently goes back as far as the stage at which developmental issues were not satisfactorily resolved. It is therefore possible that a therapist, learning more about a person's history, especially of their childhood and adolescence, will be able to locate a point or more likely a series of points at which obvious trauma occurred, which has left a 'fault' (Freud indeed compared it to a geological fault, not a moral one) in the personality structure. Balint (1968) used the phrase 'basic fault' of early damage. The following might be an example:

Chris had been delivered prematurely by Caesarean section shortly before his mother's death. After a short period with his father, he was moved to his father's parents' home, where he spent the first two years of his life.

When his father married again, Chris (who had seen little of him in the intervening years) was moved back to his father's family, where the rest of his childhood was relatively untroubled, although his relationship with his father was always strained.

In his adult life Chris found himself attracted emotionally and physically to women a good deal older than himself. His own sense of this was that he was continually searching for the mother (and the grandmother) whom he had lost so young – there was of course this double loss of the person to whom he had been deeply attached, first by the umbilical cord, and then by the process of attachment to the grandmother. Through his therapy he was able to return (in imagination and in actuality) to places associated with his mother. In his therapy particular attention focused upon the breaks (for holidays) and eventually upon the termination of the therapy, which itself had to be premature. The links to his separation from key maternal figures assisted him in understanding why his feelings about these aspects of the therapeutic relationship were so strong.

Where there have been particular traumatic events earlier in life, it is not surprising that they should have influenced a person's attitude to certain situations thereafter. Emotional scars stay as long as physical scars, but in some cases never completely heal. Freud's original work focused particularly on the precipitating trauma which had led to the patient's symptoms, although in the earliest days of his practice he did not always seek this trauma in early childhood, but in more recent history, as in, for example, his analysis of Elizabeth von R. (Freud and Breuer 1895/2004: 139–86) where her physical pains seemed to be linked with more recent events in her adult life. It is a caricature of psychodynamic therapy to imagine that the therapist is looking for a particular traumatic incident as the sole explanation of current difficulties. The idea that 'I must have been dropped on my head when I was a baby' is as far-fetched as the myth of instantaneous cure following the dramatic uncovering of a long-repressed incident. Nevertheless the sentiment behind such imaginings about therapy contains a sufficient germ of the truth, that the past does influence the present.

Therapists gather considerable information about a client's history from the stories that clients tell, and from the questions that clients themselves ask about their own history. But the past can also be seen actively working in the present. The difficulties that a client brings frequently represent a repetition, if sometimes in a different form, of former situations or relationships. This is what Freud meant by the phrase 'the return of the repressed'. What has been forgotten, sometimes because it was too painful or threatening to a person's self-image, can show itself in different forms. Relationship styles which clients adopt towards the therapist, particularly in the earlier stages of therapy, can reflect past relationships, a phenomenon known as 'transference'. This is not confined to therapeutic relationships, so that a psychodynamic therapist also looks for repeated patterns in the client's description of current relationships. Experience suggests, and some of the examples in this book confirm, that thinking about and re-experiencing past relationships helps both client and therapist to make sense of where they find themselves in the here and now.

One view of development that can therefore be taken from stage theory or a model based on distinct ages is that unfinished business and unresolved issues from the past often have a powerful effect on living in the present. By implication satisfactory resolution of present issues in the therapeutic relationship can help the past (and indeed the future) to be faced, renegotiated and in some respects even relived 'but with a new ending' (Alexander and French 1946).

Nevertheless, as I have already suggested, such models of progressive stages have serious weaknesses, as indeed do certain elements of research into developmental psychology as a whole (see Chapter 2). The first is that these stage models are somewhat arbitrary in their divisions of human growth and development into definite ages. Stage theories can differ considerably as to the number of stages that are posited, and where the beginning and end of each stage is located in chronological age. One of the virtues of the Levinson model (Levinson *et al.* 1978) is that it includes periods of transition between the major life stages, periods that are long enough (five years) to make it unwise to look to a particular age (age 13, for example) as the start of a particular developmental stage (such as adolescence). Another difficulty is that a linear model not only suggests that development goes in a straight line, but also appears to imply that once a stage has been negotiated satisfactorily the basic tasks related to it have been accomplished; or, using Erikson's Eight Ages, that the basic strengths have been acquired once and for all. This is plainly not so: the question of trust, the issue that Erikson identifies as central to the first age, appears in different forms throughout life, and changes its object at different stages. The blind trust of the baby is not helpful in the second age, where increased mobility means learning not to trust situations and objects which are potentially dangerous: fires, stairs and so on. Parents of the second-stage child have themselves to learn a new kind of trust, which involves being careful and watchful but not overcautious, since anxiety about danger will communicate itself to the child and probably inhibit the child's exploring and experimenting. This therefore is a type of trust that is an integral part of being a parent, which is a major aspect of Erikson's sixth age of generativity. The basic strengths or 'virtues' (Erikson's term) which form the focus of each stage continue to develop throughout life, in the new circumstances that constantly present themselves. Erikson himself recognized this, stating in a footnote: 'The assumption that at each stage a goodness is achieved which is impervious to new inner conflicts and to changing conditions is, I believe, a projection on child development of that success ideology which can so dangerously pervade our private and public daydreams' (1965: 265n).

One way of overcoming this particular weakness in the Erikson model is to picture it not as a straight staircase, but to combine the image of a series of steps with an image I have already used, that of a tower of development. By introducing a cyclical element into progression instead of the linear model, personal development might be seen as more like a spiral staircase. In effect we might then say that each of the eight 'treads' which Erikson calls the Eight Ages are repeated in each complete turn of a circular staircase, as it ascends the tower: in each of the chronological ages all the issues that Erikson identifies (of trust, autonomy, initiative, industry, identity, intimacy, generativity and integrity) are therefore repeated in the same or different form. For example, while the development of intimacy is associated in Erikson's model with young adulthood, intimacy is an integral part of the mother–baby relationship, and if it is missing in the first stage is going to make achievement of intimacy difficult at any later stage. Creativity, linked by Erikson to the mid-adult, is part of play, and therefore is also featured in the childhood stages, as in latency where it enables learning; and in Winnicott's view it is also a vital part of the infant experience, with the illusion that is fostered by the mother that the infant has created the breast (see Chapter 3, and Winnicott 1975: 239). Integrity, or wholeness, as well as acceptance of reality are similar issues involved in overcoming the splitting of early experience in Klein's view of the infant (Segal 1992: 53), as they are in Erikson's identification of these aspects as central to negotiating late adulthood.

A good example of the presence of aspects of all Erikson's ages in one stage can be found in a closer examination of the issues that arise in adolescence, where it is sometimes thought that the strengths and weaknesses from childhood are thrown into the melting pot. There is a plasticity about adolescence, which means the possibility of reworking issues. While adolescence is a definite stage in Erikson's model, it is also a major transitional time between childhood and adulthood. A number of issues become more real than ever before, because the adolescent now has the strength, the will and the status to enact what in childhood years could only be fantasies. Using Erikson's Eight Ages, the first three major themes of early childhood – trust, autonomy and initiative – are taken up in adolescence in new ways, with a greater opportunity for realizing them fully. In addition adolescents in industrial societies are in education until at least their mid-teens, so that issues from Freud's and Erikson's latency period struggle for a place among the strong reawakened emotions of earlier stages. This is one of the difficulties adolescents have to face, when strong emotions and forces threaten to interfere with educational tasks. Adolescence is a time of rapid change in moods and aspirations.

Adolescence can therefore be seen as a watershed in Erikson's model, especially if we follow the division of adolescence into three periods – early, middle and late – suggested by Laufer (1974) and others. Figure 1.3 shows how each of these successive sub-stages in turn take up themes from the first three ages. Thus early adolescence, with sexual development pushed more obviously into consciousness by physical changes at puberty, picks up the themes of sexuality from the third age. At the same time this set of issues points forward, preparing the sexual identity of a young person for the sixth age of intimacy.

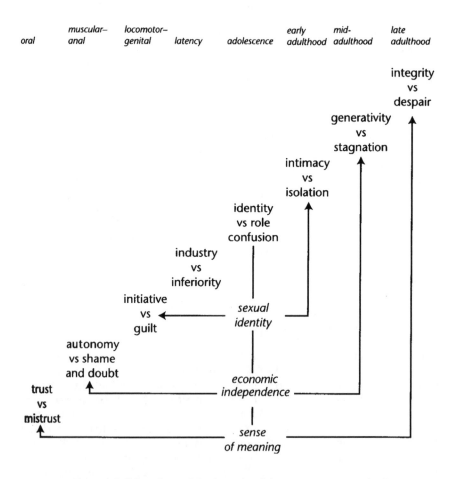

Figure 1.3 Erikson's model adapted: adolescence as a watershed

Middle adolescence could be described as being particularly concerned with issues of independence from parental influence, and moving towards autonomy and self-direction. Dynamic issues of the second age are thereby picked up with considerable force – battles of will are even harder, with physical strength and determination making young people formidable fighters for themselves. This middle period of adolescence is also the time when there is the desire for economic independence, by moving into the area of work, whether in paid employment, or in the self-motivated attitudes to work required for study through further and higher education. Looking forward, this period of middle adolescence lays the foundation for middle adulthood (Erikson's seventh age) where generativity is singled out as a major task, as a parent and/or as a worker. The late period of adolescence, where there can be intense concerns about the state of society and the world, and experimentation to find a sense of belief and purpose (including one's own identity), has obvious links with the first age, where Erikson has identified issues of trust and the emergence of the rudimentary 'self'. Yet this later period of adolescence also prefigures the final stage of the Eight Ages, that of ego integrity, where confidence in a person's overall handling of his or her life is a necessary step towards the acceptance of death. This is why it can be said that each period of adolescence looks backwards and forwards, like a true watershed.

These different aspects are described in more detail in later chapters. The point I wish to emphasize here is that it is artificial to demarcate issues and confine them to certain ages. As in adolescence, issues that appear to be particularly pertinent to each period can surface at any time. They are never resolved by passing through one age alone. Issues about sexuality, about authority, and about issues about faith, hope and integrity, all of which appear central to the period of adolescence, have appeared before in childhood, and will remain concerns throughout life.

This metaphor of the spiral staircase with a cycle of development at every age may increase the stresses in the model, but that is true to life. Using this image, the issues of childhood are thereby reintroduced in the normal process of living, and not just in those crises of adult life through which nearly every person has to pass. But where circumstances are particularly stressful there may be a return to an earlier period of stress; or new forms of stress may test the different 'strengths' or 'virtues' that Erikson identifies. Perhaps he allows for such a cyclical element in his famous remark about the final stage: 'Where adults have integrity enough not to fear death their children will not fear life' (1965: 261), although his reference here is to the connections between generations, like a series of cog wheels, where, as in family systems theory, change in one individual affects others in close proximity. The intergenerational aspect is another important qualification of models of individual development – the past to which a therapist looks is not just the individual history of the client's life, but where it can be ascertained, how the influence of the parents' history, and of the generation above them too, might play itself out in the family. Walker provides a telling example of this in her book on women in therapy (1990: 22–39); and of course systemic and family therapy has recognized the importance of a more comprehensive history than that of the identified client alone (see Allen 1994).

Modes and themes

Modes rather than models might be a better way of using Erikson's and others' models. Latency provides a good example of this. A former colleague once described it as a 'mini-cycle of development', which supports the cyclical view of development I have already suggested. Her role was one of training teachers, and using Erikson's model (particularly in relation to the virtues or strengths he associates to each age of development – see Figure 1.2) she described the task of the teacher (a key figure in the latency stage) as building up in a child a sense of *hope* so that learning can take place, and the *willpower* to see the task through, especially in the early stages when the task seems too difficult. The teacher needs to point towards a direction for learning that indicates its *purpose*, and to build on an appropriate method so that the child gains *competence*. This will lead to *independence* in learning, and a stage of *ego integrity* that generates reliability (*fidelity*), and *love* of learning and its potential for life, a *caring* attitude, and *wisdom* (Hunter 1983).

Latency, the term used to describe the fourth stage of development in Freud and Erikson, is a curious one. Freud suggests that in the latency period (ages approximately 6 to 12) developmental drives and aims diminish in intensity (particularly Oedipal issues, which should have been sufficiently resolved), and re-emerge forcefully again at puberty. Yet it is clear to any casual observer that children of this age do not cease being interested in sex; they use plenty of terms associated with genital and anal images in their jokes. They may have a 'girlfriend' or 'boyfriend' at school, even if the relationship is very different from an adolescent relationship. They may treat their teachers as substitute parents, with intense loving feelings. There will probably be authority struggles at home and perhaps at school. The intensity of all these emotions may be less strong than they are during adolescence, but it is difficult to see a child in the latency stage as other than continuing to experience the emotions and interests from the previous stages. This, as I have already suggested, is to be expected if each age involves each of the issues that Erikson identifies as significant for personal development. Some psychoanalytic writers have indeed questioned the concept of latency, such as Becker, who declared 'her intention to do away with the concept that there was a quiescent period in childhood called latency' (1965: 584).

The focus in the supposed latency stage is on learning, and learning there certainly is. Latency traditionally refers to a stage of development where the tasks of learning basic intellectual, manual and physical skills are made possible without undue interference from the concerns raised in the previous stages. But learning is not confined to this particular time at school. Learning takes place before the latency period, and afterwards: in adolescence, in training, in adult education, including learning counselling and psychotherapy through seminars, reading and supervision. Hartung (1979) in an article on learning psychotherapy builds upon the Erikson model, and suggests that in order to be able to learn, adults need to be able to enter a 'latency mode', like children need to in the latency age.

But the term 'latency mode' could as well be applied to children at school, indeed at pre-school nurseries, so that the idea of a latency stage can indeed be done away with. Children need to enter into this latency mode in order to be able to learn. When they are not overstimulated by dependency needs (which might be seen as oral issues) those who learn can feed their growing appetite for understanding and information. Not too troubled by the need for perfection (often linked to anal issues) they can find fulfilment in the satisfactory completion of tasks, and in being able to make, do or understand things well. Relaxed about cooperation and not being unduly competitive (Oedipal issues), learning presents opportunities to relate to and identify with others. In the latency mode, children and adults can learn to experiment with objects as well as with friendships and social groupings; to tolerate the frustration of results taking time; to ask questions, and look for proof of observations and explanations; and to alternate between passively receiving instruction, and actively investigating. But if children or adults are too stimulated at the same time as they are learning by other emotional issues (and Hartung illustrates how this can happen over issues of dependency, authority and rivalry, as in the first three stages of the Erikson model), then it becomes very much more difficult for them to learn, and thus maximize the opportunities presented by the teacher.

Furthermore, the difficulties that can interfere with the latency mode apply to children and adults alike. The child who is able to control bowels and bladder is freed to engage in a whole range of activities at school, whereas the child who is still soiling is likely to be so concerned with problems of staying clean and dry that there will be less time at school available for concentration upon all the learning activities on offer. An adult in a learning environment who is too concerned about perfection may then find it difficult to complete written work. A child who is concerned about the arguments between parents at home may find it very difficult to concentrate upon tasks at school. Similarly an adult who is going through a crisis in a personal relationship may find it very difficult to learn in a retraining situation. If there is continued overstimulation of other issues, attitudes to learning as well as the learning itself may be influenced detrimentally. Although some children and adults sometimes use their work to defend against worries, most people, of any age, find it hard to concentrate when there are more pressing issues on their minds.

The concept of the 'latency mode' is an important one. It represents a quite distinct way of looking at what Freud calls a 'stage', which is different again from the 'inclusive' mini-cycle of development which Hunter suggests, and which I have myself put forward above, as a possible way of looking at each age of development. The idea of a 'mode', such as a 'latency mode', is a way of looking at and using the Erikson Ages, which is a potentially valuable one. Just as we have to enter into a latency mode to learn, so other aspects of relating to other people and other objects in the external world, as well as relating to ourselves, involve us in other 'modes' of being and doing. It might be possible therefore to speak of a dependent mode, or an autonomous mode, a mode of intimacy, or creativity, each one of which may involve different qualities and strengths, and different ways of relating. That way we remain informed by the more traditional stage models but use them more widely than they may seem to suggest.

Just as modes may therefore be a good way of using models, so developmental themes may be more useful than developmental stages. This certainly links in with other traditions of psychoanalytic theory, in which the apparently clear steps of a stage model have similarly been replaced by concepts such as that of 'positions' as found in Melanie Klein's writing. While she claims to take up Freud's mantle, she alters his stage theory so that it bears her distinctive stamp. She demonstrates another way of looking at development that opens up further possibilities for the way in which psychodynamic concepts can be applied in practice. If in the past there have sometimes been battles about orthodoxy in the psychoanalytic tradition, particularly between the followers of Melanie Klein and the followers of Anna Freud, those of us who are outside the professional psychoanalytic societies can enjoy the opportunity to use the variety of insights that their arguments and discussions provide. Psychodynamic therapists and counsellors can be broad in their use of theory, without sacrificing the depth of knowledge which is represented by what is indeed a rich, if sometimes contentious, psychoanalytic tradition.

Julia Segal observes that Melanie Klein found too limiting Freud's concept of stages of development, through which a child passed 'in well-defined order' (1992: 33). Although she concurred with Freud that children's interest is focused upon oral, anal and genital concerns, 'there was constant movement from one to the other and back again' (p. 33). The similarities to my adapted Erikson model are immediately obvious. Klein describes two particular sets of attitudes that react to and act upon these concerns, which she calls the 'paranoid-schizoid position' and the 'depressive position'. Unlike Freud's stage model, which supposes moving from one set of concerns (oral) to new tasks (anal, then genital or Oedipal), Klein does not believe we are ever free of these issues: adults as well as young children oscillate between these two 'positions' time and again throughout their life, indeed in the course of any normal day.

I shall explain these positions more fully in Chapter 3, but at this point I refer to them to illustrate the way Klein suggests continuity of developmental concepts through all stages of life. She uses the term 'paranoid-schizoid position' as a way of describing the early state of mind in the newborn infant and in the first few months of life. Here good experiences and bad experiences are not yet understood as emanating from the same nurturing object (the mother's breast). Instead there is in phantasy (this particular spelling of a very important concept is Klein's) the perception of an ideal breast that provides food and comfort when it is needed; and a bad breast that withdraws, or is unavailable to the baby when it is most wanted, and so is endowed by the child with an attacking quality. This attacking quality is reinforced, Klein believes, by the projection on to the breast of the child's rage at being frustrated. Thus the child feels persecuted by this bad breast, putting the young infant temporarily into a paranoid state, largely of its own making.

While we have to be careful, in any study of children, not to attribute to them adult states of mind without real evidence (and such phantasies as Klein supposes are virtually incapable of proof, and can only be surmised from other evidence), the term 'paranoid' as used by Klein can refer to the infant's state of mind; or to the paranoid schizophrenic who believes that everyone is against him and that the world is a hostile and dangerous place; or to the persecutory feelings that we can experience when we wake on a Monday morning (or any morning?) and think, 'Do I have to get up? I don't feel like facing "out there". I'd sooner stay here where I am, cosy and warm'. These are of course different states in their intensity and their degree of permanence, but they are all related to the early experience of the infant as Klein describes it. Similarly the term 'schizoid' applies to experiences throughout life. In infancy it refers to the way in which the breast that is perceived as persecutory is split off from the breast that is perceived to be beneficent. Schizoid feelings can range (and here I extend the term to include the way Fairbairn and Guntrip employ it) from the infant who needs to protect the vulnerable self from attack to the adult person who is totally cut off from others, since others are perceived as dangerous because of their hate (Klein) or because of their love (Fairbairn/Guntrip), through to the state of mind that says, 'Just leave me alone for a while. I need some space to myself'.

Klein's term 'depressive position' is first used of the child's growing perception that early good and bad experiences come from the same source. It has little to do with depression as it is normally understood. The child begins to integrate experience, able to contain loving and hating feelings, without the fear that the hating feelings will destroy the loving feelings. I shall explore this concept more fully in Chapter 3, and at this point wish to stress that the 'depressive position' similarly is one that we experience throughout life, as we work through phases of paranoid-schizoid experience, and phases of more constructive and integrated experience. Julia Segal sums it up as follows:

> Under the pressure of frustration of various kinds, the attacks of the paranoid-schizoid position continue throughout life, though mitigated more and more by a sense of love and reality which can no longer be denied ... Klein saw the conflict between love and hatred as the motive force for much of what happens in life.
>
> (1992: 39–40)

The ongoing conflict between love and hate, which Klein places at the centre of her theoretical system, is a reflection of the basic conflict that Freud also put forward between *eros* (love) and *thanatos* (death). Sexual desire (libidinal drives) is only one of the several forces or drives within each person. Aggressive drives are also part of our make-up, as Freud came to see in his later writing (Freud 1920/2003); and apart from their dominant place in Klein's work, there is a similar sense of the continuity of a theme in Anna Freud's 'developmental lines' (1973: 59–82), where aggression is seen in various forms in the different stages: biting in the oral stage, sadism in the anal stage, domination in the phallic stage. While Anna Freud's 'developmental lines' are more obviously linked to a stage model, she makes important distinctions which merit further consideration. For example, she makes it clear that the various developmental lines progress at different speeds. She also writes: 'The interactions between progression and regression ... [and] ... the disharmonies, imbalances, intricacies of development, in short the *variations of normality*, become innumerable' (1973: 94, original italics). Her position, if closer to her father's than Klein's, nevertheless lends some support to a more fluid use of stage theory in working with individual children and adult clients.

A further example of the continuity of an issue can be seen in attachment theory. Again this is more fully explained in Chapter 3, but in this context it is important to note that modes of attachment are relevant not just to infancy, but throughout life – indeed this is one of the important differences between the terms 'attachment' and 'dependency'. While dependence may be necessary from time to time, in a kind of regression to the security of infancy, attachment is a concept that is more capable of positive or negative consequences. Attachment issues remain throughout life. There is no getting away in all these theories from the importance of the foundations laid or not laid down in infancy and childhood, but attachment issues can be understood in relation to later relationships too. The title of the book *Attachment Across the Life Cycle* (Parkes *et al.* 1991) illustrates this perfectly.

Past and present in practice

We are now in a position to see how these different aspects of a psychodynamic model can be employed: that is, how the therapeutic relationship, models of human development, and the theories of personality structure come together in practice. Although in the earlier vignette the client, Chris, used the history of his birth and early childhood to reflect upon his present ways of relating to others, the adaptation of the developmental models put forward in this chapter is capable of yielding much more than through actual history alone. Wide use can be made of ideas and images linked to psychodynamic theories of human development. With a sense of the content of these major themes (or modes, or positions, or lines or stages, since they can all be used in this creative way), the therapist has a treasury of possibilities with which to understand, relate to, and communicate with the client. Linking past to present can be enlightening (psychodynamic therapists call this 'insight'), although showing how the past can be present in the therapeutic relationship itself is frequently the most challenging and formative experience of all. The relationship between client and therapist is, as Freud put it, 'a living laboratory'; or perhaps more aptly a 'stage' upon which in part is re-enacted (with the therapist) the story of a person's life:

> Diane presented two issues at the start of her first session of therapy. The first was that she was binge eating, and then making herself sick. The second was that her husband had left her, and she was unable to get him to say anything about his future intentions. He was unwilling to pronounce the relationship between them over and finished, but he would not return to her.
>
> She did not say much about her childhood and adolescence, nor did the therapist ask any particular questions that might help him see whether the past might throw light upon the present. It was too early for that. Diane talked very fully about how she was reacting and feeling in

her current situation; and the more she said, the more the therapist was able to connect up her words with one of the presenting symptoms: her problem with food. Eating is clearly connected with 'feeding' and therefore perhaps with themes that are typical of the oral stage of development. He began to play with the language and images of the oral stage to see if this might throw light upon the way Diane felt and acted.

Diane told the therapist, for instance, that she desperately wanted her husband to come back so that she could have a baby to love: it would be sufficient for him to return long enough for her to become pregnant. She didn't appear to want a baby in order to tie her husband to their relationship. She also described their relationship when they were living together as one where she mothered him so much, and did everything for him, that he had said he had begun to feel hemmed in and dependent upon her.

As the session went on, the therapist began to experience Diane as very demanding. It wasn't that she was asking a lot of him in any obvious way: she talked very freely, and that should have made it easier for him. But she spoke at such speed and length that it was often impossible for the therapist to get a word in edgeways, and it was difficult to bring the session to a close. At the end, when she had left the room, the therapist felt quite drained; and this happened at the end of subsequent sessions, convincing him that this was something to do with Diane's impact upon him, and not his own tiredness. It was unwise in these early sessions to make explicit his countertransference (feeling drained), but he used his awareness of it to consider the possibility that Diane needed to feed off his presence and his time, perhaps trying to build herself up in a way that no amount of physical eating could achieve.

What he did wonder more openly was whether Diane might need to *give* so much love because she *needed* love so much: 'You seem to put your unloved self into your husband, or into the baby you so much want, and try to love your self. I think you feel so empty inside, now your husband has gone away, and when you have no baby to feed and look after, and you are trying to fill that void by eating'.

Diane reacted to this interpretation with real understanding: it clearly made some sense to her. This was reflected in the sessions that followed, in that she talked about herself differently. She started to make what were now quite appropriate demands upon her husband: she asked him where she stood, and made him take a share in sorting out their money problems. They both began to accept responsibility for some of the domestic issues that had arisen since their separation. She began to make legitimate demands for herself, rather than to act them out through oblique, obscure, unsatisfying and potentially damaging means. Her eating steadily came under control, and she talked of beginning to feel a sense of her self once more. It was as yet a shadowy self, but she felt she had 'more substance'. In fact, Diane said, that while before she had lived from point to point through each day – breakfast to lunch, lunch to tea, supper to bed – she was now able to look and plan further ahead. While before 'my arms and legs seemed all over the place and not to belong to me now I am beginning to come together'.

What is of real interest here is not her history (since the therapist knew very little of it) but the words Diane used, the feelings she evoked, and the images that came to the therapist's mind. This example shows how the 'oral stage' in a Freud/Erikson model can be used as a key to consider what we might call a psychodynamic picture of this client. The therapist did not know (and even if the therapy had been longer he may never have known) whether Diane was starved, or felt starved of love during her infancy. It did not matter, except as a question of intellectual interest, whether she had been or not. What helped the therapist, and consequently the client, were the associations he had to Diane, to her presenting issues, and to her language, which linked with his knowledge of the issues around feeding, emptiness, making demands, boundaries, the fragmented self and so on. He was able to reflect back to her aspects of how she might feel, which she could accept, and which provided her with a different experience of herself. Perhaps she felt understood on a deeper level and not just at the level of presenting problems. If there had been some confirmatory knowledge from Diane's past, which supported the impressions he was receiving, the therapist might have wanted to add a tentative explanation to his interpretation of her emptiness. He had noted, for example, the short time span of her day and her living from meal to meal (three to four hours, reminiscent of early feeding patterns); and the image of her body being 'all over the place' was for him so like a baby's flailing limbs.

In this example, the oral and young infant imagery is the most obvious, although it is also possible to look at Diane and her issues from the imagery of another 'stage', or, as I prefer to call it, of another 'theme'. The oral theme can be matched by an anal theme – or at least images and associations that link to that stage of development, with its key features about order and control. It was obvious that Diane liked to organize her husband, and that he was a more disorganized person who needed to break free from her oppressive control. She described how she needed to keep people happy by saying what she felt they wanted to hear, so she was unable to be assertive and autonomous enough to be her own person. She dressed very smartly, even when she said she would have otherwise preferred to wear casual clothes. It was as if she had to look perfect for any casual visitor who might come unannounced. Her rapid speech in the session might have been interpreted as a way of keeping the therapist in his place, and controlling how much he was permitted to say. In this respect there was some confirmatory evidence of this anal stage material from Diane's descriptions of her parents: her mother was very con- trolled and could not show her feelings, particularly when she felt others might criticize her for them, and her father appeared to have been a strict disciplinarian and a severe authority figure. The therapist might therefore have chosen to make his opening interpretation around this 'control' theme, although he felt that the feeding imagery indicated that Diane had shifted from being controlled and controlling when she had been living with her husband, to a mode of being (an earlier stage?) in which she was not in control of her eating, and unable to make appropriate demands.

And what about a third theme, one that might be linked to the phallic or Oedipal stages of development? Were there rivalry or sexual issues here? Diane's husband left her in the first instance because he had a relationship with another woman. This was clearly a three-person situation, typical of problems related to that theme. But for the therapist that was almost the sole identifying issue around that theme. With some clients, the material brought to therapy can be understood in two or three different ways, as if looking through different lenses at the presenting material. But to avoid confusion in the therapist and for the client, it helps to listen carefully for the predominating theme in each session, and to address thinking and explicit interpretation to one set of issues at a time.

The presenting past is therefore seen not only in the details of a client's personal history (as this becomes known it often highlights the issues), but in the way that history may be relived in the present. The 'here and now' of the therapeutic relationship provides some of the clues that are necessary to enable the present to be better understood; and when these different elements can be related to each other, the picture becomes clearer. Psychodynamic theory includes a concept known as 'the triangle of insight', in which past and present, relationships outside therapy and within therapy, and in the external world and internal world, can be linked. The triangle of insight (see Figure 1.4) describes both a way of thinking about the client and a type of interpretation that is open to the therapist, which can lead to linking the client's experience of past relationships with significant people (including the way they have been internalized so that they 'live on' inside the person), with the client's current relationships to others both in life 'outside' the consulting room, and in the relationship with the therapist.

Making links between a client's current relationships and the relationship with the therapist is of course not uncommon in some other therapeutic orientations. It is perhaps the attempt to bring in all three points of the triangle that distinguishes the emphasis in psychodynamic work from other orientations. Some examples of linking are:

- between the two points of the triangle 'out there' and 'in here': 'You've been saying today that you get very anxious when things in your room are out of place. I feel you are anxious here too, especially when I can't make things neat and tidy for you'.
- between what a person describes in his or her current situation, and a past event or relationship: 'You've been saying today that you get very anxious when things in your room are out of place. That reminds me of something you've said before, that your father was very fussy when anything got untidy at home when you were a child. It's as if he's still there, in your room, or inside you, commenting on how untidy it looks'.
- between the client's reported past and the present situation with the counsellor, known in psychodynamic theory as 'transference', for example, 'You say your mother always went around tidying everything up after you as a child. I wonder whether you're also saying that you wish I could put everything in order for you here and give you a neat answer'.
- most completely there is reference to all three points of the triangle, which is what Freud calls a 'construction' rather than an interpretation (1937b/ 2002): 'You are clearly feeling that your life's a mess. It feels impossible to put any order on it. I think this is made worse because your father always

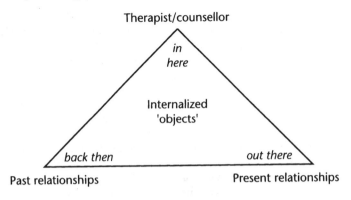

Figure 1.4 The triangle of insight

insisted that you have everything ordered when you were a child, and your mother would make sure it was, to protect you from his rage. I'm wondering whether you're feeling really frustrated with me because I don't seem to be helping you to get everything sorted out?'

When relevant links can be made, whether it is between two or three points on the triangle of insight, this often brings relief, not least at being understood at a deeper level. But insight is not normally enough. Although much emphasis has been put in the past on the mutative interpretation in psychoanalysis (see Strachey 1934), there is now much more recognition of the centrality of the relationship between the therapist and the client, which provides a place where old patterns of relating are re-experienced and new ways of relating are tested out (Meissner 1991). The therapeutic relationship provides what Winnicott (1965b) calls, in relation to mothering, a facilitating environment, but this is not just by providing good parenting. Therapy cannot but also mirror parenting that was far from ideal; like the absent or preoccupied mother, a therapist is not always on tap; like the parent who inadvertently fails to give enough reassurance, the therapist fails to provide enough ordered answers; like the controlling parent, a therapist sets limits on the time and availability of sessions; and like the parent in the Oedipal triangle, he or she is not available to become the partner with whom the client might wish for an intimate relationship. Negative experiences from the past – frustrations, rejections and disappointments – will often be relived in the therapy relationship itself, providing the potentiality for the therapeutic experience to evoke, and in the end contain, good and bad feelings, dangerous fantasies, disturbing thoughts, as well as the fondness and freedom of a maturing sense of relatedness.

Summary

The themes that form the majority of this book present material from childhood and adult life from which formulations might be made, illustrating the way the three main childhood developmental stages throw up themes that can be seen operating in positive and negative ways in adult clients. What has been called the oral stage highlights themes related to trust and attachment, although as already indicated these themes continue to operate throughout life. That which has been known in Freudian terms as the anal stage highlights issues about authority and autonomy, again which appear consistently in adult life. Moreover, cooperation and competition present in a major way in the symbolism of the Oedipal conflict and other issues related to what has been called the phallic phase. These themes will therefore be illustrated in the content and process of the meetings between a therapist and a client.

These themes will form the substance of Chapters 3 to 11. Chapter 12 presents an overview of how these themes are seen at various points of the therapeutic relationship. The Appendix provides a type of summary, listing under each theme many of the difficulties that clients present or describe; providing pointers to the type of relationship the client tries to create with, or seeks from, the therapist, and suggesting ways in which the therapist may need to be particularly attentive to the needs of the client. It hints at what might make for satisfactory and mature development, which may be said to be a major therapeutic aim. The different sections of the Appendix, when related to the actual history of the client, may help point to the different links that may be made through 'the triangle of insight'.

All this is both time-bound and culture-related. I shall examine this qualification in Chapter 2. I do not expect every reader to agree with all the possibilities to which psychodynamic and practice point. Each therapist has their own value system, even if some like to think of themselves as neutral. Readers will wish to refine and amend these themes in the light of their own experience and philosophy. And, as I will argue in the next chapter, each client must be treated as a unique individual, and clearly every therapist needs to develop an individual view of what constitutes healthy and damaged development. My own experience is that psychodynamic theory helps the development and clarification of such a view, and can indeed be translated into therapeutic practice to the benefit of both client and therapist.

QUALIFYING
INTERPRETATIONS

The relationship between the present and the past is a fascinating one, which needs to be examined more carefully if the three major themes in this book are to be used wisely and sensitively in therapy.

The concept of the past influencing the present owes something to the argument of cause and effect. Older philosophical thinking (metaphysics) used this as one of the arguments for the existence of God: that wherever there is an effect, there must be a cause, and since behind every cause there must be another, this sequence extends into infinity until the prime cause (God) is reached. Psychologists and psychotherapists similarly often look for cause and effect, although as in philosophical theology, any argument that pursues just one single line of cause and effect is too limited and unconvincing. To suggest that psychodynamic theory seeks to uncover a single trauma is a caricature of a much more careful and painstaking approach. Freud's original case histories show that he was rarely content with a single explanation for the presenting symptoms that many of his young women patients presented in their initial consultations with him. Elizabeth von R., for example, might attribute the pains in her leg to walking, and Freud likewise initially to the place where her sick father's leg rested when she was nursing him, but the most effective interpretation which he made appears to have been when he brought together a number of different precipitating factors (Freud and Breuer 1895/2004: 170–1).

A straightforward quest then for the single source of a presenting issue is like trying to find the source of the water at the mouth of the Amazon in a single Andean spring. Even when connecting past and present in an almost literal way, through the hypothesis that the past must influence the present, the therapist should never assume that he or she, or the client, can be content for long with a single explanation. That type of detection may appeal to the amateur sleuth, but is scarcely sufficient in seeking to understand the complexities of human nature.

The connection between past and present is made even more complex, because as well as our experience of the present being influenced by our past, we also have to recognize that our memory of the past is influenced by the present. Our perception and interpretation of people and events have a strong subjective element in them. The way we view the past can be distorted by current circumstances. For example, when we feel depressed, we tend to remember other occasions when we felt bad, and may perceive past events in that light: 'I remember that dreadful holiday after my mother died'. On another day, in another conversation, when we feel brighter, that same holiday may appear totally different in the way it is remembered: 'We stayed in some brilliant places during that holiday we went on after my mother died'.

As individuals we construct our personal history in much the same way as a nation or a people constructs its national or cultural history, in order to support our way of seeing things. However objective we try to be, and whatever facts we try to put forward to inform our judgements, all historical views are inevitably biased, since they consist not simply of facts, but of selected facts, one weighed against another, to support a particular position. No wonder then that a French view of British history, or a Scottish view of English history, or a Black view of British foreign (or social) history often challenges the commonly held view that the white British person has of his or her country's past. This bias in both the telling and the interpretation of history applies similarly to the way clients construct their personal stories, and to the way therapists hear and interpret them. As one study of contemporary thought suggests, history 'is always written from the perspective of the present; history fulfils a need of the present' (Lechte 1994: 111).

It does not follow, however, that history is irrelevant. How people remember their history, how they relate their history and how they construct their history is a potentially valuable way of understanding them as they are now, or at the point of time in which they are telling their story. It is nevertheless impossible to 'take a history' (as psychiatrists and some therapists do) once and for all. The history will change, sometimes subtly, sometimes with dramatic new revelations, as the person changes, and as the therapeutic relationship passes through its different phases. Sometimes there are new memories but all the time there are possibilities of new interpretations, fresh ways of constructing experience, which may or may not be the total picture of how it actually was. While not detracting from the need for therapists to affirm that certain events happened, and that memories are not playing tricks (especially in trauma work, such as with adult survivors of child abuse), there must always be open debate about the historical reality of all memories, or of constructions put upon them. This is true of academic cognitive psychology, with its assertion that we do not fully understand memory. This must also be borne in mind in the debate over Freud's ambivalent position about sexual abuse. Arguments criticizing Freud over his revised view of the reality of abuse (arguments that are often inaccurate, see Jacobs (2003: 111–14)) obscure the fact that in a psychodynamic approach to memory and constructions of personal history, there is an interweaving of fact and fantasy, actuality and interpretation: fact and fantasy can both be experienced as real, and actuality and interpretation are both essential aspects of the work. As Freud (1937a/2002) observed in one of his last papers, one of the reasons that analysis is interminable is because interpretation and reinterpretation remain unfinished for as long as we live.

Freud's work, despite its obvious weaknesses a century on, contains certain elements that make the psychodynamic therapist cautious about the status of knowledge: for example, unconscious processes include the repression of unacceptable thoughts and feelings, and make it impossible ever to know ourselves or others 'as we really are' (if indeed that phrase actually means anything). We are constantly interpreting and reinterpreting ourselves and external perceptions, not infrequently opting to see the world as we want to see it rather than the way other people see it. It is questionable whether it is ever possible to say with conviction that we see something 'the way it really is'. Human relationships are dogged by the problem of misperceptions and misrepresentations, leading inevitably to the conflicts that arise between individuals, groups and nations, each claiming that the way they see things is right and that the way the other sees them is wrong.

It is inevitable then that clients present themselves and their history from particular perspectives which sometimes may need to be questioned (at least in the therapist's thinking, although not necessarily out loud), and sometimes may need to be validated in the face of the clients' own doubts about the accuracy of their memories. But it is not only clients who look through various distorting lenses at themselves and their past: therapists too can misinterpret and misunderstand the client's story; and any approach that tries to use what may look like 'facts' in development theory can be either dangerous or dishonest.

I take it for granted that one prerequisite for all psychodynamic work is that a therapist engages in the continuous task of self-analysis, or self-reflection, through personal therapy, through supervision, and through the 'internal supervisor' (Casement 1985). We only ever perceive 'through a glass darkly', because personal factors affect the way we see everything. Even a period of personal therapy can never rid the individual of their subjective outlook; and indeed why should it? What it hopefully does is to highlight our propensity to distort, and our particular personal bias. Awareness of the ways in which the therapist's perception can be influenced by different factors minimizes the risk of believing that the therapist and her or his theoretical base must be right. The therapist's authoritative position is powerful enough in the eyes of the client without having to add grandiose self-deception. Many clients at first, and later in times of crisis, want the therapist to know all the answers, and they are ready to 'swallow' anything. (Notice the first theme of trust, with its oral metaphor of swallowing, as well as the second theme of authority appearing already.) When a therapist misinterprets a client, as inevitably he or she will, the situation is ripe for misuse of that powerful position, especially since therapists tend to put their interpretations across in ways that are warm, caring and beguiling. Freud recognized the possibility of the analyst being wrong and if that is the case 'at some appropriate moment we can tell the patients as much, without loss of authority' (1937b/2002: 215). In the same passage he stresses the danger of 'leading the patient astray by the power of suggestion, by "talking him into" something you yourself believe in' (p. 215) and he asserts somewhat immodestly that he has never done such a thing. At times, however, he does appear to want to convince his patient that his view is the correct one. I shall return to this aspect of his work later in the chapter.

Therapists should learn through their own therapy therefore how easy it is for them to be biased. They may learn the particular ways in which they can in their countertransference reactions subjectively interpret particular material, and this should alert them to their capacity to mishear and misunderstand. Their formal training also involves academic as well as personal knowledge – about technique, about personality structure, and about human development. The vast literature about therapy serves this quest for knowledge, and it is of course my own intention in these chapters to make a further contribution to that search for greater understanding. I bear in mind that some of the leading writers in psychoanalytic literature have made it clear that there is also much that they do not know, and that therapy all too often involves tolerating 'not knowing'. Masud Khan commented on Winnicott, for example, that he had a 'monumental capacity ... to contain unknowing' (Winnicott 1989: 15). But the sheer volume of the literature on human development and personality structure may appear to carry a different message, that because there is so much written there must be so much known. It is difficult to 'not know' when so many books appear to claim expertise. Winnicott (1965b) wrote: 'It is more difficult for an analyst to be original than for anyone else, because everything we say truly has been taught us yesterday (i.e. by patients)'. This is an interesting statement, and one in the end that is essential to bear in mind, since it is learning from clients that constantly informs every aspect of the therapist's work, and carries the possibility of enhancing or correcting the misinformation picked up in training. Yet it is also a statement that needs unpacking, since the bias of the therapist, and the prevailing societal values and structures in the period of history in which he or she works, inevitably mean that learning tends to be selective, and that it is often made to fit preconceptions. Thus Freud's patriarchal view of women, or Winnicott's relative lack of reference to fathers in his work are both examples of the way in which ideas are influenced by the time in which they were written. Winnicott acknowledges that he is taught by his patients, but is less aware that the way he interprets what he believes he is being taught is also informed by the values of the society of which he too is a part. This interplay of different pressures upon thinking makes it essential to be cautious about 'learning from the patient' (this phrase is also the title of Casement's (1985) valuable book). Therapists interpret their clients' material not just in the light of personal bias, but also in the light of preconceived ideas which their training has taught them, as well as in the context of their social and political milieu. It is these influences that need where possible to be identified, in order to ask the questions that can validly be asked of developmental models generally, and of psychodynamic theory in particular.

Science or art?

Freud dearly wished the discipline of psychoanalysis to be a science, although he suggested himself that some areas of scientific enquiry, such as biology, can never be as exact as others. The life sciences are generally less precise than the material sciences (Freud 1925a: 242). The scientist in Freud nevertheless seems at times to make universal statements on the basis of fairly limited evidence. While he is far less dogmatic in his writing than many people suppose (he frequently admits the limits of his knowledge, and anticipates the day when some of his theories will be overturned), some of his followers have not been so open-minded or so prepared to disagree with him. Others have questioned aspects of Freud's theories, acknowledging his skill as an observer, but putting forward different ways of constructing theoretical models from the same observations.

Psychological and sociological research perhaps involves even more variables than life sciences such as biology and zoology. The information from research in these areas often acts as a guide to the way people think and behave, but it is less precise about the individual person than, for example, the chemical physicist can be about the structure of a particular atom. The social sciences themselves debate whether they are more an art than a science, although over this century they have emerged as a different type of discipline to traditional science on the one hand or the arts on the other. Psychotherapy and counselling may be located in that part of the map of knowledge, the social sciences, rather than in the physical sciences, even if it is in the latter sector that many university psychology departments like to see themselves.

Malan entitles one of his books *Individual Psychotherapy and the Science of Psychodynamics* (1979). Storr on the other hand entitles one of his *The Art of Psychotherapy* (1979). Art and science both start with observation, but then they diverge. Both interpret their observations, but science does this in order to explain, and to explain in such a way as will hold good until it is disproved. Art also interprets, but does so to convey varieties of experience, each interpretation being unique. A work of art, unlike a scientific experiment, cannot be repeated, even if it can be copied. Science on the other hand relies upon replication in order to validate its hypotheses. Much of this has bearing upon how therapists understand the status of their chosen theory, and how they use it. Psychodynamic ideas, including the themes in this book, can be applied to many situations and to many clients, but they must be interpreted in the light of the individual circumstances of each person. This leads to a uniqueness (as a fingerprint or DNA are also unique) in personality and in history, that may be similar to, but is never the same as, another's. It is this perhaps that makes therapy such a fascinating occupation, since every enquiry is different.

Inevitably, as Rayner observes in the second edition of his book *Human Development*, the helper who is 'case-loaded' pays a price, since 'his ideas are only tested informally through his experience, reading and conversation with others. [His ideas] do not meet the criterion of formal testability in an experimental design which is espoused by the research psychologist' (1978: 16). In the third edition Rayner explains that his book is 'largely based upon the intimate, detailed work with individual people originated by Freud' (1986: 7), but that his book 'is not a gospel, it is limited in its data and vision. Think of it as asking pertinent questions, let yourself argue with it, think for yourself' (pp. 10–11). This writer would echo those words.

Winnicott and Casement write, as cited above, of learning from their patients. We read that Freud's early discoveries were almost dictated to him by patients who demanded that he hear them rather than ask them questions about what interested him (Freud and Breuer 1895/2004: 63–4). Therapists therefore encourage people to tell their stories, to describe their thoughts and feelings, and to share their experiences, even to put forward their own explanations. None of this is scientific theory, although it may be raw material for more generalized observations. In other contexts these stories could form the basis of a novel, a poem or drama. D. M. Thomas in a note prefacing his novel *The White Hotel* (1981) goes so far as to say of Freud's writings that they are 'masterly works of literature, apart from anything else', a quality that Freud recognized when he described some of his case histories as being like novellas. Thomas's fictitious case history is itself a masterly pastiche of Freud's style, which reflects with fascinating accuracy Freud's careful exploration of words, images and symptoms. He describes Freud as 'the discoverer of the great and beautiful modern myth of psychoanalysis. By myth I mean a poetic, dramatic expression of a hidden truth: and in placing this emphasis I do not intend to put into question the scientific validity of psychoanalysis' (1981: 6). He may not intend to, but it is right to question the scientific validity of Freud's work – some of which has received confirmation through psychological and neurological studies, while other ideas have fallen by the wayside. Myths tend to start as early attempts at explanation (for example, of how the world came into being), but they are much more than this. Jungian therapists appear to give more attention to myths and symbols (both collective and personal) than do most other therapists; nevertheless psychodynamic therapists generally attach particular significance to the use of words and images: they are pointers to the way in which a person consciously constructs experience, and unconsciously processes hidden feelings and thoughts. We might say that we all live out various myths, whether they be stereotypes about others, or in the ways we construe ourselves. Many of our intellectual constructs are myths, expressions of a hidden truth, even if some of them can also be justified as having apparent objective validity.

Language and imagery lie at the centre of many therapeutic approaches, but nowhere perhaps as thoroughly examined as in the psychodynamic and psychoanalytic tradition. Words with more than one meaning (such as puns and homonyms), metaphorical thinking, symbols in waking life as well as in dreams, and narratives form the basis for constructing our understanding of individual people. Each person has a unique story to tell, using both idiosyncratic and shared images with which to illustrate it. Psychodynamic therapists try to discern what the symbols, words and stories might mean to each person, what 'truths' they may portray, or even mask. It is not unlike hearing a poem or reading a novel, and asking what the author is trying to convey of the way he or she sees the world, or this dilemma, or that relationship; or what the author is trying to express of his or her own personality, thoughts and emotions. No wonder psychoanalysis has become an important tool for literary criticism and film theory. Psychoanalytic thought is also given more credibility by many sociologists, in contrast to the scorn often heaped upon it by academic psychologists.

Like good art and literature, psychodynamic theory becomes relevant when it speaks (as often it appears to do) to our experience: 'I have felt that'; 'I know that fantasy myself'; 'That helps me understand myself'. Like great art and literature, good theory also leaves room for individual interpretation. The artist, the writer or the composer provides an opportunity for each person to fill out the composition in her or his own way, so that it becomes special. Psychodynamic ideas similarly are approximations and pointers, which should leave space for the individual client and the individual therapist to make their own. Even the language used in the theory should not be taken literally. Just as metaphor and simile are common features of everyday speech, so they are constantly present in the therapeutic dialogue in phrases such as: 'It feels like . . .', 'It is as if . . .'. Images are there to be played with, not translated into psychological concepts:

> Eddie said of himself in one particular session, 'It feels as if I'm drifting through life'. I thought about the phrase 'drifting', and then reflected on how drifting takes place on currents, and not at random. I thought of the way his parents wanted him to move in a particular direction, so that his drifting might be passively going their way. When I replied I therefore said, 'Yes, drifting . . . but drifting perhaps on an undercurrent of what others have always told you what you should be doing'. Perhaps he was also finding difficult my implicit permission for him to drift in the session.

Each person has his or her own imagery, as each has a unique experience of growing and living. At the same time there appear to be certain symbols that have universal appeal: light and dark, the circle, the pillar, the mountain and so on. Perhaps many of these universal images have been borrowed from the natural world and reflect the importance of the external environment, but analysts suggest that such powerful images also describe our internal world. Jungians in particular connect such symbols to the collective unconscious and to archetypes. A different view of imagery is put forward by Rayner who argues that many metaphors and symbols are linked to childhood fantasy. He gives examples of such fantasy in everyday speech, for example 'the evocative language of oral activity' in phrases like: 'I've bitten off more than I can chew', 'She's sweet', or (as I noted above) 'I can't swallow that' (1986: 43). There is of course a danger that this type of psychoanalytic thinking (whether Freudian or Jungian) can lead to standard interpretations of symbols, most commonly, for example, of the unconscious, of mother or father, or of the penis, the breast or the womb. Sometimes such meanings appear to make sense, but it is every therapist's dilemma just how much weight to give to the individual, and how much to the general interpretation of the words and images that the client shares.

Just as language or symbols can be understood as having certain meanings in common, but must also be allowed a more individualistic interpretation, similarly all discourse about personal development and character needs to honour the uniqueness of the individual on the one hand, and acknowledge the possibility of common elements on the other. Human beings, indeed living things, have much in common: we are all born; we need special nurturing for a considerable time (although by whom and for how long varies from culture to culture and from class to class); we develop physically at roughly the same pace (even though this depends to some extent on nutrition as well as socioeconomic circumstances); we share certain basic needs (but there may be some dispute about which are basic and which are culturally conditioned); and we age and die. That much (perhaps more) it can be said we hold in common. But already my bracketed qualifications show that there can be significant differences over something as apparently straightforward as physical development. Each person lives in a society, with cultural norms and societal expectations, and even a single culture can contain a number of subcultures, in which experiences are treated and understood differently.

While it is therefore possible, and largely helpful, for the therapist to learn from psychological and sociological studies (whether of large cohorts, or through casework and the individual 'living human document' favoured in psychoanalytic writing) there must be caution about the use of such learning. As Burman writes, 'ideas are tools for change, and they are certainly used to prevent change' (1994: 188). For example, Maguire draws attention to the way in which a strongly biological version of Freud's work was assimilated into the medical establishment in North America, 'where it was often used to bolster conservative ideals of "women's place"' (1995: 53). Burman's critical analysis of developmental psychology leads her to 'hope that at the very least some caution about the indiscriminate application of general models should follow' (1994: 188).

It is therefore vital, particularly with psychodynamic theories such as this book expounds, to recognize that all our knowledge is conditioned by the society in which we live. Burman illustrates how 'paradoxical, mixed conceptions of developmental psychology testify to the different aspects of its history' (1994: 9). She relates, for example, how in the late 19th century, when the observation of children was first taken seriously, only men were presumed objective enough to undertake this, since women would be too involved with children to make good scientific observers. The idea that a woman might understand children better because of her ability to relate closely to them was foreign to these male intellectuals (p. 12). Among numerous examples that illustrate the need to be discriminating about what passes for evidence in developmental psychology, Burman also cites Bowlby's (1947) wartime studies of maternal deprivation. Like other critics of Bowlby she shows how his studies not only imposed upon mothers the sole burden for the development of children, but also made apparently negligent mothers appear responsible for their children's psychopathology and criminal behaviour. Although attachment theory found considerable support some 50 years after this research, Bowlby's findings meant that no account had to be taken of the prevailing economic and social forces, even though these might provide more cogent reasons for understanding crime and mental distress.

Similarly in the 1990s, British government statements appeared to indicate that children of single parents did less well educationally, not (as could be put forward as an alternative explanation) because of lack of resources, but because of their single-parent status. Those who manage society instinctively know how to use psychological pressure.

It was not simply the distortion of Bowlby's research (for example, extrapolating from institutional care to maternal care) that provides a warning. It is also the use to which it was put: for example, apparently justifying the need for women to return to their home and children. They had proved their value as a workforce during the war, but conveniently for society (or at least the male half of society) this type of research justified women vacating their jobs, and making way for the men who were returning to civilian life (Walker 1990: 29). The lesson must be drawn from the brief history of psychology as an applied discipline, that its observations are inevitably influenced by their historical context, and in turn may be reinforced by political and economic requirements.

Historical context and societal forces also influence the way in which normality and abnormality are understood. Homosexuality, for example, was an official diagnostic category in psychiatry until the third quarter of the 20th century. Or, to take another example, the understanding of schizophrenia, or even of people to whom the label of madness has been applied, differs not just from culture to culture, and from one generation to another, but also within one generation of psychiatrists (see, for example, Laing 1967). Mental illness can even be used to silence political argument, as it was in post-Stalinist Soviet Russia, where the mental hospital replaced the labour camp as the means of dealing with dissent. Or consider the phenomenon of speaking with spirits. This can be interpreted quite differently in various societies. In African Caribbean groups such phenomena are seen as natural and able to bring about healing; in some other religions speaking with spirits may be either a sign of particular sanctity, or of Satanic possession, depending upon the extent of the spirit-possessed person's orthodoxy; and in Western secular psychiatry, such phenomena are quite likely to be seen as a sign of auditory hallucinations, or when shared by a group, as mass delusion.

Further examples of the caution that needs to be applied to any study of human development and character arise in relation to gender, culture and race. Gender issues in counselling and therapy are examined further in Chapter 9, but at this point it is important to note how many studies of human development (especially of psychosocial stages) have been based on hypotheses by male scholars, using norms that may legitimately apply to men, but do not necessarily apply to women. An example of this is the sequence of Erikson's fifth and sixth ages, where he suggests that identity (becoming oneself) has to precede intimacy. He fails to draw a possible distinction between young men and young women. Feminist psychodynamic therapists distinguish between a general tendency in men to wish to separate and to be separate, and in women to wish to relate. 'The male's self ... becomes based on a more fixed "me" – "not-me" distinction ... By contrast, the female's self is less separate and involves a less fixed "me" – "not-me" distinction' (Chodorow 1989: 110). This makes for a different take on intimacy, although if Erikson's ages are not taken as a stage model, but as I argued in Chapter 1, as highlighting important psychological characteristics, achieved and expressed in different ways at different times, both separateness and intimacy have a legitimate place in different sets of relationships.

Another important example of the significance of gender difference in psychological research arose from Kohlberg's (1981) study of moral development, when he researched the basis upon which people make moral decisions. His own studies appear to rate men as more highly developed in their moral thinking than women, but this is because he assumed (as a man) that justice is the highest ethic. Gilligan, one of Kohlberg's colleagues, was puzzled at this finding, and found in her research that women think more in terms of care than justice, and that mature moral thinking combines fairness and care. Women, as the title of her book proclaims, speak *In a Different Voice* (1982). This distinction in moral thinking had already been observed by Freud (1925b: 342) as well ('for women what is ethically normal is different from what it is in men'), although he put this down somewhat pejoratively to a less developed super-ego. Whether this explanation is sufficient is doubtful, but given that he equates super-ego development with the resolution of the Oedipus complex, and that feminist psychoanalytic thinking has followed him in recognizing significant differences in mother–son and mother–daughter relationships (see Chapter 5), Freud's early views seem to have received some confirmation two generations later, without the rather patronising tone which he appears to adopt.

Not only are there possible gender differences in psychological development and character. Erikson recognized, as did other analysts who emigrated from Europe to North America, the significance for personal development of cultural differences. In *Childhood and Society*, for instance, he contrasts two North American Indian tribes, the Sioux and the Yurok (1965: 127–41, 169–80). He links the economic and environmental conditions of each tribe with their ways of rearing children: in the case of the Sioux he shows the similarity between living in conditions of abundance of the prairies and the generosity of Sioux mothers in breastfeeding, together with their lack of concern for rigid anal training; and in Yurok culture Erikson observes how the salmon fishermen of the Yurok have to protect the cleanliness of the river and conserve the stocks of fish, which appears to be reflected in their child-rearing, both in greater oral prohibition, and what might be called 'anal' features such as cleanliness in toilet training, all of which links to conservation. In recognizing the inseparable link between economic, environmental and family conditions Erikson reminds us that we must look for the same relationship in working as therapists with clients in and from different subcultures. This includes awareness of the dissonance caused when those who have been brought up in one culture are compelled (by social pressure as well as economic circumstances) to adapt to a different set of norms and values.

These cultural differences in child-rearing patterns are important. Whether one method of child-rearing is superior to another in its care and in its promotion of personal development can only be answered from within a culturally determined position – in other words, most of us are biased towards thinking our own culture's values are normal, and that different child-rearing practices elsewhere will either cause psychological problems, or lead to different characteristics in adult relationships. This can be shown to be both true and untrue! For instance, the book *Children in Collectives* records the visit of a largely American group of child psychiatrists, psychologists and analysts to Israel to study and discuss the effects of the kibbutzim on growing children. It is clear from the record of their observations and the discussion of them that 'psychologically and psychopathologically, there appeared to be very little difference between the kibbutz and the non-kibbutz child, even though they had been brought up in radically different ways and in radically different surroundings' (Neubauer 1965: 128). While there clearly were 'radically different' practices, such as the separation of babies from mothers, group care, different sleeping arrangements and so on, many of the issues underlying the concerns of the observers and the kibbutzim themselves were similar: for example, the need for a constant and reliable figure for the baby, questions of transference, sexuality and Oedipal issues. 'None of us was really talking of all-or-none phenomena – that is "no-one but the mother" or "the mother not at all". We were concerned with *degrees* of contact, with a *spectrum* of mother–child transactions' (p. 130, original italics).

Yet what are we to make of another way of child-rearing, as in the Alorese tribe in the former Dutch East Indies? Here the newborn baby is left during the day in the care of a sibling or adult relative some two weeks after birth, when the mother returns to work in the fields. During that time the infant is not fed at the breast, despite attempts to suckle. When the mother returns in the evening, the baby is nursed and fondled all evening, but this does not make up for the lack of nursing while she was away working. By one year of age the infant has to beg for food during the day until he or she is old enough to forage. The effect of this irregular care pattern is seen in the rage shown by children between 2 and 5 years old, at which point 'the ineffectual rages cease' (Munroe and Munroe 1975: 42).

The effect of this on the adult Alorese is not surprising, and using psychodynamic theory might even be predicted. Interpersonal relations are shallow, grief is brief, marriages are brittle, suspicion and distrust are endemic, and the Alorese are noticeable for their passivity in the face of problems (pp. 42–5). Interpretation of Western Rorschach tests used with the Alorese show these same characteristics. The data are clear: the effect of childhood on the adult is obvious; and even Western psychological tests prove valid in use with this tribe. But are we able to assert that the Alorese are not good at child-rearing as we shift from observation and explanation to making value judgements? The Alorese way of life is very different, partly determined as it is by the particular agronomy; their norms are different. An adult who dwelt upon feelings or who developed close relationships might be viewed by them as deviant. Other practices of child-rearing might be viewed by the Alorese as overindulgent.

But then is female circumcision, clitoridectomy, or the masturbation of infants to help them to sleep acceptable because it accords with a different set of cultural norms, or not? Or in our own society is it acceptable to send little children away from home to school? These are not just political questions. They are areas of concern where feelings run high, but where knowledge and interpretation is relative. Just as Erikson does not appear to single out either the Sioux or the Yurok Indians for preference in their child-rearing patterns, so the therapist cannot assume that there is only one type of development or one definition of maturity, but at the same time a therapist will have personal and culturally determined assumptions and beliefs about what is right and what is wrong. It would be difficult, for example, for a therapist to find any grounds for defending child abuse, even though in some cultures, and perhaps even at some points in Western history, different forms of abuse – sexual, physical and emotional – have been thought to be acceptable.

Clearly these questions are particularly important when working with clients from different races and cultures, but they are also important in reading psychodynamic, psychoanalytic and psychological texts. Children brought up to different cultural patterns, or by single parents, or by gay or lesbian couples, or in a kibbutz may develop different strengths, or show different vulnerabilities from children brought up in so-called 'normal' situations. These areas of divergence must be borne in mind throughout this book, even when they are not specifically explored. Inevitably any one writer works from her or his own experience, knowledge, and cultural background. In time different studies will trace aspects of psychological development from other perspectives, but they must also be carried out by those who know that perspective from inside.

There will always be a series of questions about the concepts in psychodynamic theory (for example, the incest taboo and the problem of Oedipal relationships), and whether they are universally applicable. Melanie Klein writes of a discussion with an anthropologist who objected to her assumption of a general foundation for character development (1975: 262–3). She appears to find common ground in the relationship to the primal good object, the mother, whatever other 'distortions of character are accepted or admired'. Her use of the word 'distortions' is an interesting one, as if, despite her belief that there is a common foundation, anything that differs from her own view of character is in some way deviant. On the other hand, in her example she uses the idea of the tent and the sanctuary in another community as a symbol of the good and protective mother in her own. What we may find is that some of these psychodynamic concepts are metaphors or symbols of aspects of relating, which have value as long as they are always open to translation into other cultural patterns. There may even be archetypal patterns such as Jungians maintain (see Samuels 1985a: 23–45).

There are other texts that concentrate upon the issues I raise here about cross-cultural and gender awareness, bias and prejudice (e.g. Pedersen 1994; Burck and Speed 1995; Maguire 1995; Lago 1996). These discussions are vital for a fuller understanding of the theory and practice of all the therapies. I particularly wish to underline the need for therapists to be aware that explanations of personal development are open to similar bias.

Labelling and naming

One of the features of the cultural bias of Western psychotherapy and counselling is its individualistic stance. Despite the balance provided by systemic and family therapy, individualism might also be typical of the Western view of the person, as well as being indicative of a particular political climate. Lago (1996: 78) neatly summarizes this culturally determined outlook. Nevertheless, while in no way wishing to neglect the individual's relationship to others and to society as a whole, as a therapist I also wish to validate the uniqueness of each client's personal history and present circumstances. Even when we have taken into account the relativity of much psychological knowledge, recognized the influence of gender and cultural variations, owned conscious and unconscious bias, and accepted the political and social contexts in which therapists function, it is important to look at how we apply theories of personal development to individual clients. There is a danger, in a text that sets out ways of identifying major psychodynamic themes, of promoting a type of 'pathology spotting', or labelling of clients, which fails to do justice to the individual.

This is especially tempting when it can feel more secure for the therapist to want to impose order on the chaos or disturbance that comes with a client's story. There is safety in labelling people; and there is a false security in technical language and jargon, of which there is plenty in psychodynamic literature. Such technical and impersonal language is of course present in the medical and psychological disciplines from which psychotherapy sprung. Therapists can sometimes feel that their own explanations are lacking in scientific rigour; and in their communication with colleagues in medical or psychology settings, they may feel obliged to use a technical vocabulary and diagnostic categories. When others are using words such as psychotic, neurotic, character disorder, borderline personality, bi-polar disorder, and obsessive-compulsive disorder, like the rest of us use prepositions and conjunctions, therapists who are trying to prove their value and demonstrate their expertise do not simply have to learn to understand these terms; they may also feel under pressure to adopt them as labels for their own clients.

Categorization, which labelling to some extent represents, is of course an inevitable part of every intellectual discipline. This chapter has already cast doubt on how objective research can be in this area of human enquiry, although in practice therapists have to a certain extent to use theories and technical terms to communicate more clearly and precisely with each other. Yet it is important to challenge some of the assumptions that go with the use of categories, labels and technical language; and there is a more relevant and effective way of using this process of identifying where the client is.

I have already shown in the example of Diane (pp. 22–5) how one client's material can be approached from a number of different angles, and interpreted in the light of a number of themes. What the therapist perceives, and sometimes what the client chooses to present, can vary due to the individual characteristics and bias of the therapist, and sometimes from interview to interview. Therapists whose work permits them access to medical case notes, particularly the fat files of patients who have seen several consultants, doctors or psychologists, may be aware of how many of them have been placed in a variety of diagnostic categories. I recall one client, whose notes I saw, who had been diagnosed in four different ways by the same psychiatrist on four different occasions! Given the qualifications I have already made about the status of this type of knowledge, that should not be surprising.

There is nonetheless some value in being able to identify the right label, if we mean by that a tentative 'diagnosis'. Such a medical term does not sit neatly in psychotherapeutic discourse, but it is important for therapists to assess whether or not a client is suitable for therapy. This means having some knowledge of pathological states, even if there is inevitably also some questioning of the validity of psychopathological discourse (see Davies and Bhugra 2004). In the context of assessment a certain amount of labelling is inevitable, although this is more likely to take a firmer form when the client is not suitable than when the client is – in the latter case the ongoing work provides opportunities to refine understanding of the psychopathology, which in any case is translated into everyday terms in communicating with the client.

Effective labelling may at times also help a client. In another context, for example, it is reassuring to the patient with a pain in his chest to be told by his doctor that it is not cancer or heart trouble as the patient perhaps feared, but that he has strained a muscle decorating a high ceiling. Or if the cause of the pain is indeed more serious, it is probably not only the doctor, but also the patient, who will want a definite label to be attached as soon as possible. Even when the prognosis looks unfavourable, identifying the illness may carry some reassurance for the patient. Therapists have less opportunity to provide such definite information, although it can be extremely relieving to a client to be assured that he or she is not 'mad'. Knowledge, however, in this area of work, is always much less precise than it is for example in medicine or the law. In psychodynamic theories it not always desirable to share this knowledge in that form with clients: while saying, 'You are clearly depressed' may be an effective empathic response, even if it does not constitute a very clear diagnosis, saying, 'I can see you've got a narcissistic personality' is not going to get the therapeutic relationship very far!

The themes that I explore in the following chapters are not intended as means of labelling or of diagnosing clients. My aim is rather to provide a way of looking at, and understanding, the therapeutic relationship as it concentrates upon a person's inner world, with all its emotions and internal objects. Since this is an area that contains both less easily definable as well as contradictory information, and intense and often disturbing feelings, the various themes and sub-themes may sometimes provide a sense of security, a reference point in the midst of bewilderment, to which a therapist might look, and from which there may come some sense of direction. As long as the themes and the terms used within them do not become simple catchphrases, but represent a way into the complex network of presenting problems and past issues, they can also provide a range of possible clues to look out for in the material with which the therapist is presented. The label 'depression', for instance, is little use in itself, but might lead the therapist to look further at a number of possible factors, for instance a sense of loss, or guilt, or self-loathing, or repressed anger, or an overzealous conscience, or a morally or physically punitive upbringing, or any combination of such factors.

The label in these circumstances is not used to foreclose the issue, or to mollify the client, but to widen the horizon, and to trigger off a series of associations and questions which can extend the therapist's thinking and awareness. But there is another approach that might be used, which obviates the disadvantages and dangers of labelling, and provides more opportunities for translating the general theories of psychodynamic psychotherapy and counselling into the particular work with each client.

While there is some value in labelling, and in learning both the language and the method that psychodynamic practitioners use, the idea of identifying what is happening in the client and the therapeutic relationship is capable of a much greater richness of understanding than any generalized application of theory permits. There is an alternative term, which also promotes a distinctly different concept, and which appropriately (given the need to think across cultures) is seen in many non-Western societies. It is the concept of 'naming':

> The different use of the concepts of labelling and naming is illustrated by a client who had seen me for quite a long time. Freda opened one session by asking, 'What's wrong with me? Am I a manic depressive? Am I neurotic? Do I have an anxiety state?' I was rather concerned how best to answer this, wondering what kind of answer she wanted from me. I decided to reply honestly (and partly because I was not sure I really knew the answer!) that I was not normally interested in attaching such labels to people. To my relief Freda replied that if I did, she would want a category all to herself! The reason was obvious: she came from a large family, in which she was the middle child. Time and again she had talked of situations both in her family and in present relationships where she felt that she did not matter. She saw herself as always left out of invitations to parties, she felt people ignored her, and she recalled how her parents had teased her when she showed early signs of intellectual promise, which marked her out from their other children. She desperately wanted recognition, and yet she also felt guilty when she got it. She wanted to be treated as a unique individual. And she was prepared, had I labelled her, to insist on that too in any 'diagnosis'.

It is the uniqueness of the individual that lies behind the ancient concept of 'naming'. Ursula Le Guin, in her fantasy novel *A Wizard of Earthsea* (1971), employs this concept in a remarkably powerful way. Although each person, each animate object and each inanimate object has a common name – one that is used in normal speech – each also has a special and secret name. In the case of animals and objects this name has been passed down from ancient times in ancient speech. People are given their true name either in infancy or at puberty.

Salman Rushdie uses a similar concept, in his case clearly part of Muslim thought, in his novel *Haroun and the Sea of Stories* (1990). In one scene the Water Genie asks Haroun to pick a bird to travel upon. Haroun looks around the room but only sees a peacock carved in wood. The Water Genie tells Haroun that he can choose what he cannot see:

> A person may mention a bird's name even if the creature is not present and correct ... A person may even select a flying creature of his own invention ... To give a thing a name, a label, a handle; to rescue it from anonymity, to pluck it out of the Place of Namelessness, in short to identify it – well, that's a way of bringing the said thing into being.
>
> (p. 63)

There is a positive and a negative side to this concept of naming and bringing into being. Haroun clearly benefits when he can name his means of flying; but by the same token naming may bring the more feared imaginations into being. I shall return to this danger later. Naming is an awesome act, and this is seen in the way in which Ursula Le Guin develops her story. She observes that those who are wise are able to control objects and people only when they are able to give them their true name. Because of the power of the name people only give their true name to those whom they can trust: 'A man never speaks his own name aloud, until more than his life's safety is at stake' (1971: 46). The giving of your name to the other gives the other a certain power over you.

Such a fictional concept has been shown to have a real basis in many cultures, in Africa, in the East and the Middle East and in Polynesia. In his book on psychology and religion, Leslie Weatherhead similarly writes about the significance of a person's name. He describes how in the East giving one's name is felt to be the surrender of power to another (1963: 64). He cites as evidence a number of Indians in a regiment in which he served in the Great War, who would not give their true name lest their officers should acquire an uncanny power over them. In case of their death they kept their true name in a little cylinder on their person. Similarly, he says an Indian bride would not give her true name to her bridegroom until after the marriage ceremony. Weatherhead is particularly interested in the way these examples reflect the significance of naming in the Judaeo-Christian tradition. He cites the story of Creation and Adam naming the animals, this giving him power over the rest of Creation. He refers also to the episode in the Old Testament where the angel wrestles with Jacob and asks Jacob his name. Jacob gives it, but when he asks the angel his name, none is given. Similarly the power of the name is seen in the New Testament, for example in the healing of the man possessed by many devils. It does not matter whether this story is true or not. As I have indicated earlier, myths contain hidden truths. What is crucial in that story is the question, 'What is your name?' and the devils' reply, 'Our name is Legion', because it is this name that gives Jesus power over them.

The power involved in the act of naming is the central feature of Le Guin's story *A Wizard of Earthsea* (1971). The story is of a young hero, Sparrowhawk, who, in a fit of youthful pride, conjures up a shadow from the dead, which nearly destroys him. The shadow follows him and he tries to flee from it, without success. An old wizard, the one who had given Sparrowhawk his true name, tells him that he must stop running, and turn and face the shadow, and name it. Sparrowhawk protests, 'The evil thing, the shadow that hunts me, has no name'. '*All* things have a name' is the reply. Sparrowhawk turns and now becomes the pursuer, while the shadow becomes the pursued, until at the ends of the earth he names it. Without revealing the climax of the story, there is enough here to show the relevance of this concept of naming for therapy.

Naming forms an important part of the therapeutic process – and is far more relevant to the individual client than labelling. First, an essential part of the initial or early sessions is when clients are able to name what is troubling them. This process not only brings inner distress into the open, but it also begins the process of removing the fear and anxiety aroused by and associated with their present experience. Naming starts the process of owning and controlling the person's fear of what is happening to them, in their external or internal world.

Second, naming is seen in the way the therapist responds, in recognizing individuality, in treating the client not as 'another depressive' but as a unique individual, with her or his own particular problems, and her or his own life experience contributing to those problems.

Third, naming provides the opportunity of naming those parts of the self that frighten the client. In the ongoing process of naming, as in the initial naming of what troubles them, clients can experience considerable relief from the power that these parts of themselves have over them. Such naming takes place in a variety of ways. Parts of the body, for instance, may be given their proper name by the therapist or the client, and rescued from their association with guilt and shame – particularly the sexual. Words like 'homosexual', 'gay/lesbian', 'masturbation', which even in a more liberal society still trouble many cease, when named, to hold quite the same power in an individual's conscience. Similarly other parts of the self, 'forbidden' feelings like hate, jealousy, revenge, envy, even perhaps for some people love, when named come within the compass of an individual's control, rather than being repressed or suppressed. Anxiety and guilt about feelings, actions, thoughts, parts of the mind and parts of the body are lessened as each one can be named and brought into the open.

However, this is a subtle process. It is not enough, any more than it is enough with simple labelling, for the therapist to hammer the client into submissive acceptance by technical language or by clever interpretation. Naming takes place when something that is already known by the client is given that final push into consciousness or into words. In her novel *Possession*, A. S. Byatt writes of the recognition that takes place when we see something that at the point of seeing we realize was always there:

> Now and then there are readings which make the hairs on the neck, the non-existent pelt, stand upon end and tremble, when every word burns and shines hard and clear and infinite and exact, like stones of fire, like points of stars in the dark – readings when the knowledge that we *shall know* the writing differently or better or satisfactorily, runs ahead of any capacity to say what we know, or how. In these readings, a sense that the text has appeared to be wholly new, never before seen, is followed almost immediately, by the sense that it was *always* there, that we the readers, knew that it was always there, and have *always known* it was as it was,

though we have now for the first time recognised, become fully cogni-
sant of, our knowledge.

(1990: 471–2, original italics)

There is no magic, no secret formula, no clever interpretation that can
reach that depth of a person unless that person is already near to self-recognition. 'A mage can control only what is near him, what he can name exactly
and wholly' (Le Guin 1971: 60). Therapists can only speak of what is known
(how can they presume to do otherwise?), not from a theoretical background
but from the client, however much theory may inform their practice. Theory
sometimes contains truth, but sometimes also proves to be wide off the mark
in the case of an individual client. Unless it is translated into that person's
current presentation, it is likely to give rise to interpretations that make the
therapist feel more secure than the client. Naming on the basis of theory
alone may give the therapist the feeling of being helpful, but it probably also
colludes with the client's fantasy that as an expert the therapist has only
magically to 'speak the word' and the client will be healed. Interpretation,
especially if it is based on guesswork and not what the therapist 'can name
exactly and wholly', may even give the therapist the sort of power over the
client that the person most fears. It is vital, when naming takes place, whether
by the therapist or the client, that power should remain with the client, and
that power should be based on self-recognition. As therapists we must not
replace repression with oppression. Winnicott writes that premature interpretation 'annihilates the creativity of the patient and is traumatic in the
sense of being against the maturational process' (1971: 117).

One of the misconceptions about psychoanalysis and psychodynamic
psychotherapy is that analysts and therapists make standard interpretations.
It is true that at times it seems that Freud equates all dream symbols with
representations of sex; and that Melanie Klein in some of her case histories
appears to make what can only be called leading interpretations. Psychoanalysts in particular tend to write for other analysts, and often frame what
they have to say in technical language, failing to give us a true picture of the
give-and-take of the consulting room. In what is otherwise a rather technical
book on group analysis, the French psychoanalyst Anzieu underlines in his
opening pages that 'in everyday practice ... [the analyst] expresses himself as
much as possible in everyday language' (1984: 4). Freud writes about the need
to get close to what the patient is trying to express, rather than interpreting
indiscriminately. In one of his papers on technique he warns against the
analyst imposing ideas upon the patient:

> It is not difficult for a practised analyst to identify clearly the suppressed
> wishes of a patient, even from the nature of his complaints and his case
> history ... I have heard that there are analysts who brag about such
> instant diagnoses and rapid treatments, but I should warn everyone
> against following such examples ... Even in the later stages of the
> treatment you must be careful not to communicate the explanation of a
> symptom or the interpretation of a desire until the patient has reached
> the point where he is only a short step away from seizing upon this
> explanation for himself. In earlier years I had plenty of opportunity to

discover that communicating an explanation prematurely put a premature end to the therapy, both because of the resistances it suddenly aroused, and because of the relief the explanation brought with it.

(Freud 1913/2002: 60)

Freud appears to have forgotten this in one of his very last papers, where he asserts that the patient is always able to reject the wrong construction, and that no harm will be done if the analyst makes a mistake. He adds that if the analyst realizes that a mistake had been made 'we can draw the conclusion that we are wrong, and at some appropriate moment we can tell the patient as much, without loss of authority' (1937b/2002: 215). He is aware of the danger of the power of suggestion , but if there is some 'mishap' like that 'the analyst must have behaved very incorrectly' (p. 216). Suggestion is clearly a worse offence than making an erroneous construction, because Freud, while owning the latter, says of suggestion that such an abuse 'has never once occurred throughout my career' (p. 216).

What Freud fails to underline in this paper, written only a few years before his death, is just how powerful the authority of the analyst or the therapist can be, particularly where the process of naming is involved. The description of naming which Rushdie's Water Genie gives Haroun contains an implicit notion that anything can be created by naming it: 'A person may even select a flying creature of his own invention ... in short to identify it – well, that's a way of bringing the said thing into being' (Rushdie 1990: 63). Therapists will know clients who have been damaged by carrying around with them a psychiatric label which some tactless doctor or psychologist has given them in the past – the correctness or not of which is immaterial. If naming is therapeutically so much more powerful than labelling, then wrongly used it is by the same token more dangerous. It is not difficult to see how a therapist can create in the client what may indeed have been dimly part of the client's unconscious, but which should have been allowed to remain there, by being strictly contained within the boundaries of the therapist's imagination. In his late years Freud clearly looks back and recognizes the power of suggestion, and condemns it, as well as insisting that at the right time wrong interpretations need to be owned as such.

Another old man, a very knowledgeable but largely self-taught naturalist, once spoke (in a personal communication) about what he called 'sweet power'. This is not power over others or, in the context in which he was speaking, power over the environment. 'Sweet power', he told me, comes from being able to stand at a particular point in the country, and looking around, naming the geographical and natural features, being able to recognize the plant and animal life, and the relationship of the parts – including the observer – to the whole, in that microcosm of the natural world. It is perhaps something like the naming of the beasts in the Genesis story of Creation. It is not merely a scientific exercise, nor (he made it quite clear) is it a way of showing off knowledge, as some labelling or diagnosis can be. It is a process whereby a person feels in touch with, and in tune with, the environment of which he or she is but one part. Ursula Le Guin puts similar words into the mouth of the old wizard in Earthsea:

'When you know the fourfoil in all its seasons, root and leaf and flower, by sight and scent and seed, then you may learn its true name, knowing its being; which is more than its use. What, after all, is the use of you? Or myself?' Ogon went on a half-mile or so, and said at last, 'To hear, one must be silent.' The boy frowned ... kept back his resentment and impatience ... For he hungered to learn, to gain power.

(1971: 269)

There is another aspect of 'naming' which links with the frequent reference made in this chapter to metaphor. I referred above to the Genesis story of Creation, and to the power given to Adam to name the creatures. One interpretation of this is to see in the act of naming that Adam was not himself the creator, but was given a share of power over Creation. In one of the poems in *Possession* A. S. Byatt alludes to this Genesis story, echoing in her own way the power of naming which Rushdie and Le Guin also describe:

The first men named this place and named the world.
They made the words for it: garden and tree
Dragon or snake and woman, grass and gold
And apples. They made names and poetry.
The things were what they named and made them ...

The significant words follow:

... Next
They mixed the names and made a metaphor
Or truth, or visible truth, apples of gold.
The golden apples brought a rush of words
The silvery water and the horrent scales
Upon the serpentining beast, the leaves
All green and shining on the curving boughs
(The serpentining boughs) that called to mind
The lovely gestures of the woman's arms
Her curving arms, her serpentining arms ...

(1990: 464)

In this beautiful playing with words, Byatt reminds us that 'naming' (and indeed 'labelling') is itself a metaphor, and that all language is a means of trying to bridge the gap between inner experience and outer reality. It is also important to recognize that therapists and clients use words, as indeed a writer uses words, because it is probably the most convenient means of expression. Nevertheless what therapists, clients and writers identify and name is still only an approximation to inner experience. Since psycho-dynamic theory is full of metaphor, there is a point with clients when it becomes essential to make it clear that what they and we speak and name may be better than a label, and may carry more force and feeling than a label, but that it is still only a fallible and one-dimensional expression of the inner world. As the analyst Bion once wrote, psychoanalysis is 'a stripe on a tiger' (Eigen 1998: 16–17). For a fuller discussion of the various modes of knowledge and belief from a psychodynamic perspective see my book *Illusion* (Jacobs 2000a).

Summary

Given this important proviso about psychodynamic language and the power of the interpretation, we may summarize the argument of this chapter: psychodynamic theory meets our desire for greater knowledge as therapists, and aids the exploration and description of the inner and outer worlds of human relationships. Much as this knowledge may prove valuable, but it has limitations, not only because of what is not known, but because even what appears to be known is embedded in societal, cultural, and gender assumptions, which must always cast some doubt upon the permanence or objectivity of these and other theoretical concepts.

Seen as metaphors, sometimes even as symbols, which can enhance the art and skill of the therapist, psychodynamic concepts and language have much to offer therapists and clients, although they will usually need to be translated into more commonplace language for most clients. The terminology itself may promote clearer communication between practitioners, although using the theory and language to label clients runs the risk of giving therapists power over their clients. There is always the risk inherent in any categorization of losing sight of the individual, but there is also the danger of burdening the individual for life with a misleading or even damaging self-image.

Naming, on the other hand, ultimately provides deeper security to clients, for in the end they are helped to do the naming themselves. Naming gives them a sense of control that is based less on head knowledge and more on insight and on acceptance of more hidden parts of themselves. Naming recognizes and explores the 'being' and the uniqueness of each individual, for ultimately it is by name we are known, not by label. By recognizing how even naming itself is a metaphor and that what we name are also metaphors, then we are less tempted as therapists to use our knowledge to become as gods.

Developmental models and themes provide many clues to possibilities which ultimately only the client can confirm or deny. If the themes inherent in the course of personal development are to have any value, it will not simply be because they promote knowledge, but because they can be integrated with that intuition and sensitivity that therapists have acquired in their training. Combining the knowledge of the theorist, the insight of the artist and the humanity of the therapist is a delicate skill. Theory only serves therapists and counsellors well if it serves the client well. It is primarily clients who make theory, and not theory that makes therapy.

TRUST AND
ATTACHMENT:
FOUNDATIONS

The significance of past experience (both as objective facts, as well as subjective perceptions) applies as much to the earliest weeks and months of infancy as to any later time in a person's development. There might even be ante-natal influences as well (see, for example, Piontelli 1992), although it is post-natal experience of mother and baby that is more commonly discussed in psychoanalytic literature (see, for example, Breen 1989). While talking with mothers is clearly one way to understand the earliest relationship in anyone's life, a combination of infant observation, of attempting to conceptualize on the basis of what children and adults experience later, and increasingly the support of neurological and psychological studies of infants (Gerhardt 2004) provides the potentiality for many variations on theories of the infant's emotional development, and its significance for later life.

There is within psychoanalysis, as elsewhere, debate about the influence upon personal development of nature and nurture: how important relatively is genetic inheritance, natural temperament, and the environment in which the child grows, especially that provided by parents or parental figures? How important is actual experience versus felt experience? Melanie Klein, for example, appears to stress what a baby experiences, whatever the actual mothering that the baby receives, suggesting universal experiences about splitting, about aggression, and about reparation, even if the early environment is benign. Others, such as Bowlby, Fairbairn and Winnicott emphasize environmental factors; for example: 'Environmental influences can start at a very early age to determine whether a person will go out for experience or withdraw from the world when seeking a reassurance that life is worth living' (Winnicott 1988b: 128).

Recognizing the significance of these early relationships is vital in psychodynamic therapy. There are, first, parallels between the start of a therapeutic relationship, and the relationship of mother and baby, the recognition of which in no way infantilizes the client, but instead promotes the sensitivity of the therapist. Second, the way in which people make or break other relationships, particularly close or intimate relationships, similarly often has parallels to the way in which early relationships have been experienced. We might use different terms to describe what appears to be a mature way of relating: trust or hope (as in Erikson's first age), towards independence (Winnicott), secure attachment (Bowlby), the depressive position (Klein), but whatever term is preferred, each of these theorists sees its foundation in the earliest weeks and months of life, promoting the ability to relate well in adult life. Third, achieving an understanding, both intellectual and imaginative, of what may not go so well in infancy promotes empathy for those who suffer long-standing and severe disturbances, some of whom may not be suitable for other than the most skilled and experienced therapists. The effects of early deprivation (and privation; see Winnicott 1975: 306–15), abuse and neglect, at least from a psychoanalytic perspective, contribute greatly to profound psychotic and schizoid characteristics in later life. Although we have to be very careful of interpreting childhood from the perspective of the adult, one aspect of the richness of psychoanalytic writing on infancy is that it provides a language with which we can imagine the inner world, perhaps indeed of the infant, but more obviously the inner world of the distressed adult.

Yet it is very difficult, perhaps in the end impossible, to imagine precisely what an infant experiences in her early days, weeks and months. Infancy can be idealized, so that it is imagined as a time of bliss, a round of sleeping, feeding, and being bathed, simple play and sleep again. Parents of young infants know that this is not the case, although they may forget their own empathic pain as later years raise different issues. This early age of innocence is only innocent inasmuch as a baby does not know what the adult knows; and how much more difficult that makes it we can imagine for the baby, but also for the parent, who cannot as yet reassure with explanations. A more dynamic picture of a baby is far more complex, and although those who read Melanie Klein may at times find it difficult to believe the horrifying picture she appears to paint of the infant's thoughts and emotions, what she does express is the possibility (though for her the certainty) that babies may experience terrifying images. If we may doubt some of her interpretations, we also have to pause and remember those times when we have witnessed a baby's 'rage', and been made only too aware of how powerfully a baby can make her demands felt. If 'rage' appears too strong a word, adultomorphizing the infant or even projecting one aspect of a tired parent's feelings on to the child, Gerhardt's words nevertheless underline the strength of a baby's feelings:

> Feelings start at a very basic level. A baby experiences global feelings of distress or contentment, of discomfort or comfort, but there is little nuance or complexity involved in his processing of these feelings. He doesn't yet have the mental capacity to do complex information processing.
>
> (2004: 19)

It is not easy to *unlearn* years of experience and perspective, in order to imagine what it may feel like to be a newborn child: a state where there is virtually no knowledge, and not yet enough experience to constitute memory and learning. As adults we have many frames of reference. We know, for example, that night follows day, and we can visualize summer when it is winter. We have memories which support our knowledge so that we can recall times and seasons, and we know that they will return. At the same time some painful feelings can be so strong that it is impossible to imagine that good feelings will return – and if that is true for adults, it is probably no less true for infants and children. It is of course impossible to imagine a time when we knew nothing, and did not know how to make sense of each new experience. For a newborn baby this lack of knowledge gives rise to 'fantasy': primitive attempts to make sense of experience, without any knowledge as yet of 'reality'.

Perhaps the closest we get to this in imagination is when we are due to visit a new place, or to meet a person with whom we have only spoken on the phone. We form an idea of what the place or the person will be like, and very often we are surprised that the reality is not at all like we imagined it in our fantasy. The disjunction between fantasy and reality may even (temporarily) be quite disturbing, although we quickly adjust to the new situation. As adults we take for granted this ability to imagine, or, to use psychodynamic language, 'to fantasize'. We have sufficient knowledge and experience for our fantasized expectations not to become too wild. Similarly most day-to-day experiences in adult life can be assimilated readily into some frame of reference. But none of that is yet available to the infant, even though she will hopefully learn that the world (the only world to her) is a safe enough place.

It has been long recognized that the extended period of dependency of the child upon its parents makes for particular features in the process of development. For a considerable time (although it often feels longer than in fact it is) babies need others to feed them, to give them security and warmth, and to make them comfortable – and that is just the physical level of parental attention. They also need a relationship that conveys all this on a different emotional level. Psychoanalytic theory has itself developed, from what at first seemed to be more about satisfying self-preservation drives such as hunger, to stressing that it is not just being fed that matters, but how the total relationship with the carer which is only partly conveyed through feeding, is of cardinal importance.

There are nonetheless differences between analytic theories, for example, over their understanding of the precise nature of the early relationship between baby and mother. ('Mother' is the most common and straightforward term to use here, although of course 'mother' may include a father who takes an equal part in childcare or mother may not be the natural mother.) Before birth, of course, mother and baby are intimately linked physically, and in most cases emotionally as well inasmuch as the pregnant woman experiences her baby as a welcome if sometimes physically uncomfortable part of her. At birth the physical link is, in one sense, severed. But are mother and baby still intimately linked psychologically, as if they were one person? This is what Winnicott appears to claim, when he writes that 'there is no such thing as a baby' (1964: 88), but rather a nursing couple in a type of symbiotic relationship, as if the baby does not (and cannot) exist on her own. Yet Daniel Stern, as much an observer of babies as Winnicott, finds this idea of undifferentiation between mother and baby 'very problematic ... At the same time ... it has great appeal' (1985: 240). Winnicott's image appeals perhaps because it touches an early memory although we cannot know whether this memory is of the womb or after birth. Or is it a fantasy which appeals to the comfort of the oceanic feeling in an adult life where isolation is often felt as a threat?

Self and not-self; me and not-me

The difficulty of imagining the infant's state of mind is illustrated by this question of the nature of the relationship between the new-born infant and the mother. I have already drawn attention to a baby having no initial frames of reference, and having to learn over a period of time how to place her very different experiences of comfort and discomfort in perspective. But how might a baby 'understand' these different experiences? Take feeding, for example. A baby is hungry, and the hunger may even be painful, until it is relieved when her sucking makes contact with a nipple (or a teat) and the hunger is relieved by something warm, sweet and wet. Or other uncomfortable feelings are relieved when held in something warm and secure. The reader's picture here is immediately of a mother's breast, or the bottle, or a soft blanket, or a mother's arms. But a new baby has no such knowledge. Milk, a blanket, mother's skin – none of these have as yet any objectivity. A baby does not know whether they belong to her or are outside her – it is not even a question the baby asks. In this sense it can be said that all experience is unitary: there is no division between 'me' and 'not-me'. A baby's thumb (in her perception) may be no more or less attached to her than the mother's nipple. The boundary between what is me and not-me, between self and not-self, the space between the body of the baby and the body of the mother – all these are only gradually distinguished. Winnicott even suggests that a baby may imagine that she has herself created the breast, when a mother is sensitive to her baby's needs and places her nipple on the baby's lips just at the right moment when the baby wishes a feed (1971: 1–10).

Winnicott in fact does not like the term 'symbiotic', since it is too biological a concept to be acceptable (1971: 130) – although Margaret Mahler does use the word (1958: 77). It is a misnomer since while a baby cannot survive without mothering, a mother can survive without her baby, although not of course without real pain. Viewed psychologically, however, it may still be the right word to use of some mother–baby relationships. Most mothers, in the period of pregnancy, birth and early weeks, are primarily preoccupied with their baby – Winnicott calls this 'primary maternal pre-occupation' (1975: 300–5). This is not just because of their baby's demands, but because they need the baby as much as the baby needs them. Some mothers describe this as 'being in love' with their baby. Danah Zohar writes of her pregnancy:

> I experienced what for me was a strange new way of being. In many ways, I lost the sense of myself as an individual, while at the same time gaining a sense of myself as part of some larger and ongoing process.

At first the boundaries of my body extended inwards to embrace and become one with the new life growing inside me. I felt complete and selfcontained, a microcosm within which all life was enfolded.

I experienced myself as extending in all directions, backwards into 'before time' and forwards into 'all time', inwards towards all possibility and outwards towards all existence.

(1991: 193)

This description is perhaps an example of the 'oceanic feeling' referred to above. We catch glimpses of a similar state when for a fraction of a minute time itself seems suspended and we feel a sense of harmony which cannot adequately be conveyed in words: the harmonies of music sometimes express it better. It is also seen in the confusion of space and time boundaries which can result from the use of hallucinogenic drugs, both in good and bad 'trips', although it is generally the bad experience that might bring people to the counsellor or therapist:

Gemma had been slipped LSD in a drink. She described the terror of time sliding backwards and forwards, together with a frighteningly vivid conflation and confusion of herself with two people whose deaths she had witnessed years before. At one moment she felt she was them, at another that they were her, and she was convinced that she was going to die too. Fortunately this was an isolated incident, and after she had been able to describe the terror, she was able in a more grounded way to look at her memories of these two deaths, and some of the (unjustified) guilt she was still experiencing over them.

The effects, or even the after-effects, of drugs may be responsible for this type of frightening experience. But confusion over the boundaries between self and other, or over time or space, has other possible explanations. For example, it may be a sign of a deep level of disturbance, of a type of psychotic merging with the environment or with other people, and in itself an indication that such a presentation may not be appropriate for counselling, or for any but the most specialized form of psychotherapy. So when a client refers to this type of confusion of boundaries, particularly to feeling apart from the world about them, or even from their own body (such as physically experiencing looking down upon their body), a therapist needs to consider various possibilities:

- it may be an example of dissociation (often linked with a history of severe trauma or abuse; see Walker 1992: 182–5 for examples);
- or of what is described often as a 'borderline personality', where generally the person can relate to the therapist, but describes experiences that can feel to the client and to the therapist as 'over an edge', too far out of touch with reality;
- or of psychotic disturbance, particularly when the person apparently has no awareness that what they are describing is strange; or when, even if they are disturbed by the content of their thoughts, they are not actually disturbed that they are functioning in such a way.

It is vital to be aware of these levels of disturbance, particularly since counsellors and therapists are at times asked to take on clients who in an earlier generation would have been referred and cared for elsewhere. In the first two instances (dissociation and borderline personality), developed skills, considerable experience and good supervision are essential in the therapist. An overinterpretative technique might trigger off psychosis. In the third instance of psychotic states, psychiatric assessment and cover is essential if the choice is made to work with such presentations. Where there is evidence of drug or other substance abuse, again specialized help might be necessary (although see Reading and Jacobs (2003) for possibilities for the generic therapist).

Such examples show that merged or confused boundaries demonstrate that the symbiotic relationship is not all bliss. Mothers usually experience the pain of their troubled babies. Some mothers, it is important to recognize, do not view their pregnancy and/or their newborn baby with joy, and pregnancy and/or birth may lead to a particular type of depression with consequent effects on the child (Murray and Cooper 1997). Some psychoanalytic writers, such as Bowlby and Winnicott, have been tasked by feminist critics as having idealized mothers on the one hand, and put an enormous burden of responsibility upon them on the other hand, and thereby contributed to women feeling inadequate and depressed if they do not experience the pleasure of being a mother. Yet the criticism of idealizing motherhood is not altogether fair, since psychoanalytic descriptions of the mother–child relationship make it quite clear that motherhood engenders hate as well as love: for example, Winnicott (1975: 201) lists a number of reasons that a mother can be said to hate her baby, which he links to the hate that therapists can also feel for their patients. Dana Breen describes in detail the different experiences in pregnancy and the early weeks from actual conversations in *Talking with Mothers* (1989).

This confusion of self and not-self is also a part of all relationships. It will not always be troublesome: indeed in one form, empathy, which means getting under the skin of another person and trying to experience what they are experiencing, is obviously seen as one of the essential aspects of therapy. There are many ways in which one person 'enters into' the experience of another, and it makes sense to link some of the psychological phenomena to the very close sympathetic relationship of mother and baby. The opposite of merging is splitting off, and when, for instance, we attribute to another person a thought or feeling that we cannot see is in fact a part of ourselves, this is known as 'projection'. A similar phenomenon is 'projective identification'. This can be experienced when we find ourselves having feelings that in one way seem to be ours, but at the same time make us wonder where they have come from: 'Why am I reacting to this person this way?' There are, of course, different explanations for this, but in projective identification it is suggested that such feelings have been 'put into' us by the other. I may therefore disown my angry feelings for my partner, by 'making' her the one who becomes angry with me (and most subtly of all, without her realizing, or even me realizing, that I have made this happen). Projective identification is not unusual in close relationships, such as between sexual partners, and can occur in the therapeutic partnership.

Projection and projective identification are reckoned in psychodynamic theory to be early (or 'primitive') defences, although in infancy they are thought to be natural defences against pain or terror, which have to be put elsewhere, according to Klein, for example, into the breast or into the mother. Segal describes this:

Projective identification involves a more active *getting rid of* something belonging to the self into someone else ... It can be a very powerful means of communication of feelings (used by babies or small children before they can talk, for example). It can also be used as a destructive attack, with nasty or unbearable or 'mad' parts of the self evoked in other people to destroy their comfort, their peace of mind or their happiness.

(1992: 36, italics added)

The therapist needs to be ready to receive such projections and monitor such projective identification, to hold the experience (as a mother also contains what her baby throws at her) and at the right moment, when more able to accept the projected feelings, to help the client receive them back. They can be helped to own their feelings. Clients too may have been at the receiving end of projections and projective identification, where they have swallowed what others have said about them, or taken on board others' projections. In such cases they can be helped to recognize how others have contributed to their difficulties. They may then temper their sense of overresponsibility for things that have gone wrong. As a therapist described her client in supervision: 'It's almost as if she became part of her father's mental illness'.

In these different ways we see the significance of the concept of self and not-self, or as it is often put in psychodynamic theory, 'me/not-me': we learn gradually to distinguish what belongs to me, and what belongs to 'not-me' – that the breast belongs to mother, not the baby, that what is outside the body is an object in its own right, not as Winnicott puts it a 'subjective object' (1971: 130) Winnicott also calls this a state of 'I am', a stage of being that comes before doing (p. 130). This sense of identity is also seen in the way the term 'self' is used in everyday language: 'I seem to have lost myself'; 'I don't understand myself'; 'I am not myself anymore'.

The concept of the 'self' certainly has complex psychological and philosophical problems attached to it (Brinich and Shelley 2002), but ordinary life also is full of different types of problems around the self. The self can get lost, for example, in love. When people fall in love their personal boundaries seem to merge. Absence of the other 'half' (the term is an interesting one) is like losing part of oneself. The language of love (as much as the act of love) frequently expresses the interpenetration of each one by the other. If this phase of love is perpetuated, without separateness being re-established, a person may fear losing himself or herself in the other:

Harry became desperate when he realized how his love for Isabel made him so dependent upon her that she was able to play him along, always calling the tune. He needed Isabel so much that he was afraid to say anything which might destroy the relationship. At the same time he felt resentful at being treated like an object that could be picked up and dropped at her whim. Things got to such a pitch that he resolved to break off seeing her, and was able to do so. Immediately he felt so different that he told his therapist, 'I have got my self back again.' He had feared being desolate and alone, but found himself able to relate to others much more easily. Harry was then, and only then, able to see parallels between the confusion of his self with Isabel's, and the relationship between his parents. He remembered a time when his father was cutting a piece of wood, but cut it to the wrong length. Father had immediately blamed Harry's mother, with the result that Harry was bewildered. He could not understand what his mother had done. His mother also confused him, because she would say, 'If you do this, or don't do that, you'll kill me'. He remembered feeling puzzled as a child about how such things could happen, and what it meant about the way people interacted. He had had to distance himself from his home before he found any sense of identity for himself; and he had lost it again in his relationship with Isabel. One of the aims in his therapy was to help him to establish the boundaries of his own identity. Only when he had done this would he be able to get close to another without fearing the loss of himself. In that sense he was an example of Erikson's model which suggests that identity needs to be achieved before intimacy. But another way of looking at this is that following the intimacy of the mother–baby relationship separateness needs to be achieved.

Omnipotence and narcissism

In his theory about the early relationship between mother and baby Winnicott suggests that a baby is born with a mental conception of the breast. Suckling is of course an instinctive action, or reaction to the presentation of the breast. The baby searches for something that should be there, and knows what to do as soon as she has found the nipple, which to the observer has of course been presented to her by the mother. But Winnicott's observation is about more than an instinctual process: it is also an important mental process. When a mother presents her breast to her baby, and her baby is looking for the breast, Winnicott (1988b: 100–3) suggests that the baby 'thinks' that she has 'created' the breast. This description is course metaphorical, hence my placing of some of these words in inverted commas. We can scarcely call this 'thinking', as (for example) the reader is presently thinking. But Winnicott is making an observation which is particularly relevant for understanding the nature of omnipotence as well as of creativity (which Erikson places in the seventh age, but is apparent here, at the start of life).

'I thought it, and it was there'. Finding the breast of which she had conceived perhaps leads a baby to believe in the power of her thought, or of her wish to make things happen. She is, in a sense, omnipotent: 'I have only to think it, and it is there'. This type of thinking lays a basis for later belief in oneself, for trust and for faith – these terms might at this point be interchangeable. While we may think of these early months of life as engendering trust in the mother (and indeed this must be part of the experience), the baby's sense of being able to create something lays down an even earlier sense of trust: belief in oneself. Since mother is not yet perceived as a separate person, this trust is in 'everything': the baby, the mother and indeed the whole (if tiny) world the baby experiences. 'When I want it, it is there'. In fact, this early sense of omnipotence will not last. Winnicott calls it an illusion: the first of a whole series of illusions which we experience throughout life. One of the mother's tasks is to provide the basis for such an illusion to take place; and if she can do that, it is a little later her task to help her baby towards disillusionment, as the baby learns that the breast is not always there, and that things are not always there for the asking or the wishing. But at the beginning it is the mother's provision of herself, at the point at which a baby seeks the breast or needs to feed, that creates this sense of confidence in the emerging self, and which forms a foundation for a maturing sense of self – what Winnicott (1965b) calls 'the maturational processes'. By contrast, a baby who does not find her needs met not only feels frustrated, but is also denied an early lesson about her ability to create.

There are two ways in which these ideas can be seen in clients. Some people have a sufficient sense of confidence in themselves, which was laid down in infancy and no doubt reinforced in their childhood. They believe in themselves and trust others, and in some sense have confidence in life itself, even if they know life can be unpredictable. Others incline to pessimism or cynicism, even when life is going well. Those who have confidence in themselves do not think they can make everything happen; but they know that (often as a result of working at it) some of what they wish for can happen. There is in them a basic optimism that life is on their side, and that it is worth living. They may be knocked by events, but the therapist senses enough basic strength or confidence in them to merit some optimism also in the therapeutic process. This can be contrasted with the much more difficult task of working with those whose view of themselves is either bleakly pessimistic ('I never get anything I want'; 'I am powerless, and can do nothing'); or the opposite, frighteningly omnipotent: either frightening to others ('I am going to have whatever I want'); or frightening to themselves ('I thought that, and so it must have been me that caused it to happen').

An example of such an omnipotent fantasy could be seen at work in John. He had met the girl of his dreams, but his difficulty – as his therapist saw it – was that it was all a dream or a daydream. John believed that she would marry him, but she (who had also seen the same therapist because she was unable to handle John's attentions) was clearly angry at the way he was pestering her – not quite as threatening as stalking her, but almost as troublesome. She had tolerated his calls at her flat, but she made it quite clear that she already had a relationship. She had said, 'Let's just be friends', even though she did not like John at all and only felt sorry for him. But such a slender straw was enough for John to cling to; he read this as her wish for a relationship being the same as his; and he redoubled his efforts. She moved and refused to answer his telephone calls. He wrote, but she did not answer, until one day she grew tired of his persistence and replied, to tell him about her new job. Once more

John grabbed the straw, and sent by return an erotic love letter. Nothing could shake John's conviction that he was going to marry her. 'But he's not in love with me', she said despairingly, 'he's in love with himself'.

John was certainly in love, but he was in love with an illusion, an object of wish-fulfilment, an idealization of this young woman and of their relationship. When John himself saw his therapist he provided an opening in what could so easily have been an intractable situation when he said, 'It's God's will that I marry her'. John had a religious faith, which enabled the therapist to address him from a different angle: 'You seem to be very sure that you know God's will … Perhaps you are trying to tell God what you want'.

This oblique reference to John's wish for things to go his way (even taking on God's omnipotence) implied that he did not stop to think what the other person might wish. The shock tactic of this intervention seemed to make a slight impact upon his thoughts about the girl. Perhaps suitably reminded of his own fallibility John replied at that point, 'Perhaps I should wait and see what happens between us, and try not to push it too much'. The therapist was not very confident that things were resolved, but thought it was a step in the right direction.

This omnipotent way of thinking is reminiscent of a baby and her mother, who is in many ways the baby's only world, and suggests that the small world of the baby is, as Balint describes it, a 'primitive, harmonious, inter-penetrating mix-up' (1968: 72), although of course sometimes the mix-up is not always harmonious. It is quite hard to imagine what it might be like for a baby, when this is the only 'world' she knows. 'The horizon of the baby extends at first a few inches, and later only a few feet from his body. Its adequacy is determined by the very restricted exchange between mother and child' (Scharff 1988: 15). When the baby feels good, even though the source of that feeling is not yet clear, the world as a whole is good; when she feels bad, everything is bad. It is like being caught in a hall of mirrors, which almost infinitely reflect either good or bad feelings. It is this that is a baby's first experience of her environment. That little world enlarges of course as the child grows, but first impressions count for much, especially at such an impressionable stage. It is probably an all-or-nothing existence, which is not altogether an unfamiliar experience in adult life:

> Kate was talking about the last few months, which she had spent in Africa: 'When I first arrived I was almost worshipped by the people in the village. I was put on a pedestal, and I felt really great. But after a couple of months they got used to me, and me to them, and I started to feel ordinary, well, not ordinary, but really criticized by some of the people there. I'm like that. Things can be pretty wonderful, and then all of a sudden they go off, and I have to find something new. I'm an all-or-nothing person.' Perhaps this linked with the issues that she first brought to therapy: alternately overeating and then starving herself: all or nothing.

There will be times, then, when everything feels very good for a baby, but also times when everything feels bad. It is impossible for a mother to be ever-present or ever-attentive, even though most mothers are very alert to their baby's needs. The points of frustration are important for the baby's development, the beginning of learning that in the end there is nothing simply on tap. There are some pains which mother can do little to relieve, when nature must simply take its course, and her baby will not be comforted, however hard she tries. All this is part of the disillusion that a baby experiences, which Winnicott stresses is a healthy part of development. Mothers try to provide containment, but also to filter reality to their babies in tiny portions, according to what they can bear. What matters is that the mothering is reliable and dependable, so that where there is pain there can also be comfort, and that where there is waiting there is also satisfaction.

It must sometimes feel impossible to get it right, because too anxious a mother may also give rise to an anxious baby. It is not only the neglectful mother who nurtures the seeds of doubt. A mother may be too preoccupied with her baby, for too long 'lending her own self to her infant' rather than encouraging the development of the infant's self and 'recover[ing] her self-interest' (Winnicott 1965a: 15). Winnicott uses the phrase 'the good-enough mother', or 'the ordinary devoted mother' (1988a: 3–14), meaning by this one who is attentive and adaptive to her baby's needs, but one who also knows when she is not wanted; one who contains the painful feelings in her baby, but who gradually introduces the wider world, so that it gradually impinges upon her infant. She provides the foundation for the emerging view of the world that in later life is recognized as sometimes heavenly, and sometimes hellish, and on balance a good-enough place to be. Trust in oneself comes from a dependable mother-figure, whose reliability gives rise to a broad sense of trust in the ever-widening world beyond her.

Issues about trust and reliability are present to some extent in every client. The parallel between the reliable and sensitive mother and the reliable and sensitive therapist is obvious here, although only in the work that some experienced therapists undertake with deeply regressed clients is there any real replication of the daily attention that a mother gives her child. The reliability of the therapist is maintained by keeping to appointments, by being able to listen without making the client anxious, and by being able to contain 'bad' experiences and feelings. The therapeutic relationship provides the milieu in which, in Alice Miller's words, there is 'freedom to experience feelings which are spontaneous. It is part of the kaleidoscope of life that these feelings are not only cheerful, beautiful and good, but that they can display the whole scale of human experience including envy, jealousy, rage, disgust, greed, despair and mourning' (1979: 72).

This need for reliability perhaps goes without saying. Yet no therapist can be so reliable as to be constantly present for the client. Apart from illness and those occasional but unavoidable times when they cannot keep an appointment, therapists build breaks into the contract, both through regulating the frequency of appointments, and through holidays. Neither can therapists hope to avoid lapses of concentration, or the failure to understand, any of which shows therapists to be fallible. They cannot fulfil the wish some clients have for a substitute mother. Such moments of 'failure' provide important points to take up clients' feelings of disappointment, anger or sense of loss in relation to the therapist. When such feelings can be vented, they can some-times be linked to past experience (without in any sense letting the therapist 'off the hook'); or they may be opportunities for looking more deeply at past disappointments.

In some writing on counselling and therapy (more often from a humanistic perspective) there is a tendency towards idealizing the role of the therapist, who provides the right conditions that will enable the client to develop. But this is only part of the picture. While therapists should endeavour to provide what Winnicott calls (in respect of mothering) 'a facilitating environment' or the 'environment-mother' (1965b: 75), therapists inevitably fail to do this, and in failing to do this also provide a model of responding to failure. To describe the therapist–client relationship with any accuracy, especially in terms of trust and reliability, we need to set alongside each other two con-tradictory statements of Winnicott's:

> It is the mother–infant couple that can teach us the basic principles on which we base our therapeutic work.
>
> (Cited in Guntrip 1968: 361)

> He can never make up to clients for what they have suffered in the past, but what he can do is to repeat the failure to love them enough . . . and then share with them and help them work through their feelings about his failure.
>
> (Cited in Malan 1979: 141)

Kohut also places importance upon the empathic therapist being able to deal with failing to be as empathic as the client wants and needs.

In reaction or response to mothering which is either neglectful, that is which fails to allow the omnipotence to be experienced in the first instance, a child may become either clinging or withdrawn, or as I will explain further below, narcissistic. One expression of any of these characteristics can be seen in those who cling to drugs, alcohol or food, or to dependent relationships; or perhaps who live in a withdrawn fantasy world, in extreme cases showing psychotic fantasies, as if only their own created world is a safe place to be. Others may withdraw from intimate contact with people, less schizophrenic than schizoid. The earlier the disturbance in mothering, the greater the need for long-term therapy or for other specialized help. But there will be less extreme examples of withdrawal or dependency in any therapeutic practice:

> Lara had fallen in love: everything was heavenly; her boyfriend was 'super', her work going 'very well'. Even her terminally ill father had begun to rally. But none of this eased her problem of overeating. When she was on her own she ate and ate. She could not see anything that caused it, except to acknowledge that the only cloud on the horizon was her fear of being let down when she was so happy. A previous boyfriend had left her when she had least expected it. Her therapist wondered whether eating was a way of trying to store up happiness. He made several interpretations along these lines, although they had no effect on her voracious appetite, until one session in which he suggested that it was almost as if she were saying of her boyfriend and her father (both of

whom she feared losing), 'I'll eat you up – I love you so much'. This remark appeared to have a dramatic effect, because from that session on Lara's eating became more normal. She was also able to move towards getting in touch with her discontent at her boyfriend's lack of consideration for her.

In this instance the therapist knew little of Lara's early life, upon which to base any idea about her early experiences of dependency. He concentrated on the present situation, but he used words that appeared to express one of the presenting issues.

In the following example, the family history had some relevance, in what was a short-term contract:

Mike had fallen in love. This had created some turmoil for him, because he was a 'fiercely independent' late adolescent, following his father who had laid great stress upon that particular virtue. Mike's father was the child of a broken home, and had been shunted from one part of the wider family to another, and from one institution to another. Subsequently father had been successful in his career, and he brought his sons up to think of career first, and relationships a long way second. Mike too had been successful to date, ahead of his peers in many of his achievements, but afraid of being caught up in a close relationship. He was not only worried what his father would think; he was scared in case he ceased to love his girlfriend, or she stopped loving him. Mike described their relationship in this way: 'She has got into the pool, whereas up to now I have only allowed my close friends to dip their feet in'. The way she had 'got inside him' was a disconcertingly new feeling, though it only appeared temporarily to throw him.

Some clients fear dependency on their therapist or on the therapeutic process. This may be expressed openly in the first session, but may be expressed obliquely, as in the reference made by one client to the anxiety he felt about becoming dependent on the tablets the doctor prescribed: he may also have been referring to an anxiety about therapy as well. There may be clues to anxieties about dependency in the client's pattern of relating to others:

Nan said in her first session that she tended to see people two or three times, and then broke off relationships. The therapist was therefore alerted to the possibility that this might also happen with her. Indeed after four meetings Nan aired the idea of stopping. The therapist reminded Nan of what she had said in the first session, and looked with her at her present anxiety about closeness.

Nan illustrates the withdrawn person well. She feared close relationships, but deep down longed for comfort. She sought therapy because she was so isolated, spending much of her time on her own, eating and sleeping. Her early history demonstrated that her infancy had been traumatic. She had been born prematurely, and her mother died soon afterwards. Her first weeks of life were spent in an incubator, and it was several weeks after that before she left hospital, because her father had been looking for somewhere to place her. So she was rejected by both her parents, one unintentionally, the other intentionally. She went into a foster home, where food or a dummy was used whenever one of the children was upset. When Nan's father married again, and she was taken back by the new family he now had, she rejected her stepmother. Nan later experienced further losses of other members of the family whom she had allowed to become important for her. Little wonder that she could not allow herself to depend upon another person, for fear of losing them. She found herself hating people once she had got to know them a little, and this seemed to be a way of forestalling any rejection they might first make of her.

This last example is typical of the personality type that is known in psycho-analytic terminology as 'schizoid'. A schizoid person maintains an emotional distance, even in what might otherwise be a close and intimate relationship. Although long-term therapy may be necessary for shifting a schizoid pattern of relationships, such clients can of course seek counselling for other reasons than their relationships, in which case short-term work may be possible. Where it is possible to build a relationship with such a client of sufficient trust, long-term therapy for the deeper issues becomes a possibility.

Sometimes a client uses an intellectual defence in order to avoid closeness, which may prove difficult for the therapist, since the 'feeling mode' is kept at a safe distance. This is again often found in the schizoid character:

Oliver found solace in his books, and passed his exams at school well ahead of his own age group. He had been brought up in a home where there was not simply material poverty, but also extreme poverty in the quality of relationships. His parents' constant rows drove him to his room and to study. At school he made friends, but never close friends. It was not until his mother died that the dearth of love in his life hit him, although his presenting problem was actually about his inability to progress with his doctoral thesis. He tended to talk intellectually in his sessions, looking all the time for explanation – and always in a most affable way – but unable to get near to any feelings of sadness or of closeness. The most obvious feeling he experienced was anxiety about closeness, but he avoided that socially by keeping people at a comfort-able distance. It took many months before he could begin to show any glimmer of sadness; his therapist did not push for feelings to emerge, but rather used the 'intellectual' style of the sessions to point out constantly the fears that Oliver might have. Helping those who have deeper levels of pain can take a very long time, and requires respect for the defences that protect them.

If one of the difficulties in working with a detached person is creating a relationship in the first place, the opposite is true of the clinging, dependent client, who might be said to latch on to the relationship offered by the therapist, and hungrily demands more and more time, help and attention.

Peter had been four years in therapy in an outpatient department of the local psychiatric unit when he came to the local counselling centre. The therapy had terminated six months before, and he was still feeling depressed. What was noticeable was how quickly he raised questions about what he and the counsellor would do when it came to the summer break; how difficult it was to get a word in edgewise with him (although he also did not give away much about his deeper feelings); and although he was on the surface very warm and friendly, the counsellor soon recognized how difficult it was to end sessions. Peter always wanted to take them over time. One of the clearest themes that emerged was his experience of being let down when he thought he was in a committed relationship, and the counsellor tried to identify this as the main anxiety Peter felt about any discussion of endings.

A therapist can easily feel 'drained' and empty, frustrated and angry, perhaps mirroring in her or his countertransference the dependent client's own feelings of emptiness and anger, neither of which can be assuaged. But dependency takes many forms, and the inner compulsion to make demands can make some people feel so guilty or ashamed that they become afraid of expressing their needs, or are constantly apologetic about 'taking up your time'. They are afraid of their hunger for love in case it drives people away, which, of course, in relationships generally is what a demanding person often does.

Really damaged and demanding clients may call upon the therapist at all hours. Training as a therapist provides little experience in handling this type of client, who in one sense appears to have regressed to the position of an ever-hungry baby. Where such demands are experienced, therapists need to be able to preserve their own and their client's boundaries, remaining steady but reliable over time limits and frequency of meetings. It is important to remember in such cases that more frequent meetings do not usually stem the demand, and may even encourage a deeper regression, suggesting that boundaries can be pushed even further. Supervision is clearly vital for working with such situations.

Less regressed, but similarly demanding clients may indicate their need and their discontent through quiet grumbling or open hostility. If this can be brought out into the open and accepted by the therapist, without retaliation on their part, a client can often appreciate the security of firm boundaries, whereas wavering and flexible times often make the client feel even more anxious. A reliable and stable therapist who is not shaken by the client's demands or by their attacks enables a client to feel more secure and less fearful that the needed relationship will be snatched away. A therapist who constantly tries to reassure by acceding to requests can make a client feel anxious and guilty. Winnicott writes: 'In the analytic situation the analyst is much more reliable than people are in ordinary life; on the whole punctual, free from temper tantrums, free from compulsive falling in love, etc.' (1975: 285).

It needs to be said, however, that it is easier to write about the balance between setting limits and showing care than it is to effect it. It can be difficult to weather the storms that blow up, hard on both the therapist and the client. Until a client feels secure in the relationship with the therapist, and understands that the frustrations involved in the relationship are not the therapist's retaliation towards the client as 'bad' or 'needing to be punished', it is difficult to move from the intensity of the therapy relationship itself to look at other relationships outside the session, and to wider areas of concern.

The link between being 'bad' and being demanding is seen in the following example:

> As a child, Quia clung to her mother for many years at those times when mother was home from the mental hospital. She was a frequent non-attender at school, until the age of 10, when she overheard her mother saying to a neighbour that her most recent spell in hospital was because she was worried about Quia's clinging behaviour. Although it was initially mother's absences that had made Quia so dependent, the situation was now turned on its head; it appeared to her that it was her demands that were driving mother away. She also recalled an early occasion of mother's absence when an aunt with whom she was staying refused to let her see 'Watch with Mother' on the television, because she had not 'performed' on the potty after lunch. We might restate that situation as: 'If I cling on to what is in me (i.e. my faeces), that prevents me seeing mother too'. After Quia had heard mother speaking to the neighbour she determined to become self-reliant, and went to school without making any fuss. But the problem had been pushed underground, because in her first session with her therapist she several times used the phrase, 'You can't rely on anyone'. The therapist observed that Quia was probably wondering if she could even rely upon her, but in this instance even this was not enough to help her return for a second session.

Reliability and dependability are of course important with all clients, although not everyone reacts negatively to changes or unpreventable disappointments on the part of the therapist. With demanding clients it helps them to learn that however badly they think of themselves this does not alter the constancy of the therapist. With those who are fearful of making demands or and allowing themselves to become dependent, the steady attention of the therapist may help them to make the first moves towards the trust that they need to engage in other aspects of the therapeutic relationship.

It may be easier to understand the expectations of demanding clients if they can be seen against the backdrop of a natural and normal stage in early infancy, before a baby needs to learn about limits and boundaries, or to come to terms with the realities of other people's independence. There is no reason that babies should not enjoy the same privileges, which Winnicott described to new mothers as being their right: 'Enjoy yourself. Enjoy being thought important. Enjoy letting other people look after the world ... Enjoy being turned in and almost in love with yourself ... Enjoy having more right than you have ever had before or will have again to do just what you feel is good' (1964: 26). Freud put it similarly when he used the phrase in his paper on narcissism, 'His Majesty the Baby' (1914: 84), interestingly linked to the narcissism of parents who see their child as destined for great things. It is perhaps unfortunate that psychoanalysis uses the term narcissism as a natural phase of development, because in common usage it has pejorative undertones. It is, however, in psychoanalytic theory distinguished from that narcissism which we equate with selfishness by being called 'primary narcissism'. There it means that infants need to have sufficient narcissistic 'supplies' for themselves (to use a somewhat unsatisfactory psychoanalytic image) before they can develop concern for those who care for them. It is from the security of being loved that we acquire both the confidence and the wish to love others. This is one aspect of secure attachment to which I shall return in Chapter 4.

In adults it is this same unfulfilled narcissistic need that lies behind what we call egocentricity. The narcissistic person, so often criticized as being self-centred, and appearing to be only in love with self, has not in fact acquired sufficiently strong a sense of self-love to be able to feel and express concern for others and for their well-being. What appears as self-opinionated talk frequently masks lack of confidence, vulnerability and lack of self-esteem. Although a narcissistic adolescent or adult can easily become at the very least a bore and at worst an object of hostility, we might be more tolerant if we could understand that what we call selfishness is in fact a sign of the opposite, a depleted sense of self.

> Raoul was described by a psychiatrist who had once seen him, as one of the most narcissistic people he had met. Popular opinion might venture that it was being an only child that had 'spoiled' him (the word carries an interesting *double-entendre*); but in fact Raoul's mother had had little time for him, and had sent him out of her room whenever he went to talk to her when he was small. He keenly felt the status of an outsider, which in his case was reinforced by his nationality and his religion. One of the issues he presented was his anger with others whenever his 'private space' was threatened: for example, when he lost sole use of his office at work and had to share it with another; or at the presence of his (third) wife in the living room, bedroom or kitchen which he felt interfered with his wish to watch television, sleep or cook a meal; and when doctors refused to take his hypochondriacal symptoms as evidence of physical illness. All this made Raoul go wild. He saw himself as looking after his wife in a generous and selfless way, although it appeared that she represented a part of himself that wished to be looked after. In his fantasies he had devised schemes for robbing banks of money – they had plenty and they would not miss it. He was always looking for an ideal job with high status, yet he gave up opportunities where he could have done very well for himself after only a short time, whenever negative aspects of the job appeared. Although Raoul liked to think of himself as important, he was taken aback when the therapist offered to see him for the year that Raoul was to be in the locality: he clearly believed that no one would ever offer so generous a time. Indeed it took that year before he began to recognize how badly he had treated people. It was only in the penultimate session that he acknowledged how he had made each of his three wives feel insecure. The therapist pointed out that Raoul too, as a child, had been made to feel insecure, and that much of his behaviour sprang from his insecurity. It was important to support his self-respect at

those times when he was able to be honest with himself, (because the inflated sense of self hid a fragile and frightened person.)

Kohut (1971, 1977) is one of several psychoanalysts who have made a particular contribution to working with what we should more accurately call narcissistically damaged clients. Josephine Klein explains his thinking in an admirably clear chapter called 'Feeling Grand' (1987: 203–27). In summary, a baby needs to 'feel grand', as she does when her needs are met by the parent. But where there is narcissistic injury, the child may grow into a 'grandiose' person, (as if they are always struggling to feel grand, but never succeed in this, whatever their external achievements.) Kohut's clinical practice suggests generous empathic responses to the narcissistic client as the main form of intervention, without attempting to make the usual type of interpretations in which a client is encouraged to link present feelings to past experience. The exception to the empathic response is when the therapist in some way fails in being empathic and has therefore been unresponsive to the client's needs. The client is at such times particularly encouraged to look at the limitations in the imagined grandness of the therapist. Thus the therapist concentrates upon accurate empathy; and only as a second stage, when the client feels really understood, upon explanation.

Since a narcissistic person has a fragile sense of self, which constantly needs boosting, there may be real difficulties for the self-absorbed person in mid-life, when physical well-being begins to wane, illness becomes more common and the signs of ageing are more apparent. Since primary narcissism is enhanced by the mirroring relationship with the infant's carer(s), secondary narcissism, where self-image remains an issue, is clearly threatened by events such as these.

In an article on mid-life, Chessick describes one such person: a 48-year-old married woman, unusually talented, who presented with tension and arthritic pain in various joints, and a morbid fear of growing old and dying. In her relationships with her husband, her teenage children and with friends there were no major disturbances. But her history revealed a mother who had resented having her as a baby, because of the mess that was inevitable with an infant. But both mother and father had encouraged the growing child in her considerable musical and other talents, although this left her little space for ordinary play. Her parents fostered her 'infantile grandiosity' and fostered a sense of her being 'outstanding and unique', which must have been a welcome change from feeling mother's rejection of her (at least in some respects) as a baby. Instead she found her sense of self through having to be brilliant at everything, and through being praised for it.

In her adult life this had up to now worked well enough: she gave many successful musical performances. But with the growing evidence of ageing, in terms of her physical appearance and creative power, her arthritic joints making her playing music less fluid, and the death of some friends and relatives, this woman had to face weakness and limitations in the immediate future, and mortality in the long term. Chessick writes that she was 'what we might call a "successful narcissist" until the second half of her life', but her sense of self was bound up in body image, and in achievements that were now less easily achievable. The sense of self she had developed as a child and as a younger adult could no longer be sustained. Her therapy, over four years, proved successful, partly through her coming to understand the deprivation in her child-hood and her need for 'empathic soothing and relaxation in the parent–child interaction'; partly because she was able to internalize the actual experience of this which she received from her therapist.

(All quotations in this example are from Chessick 1983: 5–12.)

Winnicott describes this type of personality as a 'false self', and suggests it is not uncommon: 'The defence is massive and may carry with it considerable social success. The indication for analysis is that the patient asks for help because of feeling unreal or futile in spite of the apparent success of the defence' (1965b: 134). In Winnicott's terms we might understand the above case as being a major crisis of disillusionment, because the prospect of death, certainly no respecter of persons, and the thought of dissolution of the self, puts an intolerable strain on the illusion of omnipotence. 'Death exposes the superficiality and triviality of many of the ambitions and aspirations on which men spend their energies' (Macquarrie 1966). Letting go (in many of life's events) is more gracefully accomplished when we feel secure enough in ourselves. In dying, and in loss and disappointment of all kinds, acceptance is more possible (although never easy) when we have a strong enough sense of our own value and the value of others to tolerate the wounding of our nar-cissistic pride. Some will react angrily, even showing paranoid concerns about ageing and death, as if both are 'out to get me' and have to be defeated: a quite different reaction to that will to survive which can bring some people through life-threatening situations. Other narcissistic personalities, on the other hand, might be able to bask in being looked after and cared for, as if they were once again children – as long as this caring is sustained, because even the contented older person, enjoying such nurturing, can of course turn bitter and demanding if the care is not as continuous or as great as is needed.

Pride is often a defence against feelings of worthlessness. (I refer here to inflated pride, because there is also a sense in which children and adults need to feel proud of themselves and their achievements.) The narcissistic client may find it difficult to accept what the therapist says, not simply because it appears critical, but because it strikes at the root of his or her being. What I am describing here is different from guilt, although it is near to shame. People who show evidence of narcissistic damage may feel bad about their whole self, whereas when they feel guilty or in some instances ashamed, they are more likely to dislike or feel bad about one particular aspect or action. Broucek concludes an article linking shame to early narcissistic developments with these words:

> Shame experiences disrupt the silent automatic functioning of the sense of self, and shame is therefore considered to be the basic form of unpleasure in disturbances of narcissism. The grandiose self is viewed as an evolving compensatory formation instigated in large part by primitive shame experiences.
>
> (1982: 377)

There appear from time to time some clients who so enjoy talking about themselves that therapy seems to feed their narcissistic needs in a rather unhealthy way. Talking about themselves may be confined to what they think is more acceptable to the therapist, as they defend against deeper feelings of worthlessness. But there are other clients who, far from seeking praise and attention, demonstrate a real devaluing of their self-worth. This is typically heard in the protest, 'You must have people who are much more in need of your time than me'. This may indeed partly be a defence against self-exploration, but it is often also a demonstration of inability to claim time and attention for themselves. They may be afraid of their wish for love and affection, in case it is never achieved, or in case it is lost as soon as it is found; their low self-esteem is a form of self-denial, which may partly seek to prevent intense feelings of later disappointment.

Simon expressed doubts early in the first session about therapy being self-indulgent. He went on to talk at length of various family situations in which, as a child, he had to defend his mother against his father, and his sister against his mother, and look after a sick brother. Such concerns meant that in late adolescence he had to abandon his own plans and wishes. He could see how he had had to assume an adult's responsibility for others, which did not permit him to enjoy his own childhood. The therapist related all this to Simon's difficulty of having anyone for himself: 'You seem to be saying that no one cared for you. You had to care for them, and you aren't at all sure you can allow someone to show care for you'. Simon's eyes filled with tears, confirming the accuracy of this intervention.

A middle-aged woman introduced herself to the therapist as 'second-hand Topsy'. In the session that followed there were many examples of allowing others to be indulgent at her expense. When the therapist had to alter the times of their meetings for two sessions running, she acquiesced and denied any feeling of being put out. She was grateful that she was able to see her at all. 'You have to put yourself second here too, even though it would be natural to feel something about my changes of time', the therapist observed, 'just as you put yourself second with others'. Topsy often said that she felt selfish coming to therapy, although later she was able to accept that she could sometimes put herself first. She found it difficult to relate freely to others: she was continually concerned not to offend them, needing to make sure of their favour, but at the same time suffering because they (often themselves more obviously narcissistic) took advantage of her.

The complaint that psychotherapy is too self-centred, individualistic and introverted is less voiced than it used to be but it contains some truth. Therapists tread a narrow path which involves giving generously of their attention to clients, and encouraging in them an awareness of their own needs; yet also challenging them to look at areas of emptiness and of distress, as well as at their impact (or lack of it) upon other people. Given that the term 'narcissistic' is used in two quite distinct ways in psychoanalytic discourse, the one positively to describe an essential aspect of development, and the other somewhat pejoratively to describe a form of inflated esteem, this double meaning of narcissism has to be borne in mind. When a client shows concern for others, is that because he or she is more worried about their own narcissistic needs being met? Or is it that rewarding moment for the therapist when what was formerly an egocentric concern is now a genuine reaching out to the needs of the other?

Development of this sense of self is obviously enhanced through the relationship with those who care for the infant. Learning about that relationship involves learning to integrate different experiences, which the next chapter considers, as the infant progresses towards a sense of secure attachment, and with that achievement, into negotiation of the next theme of authority and autonomy.

4

TRUST AND ATTACHMENT: TOWARDS AMBIVALENCE

Idealization and splitting

In the early stages of life, as described in Chapter 3, with good enough nurturing a baby acquires an early sense of well-being in the face of the natural vicissitudes of experience, so as to be less afraid of the world that is around her, or the inner world that is part of her. Hers is as yet a very small world, but it is her whole world. Her experience is very limited, but it is all she knows, and it is upon this that much else has yet to be built.

In the face of distress and discomfort, especially when it is more than the disposition of the baby can tolerate (because individual babies tolerate different degrees of stress), various ways of trying to find and maintain a basic sense of a good self and a good world may be adopted. These ways of defending the self can be seen more clearly in adult frames of reference than they can actually be observed in infants. So, for example, a dependent person continually needs to 'top up' a rapidly draining sense of worth; a withdrawn or schizoid person tries to keep well away from the risk of rejection and the wish to be dependent; a narcissistic person surrounds the undervalued self with self-praise and flattery, or may indeed put others first in order to meet his or her needs by projecting them into others.

I indicated in Chapter 3 that a particularly significant aspect in developing a harmonious sense of self is learning to integrate good and bad experiences, so that a growing child learns that while life is good, it is not invariably good, but that it is not all bad either. On balance, for most people, the good outweighs the bad (although what is felt to be good and what is felt to be bad is partly culturally determined varying from society to society, and from age to age). If we are to make realistic assessments of the relative merits and faults of ourselves, of others and of the situations in which we find ourselves, we have to learn a sense of perspective and balance. This is probably a lifetime's task, and writing of her own adolescence in *Lark Rise to Candleford* Flora Thompson records that 'older people saw things more in proportion, for they had lived long enough to learn that human nature is a curious mixture of good and evil – the good fortunately predominating' (1973: 479). It is not surprising therefore if it is difficult to learn this in the early months of life.

In normal discourse the term 'ambivalence' is often used to mean mixed feelings, but psychoanalytic discourse uses it slightly differently. It means the capacity to contain more extreme swings of feeling and reaction, and then to hold together these opposite emotions or 'affects', such as love and hate. For some people, relationships are 'all or nothing', by which we mean that if they are not all good, they then become all bad – just like the infant's experience of pleasure and frustration that we tried to imagine in Chapter 3. Many people find it difficult to reconcile quite contradictory reactions to the same situation: for example, anger and sadness at times of grief; or pleasure and envy at another's success; or relief and anger when someone has caused us worry and all then turns out well. Flora Thompson, following her words quoted above, continues that 'tart and tears should be separated by at least a decent interval' (1973: 479). Adolescents, as I observe in Chapter 5, can swing hugely both in mood and in their views. How much more might infants and young children find different experiences confusing and puzzling, evoking contradictory emotions that might be difficult to reconcile.

It is possible to imagine what it is like to feel full and comfortable and therefore complete at one point of time; and hungry, cold, frightened and angry at another. It has been suggested by child analysts such as Melanie Klein (Segal 1973) that a baby copes with these different experiences, which as yet cannot be understood, by splitting: believing that good experiences have come from a good mother, and that bad experiences must come from a bad mother, thus separating into distinct compartments their own positive and negative feelings. This way infants might isolate their bad feelings (that is, what they feel within themselves as well as what they feel towards the 'not-me') so that they cannot damage the good feelings. We must not of course confuse 'feeling' with 'thinking', although perhaps in the infant these two processes may be much closer than in an older person. Although it may be difficult as an adult to imagine such a way of dealing with confusing experiences, it may be helpful to see splitting as a primitive form of logic, which is somewhat like a computer programme, in which everything has to be split up into clear-cut compartments. Computers cannot cope with contradictions without crashing. Human beings find similar difficulty with holding together strong conflicting feelings.

This type of 'primitive' thinking or feeling is not confined then to infants and children. Some religious belief systems resort to a form of splitting in an attempt to resolve the problem of how a good God can allow evil: so a 'demi-god', Satan, or a devil, is held responsible for everything that is bad, enabling God to be preserved as the source of all that is good. Despite their claims to be monotheistic, such religions encourage a type of dualism: the belief in two gods, each with a different attitude to creation, although other religious systems posit a god or a goddess who stands for both creation and destruction. Splitting was also seen in much 'cold-war' political rhetoric, where it was combined with paranoia and projection, and in some of the other political tensions between ideologies. The external enemy is pilloried as all bad, threatening the all-good homeland; or one section of society promises to save 'us' from the machinations of 'them', 'us' being all good, and 'them' being all bad. Realistic appraisal of others is not as common as we would like to think, even among apparently thoughtful men and women.

At its most extreme, such splitting therefore leads to the idealization of one party, and denigration of the other. A therapist may be idealized, while clients can denigrate themselves, or perhaps their partner, as lacking in understanding, uncaring, and unhelpful. When faced with such idealization, therapists can respond in a number of ways:

- they may observe that they are being put on a pedestal, elevated into a perfect person/object. It is of course a tempting position to occupy, but a false and dangerous one;
- they may suggest that the client is endowing them with all that is good but is denying his or her own value and strengths;
- they can identify the negative feelings that are being voiced towards those outside the therapeutic relationship as applying in the here and now, although the greater the idealization of the therapist, the more rigorous is likely to be the defence against admitting discontent and anger towards the therapist;
- they may try to balance the picture by pointing to positive features in those people whom the client runs down, so that ambivalent feelings can be more fully recognized in those relationships.

There may be occasions, albeit fairly rare in short-term work, but apparent in some longer-term and more intensive therapy, when this idealization can become so highly charged that the therapist is worshipped like a god, with strong needy and dependent feelings focused upon him or her. One indication of such strong feelings is a sense of how impossible it is to meet the expectations of the client. This has been called the 'eroticized transference', although the term is a weak one, since the origin of such feelings in the client appears to be less connected with genital sexuality than with early dependency needs. It has also been called the 'delusional transference' (Little 1958, 1986). Sexual feelings may be felt and indeed expressed, although it would be a mistake to see such a highly charged relationship as purely about the physical expression of love. Such situations are delicate, partly because there is also explosive anger not far beneath the surface, which needs to be handled with sensitivity. It is impossible to give general advice on handling these intense relationships, except to observe that in such cases the therapist has to maintain firm but caring boundaries, and has to be prepared for the fiercest of attacks from the client for doing so. There are also suggestions in the literature that where there are signs of this type of psychotic transference, where the reality of the therapeutic relationship and its limitations is becoming impossible for the client to work with, a more face-to-face, management style is necessary before therapeutic work can continue (see Rosenfeld 1978). Such situations, which may arise more frequently with those diagnosed with borderline personality disorder, obviously require specialist supervision, with a therapist who is experienced in more intensive psychotherapy. (For a fascinating discussion of this phenomenon see Alexander and Jacobs (2006).)

Hate, rage and paranoid feelings

The child – or the child in the adult – struggles to preserve the good against the ravages of bad experience, and idealization is one defence. It is difficult to know whether the opposite of idealization is narcissism (self-idealization), hate and denigration, or paranoia (projected hate). Like the person who idealizes, the person who expresses paranoid ideas also uses the defence of splitting, although in this instance he or she projects all the bad feelings away from the self, seeing either the world, certain individuals, or people generally as hostile and persecutory, set on attacking the innocent and good self. Such a person is struggling to keep negative feelings at bay, by denying ownership of them and putting them into others. In extreme cases paranoia takes the form of paranoid delusion, where the person perceives plots and machinations, human or otherwise, which are 'real' to the client even if the therapist can understand them as fantasy. Such extreme fantasies suggest of course the need for psychiatric assessment for those who express them, and extreme caution in accepting them for therapy without the support of a therapeutic team. Yet making a referral, even for an assessment by a specialist, can be very difficult. While the idealizing client might experience referral as a rejection of their love, paranoid clients may see it as confirmation of the plot against them, and as a way of delivering them into the hands of the enemy, especially if they have received psychiatric treatment in the past. The skill of referral lies in trying to become and remain a good-enough person, supporting every hint of the central rational part in the client, so as to quell, at least temporarily, any irrational fears. Careful choice of words, a gentle manner, avoidance of irritation, and refusal to show panic oneself are all helpful. This is easier to recommend than to effect when under pressure, although it is important to recognize that a seriously disturbing person is also feeling under great pressure. Empathic responses, without colluding with irrational ideas, may help create sufficient trust for a referral to be made: this is a significant role for any counsellor or therapist, even if it is a fairly brief one. Where it can be carried through well, a referral provides an example of an alternative experience and world-view, more positive than the one which the client has come to fear. Badly done, it simply confirms a negative world-view and makes the task of the next helper even more difficult.

Although paranoid delusions indicate one extreme, paranoid feelings are a feature of everyday experience, even if they do not usually render us suspicious or hostile for long. When life takes a turn for the worse, it is not unusual to project our frustration and anger outwards, and to wonder why others, or indeed why life itself, should have it in for us. This is a common way of dealing with negative feelings, since paranoid thoughts are a defence against dealing with one's anger or hatred. In some psychoanalytic thinking paranoia is also interpreted as a way of defending against forbidden love: 'I love him. No, that is forbidden. Therefore I must hate him. No, that also is forbidden. Therefore he hates me' (see Freud 1911/2002: 53).

I have some concern about the way the word 'hate' is used so frequently in psychoanalytic writing in relation to infancy, although I do not dispute its appropriateness in the child and the adult. Winnicott's list of reasons that a mother might hate her baby, for example, while accurately conveying situations in which hate might be possible in the mother, might as well describe moments of frustration, irritation, and anger as the full-blown feeling (1975: 201). But then parents can momentarily hate their babies (and each other), and children can hate their parents. But might _rage_ be a better way of describing the obvious emotion that babies can express? Melanie Klein and Winnicott, among others, suggest that babies can hate their carers, although the underlying motivation for the affect appears different in each of their theories. Klein writes of the primitive fantasy of destructiveness which is a response to the threat of annihilation of the infant self. Winnicott sees destructiveness as one aspect of the struggle for life, a 'combined love-strife drive' (Abram 1996: 10) that relates destruction and construction.

Hatred is for most people a short-lived, intense, and often guilt-producing emotion. The paranoia of some severely damaged clients, hatred projected out and then felt to be coming from others, is not momentary, and because it is so pervasive it often has the effect of making others wary and rejecting, which of course compounds in reality what are otherwise paranoid fantasies. It is important to discriminate between paranoid feelings, which have little basis in present reality, and more justifiable ones. Attitudes in society towards racial minorities and around gender issues often are prejudiced, and may give some substance to a client's paranoid anxiety. There are equally other forms of prejudice and discrimination of which every therapist should be aware: against disability, sexual orientation, religion and age. At the same time, we cannot rule out the possibility that some people invite or incite hostile reaction, or interpret current situations adversely on the basis of earlier experiences which were all too real, but are not now so. Such situations are often complicated, such as when clients with some degree of paranoia select as their persecutory figures people who genuinely demonstrate hostility to them. Therapists therefore need to disentangle genuine from fantasized examples of prejudice, and to help clients to own and express their own feelings of anger, even when their paranoid feelings have some basis in reality. The history of psychoanalysis and psychotherapy contains too many examples of experiences being misinterpreted by therapists as fantasy, when they were only too real: therapists had better be cautious in attributing cause and motive to the victim rather than to the persecutor.

Paranoid feelings are a particular way of handling negative emotions. The nature of anger and the origins of the capacity for aggression are still much debated, particularly how much aggression is innate and necessary for development and survival, and how much it is a response to frustration or fear. For example, the following theories have been suggested, within psychoanalysis and in other disciplines:

1. _Biological-instinctual theory_: Such a view tends to regard aggressive behaviour as representing an intrinsic, inherent component of man's nature, the result of the process of natural selection (Lorenz 1966).

2. *Psychoanalytic theories*:
   a) Some consider aggression an innate part of man's constitution, an instinct for destruction; an anti-life, anti-self force; an impediment to the development of the ego; the ego's protest at the presence of impediments in the environment;
   b) Some ego psychologists see aggression as a reaction to the conflicts inherent in the process of adaptation, a reaction to unpleasure and depressive affect;
   c) Some view aggression as motivated by the striving to overcome an obstacle;
   d) For self psychologists, aggression is a reaction to narcissistic threat, a signal of potential injury to the self;
   e) Balint (1968) roots aggression in a failure of fit between the child's need for absolute dependence and the response of the mother, hatred serving as a barrier to protect the ego from 'people who do not love us';
   f) Most British independent analysts see the life motive (libido) as having primacy over aggression and, therefore, infantile aggression as part of a healthy struggle to oppose pathological interactions. Winnicott (1971) maintains that aggression originates in the prenatal activity of the infant where aggressiveness is almost synonymous with activity: 'We need a term such as life force'. Aggression contributes to the development of the self (see also Heimann and Valenstein 1972).
3. *Frustration theory*: This view maintains that aggressive behaviour evolves from interference with ongoing processes and/or gratifying behaviour. Supporters of this view are quick to add that the response to frustration is often a learned response. Some psychoanalytic theorists see aggression as a reactive and protective phenomenon provoked in the individual by external circumstances, which in varying ways lead to frustration.
4. *Social learning theory*: According to this theory, aggressive behaviour results from the nature of child-rearing practices and other vicissitudes of socialization and group integration processes. Evidence for this point of view is organized from data gathered by sociologists, anthropologists, and psychologists oriented towards learning theories.

Anger can of course take many forms, although for the therapist it is extreme expressions of anger that are likely to be a major concern, such as the angry client whose forceful expression or threats actually scare the therapist.

Malan (1979: 189) observes that there are certain patients who show the following linked phenomena:

- a history of emotional deprivation, sometimes severe, often occurring relatively late in childhood;
- impulses of almost unbelievable primitive savagery and destructiveness, side by side with love of equal intensity;
- incontrovertible cumulative evidence that the deprivation is felt to be mainly directed towards the mother;
- prominent themes to do with breast-feeding.

It is of course difficult in some ways to imagine a baby's experience of frustration. We do however observe how a baby's whole body can become contorted with what we would call rage. If the force behind her physical expression, kicking and flailing limbs, were translated uncontrolled into an adult body, the damage that could be done would certainly be immense. Malan asks if it is possible, given that aggression is millions of years older than personal love, that a baby's first relation to her mother is aggressive rather than loving? (And, we might add, getting rather than giving?) If the mother then in some way fails to meet the demands of the baby, could it be that her baby then thinks that her aggressiveness (or her greed) has in some way damaged or even destroyed the good mother?

If such statements appear extreme, we need to remember that the nature of much psychoanalytic description is symbolic. It is only when we pursue such ideas in the experience of the child or adult who can verbalize internal experience, that we conceive how there might be parallels in infancy. For example, as an adult, I may be kept waiting by someone who does not arrive as we had arranged. If this person is special to me, I begin to wonder at first if they are all right. I may then wonder if they are hurt. It may not be long before concern gives way to frustration: how dare they keep me waiting! Then, perhaps, there follows a different concern: did I say or do anything last time that might have put them off?

The reader will be able to add other constructions and fantasies in the period of being kept waiting. When the person arrives, such ideas are fairly soon forgotten in the relief at seeing them again, although the resentment may continue rather longer beneath the surface. Children are not always so good at dissembling or disguising their feeling, and Bettelheim (1978) observes how much the thoughts of revenge in the mind of the fairy-tale 'genie in the bottle' may reflect a child's feelings:

> This is exactly how a young child feels when he has been 'deserted'. First he thinks to himself how happy he will be when his mother comes back; or when sent to his room, how glad he will be when permitted to leave it again, and how he will reward Mother. But as time passes, the child becomes angrier and angrier, and he fantasizes the terrible revenge he will take on those who have deprived him. The fact that, in reality, he may be very happy when reprieved does not change how his thoughts move from rewarding to punishing those who have inflicted discomfort on him. (p. 29)

Feeling hungry or uncomfortable, the baby cries, but mother does not immediately respond. Her frustration rises, and her cries become more angry and frightened. Still mother does not come. What does the baby make of mother's absence? If adults can put wild constructions upon a person's lateness, it is quite possible infants and children will too. Various fantasies are suggested by child analysts, in that a baby may wonder: is it my need for her, my greed for her, my frustration with her, is it my anger with her that has driven her away? Of course mother eventually comes (only minutes late in her eyes, but an eternity in the baby's), and such thoughts are largely set to rest. The repetition of this experience enables most babies to learn that mother comes, even if they have to wait, as surely as an adult knows the sun will rise each morning. Yet in babies with low levels of toleration, or where the intensity of the frustration continually goes beyond what they can take, a residue of fear may be left that it is they themselves who have driven mother away.

Perhaps this seems to some readers far-fetched. Perhaps not, when we remember mythical tales in animistic societies that purport to explain what has happened to the sun as it rises and falls in the sky, or the fact that an uninformed people may hold themselves responsible for the sun's disappearance and reappearance in an eclipse. Neither is it far-fetched when we recognize that in bereavement the words 'if only I hadn't thought, said or done that' can be the precursor of thoughts that in some way the bereaved was responsible for the death. Nor, yet again, when we remember those occasions when we have become so angry that we have wished someone dead. Of course we did not mean it, but that is easily said as long as the person survives and reconciliation lays the thought to rest. It does not prevent memories of such thoughts surfacing when a death occurs; and some adults feel, even if rationally they know otherwise, that their death wishes might have been responsible. It is not so far-fetched to surmise that the mind of the infant and child might also make false assumptions, including those suggested earlier. Theorists differ in the relative weight they ascribe to anger, greed, or even love, as the imagined cause of loss, but they all accept the enduring power of such fantasies.

As the degree of idealization seems to be equal and opposite to the force of negative feelings, unconsciously repressed, and sometimes split off onto another person, so rage seems proportionate to the degree of need and its consequent frustration:

Urwin collected clocks and watches – his room was full of them. But whenever he detected a blemish in one he had bought, or when one of his time-pieces went wrong, he got into a frenzied rage, in which he smashed the offending object to pieces. His early history threw light on his behaviour. His parents had divorced soon after he was born, and he was sent to live with a spinster aunt who spoiled him and, in his own words, 'let me get away with murder'. He was visited occasionally by his mother, and once by his father. It was his earliest memory that father had tried to comfort him when he was distraught by holding a watch to his ear, soothing him to sleep with its rhythmic ticking. From the age of 3 Urwin remembered wanting clocks and watches, and when she visited him, his mother would bring him old clocks that no longer worked.

We have to guess that the old aunt, while giving him much, was unable to give him the body contact and the nurturing that he needed. Being 'Victorian' in her own upbringing, she may even have been of the school that babies should not be given too much attention. Father's watch became a symbol of closeness, comfort and intimacy; perhaps of the beat of the heart beneath the breast? It resembles Winnicott's 'transitional object' (1975: 229–42), a representation, like a thumb or a teddy bear, of mothering. But while most children grow away from their transitional object, Urwin was always looking for the perfect one. He could not get enough watches in his search, and when the objects he thought were perfect showed their obvious imperfections, they had to be destroyed. Urwin was not so disturbed as to think that the clocks and watches that were imperfect actually became persecutory objects (as does the Duke in James Thurber's tale *The Thirteen Clocks* (1962), where time itself is the persecutor). But the line between thinking and paranoia was thin. It was only Urwin's fear of his new father and his mother, when she remarried and he returned home, that prevented him from smashing them up when they frustrated his wishes. It was ominous that his old aunt had been the person he continued to attack physically right into adolescence. As he became more frightened of his aggression, he sought help.

When a therapist works with a client who demonstrates or fears this destructive anger there are a number of key aspects to be borne in mind:

- help the client to keep hold of characteristics and achievements that are positive and good, presenting that side of the picture alongside any reference to aspects that might otherwise overwhelm the client with fear or guilt;
- encourage the client to verbalize the anger in the session, rather than act it out in self-destructiveness or damage to objects or people outside, perhaps observing how expressing it verbally in the safety of the session harms no one;
- demonstrate, through the relationship with the client, that verbally expressing anger (especially towards the therapist) or describing destructive fantasies does not destroy either the therapist or the client, or their relationship – the client can even 'bite the hand that feeds', and learn that it will not be taken away;
- where necessary (and the threat of this happens only very occasionally) maintain a firm stance against any physical expression of destructiveness in the session;
- make connections between the past and the present that may explain the intensity of the anger or the guilt about experiencing it; at the same time draw a distinction between what was an age-appropriate response in infancy or childhood and what is inappropriate now (in Urwin's case, the imperfect watch is not his mother as he experienced her as a child);
- support the client in expressing appropriate anger to the right degree about current situations: Urwin was in therapy for some time before he was able to go back to the shop to complain about a clock that turned out to have a fault;
- clarify the distinction between realistic guilt, resulting from expression of anger that has hurt others (such as Urwin's aunt), and inappropriate guilt, where the damage is much more to the client's sense of well-being;
- where there appears to be reason for realistic guilt, encourage and support the client's wish to make direct or indirect reparation: being able to mend

situations and repair relationships is a sign that destructiveness need not be final;

- remember that beneath the anger there is probably deep sadness, emptiness or a profound sense of helplessness and weakness, all of which are defended against by rage. The person who is wounded may prefer to respond angrily rather than show how hurt or weak they really are. Acknowledging their own pain may help them more;
- certainly not last, acknowledge that therapists and counsellors also hate their clients, especially those who make them feel incompetent or afraid (Winnicott 1975: 194–203; Prodgers 1991). Appropriate channelling of aggression in the therapist towards therapeutic ends will minimize the split between the 'bad' client and the 'good' therapist;
- finally, Malan adds an observation to those listed above in relation to severely damaged clients and aggression: 'that integrating the love and hate leads to moments of extraordinary transformation, in which the world, both past and present, changes from "bad" to "good"' (1979: 189).

Those who act out their aggression are in the minority amongst the normal client group with whom therapists and counsellors work, unless practising in a forensic or mental health unit setting: many clients in a generic therapeutic practice find it more difficult generally to show feelings; controlling them is less of an issue. Indeed a good number of clients who find it difficult to express their hostility openly fear that if they do so, they will be too destructive. Their aggression is often turned instead upon themselves, in depression or in self-damaging behaviours; breaking off relationships, for instance, before they get angry with others; or in more difficult cases, self-harm.

Vickie was more typical than Urwin. She had great difficulty acknowledging her own anger, more usually feeling that it was others who were angry with her. She was constantly trying to please others in order to stay in their good books. After a year's therapy she was able to acknowledge her destructive fantasies, and even said to her therapist on one occasion, 'If you say that again, I'll go for your jugular'. Having said what she felt, she went on to say, 'It's been good to find the anger in me, and to begin showing it here without feeling so guilty'.

Envy Klein

There can be an angry, sometimes destructive, component also in envy, an emotion that is particularly related in Kleinian theory to infancy. Envy is similar to, but not the same as, jealousy, since the latter normally involves three or more persons: for example, where a husband is jealous of his wife's attention to their baby. Envy more usually describes a two-person situation, where one person envies what another person has and which they do not believe they themselves possess: usually an object, or a quality, rather than the 'possession' of a third person. Melanie Klein uses envy in this sense, such as a baby's wish to possess all the good milk in the breast, while Freud uses it in a similar sense when he writes of penis envy in women (and as will be seen in Chapter 9, others have suggested envy in men of the breast or the womb).

Klein sees envy as innate, and closely linked to aggression: 'I consider that envy is an oral-sadistic and anal-sadistic expression of destructive impulses, operative from the beginning of life, and that it has a constitutional basis' (1957; see also Segal 1973). Yet there is no single psychoanalytic view on the origin and characteristics of envy, and it is also possible to see it as a product of a sense of being small, and helpless, yet aspiring to want to develop and grow – to have what the other or others have. Unresolved it can lead to feelings of inferiority, sometimes accompanied by the wish to destroy what others have on the principle: 'If I can't have it, then I'll make damned sure he doesn't have it either'. Joffe believes that envy can be accompanied by admiration, and that envy, unlike depression, carries a sense of hope. Its presence signals aspiration (1969: 533).

> Wanda told her therapist how angry she had been the previous week. She had returned from a break to find him sun-tanned and relaxed, and she felt he was not even listening to her. She envied him such a good life, when hers seemed to be full of disasters. She denied that she wanted him to suffer as she did, but the therapist nevertheless took up Wanda's anger with him for being away and withholding his attention from her. He later linked her feelings about his inaccessibility while on holiday with the anger she felt at her mother's withholding herself from Wanda when she was little and mother was so often ill. His own looking so well, of course, compounded the situation. But her envy also gave an indication of what she would like to achieve for herself.

That there can be a destructive component in envy can be seen in the following example, which also has clear indications of jealousy, because whenever Xavier got close to a woman, he found himself so possessive of her, and so jealous of other men, that it always led to the break-up of the relationship. One of his therapy sessions illustrates the type of envy that Melanie Klein describes. It has to be said that the rawness with which Kleinian ideas are expressed in the literature is not necessarily the way to put it in practice, because they can seem over-strong and puzzling to the client; but in this (and other instances, of course) they really can provide the most helpful images of what the client has felt or is experiencing:

> Xavier was remembering incidents in early childhood. When he was five he was taken by some slightly older boys to a wood which was out of bounds. They were going to collect birds' eggs. The other boys said there were dinosaurs in the wood, and hid behind bushes making roaring noises. Xavier became so frightened that he ran home, and arrived there crying. He could not tell his mother why he was upset because he should not have gone to the woods in the first place. In her frustration with him, she shook him to try and find out what had happened. When he wanted comfort from her, she only succeeded in making him more frightened.
>
> The therapist responded, 'Perhaps it also felt bad to have stolen birds' eggs'. Xavier paused, agreed, and then went on: 'I've just remembered

something else, but I'm too embarrassed to tell you'. The therapist tried to understand this resistance, saying, 'Perhaps you are afraid if you tell me that I'll then shake you like your mother did'. This appeared to free Xavier to speak of this further memory. When he was very young he was sent off to bed early, and lay in bed thinking that he wanted to cut off his mother's nipples. He went on himself to wonder if what he felt then as a little boy, and re-experienced now in his possessiveness of girlfriends and his jealousy of other men, was associated with the birth of his younger brother, who always (so Xavier felt) received more understanding from their mother than he felt he did. He also wondered whether brother's arrival had meant that he felt pushed away from his mother's breast. Xavier's thoughts certainly made sense to the therapist and were consonant with Kleinian theory. We can speculate further, although in the session it was not immediately relevant to Xavier to express it openly, whether stealing birds' eggs, and then experiencing guilt (as a result of the persecutory dinosaurs?), was linked to an envious wish to destroy the eggs in mother's body (another aspect of Klein's theory of envy and aggression), and so prevent a rival appearing on the scene. Such associations in the therapist's mind needed further evidence from the client before they could be shared, especially since the therapist was keen that it should be Xavier who made these links, not herself.

Psychoanalytic thinking sometimes associates the expression of aggression with the three psychosexual stages (oral, anal and phallic): witness Klein's words quoted above about 'oral-sadistic and anal-sadistic expression of destructive impulses'. Klein might be said to have done for infantile aggression what Freud did for infantile sexuality, resulting in the same horrified responses from many who cannot conceive of babies and children as being either destructive or sexual, but pointing the way to fantasies and feelings that can be related to what some clients experience and express.

It is perhaps unfortunate that these terms are associated primarily with adult behaviour and responses, or with the intentional and active expression of aggression in children and adolescents. When related to infants they are less easy to comprehend. Since most therapists do not work with young children it may be they cannot substantiate Klein's ideas with that age group; but Klein's expressive language often describes well the sadistic aggression of those who have reached an age when they can wreak havoc with others' lives and property. When Klein refers to oral sadism she includes both the fantasy of tearing at the mother's body with teeth and nails, as well as the reality (which Winnicott observes with a more optimistic slant) that 'the baby hurts her nipples even by suckling' and 'he tries to hurt her, periodically bites her, all in love' (Winnicott 1975: 201). But we can also think of the way adults can produce 'biting criticism'. Anal sadism is associated with defecation and the way in which this too can be used as a 'weapon', but we also speak of being 'shat upon' by others. Phallic sadism is seen in rape, abuse, and other aggressive sexual relations, particularly where the penis (or its substitute) is used to hurt and damage (see Chapter 11).

These violent images (and Klein's interpretations are full of them) make real sense when linked to aggressive and destructive impulses, fantasies and actions as they are described by adult clients. The link to infancy does not have to be made explicit, and there may indeed be little evidence of early history with which to make such links. Nevertheless early trauma can be a feature of those who act out their destructive impulses, and if often the link is not clear, the metaphors are still useful:

> Yvette was a desperately unhappy young woman. She found making relationships very difficult, and her shyness and awkwardness in company tended to put people off. She admired people from afar but could never approach them. Once she entered therapy she became deeply attached to her therapist, and as a result huge storms arose whenever the therapist had a break or rearranged a session. Yvette's attacks on the therapist were bitter and cruel: she accused him of deliberately taking her on in therapy in order to torture her with the pain of his absence; she at times rubbished everything he said, that it was all therapy-speak, and worthless; she made one or two attempts at suicide just when the therapist was going away; she threatened suicide at other times and left him in suspense until the next session; she would slap at her face and head in the session (although the therapist firmly asked her to stop acting out in this way); she sometimes sat silently and shot vicious looks at him from her chair.
>
> All in all Yvette succeeded in making her therapist feel dreadful, drained, and worthless. All attempts at understanding this from her past met with a blank refusal to believe the past was of any importance. Although there were some occasions when Yvette might have felt furious with her mother or father, most of these fell within the usual range of family events; and since she was the youngest there was not even the birth of a sibling to explain just how thrown she was by breaks or changed arrangements. When invited to reflect on why she might react this way Yvette's fury could see no point in exploring her history.
>
> Alternating with these episodes (and there were many of them) were other sessions when she was charming, or when she was good to be with. She never seemed to show concern for her previous behaviour at these times, but she would make things right by her manner. The therapist nonetheless felt that this was not true 'depressive position' concern but an attempt to make things better so that Yvette should not lose him altogether.
>
> This style of therapy went on for many months and eventually an ending had to be faced, because the therapist was leaving the area. The attacks intensified, and it was all he could do to sit out the sessions, interpreting when he could, but feeling that at such times his words were unheard, or if heard were spat out again and turned against him. Perhaps what made it worthwhile was that in her outside life things were steadily if slowly changing: she began to make friends; she received praise in her work; she became more bold in arranging to go out socially and so on; although none of this would she acknowledge as progress. And some time after they had finished (and the last session went reasonably well)

Yvette got in touch with the therapist and genuinely shared some really good news about her first intimate relationship.

The example bears out Julia Segal's comment on the Kleinian approach of allowing fantasies to be expressed in a relatively uncontrolled way. Having referred to therapy with children, she goes on:

> With adults, too, expression of fantasies can be facilitated in therapy. Lack of restriction on what is said and felt is combined with firm holding of safe boundaries. These reduce the fear of powerfully loving or aggressive feelings spilling over into action. If the therapist is firmly in control the patient can 'let go' more. If the therapist can recognise unwanted feelings and ideas, the patient may be able to too.
>
> (1992: 61)

Klein's powerful imagery is immediately recognizable in the behaviour of some clients (especially in forensic work). It is also possible to detect it, if they are honest with themselves, in many people's fantasies. These destructive feelings can also be seen in infancy, where they are expressed in nightmares, in some aspects of play, and most clearly in the delight of children in stories that often have a somewhat sadistic quality to them. The traditional fairy tales (of the Brothers Grimm for instance) and their modern equivalents often contain in symbolic language issues around the developmental conflicts first encountered in our early years. Perhaps this is why such gruesome stories are so popular, even as bed-time stories, when they might be thought to fuel nightmares. Perhaps the expression of these feelings in fact clears the way for sweeter sleep.

One modern example of this type of story is *Where the Wild Things Are* by Maurice Sendak (1970), which is well worth looking at, since its illustrations powerfully support its highly significant text. When it was first published, it evoked a minor storm of protest from some protective parents as being too frightening for their children. In this story the young boy Max behaves like a 'little monster' and his mother sends him to bed without any supper. Alone in his room Max 'dreams' (although we are not sure whether it is a dream or a waking fantasy) that he travels to the land of the Wild Things, where he tames them despite their terrifying attempts to frighten him. He then gets them to join in a wild rumpus to which he calls a halt, sending them off to bed (as he was himself) without their supper. Then he feels lonely, and wants to be somewhere he is loved 'best of all'. He leaves the Wild Things, despite their protest that they will eat him up (words he himself had used to his mother when she got angry with him), and he returns to his room where his hot supper is waiting for him.

Max's own wildness at home is thus relived and relieved in the dream, projected on to the terrifying Wild Things of his own imaginative world. Through taming them and controlling the start and finish of their rumpus, he tames the wildness that has got him into trouble. Having punished them (as he was punished and as he might have wished to punish his mother in revenge) he feels unloved and empty, and needs to return to reality, where he finds his supper, a sign that the loving relationship between the destructive Max and his angry mother has been repaired and restored.

Such a story encapsulates some of the principles of therapy and counselling, through which clients are helped to face both the strength and cause of their own feared or actual wildness, by coming face to face with it, as Max himself does when he first encounters the Wild Things; by expressing it (as in the rumpus) in the relative safety of the therapeutic setting; and by finding they can exercise control, as Max does when he commands the rumpus to stop. The constancy of the therapist, who stays with the client, even when the client has been angry with them, helps to show in action that relationships need not be broken irreparably if aggression is expressed, and that care and love, as they become internalized through time, need never be permanently cut off.

Guilt, concern and reparation

Following their expression of feelings, whether in action, or through words or in fantasy, people can feel guilty. Psychoanalytic ideas vary as to where and when lies the origin of guilt. Freud placed guilt at the Oedipal period, in the phallic stage; Klein sees guilt originating in infancy; and while Klein (1937/1975) writes of guilt, Winnicott (1984) prefers the term concern, although generally there is also agreement about the anxiety that follows the expression of aggression or other powerful feelings, leading to guilt and/or concern. Since it is my contention that these themes are not limited to a particular stage of life, the debate about the first appearance of guilt is not particularly relevant. What is more appropriate is to consider the possibility that when clients in therapy relate powerful fantasies and feelings this may be followed by anxiety, for example, lest the relationship between therapist and client has been damaged. Guilt may take the form of anxious concern for oneself, such as Yvette in the earlier example showed following most of her outbursts. She feared losing her therapist. Similarly some 'neurotic' guilt that appears out of proportion to its precipitating circumstances, seems to show more anxiety for the welfare of the self than genuine concern for the person who has been hurt. Making reparation is sometimes an attempt to restore the needed relationship, although it can, especially where guilt is justified, include genuine concern for the person who has been damaged.

It may therefore be useful to distinguish between guilt and concern, with the latter more clearly showing the capacity to imagine how the other may be left as a result of one's actions. Concern for the other, and anxiety about the damage done to the other, are indications of what Klein calls the 'depressive position'. The term is an odd one, given that it bears little relation to the clinical term 'depression'. Winnicott suggested that the term 'is a bad name for a normal process, but no one has been able to find a better. My own suggestion was that it should be called *"the Stage of Concern"'* (1975: 264, original italics). Nevertheless what the term stands for is important to grasp in psychodynamic work. In contrast to schizoid or paranoid states, the split between the 'good' and the 'bad' object, and the defence of projection, Klein posits a state of mind where others are perceived as whole persons (or whole objects as the terminology often puts it), and where the self is perceived as containing both loving and hating feelings. It is an expression of ambivalence. There is also a greater sense of reality: 'damage is no longer feared as total destruction. A good experience does not mean heaven forever; its loss is not the end of the world, but is a real manageable grief mitigated by hope for good experiences in the future' (Segal 1992: 38). To those who rightly object that a major loss often seems like the end of the world, it is important to recognize that even when the depressive position is reached (as Klein suggests it is for most of us in the first year of life), it is never a permanent state: daily life and developmental crises continuously unsettle us. Whether through large or small difficulties, we move between feeling anxious, paranoid, helpless, cut off, hateful, desperate and needy (for example) and recovering a sense of proportion, security, attachment, hope, satisfaction and love. However, the achievement of a more integrated state, with a sense of hope, having once been achieved, sets a marker for the reachievement of it, even if from time to time we descend into what seems like the deepest pit of despair. This movement is a familiar one in therapy, in which the peaks and troughs of experience can neither be engineered nor prevented, but where the achievement of a more whole sense of self provides both the goal for climbing back when things slip back, and also the strength with which to do it.

Empathy is closely linked to concern, and it is probable that the capacity for empathy is engendered in the developing concern of the baby for the one who cares for her, as the closeness of the relationship shifts into the identification of the other as a separate person, with separate needs. Empathy also proceeds from the relatively selfless concern of the mother for her baby, an intuitive capacity and emotional rapport which Winnicott calls 'primary maternal preoccupation': 'she knows what the baby could be feeling' (1965a: 15). It is this with which the infant identifies, in her concern first for the mother and then by extension for others. As the sense of self becomes more secure this is a stronger position from which to feel concern for others. This can also be described as a form of identification, in which I am able to identify with how another person may be feeling, and relatively altruistically show my concern for them. This usage is somewhat different from that form of identification in which I project my own needs on to the other, identify with the other, and then care for myself through caring for the other. In analytic terms, the infant moves from primary identification, where the distinction between 'me' and 'you' does not exist, to secondary identification, where separate identity leads to the ability to identify with the other person.

There is apparent confusion in analytic writing between terms such as 'identification', 'internalization', and 'introjection' (see Wallis and Poulton 2001). This may reflect in one way the difficulty we have in identifying and expressing what is special to us, and what belongs to another; whether we act from our own unique identity or are influenced by another who has become so much part of us that the difference is undetectable; and whether in understanding others we are ever able to understand them as they are, unless in some respects we can identify their experience with part of ours. Perhaps these semantic distinctions need not interfere with therapeutic practice, where the capacity to know what another might be feeling needs self-understanding, and a healthy questioning attitude towards our own perceptions, if we are to avoid projecting onto another those parts of ourselves that bear little or no relation to what is being offered us by them.

These concepts are therefore particularly relevant to therapists, who, when they feel relatively secure within themselves and relatively free from anxiety about themselves, are more free to attend to the client, and to the client's needs, without projecting their own concerns onto the client. Whatever else is written in these pages about theoretical knowledge, there is no substitute for that intuitive way of knowing, which is perhaps the therapist in a maternal role. When a therapist lacks a strong inner core it is much harder, not only to identify and empathize with the client, but also, for instance, to allow the expression of the frustration, the anger and the love that the client can feel towards the counsellor, or to be open to criticism and attack.

Attachment: towards relatedness and separateness

When John Bowlby, an analyst by training, first published his ideas about attachment in the journal *Psychoanalytic Study of the Child* they caused a storm of controversy with his psychoanalytic colleagues. Yet today attachment theory has attained a status in certain quarters equal to that of Klein or Winnicott. In contrast to the speculation about the power of fantasy that runs through Kleinian theory, Bowlby's research stresses the objective, the environment and the observable. As Köhler (in Brisch 2002: xix) observes, psychoanalytic understanding draws upon material gained in the therapy from free association, and the phenomena of transference and countertransference, reconstructing the patient's history; by contrast attachment research draws upon data obtained from children of specific age groups, using qualitative and quantitative methods, the study of parent–child relationships from birth to adulthood, and systematic longitudinal studies. Attachment theory grew out of Bowlby's psychoanalytic training and his work, and the concept of attachment is certainly not confined to attachment theory. As Brisch writes:

> Various psychological theories and psychotherapeutic schools have developed a variety of concepts regarding the formation and significance of attachment and the effect that separations may have on the mother–child relationship. Some of these theories contain certain parallels to or similarities to attachment theory; some of them relate explicitly to Bowlby. On the other hand there are fundamental differences as well.
>
> (2002: 53)

It is my contention throughout this book that the major themes that have sometimes in psychoanalytic theory appeared only to be linked to specific ages in fact appear time and again throughout life. Nevertheless there are some features of development that feature more strongly at certain times, and under certain circumstances, such as dependency, which is more appropriate to infancy, and less appropriate to adult relationships, where interdependence, or mature dependence are expected to feature strongly. The foundations laid in the early months of life, through passing from a quasi-symbiotic, dependent relationship to distinguishing self and other, and integrating good and bad experience also appear to lay the foundation for the type of secure attachment that Bowlby describes, albeit basing his many ideas on other theories than the purely psychoanalytic. And attachment, like the themes I emphasize, remains as a central issue of relating throughout life (Parkes *et al.* 1991).

It also seems that the concept of secure attachment forms a bridge between issues around trust, selfhood, ambivalence and concern, all of which have a close relationship to the experience of the infant in the mother–baby relationship, and the next major set of themes to be considered, authority and autonomy, including the exploratory behaviours which are a significant part of attachment theory. Secure attachment, for example, might be seen as essential if the young child is to be able to use mother as a base from which to explore the world, being willing to separate from her initially for brief periods and later to separate sufficiently in order to make new attachments with others. As an adult a securely attached person is confident of those with whom he or she closely relates. By contrast, anxious attachment can be seen in the person who clings and is overdependent upon others, because of their anxiety about the reliability of attachment figures.

Attachment theory draws upon ethology, developmental psychology and systems theory as well as psychoanalytic ideas. As other analysts have done, it focuses upon the early influences on emotional development, and how these give rise to the development and changes in attachments between people throughout life. Bowlby highlights the way a child seeks closeness with mother when experiencing anxiety, and much that attachment theory posits about the quality of attachment to the mother has parallels in what I described earlier about the intuitive, sensitive response of the mother – perhaps Winnicott (1988a) expresses it most obviously, recognizing the natural ability of many mothers to adapt to their infant's needs without the need of experts or books.

It is in the first year that the infant is able to develop 'internal working models' (Bowlby 1969) which provide a certain predictability to the interaction with the attachment figure – that is, that mother will or will not respond when he cries out for her. Yet there is another need in the infant, that is to explore, and Bowlby suggests that the infant can explore more safely and without distress if mother provides a secure emotional base. 'Secure attachment is a precondition of an infant's ability to explore his environment and experience himself as an agent and self-effective individual' (Brisch 2002: 18). There is then interplay between the attachment system and the exploratory system. We may again see here some links between Bowlby and Winnicott. Attachment theory suggests that a mother who clings to her infant may create a close relationship, but not a secure attachment, because she does not give her the scope to explore. Winnicott writes of the infant's experience of being alone in the presence of the mother – that is, a mother who is not anxious – and how healthy this is for the infant.

The quality of the infant's attachment has been classified through research into four types: secure attachment, avoidant attachment, ambivalent attachment and disorganized/disoriented attachment (Brisch 2002: 27–8). The provision of a secure base and of encouragement to explore from it typically results in children who are secure and self-reliant, trusting, cooperative and helpful, who in psychoanalytic terms might be described as having a strong ego, or having introjected a good object (Bowlby 1979: 136). In avoidant attachment there is an inhibition of attachment behaviours resulting in a greater distance from parents. In adult life this may show itself in relationships that lack emotional closeness. An ambivalent attachment might be illustrated by a patient who as a 2-year-old wanted closeness from mother, but could not achieve it due to the birth of a younger sister, and there was rage and disappointment at being rebuffed by her mother. Or in another case the patient was close to her mother but had hostile feelings towards her, because of her frustrated desire for attachment and her inability to experience autonomy and exploration (Brisch 2002: 99, 206–7). Disorganized/disoriented attachment is identified when infants show contradictory behaviours to mother's absence, which are seen more often in high-risk children who have had traumatic experiences (Main 1995).

Just as many of the features of early development are shown in later relationships, including the therapeutic relationship, so attachment theory not only informs the therapist about patterns of mother–child interaction but also extends understanding of later life stages and the issues that arise within them. As Ainsworth describes when considering attachments across the life cycle, many other interpersonal relationships 'may involve affectional bonds. These include the attachments of child to parents, the bonds of parents to child, bonds with other kin, sexual partnerships, and the bonds that may occur between friends' (1991: 33). While she confines such attachments to long-lasting relationships, defining 'affectional bonds' as those where 'the partner is important as a unique individual, interchangeable with none other' (p. 38), those who have difficulty making long-lived relationships show other aspects of attachment theory – ambivalent and avoidant attachments.

The therapeutic relationship too involves the development of a secure base. Brisch asserts that it is 'an important therapeutic task in every case' and 'is a prerequisite for enabling the patient to change pathological childhood representations of self and attachment figures through work in the transference' (2002: 235). Many of the elements that contribute to the creation of a secure base for the child have been described in this chapter and the previous chapter. Using different terms, the development of trust and the sensitive handling of the initial dependency on the therapist are an essential foundation for the therapy that follows, and where there is avoidance of or ambivalence about the relationship with the therapist, the work may prove too shallow for more profound change. The dependent, submissive or clinging client, on the one hand, or the mistrusting, distancing client, on the other, are not in an optimal position to make best use of what therapy has to offer, although of course what the therapist hopes to offer is a way out of such unfulfilling ways of relating.

I shall return to the way these themes from the earliest relationships in the life cycle are played out in the therapeutic relationship in Chapter 12, in seeking to provide a secure enough base for the work to progress. The secure base that has been described also acts as the foundation for negotiation of the themes which Chapters 6, 7 and 8 examine, where what attachment theory calls the exploratory system will be seen to have parallels in moves towards autonomy and the internalization of authority figures. First, however, in Chapter 5 I shall consider some other aspects of trust and attachment themes which are encountered in adolescence and adult life.

aloness /(loneliness) — anomie
— alienation

5

TRUST AND ATTACHMENT: RELATED ISSUES

Loneliness and being alone

The process described in Chapter 4 of the internalization of good experience, or a good object (a term that describes mother and the whole experience of mothering), together with beginning to integrate fulfilling and frustrating experiences into a whole that is predominantly positive, makes a significant contribution to the child who is securely attached, and from that base is able to explore, moving away from mother to engage with a wider world. From a slightly different perspective this secure base can be translated as containing a good enough object within oneself to be able move out on one's own, and to be alone with oneself: self-contained, as we might put it.

I refer here not necessarily to the physical proximity of others or being able to be distant from others. Winnicott (1971: 50) presents the valuable image of the mother sitting with the child playing contentedly alone. So it is possible to feel self-contained in the company of others, just as it is possible to feel lonely in a crowd. Loneliness in a crowd describes the inner feeling of being at odds with oneself, no matter how much external affirmation is forthcoming from other people. A person in such a state could be said to have become their own worst enemy (a not uncommon description of people who are depressed). The stage of primary narcissism described in Chapter 3, together with the internalizing of the love of the caretaker, enables a person to experience a general (though not omnipresent) feeling of 'being comfortable with myself'. There are of course times when this is not so: Klein's paranoid-schizoid position is a regular occurrence, although on many occasions a passing experience, followed by the return of the depressive position.

What I am describing is the inner relationship between different aspects of the self. The phrase 'I feel comfortable with myself' uses two personal pronouns, 'I' and 'myself'. The capacity to be contentedly alone relies upon this good inner relationship, which should not be confused either with narcissism

not the only reason [margin note]

on the one hand (a desperate attempt to like oneself), or with schizoid withdrawal upon the other (the need to be alone because relationships with others present too great a threat). Dunne describes well the ability to be solitary and yet content: 'What makes a man happy when he's alone and happy? What makes a child happy when he is playing alone? There may be a clue in the word "alone". The word is a combination of the two words "all" and "one"' (1979: 104–5).

In a moving passage where he draws upon the image of Greek theatre, and two actors alongside each other, Dunne goes on to suggest that loneliness can never be cured by another person: 'We are alone, you and I, and we cannot make one another unalone' (1979: 106). Winnicott's phrase fits this image, when he writes of the paradox of 'the experience of being alone, as an infant and small child, in the presence of the mother' (1965b: 30). He, like Dunne, sees this as a very positive experience, although some writers (including psychoanalytic authorities) seem to see it as axiomatic for maturity that a person has to be in a good relationship with another. Being in relationship to others is a value that our society and psychotherapeutic values support, but it is of course possible that, in Winnicott's words, in the end what we have to encounter is 'the essential aloneness of the human being' (1988b: 114), which ties up with some of the central ideas of existentialism and existential-phenomenological therapy.

The capacity to be alone therefore depends upon being content with oneself, yet not being self-content; and upon loving oneself, yet not upon self-love. It is another of those delicate balances that attempt to define maturity and psychological health. This sense of contentment with self is important both for intimate relationships and being alone. As Rayner writes, in a section on 'Being Alone':

> Looking back over the course of life from birth, we can detect a continuous ebb and flow between intimate intermingling with other people on the one hand, and self-contained, even solitary, thought and action on the other ... Without such solitary exploration a person can be little more than a cypher, an echo of others with no ideas of his own to contribute.
>
> (1986: 229)

Winnicott (1965b), Klein (1963/1975; see also Segal 1992: 40) and, from a Jungian perspective, Anthony Storr (1989), similarly link the capacity to be alone with creativity. (For a study of the ending of therapy, separation anxiety and solitude, see Quinodoz (1993).)

However, there are others for whom either the academic, intellectual or artistic life provides opportunities of living in 'a world of their own'. It is not unusual to find that some of those who have brilliant minds also find difficulty in relating closely to others – their books, their research, their laboratories, their studios, perhaps even their word processors, exercise a greater pull on them than their family at home. Whether or not this is defensively schizoid or positively creative is perhaps not for the therapist to judge, although at the right time, therapy may prove to be a means of enlarging horizons, rather than eradicating the creative and artistic spirit as some fear:

Zara had been pushed back to school at the age of 9 after a serious road accident which led to some facial disfigurement. Following the accident and a spell in hospital where she was seriously ill, her wish to stay at home close to her mother was very understandable. Yet her mother (as she later told her) was in a dilemma: she wanted to comfort her daughter, and at the same time felt she should respect the child psychiatrist's advice that Zara should go back to school as soon as possible. It felt hard for her to have to push her daughter out in this way.

But Zara did not understand her mother's concern at that time. Having to go to school, she reacted by immersing herself in her books, and staying on the edge of the groupings of her school friends. In her books she found some consolation. Her reading meant that her schoolwork progressed well, and eventually she went to university. Perhaps it was going away from home that triggered off the separation anxiety; or perhaps her intellectual defences had worn thin. But once she arrived at university she stopped going out, she stayed in her room, even in her bed, and she read novels. When she first saw the university counsellor she jokingly asked for 'magic pills' to make her less depressed. Following her mother's earlier pressure, she wanted to 'go out' because that was the healthy thing to do, but also she honestly wanted to stay away from people.

It was only later that Zara told her counsellor that when she first went to see him she was concerned about him as another professional person who might meddle with her mind. The child psychiatrist she had seen before had prescribed 'magic pills' to tranquillize her, after he had mistaken her child-like way of expressing her school refusal ('It's like a voice telling me not to go', she had said) for incipient psychosis. So the counsellor, who at first had thought in terms of encouraging her to go out and begin mixing with people, soon realized that Zara needed to be able to retreat and find some safety; and that she needed to come out in her own good time, not under pressure. He was therefore content to link the dilemma that she felt, whether to 'stay in' or 'go out', with her mother's dilemma, and indeed his own.

Fantasy and reality

Psychodynamic theory regards the inner world of the client as being equally significant to the influence of the external world upon him or her. The inner world of each one of us – which Freud mapped out as the conscious, the preconscious and the unconscious, and which succeeding generations of analysts have elaborated (Brinich and Shelley 2002) – remains a mysterious and largely unknown part of us, although we glimpse its workings and the 'internal objects' that people us. Dreams and nightmares reveal the surface of this hidden world, and in waking life tales such as *Where the Wild Things Are* (p. 83), fairy stories and science fiction feed upon fantasy and the fantastic, while even more realistic works of literature have their own fantasized characters and settings. Little wonder that literature and the arts have been such a

confused realism with naturalism

rich source for psychoanalytic enquiry from Freud onwards (see, for example Freud 1908/2003). While realism in literature and art shows us different *among* perspectives on the world as we know it, the fantastic and the surreal often symbolize aspects of the 'inner world' – like the dinosaurs in Xavier's memory (p. 81) or the Wild Things in Max's dream (p. 83). Klein believed that children relate to the world through their unconscious fantasies (she prefers the spelling 'phantasy' to distinguish these unconscious phantasies from conscious fantasies (Segal 1992: 28–30)).

Dreams are personal stories, which serve the purpose of preserving sleep, while at the same time providing a means of working over unfinished anxieties, most commonly from the previous day. Clients' dreams are not usually an easy medium to work with in once-weekly therapy, since there is often so much else in waking life to reflect upon. Freud (1900) may have called dreams 'the royal road to the unconscious', but in her introduction to a collection of papers on the significance of dreams, Flanders observes both that 'the dream no longer occupies the centre of psychoanalytical debate' (1993: 1), and that 'the focus of contemporary analysis is emphatically the dreamer, not the dream' (p. 20). Nevertheless clients do relate their dreams, and when they do they can be encouraged to associate freely to the images and situations they describe, finding their own clues to the dream's meaning. The temptation with dreams is to try to understand them straight away: yet often it is later material in the session that throws light upon a particular dream image. There is never a single meaning to a dream, and what in the end matters most is less the dream itself, than having dreamt it. Dreaming is healthy, whether or not the dream is remembered or analysed.

Whether or not the images and symbols in dreams can be interpreted, expression of them and of the feelings associated with them is in itself cathartic. Clients present symbols, metaphors and images in many other ways: in their daydreams and fantasies, in speaking about the plays, novels, films and art that have moved them as well as in their use of language. All these communications can be as replete with double meanings, condensations of meaning, and all the other means of disguised material that Freud (1900, 1901/2002) initially recognized in dreams, and later saw were also part of what he called the psychopathology of everyday life.

Fantasies of other kinds can also provide glimpses into our internal world, although they do not always have to be deeply analysed to be understood. Daydreaming of a good meal helps a hungry person go without food during the day so as to enjoy going out to dinner that evening. Picturing a loved person from whom someone is temporarily separated usually helps make the interval and absence tolerable. Imagining anticipated situations can act as a useful way of rehearsing words and actions, so as to be better prepared for different eventualities.

At other times fantasies are less helpful. The nightmare is a dream that has gone too far, when the fantasy becomes too much and uncontrollable, even in sleep. Clients also provide many examples in therapy in their waking thoughts that demonstrate fantasy constructions upon experience, which often lead to false conclusions, and may lead to perceptions of the world, and of people, as hostile or fearful, or both. Other fantasies may appear to provide security and satisfaction but, because they keep a person introverted and collude with anxieties about real relationships, impoverish the opportunities for fuller and more mature relationships.

Psychotic and borderline states

What is important in all therapeutic work is to distinguish between fantasies that are recognized as such (and which may provide the opportunity for different insights into the major concerns and patterns in a client's inner world) and fantasies that have become so real that the world of make-believe has become confused with the realities of the external world. There are some people who seek help for whom fantasy has become so close to being their reality that they are unlikely to benefit from the brief therapy that is often on offer, and who, even if they can be offered long-term help, need a very special kind of therapist. What marks out those whose reality sense has become impaired has been variously described, although it is often the therapist's own countertransference feelings and being unable to think that are the most obvious clues. In working with the majority of adult clients, therapists know that they can use metaphorical and symbolic language and that clients will understand what they mean. A common phrase in a therapeutic intervention is 'It's like . . .', or 'It's as if . . .'. Clients similarly use such phrases in describing their ideas and feelings: 'You are just like my father when you say that . . .', or 'She treats me as if I were a little girl'. Some of the fantasies that people report are introduced with a qualification such as 'I know it's silly to think so, but . . .'. In other words, they are aware that there is a difference in kind between some of their thoughts and reactions and what they would regard as more normal or realistic constructions.

Furthermore, as I have described in earlier chapters, a certain degree of paranoid feeling is fairly common, when it is known to be unreasonable, but is nevertheless uncomfortable. We all show certain schizoid traits, where we temporarily cut ourselves off from others; and there are people who avoid intimate relationships, but know they would like to be different. These states are relatively minor versions of more full-blown disturbances, such as paranoia, schizophrenia and other forms of psychosis. In these latter instances there is usually a clear sign that the client is much more inaccessible; and the feelings engendered by the client in the therapist are often such as to immediately raise serious questions about the suitability of the client for the help that can be offered by the therapist. The phrase 'as if' is missing; things are what they are, not what they seem; fantasy has become reality. There are indications of disturbed, chaotic thinking; words and ideas do not appear to connect; any sense of a personal relationship is remote.

An old 'black' joke runs: the neurotic builds castles in the air, the psychotic lives in them, while the psychiatrist collects the rent. This crude definition illustrates the difference between the neurotic person's acknowledgement of the difference between fantasy and reality (which in itself can lead to discomfort), and the psychotic person's confusion of the two. In fact a psychotic person's world and their strange ideas have their own logic and meaning, and

Laing

often serve to protect them from the feared devastating effects of the real world. One of the compelling attractions of staying in a uniquely constructed personal inner world, which becomes projected out and confused with the external world so that outer becomes inner and inner becomes outer, is that it is in one way safer than the intolerable external world.

These severe disturbances frequently appear to go back to an equally intolerable childhood, where there has been abuse and/or neglect, where not only has there been little or no chance of building up trust in a dependable world and dependable relationships, but where the nurturing has failed to protect the vulnerable infant from the genuine harshness of the external world. Winnicott observes that the failure of the environment to facilitate the maturational processes in the infant is linked to psychosis, a failure that he calls 'privation' (1965b: 226). He distinguishes privation from deprivation, where there is an initial good-enough environment, which then for some reason ceases. These differences are noticeable in any therapeutic practice: there are clients who have been started off well, and then suffer traumatic circumstances, so they have a core of inner strength which helps them climb back up; and there are those who have never had this good-enough begin- ning, who are much more difficult, perhaps even generally impossible to help other than through the use of more intense resources than the individual therapist can provide.

As with other defences, attempting to argue a psychotic person out of his or her bizarre thinking will be felt to be too threatening, and therefore is likely to be strongly resisted. Interpretations about past history and trauma may cause more harm than good. Sometimes there is a thread of thoughtfulness, or the psychotic symptoms are part of a picture that has some signs of more ordinary neuroticism, and this might suggest what is often called a 'borderline per- sonality disorder', which as the term implies, locates the person somewhere on the line between psychotic and neurotic thought and behaviour. Psy- choanalysis recognizes such a presentation; for example, Rey describes 'per- sons who have achieved a kind of stability of personality organization in which they live a most limited and abnormal emotional life which is neither neurotic nor psychotic but a sort of frontier state' (1988: 203). The experience of being with a borderline personality might be described as sensing a person who is on an edge, who could, given undue pressure from the therapist as well as from outside sources or adverse circumstances, tip over into an even more disturbing state. Yet communicating with the borderline personality is somewhat less fraught than trying to work with someone exhibiting full-blown psychotic characteristics. Where there are some signs of more realistic thinking this may be used to guide the client towards more specialized help:

Andrew presented his preoccupation with washing his hands to a counsellor in a Primary Care Practice. This would usually be understood as an example of an obsessive-compulsive disorder, related perhaps to issues about guilt and control; but in Andrew's case there were some worrying psychotic features. He believed, for example, that when he was walking down the street he might tread on glass; and when he came to take off his shoes, splinters of glass might get transferred to his hands; and that if he then rubbed his eyes, he might damage them. That was why he washed his hands so often. He asked the counsellor whether getting glass in his eyes was a possibility – an interesting invitation to the counsellor to comment, which suggested a degree of willingness to listen to what the counsellor thought. The counsellor replied that it was a possibility, and that it certainly made sense to wash his hands from time to time, but that the chances of damage to his eyes were very slight indeed. Perhaps, the counsellor asked, there were other worries? Might it be wise for Andrew to go back to see the doctor? This degree of support appeared to encourage the client to return to the doctor, who was forewarned by the counsellor, and was able to prescribe medication to calm Andrew's obvious anxiety and 'erratic' thinking. Notice that Andrew's thinking was not illogical – it had a type of logical sequence to it. But it was too literal. Fortunately words like 'might' and 'possibility' indicated less rigid a fantasy in Andrew's mind than words like 'must' or 'probability', which he might have used had he been in a true psychotic state.

Diagnostic indications as used for example in the *Diagnostic and Statistical Manual of Mental Disorders* (APA 1994) sometimes make it clear that the usual symptoms of different types of personality disorder cannot be applied to someone under the age of 18. This somewhat arbitrary line is a reminder that adolescence can be an extremely turbulent time, where what might be indications of more serious disturbance in adult clients are within the normal parameters for adolescent behaviour. The nature of the adolescent process therefore makes it difficult to distinguish between what lies within the norm, and what might indicate a more serious disturbance. Psychiatric illness is notoriously difficult to diagnose in persons of this age. What in the adult could be indications of the manic-depressive personality, in the young person might be normal mood swings. What is felt to be deviant or outrageous behaviour in adults might be seen as more usual (if not always acceptable) in an adolescent, and may even be called 'high spirits'. Dieting is the concern of many a young woman, without it having to tip over into anorexia or other eating disorders. Depression is common, without it being more than moodiness. Heavy drinking may even only be a feature of student life, part of a youth culture that can be left behind when the young person graduates.

I include this aspect here partly because the turmoil of strong feelings has perhaps a closer relationship to early experience, where impingements that cause distress come from causes that are as yet unknown; and partly because the early process of distinguishing 'me' from 'not-me' has some resemblance to a process in adolescence that has been described as finding an identity (Erikson 1965, 1968; Marcia 1975). This process can involve a period of confused identity, with a negative view of self: 'I am nobody. I'm stupid. I'm confused' are among the answers such a young person can give to the question 'Who are you?' The confused adolescent readily changes values, is vulnerable to feedback because of low self-esteem, and has difficulties in personal relationships. Although some young people may get stuck in such a position, for most of them this is a phase through which they develop. One of the virtues of adolescence is its fluidity: many young people are on the move, changing, adapting, reworking situations, making and breaking relationships, experimenting, striving towards an identity. This is why counselling young people often brings rapid results, since they are less tied by conventions, by permanent relationships and by fixed attitudes.

At the same time there are pointers to deeper disturbance in young people, which might indicate the desirability of referral to more specialist resources. When anarchic words and fantasies are acted out, a young person can be frightened of their destructiveness or self-destructiveness. Where work and relationships cease to matter or function, introversion is more extreme. Where a strong mood or behaviour pattern extends over a long period without showing signs of changing, this may indicate more serious problems. Where imagination runs riot and fantasies begin to feel too real, then psychotic features may be apparent. When unconventional dress and normal untidiness give way to a failure to care for themselves, and young people withdraw from contact with others, it is probably wise to seek psychiatric opinion (see Laufer and Laufer 1989). The following client illustrates this type of severe disturbance:

> Basil initially presented with feelings of isolation from people, but at the time he seemed to be functioning well at work, and in any case was reluctant to see the therapist, so the therapist did not pursue the missed second appointment. When he returned a year later, with the same problem, he said he was more ready for therapy, although there was more of a sense of desperation than of hope in his voice. Basil described himself: 'I'm cut off from people … it's like going down a spiral staircase and passing people on their way up … I have no sense of time … I couldn't work out what was real at the theatre last evening, whether it was happening on stage or whether it was what was going on in me … I saw a dead cat yesterday lying in the road, and went up to it and felt nothing … going from one place to another is dangerous … I'm losing my marbles…'
>
> Condensing his words in this way masks the erratic pattern of the sessions; some were clear, and others confused; in some the therapist felt they were communicating (especially when he could empathize with Basil by drawing upon images related to the theme of trust), but in other sessions the therapist, like Basil, felt hopeless and helpless.
>
> In the event, he only saw him until he could find Basil a place in a therapeutic community. The psychiatrist who interviewed Basil confirmed the therapist's opinion that Basil showed some signs of being a schizoid personality, but said that the disturbance was difficult to describe or to understand. He added, 'The problem about once-a-week therapy is not so much that it is not enough, as that Basil has to be "open" at those times. A therapeutic community offers the advantage of any opening that occurs, no matter at what time'.

There are certain presentations that, in addition to the fluctuations of adolescent mood and behaviour, present difficulties to the non-specialist: disturbing behaviours, such as self-harm and mutilation, eating disorders, dissociation, multiple personality, drugs and other severe substance abuse, in adults as well as young people. Many of these presentations have connections with the themes of trust and attachment, although control issues (part of the next theme) are also present. It is relatively easy to attach labels (see my warnings in Chapter 2) that are likely to be carried for life, whether or not they are accurate. Insensitive referrals for medical or psychiatric help can break trust in the caring professions, since doctors (like parents) may not be trusted to understand, or a psychiatric assessment suggests the fear and stigma of mental illness. It is hard for a therapist to know whether these indications of disturbance are extreme yet short-lived episodes, or more ongoing borderline features, without making further enquiries of the client. It is also apparent that sometimes a sensitive volunteer counsellor or self-help group is able to do more good than hard-stretched and therefore inadequate professional resources where the waiting lists are too long. These are extremely difficult areas for counsellors and therapists, reflecting just how hard it must be for their clients. As ever supervision is an essential resource for reviewing what is and what is not possible, and for finding support with what can be confusing and disturbing material.

The relationship of trust and faith

Erikson sees faith – in its broadest sense, not simply religious faith – as one of the needs of any society, and rooted in the mother–baby relationship. Winnicott likewise linked adult belief to an infant's trust in the mother, saying, 'The point is, can they believe? I don't care what it's about. The capacity to believe is more important than what you believe' (quoted in Rudnytsky 1991: 181). Arriving at a personal value system or set of beliefs is one feature of personal development that has to be linked to a person's sense of trust and confidence in others, the external world and the self. Lack of opportunities in work, rejection in relationships and other adverse circumstances can lead to the undermining of self-confidence, to lack of faith in the social order, and in turn to destructive attacks on self, or other people and society. Early trauma and neglect in infancy can also lead to deep cynicism and a totally pessimistic attitude towards life. There is no sense of hope, only of worse to come. In such a frame of mind it is scarcely surprising that some people can only express their frustration and lack of faith.

There are a number of studies about personal belief, which illustrate significant shifts in the way children, young people and adults express and conceptualize their beliefs. Concrete images in children develop into conceptual and abstract thinking, applied not only in their studies at school and perhaps thereafter in the major academic subjects, but also in making value judgements and in their moral thinking (Piaget 1950; Kohlberg 1981). A valuable way of conceptualizing the development of belief is Winnicott's writing about illusion. He uses this term in a rather different, more positive way than Freud (1927/2004). The latter sees religious belief as one example of illusion, a type of wish-fulfilment, that arises from the need of the adult to have a dependable father figure, the promise of life after death, and a sense of moral order. Illusions are to be given up in favour of reality thinking. Winnicott (1975: 240) suggests that illusion and disillusion alternate throughout life, representing a type of transitional phenomenon. Although a baby has to give up early illusions of symbiosis and omnipotence, the growing child develops new illusions, some of which in time also undergo disillusion, making way for fresh illusions.

The implications of this idea for a psychology of belief, and for understanding the different ways in which people construct their sense of meaning, are examined more fully in my own book *Illusion* (Jacobs 2000a; see also Fowler (1981), who draws upon Erikson, Kohlberg and Piaget, but appears not to be aware of the importance of Winnicott's ideas). There are parallels between the themes discussed in these chapters, and modes of belief. Therefore unquestioning, simple faith, typified by mythical and magical beliefs, can be associated with early trust issues. There is much evidence of beliefs that are held or understood because of the authority of others (religious or political leaders, or academic experts), which tend to mirror issues around authority, while a further mode of belief challenges authority and seeks more autonomous ideas, although sometimes at the risk of self-aggrandizement. Given the significance of narcissism in the theme of trust, it is interesting to note that Britton refers to the epistemic narcissist, 'someone who believes only in his own ideas, a counterpart in the realm of knowledge to the libidinal narcissist in the realm of love' (1989: 179). Other modes of belief include more universalistic ways of thinking, real interest in alternative belief systems, and the willingness to accept the immensity of what is unknown – some of which finds parallels in the other major theme of cooperation.

Using a different scheme, Becker (1972: 185) outlines different levels of meaning by which an individual can choose to live:

- The basic level of the *Personal* – who one is, the 'true' self, what makes a person special, whom he feels the self to be deep down, 'the person he talks to when he is alone' (this ties in with much that has been described in these chapters about a confident sense of self);
- The higher level of the *Social* – the extension of the self to include those with whom a person is close or intimate: partner, friends, and children;
- The next higher level of the *Secular* – symbols and allegiance at greater personal distance which are often of a compelling quality – the corporation, the party, the nation, knowledge (science and the humanities), or humanity itself. These two middle levels reflect other aspects of later themes;
- The highest level of the *Sacred* – 'the invisible and unknown level of power, the insides of nature, the source of creation, God'. (This level appears to represent a reflection of issues of trust and attachment to a secure base, but on a far wider and deeper scale than the personal or the interpersonal alone.)

Becker concludes: 'The ideal critique of any faith must always be whether it embodies within itself the fundamental contradictions of the human paradox and yet is able to support them without fanaticism, sadism and narcissism, but with openness and trust. Religion itself is an ideal of strength and of potential for growth, of what man might become by assuming the burden of his life, as well as by being partly relieved of it' (p. 196). His words apply of course as much to faith in political ideologies and humanism as they do to religious faith.

Trust and attachment through the life cycle

The initial experiences of the infant make all the difference between viewing life itself as essentially beneficent, or as essentially persecutory. The achievement of ambivalence comes not from an infancy or childhood that is free from frustration, but from integrating painful and difficult experiences with satisfying and pleasurable ones. Such a foundation permits the development of a multifaceted view of life and the world.

The themes of trust and attachment are repeated and tested time and again in life as the growing child moves into a widening world, engaging in other relationships and encountering new experiences. Basic trust, for example, leads to more refined forms of trust. Blind trust may be appropriate for babies, but it needs to be tempered as the child enters new situations, because the wider world can also be a dangerous place, and there are some people who are not to be trusted. Attachment too develops, with secondary attachment figures (such as the father), and attachment theory speaks of a hierarchy of attachment figures (Brisch 2002: 16). Attachment as well as secure separation enables the negotiation of a continuous process, from birth, through weaning, through taking first steps, in going to play group and school, into adolescence and on to the many other occasions for change in adult life, including leaving the parental home, changes in job and location, and the different stages of intimate partnerships.

Yet any therapeutic practice is familiar with difficulties and failures in relationships, some of which are related closely to the issues that have been part of this major theme. There is, for example, an idealized view of love that dominates popular culture, which tends to reinforce an unrealistic expectation of relationships. Therapists encounter clients who are still searching for their ideal partner; who seem neither to have learned that in most partnerships the symbiotic mother–baby phase is only one aspect of a total relationship, nor that in their search they may in fact be looking for something missing in themselves which an external other can never replace. Couples grow together as they learn to embrace and value the ordinariness of life, as well as the high points, to work through differences as well as enjoy agreement. Living with ambivalence, finding a type of 'depressive position' in a relationship, is as important to a couple as it is to individual maturity.

Some partners so much desire a symbiotic relationship that they cannot be separated or cannot permit each other individuality. There can be other difficulties where one or both partners are narcissistically concerned only for themselves, and have not developed sufficient awareness of the other's needs to accept their differences, or sufficient toleration of frustration of their own needs. It is as if the other exists like the early mother figure, simply to serve them. One partner becomes demanding, while the other struggles to meet those demands. In other partnerships one or both may be withdrawn emotionally, and find difficulty in abandoning themselves to sexual and loving feelings, and therefore to each other. In any intimate relationship there has to be shared caring (with each able to care for the other at different times), and therefore a balance between concern for the other and claiming some care for oneself. The most stressful times are often when each needs care from the other, and neither has the emotional resources to provide it. Some of these issues will be seen in Chapters 10 and 11, in relation to Oedipal situations, but aspects of Oedipal issues also appear in the early mother–baby relationship. Indeed Klein finds as much evidence for the Oedipus complex in infancy as Freud does in later childhood.

While this theme has concentrated upon the experience of the infant we also need to relate it to the mother's experience of conception, pregnancy, and giving birth, all of which have the potentiality to revive primitive memories of her own infancy. For some women pregnancy provides them with their first real opportunity to project their own needs for mothering on to their baby. If this serves the baby well at the start, keeping the baby dependent may not be so healthy later on. The need to love in order to find love may be one motive for an early pregnancy, although there are others: as a way of avoiding being alone, or even of avoiding adult relationships; as a means of gaining some independence from the family, and of making one's own home and so on. Nor should we forget that expectant and actual fathers also have their agenda, as in the following example, where the wish to find something for himself seemed important to Ced:

> Ced's casual relationship with a young woman had led to her becoming pregnant. Ced was certainly not callous, and he helped to arrange the abortion with her. This was strange since at first he seemed delighted to have fathered a child, even if it was her wish not to continue with the pregnancy. He was in fact less concerned about her feelings than his own, perhaps because his own issues in this situation were considerable: Ced's father had simply walked out on the family when he was still small, and had not been heard of since; so perhaps Ced was trying to find the 'father' in himself, and that mattered more to him than any sense of how much difficulty and distress he had caused the young woman.

Should an abortion be necessary, it obviously involves a very special kind of loss, and usually more so for a woman than for a man. Even if there is not a strong religious or moral concern, guilt can be intermingled with grief and relief. This is a very clear example of a crisis where someone experiences very different, conflicting, feelings, which create their own tension. Abortion can trigger off anxiety about murderous fantasies. Kleinian theory suggests these are common, including the desire to get rid of potential siblings from the mother's womb. If there is any reality in such a theory it is easy to see what effect this fantasy might have where a pregnancy does not come to term. There is clearly pain, and there may be guilt, which need to be expressed, and set in context:

Dora was one of those gentle people who could never harm a fly. Another side of her came out when she got drunk at a party, went rather wild, and slept with a man whom she did not even know by name. When she found she was pregnant she was very upset at the thought of an abortion, although she recognized that it was necessary. She saw a counsellor to clarify her decision, and they arranged to meet again after she had been to the clinic. Dora went alone to the clinic in another city, and she returned alone. On the train back, a goods train passed the other way, laden with military tanks, an image that stayed in her mind. She felt it applied to her; and although she knew rationally that what she had done was not murder, it nevertheless felt as though she had violated a life. Perhaps linked with this feeling was one that associated the tanks to a man's violation of her own body, however much she had in some way been a willing party. Whatever the meaning of what she saw and felt (and no one can ever be precise about a single image) sharing it with her counsellor helped, and Dora was gradually able to work through her experience sufficiently to feel more of her old self.

While there was some resolution at the time for Dora, it would not be unusual for that abortion to be causing pain years later. Anniversaries of an abortion, or of the time when a child might have been born had the pregnancy not been terminated, can be as significant as other anniversaries:

Edna constantly talked in her therapy of pets and relatives dying, or of her fear of them dying. The counsellor did not wish to hazard a guess without more evidence, but being employed within a Primary Care Practice he had access to Edna's medical history. A glance at her notes confirmed his hunch that she had had an abortion some years before, and he tried to work with her with knowledge of this in mind, even though she never talked about it.

Guilt at having terminated a pregnancy can also lead to fears of being punished through being unable to conceive a second time. This is yet another reason (in addition to dependent needs referred to earlier) that one abortion may be followed by further pregnancy and the request for a second abortion. Sometimes this appears to be an attempt to prove that no damage was done by the first abortion: but while this anxiety is assuaged, a second abortion perpetuates a cycle of uncertainty. For some women it is only the birth of a child who takes the place of the one they have lost that puts an abortion or a miscarriage to rest. While other factors of course have to be taken into account, there may be an element of reparation in some pregnancies.

Miscarriage gives rise to many levels of feeling, including those that relate to this fundamental mother–baby relationship. Miscarriage, and even more so stillbirth, involves a birth and a death at the same time, and giving up a baby for adoption, much less common now than 50 years ago, is a type of 'living death', which for the natural mother often leads to a lifetime's concern about the child who was hers; and for the child a lifetime's wondering about the circumstances that led to such a beginning. Clients who have been adopted, and clients who have long ago given up their baby for adoption – whether or not they seek the other out through the permitted procedures – suggest situations that clearly give rise to many of the different issues that this theme raises.

It is essential for professionals (doctors, nurses and clergy) to recognize too the significance of stillbirth in the care that they give to parents: allowing the dead baby to be seen and held, or photographed, encouraging the death to be talked about at the time, providing a tangible memento, naming the baby if so wished, and arranging for proper recognition of the death through a religious or secular funeral (see Case 1978; Kirkley-Best *et al.* 1982). In these particular instances of loss (abortion, miscarriage, stillbirth and adoption) there may be clues to the nature of the relationship and the degree of loss in the words used to describe the foetus/baby. 'Foetus' and 'it' are cold and more distancing terms. 'He', 'she' and 'the baby' may indicate recognition of, or the wish for, an attachment and greater emotional involvement. 'The child' may refer to the unfulfilled fantasies of the child as he or she would have been in a few years' time, or (looking back on such an event) as he or she might have been now.

When pregnancy goes to full term, with a successful delivery, there are again many different emotions. A mother has gained a baby, although she has lost part of herself; the actual baby in her arms replaces the fantasy baby whom she has thought about all during pregnancy – this is one of the reasons suggested by Winnicott, as to why a mother may in one respect hate her baby; 'nor is the baby magically produced'; the baby is 'a danger to her body in pregnancy and at birth' (1975: 201). The difference between the ideal and the real, the demands of mothering, the sense of responsibility, even feelings about the smallest abnormality in a baby, and anxiety about being a good mother might contribute to post-natal depression. Therapy provides the opening for expressing these mixed feelings, including the negative thoughts and emotions that a mother thinks she should not have, and constitutes a more natural and normalizing approach to post-puerperal depression than pathologizing and treating it with powerful drugs or electro-convulsive therapy, which is the experience of some clients.

When their children have passed through the early dependent stages and are becoming slowly more independent, parents have to learn about different aspects of trust and attachment. Their 'ideal baby' may at times be a 'little monster', and the task of parenting involves oversight and letting go, being neither intrusive nor clinging, yet careful to be available when the child runs back in anxiety, or when tired of exploring. It is not easy to get the balance right, particularly with adolescents, where these issues are likely to be lived out with some forcefulness and angst on all sides. Since much of this is also about providing the right milieu for independence and autonomy, these issues are more fully discussed as part of the next theme of authority and autonomy.

Trust and attachment are also part of the learning and the working environment, and of relationships outside the home at all levels, including that between a child or an adolescent and his or her teachers, or between employees and their employer, manager and managed, and so on. In learning, too trusting an attitude can lead to swallowing whole what those in authority say; too much anxiety can lead to rejection, spitting out, tearing apart destructively what others try to teach and pass on. Although these are clearly issues around authority the metaphors we use, such as 'swallowing' and 'spitting out', show how fundamental some difficulties may be in the learning process.

There was a time when the work environment involved a dependency culture, although the days are largely gone for most people when they can expect to be provided with a job for life, and an employer who is a benevolent provider in times of trouble and want. Yet in the process of growing up trust is encouraged in the promised goals of education and later in contracts of employment. When that trust is broken it may lead to a deep lack of faith in those who make promises and even in society itself, which is experienced as uncaring. The undermining of faith in others can easily lead to lack of faith in oneself. Where there is a split in society, and indeed in the wider world, between those who have and those who have not, it is reminiscent of the basic split that can be experienced in infancy between the hungry baby and the mother who appears to withhold all the good things she has. Since Erikson links hope and drive as the two basic strengths of this first age, it is important to remember that people without work may not just lose hope that things can be different, but also their drive to change things. It is not surprising therefore that redundancy and unemployment can give rise to debilitating depression, to withdrawal into a frightened and fractured self, and all the attendant difficulties of moving out of that state. It is not just 'what I do' that has been taken away, but 'who I am' that has been undermined. Add to this living on benefits, or on a pension (apart from problems about the actual level of the payment), and it can be seen how dependency issues may be stirred up, encouraging some to sink into a state where their single expectation is to be looked after; while others feel guilty at being dependent, and blame themselves for the way they are. Being without work (which for some people also happens when they retire) may make people feel even more helpless and infantilized, losing hope that they can make an impact on, or contribution to, society.

> Frank had been unemployed for three years. His main preoccupation was getting a job; and this had become so central for him that he could not hear what anyone else was saying to him, unless they were giving him an opening to express his feelings. His manner reminded the counsellor of a hungry baby, for whom nothing else matters than being fed. Frank had no room for concern for others and their difficulties, even if they too were unemployed. Getting a job so dominated him that until that need was satisfied he could apparently not settle to any other activity, including relating to others at home. Frank's situation is probably not atypical of the effects of long-term unemployment. In fact he changed, at least partially, when he was encouraged to get involved as a voluntary helper. This gave him a sense of purpose and self-worth, which helped him to pay more attention to the needs of others outside himself, in turn helping him to be more positive and less resentful at job interviews.

The second half of life gives rise to a set of different issues, not normally faced before, such as having parents whose ageing can make them more dependent. There are, of course, differing cultural attitudes to who should care for elderly relatives, and about expectations on filial responsibility. Illness at any age and ageing may give rise to anxieties about having to be dependent upon others. We also know that in this reversal of roles that comes with old age, ruthless games can sometimes be played, where older people are more infantilized by the younger generation than they are by their natural physical weakness. It is at this point in family relationships that the real ability of parents and their children to relate adult-to-adult is exposed and tested. There may be some reflection of these issues in even more frightening terms in the sadistic attacks that can take place on the defenceless old person by the young. These might even be examples of the acting out of revenge that a younger generation feels towards those who were once felt to be persecutory objects.

Some mental infirmities reflect psychotic states discussed earlier in this chapter. Senile dementia, for example, can lead to fragmentation of thought, where fantasy appears confused with reality. Rayner (1986: 259–60) reminds us that these fantasies are still symbolic and can best be understood when the symbols can be translated into present concerns and he provides some useful examples of this.

Some psychologists (for example, Lowe 1972: 248) have suggested a number of psychological 'types' of older person, each one demonstrating a different resolution of the way they look back on their life. Most of the types referred to reflect ways of dealing with basic issues about self and others. One type has been referred in Chapter 4 in describing a possible narcissistic reaction to ageing. Other types include the self-hating older person, who is despairing and pessimistic, who turns his or her hatred into self-contempt, and who has such a negative view of the past that death is looked forward to as a merciful release; or a different expression of hostility is seen in the older person whose anger is directed outwards, in criticism of others and in envy of the younger generation, but who is fearful of death. It is not difficult to envisage how much issues of trust and attachment are raised in ageing, as affectional bonds to family and attachments to colleagues and friends are often severed, including the prospect of severing the attachment to life itself.

Nevertheless reactions to ageing are different for the psychologically mature older person, known by some gerontologists as the 'constructive' type. Such a person has high self-esteem and broad interests that were developed earlier in life, and remains self-aware, enjoying the sense of responsibility that is appropriate to old age. He or she is eager to preserve personal integrity, and to enjoy a sense of tranquillity (like the dependent type), but (unlike the dependent type) remains aware of a sense of purpose and meaning in life, hoping for an even greater understanding of what life is all about.

Erikson describes the aim of the eighth age, mature adulthood, as one of ego integrity, a phrase that has much in common with ambivalence in the depressive position, which Klein associates with the resolution of more primitive fantasies. Ego integrity comes from looking back over life, appreciating all that has gone well, finding pleasure in one's achievements and in one's creativity and generativity, as well as the acceptance of those things that have gone wrong, and the recognition that these cannot be changed (concern without overbearing guilt). On balance the good things in life are felt to outweigh those inevitable experiences that have been bad.

Bereavement itself involves separation, with different degrees of pain and intensity depending on the quality of the attachment to the one who has been lost. Dying pushes at the limits of trust, and confidence in the self, whether or not people have a religious belief in another form of life after death. Care and counselling of the bereaved and of the dying has become a specialist area with its own large body of literature, and needing particular study (see, for example, Kubler-Ross 1969; Speck 1978; Raphael 1984; Parkes 1986; Worden 1991; Lendrum and Syme 2004).

In a society where death is so often institutionalized and locked away, being with the dying and facing death itself is not surprisingly overloaded with fantasies of the most negative kind. Even direct experience of another's death (and that is not as common as it once was) cannot adequately prepare a person for his or her own, since it is almost impossible to conceptualize it, involving as it does the dissolution of the self (or of the self as we know it, depending upon one's religious views). Rayner (1986: 238–42) suggests that recognition of being mortal and finite (which does not really occur in most people until middle age) is frightening, but that it is also a relief, because the denial of mortality can be shed. Any kind of denial engenders inner stress, and being able to throw off denial releases some of the tension.

There is a sense in which we here come full circle, back to the impossibility of being able to conceptualize not only death, but also pre-natal and post-natal experience. The type of knowledge that we have of the early weeks and months of the infant's life, addressed through the themes of trust and attachment, is a combination of speculation arising out of observation of babies, intuitive responses to infants, as well as of imaginative engagement which draws a variety of experiences of being with the young. Psychoanalysis gives form to this type of knowledge with theories, some of which extrapolate back into infancy from what older children and adults describe about their psychological and emotional states. Attachment research and observational studies add more weight to this theorizing, but in therapy itself this combination of factual information and imaginative construction needs to be set alongside how clients describe their experience, their thinking (whether logical, fanciful or bizarre) and their feelings. They may have little knowledge of their own infancy other than what they have been told. Yet the features that these last three chapters have identified may ring true for them, and enhance the sensitivity of the therapist to their felt and imagined present and past experience.

AUTHORITY AND AUTONOMY: INTERNALIZING PARENTAL AUTHORITY

The growing child and parental expectations

Another group of important themes presented in the therapeutic setting is related to that period of development that is described variously by different authors, but is generally concerned with the development of greater independence and initiative. Erikson calls it the 'muscular-anal' stage, following Freud, but making rather more explicit than Freud what happens psychologically as the infant becomes capable of much greater coordination of muscles and brain. This leads in turn to greater mobility and dexterity, to speech and more precise communication with others, and to engaging more fully with other people and situations in the child's widening world. Attachment theory uses the term 'exploratory system', and the greater mobility that physical development brings certainly enables the securely attached child to range further from the carer, and engage in new tasks that widen skill and knowledge. Winnicott likewise envisages the development of greater creativity and play.

Like the first set of themes these issues, many of them to do with different aspects of control and of becoming gradually more independent, are seen not only in the younger child, colloquially called 'the toddler', but played out in relation to different tasks and to different significant figures throughout life. If the first set of themes around trust and attachment are largely to do with finding a sense of being, the themes I discuss here are about doing, making, and acting, on the basis of attitudes acquired in the early years, reinforced within the family in later childhood and adolescence, supported or challenged in school, and becoming a major influence on the way in which learning, work, and relationships with authority in particular, are faced and worked with in adult life. People can value themselves or feel valued by others on the basis of *what they do* (or do not do), rather than on the basis of *who they are*. The division between being and doing may seem artificial, because personal identity often includes what a person does as well as what they are like. But the person with a secure basic sense of self can change what they do without altering who they are; and the person who lives only for what they do may be masking a weakened sense of who they are. Where people successfully handle the issues that arise in the context of this theme of authority and autonomy, the foundations are laid for self-esteem in terms of what might be achieved, for confident independence, and for the potentiality for the pleasure and creativity of self-expression. Negotiated less well, the same issues may lead a person instead to doubt, shame and inhibition.

Freud's early work tended to emphasize the anal aspects of this early period of development, and anal characteristics are often identified as coming from negotiation of this period of life. Graphic terms, such as 'messy', 'dirty', 'letting go' or 'holding in' clearly apply to attitudes and reactions to toilet training; but of course they apply to many other situations as well, where they are equally significant, for example, a messy room, or even a messy life; or the letting go of feelings as well as faeces. In developmental terms the second and third years of life bring immense changes, as an infant moves from relative helplessness to being able to move around, from being fed to feeding herself, from a few sounds to speaking her needs, from holding and hugging to taking things apart and putting them back together. As life proceeds the older child learns further skills, and faces the need to tackle new tasks. Attitudes to these tasks, as well as reactions from others to achievement and failure, may be influenced by and understood in the light of parental encouragement or restrictions in earlier years; and throughout adult life there are plenty of other opportunities and situations where early learning about authority and about the process of becoming autonomous play a significant part.

This theme therefore covers much more than Freud's apparently single focus upon anal eroticism and toilet training (although he also refers to the pleasure of muscular exertion in play); and more too than Erikson's extension of the tasks of this second stage to 'muscular-anal' development. Anal characteristics (being ordered – or messy; holding back – or letting go; retention – and spoiling or soiling) can also be applied to a range of other activities and interactions both in other aspects of parent–child relationships as well as in adult life.

There is much to learn and absorb in the process of growing up. Children have to work hard to make sense of what is expected of them, of what words mean, of how things work, of what being in relationship to others might involve. Sometimes what parents and significant others say is misinterpreted or misunderstood by them, and such distortions can be carried into later life. Children sometimes struggle to make sense of bewildering words by changing them into something that sounds familiar to them and which makes more sense to them: such as versions of phrases in the Christian *Lord's Prayer*, where 'Thy kingdom come' becomes 'Vikings will come' (there having been a project on Vikings at infant school); or 'Lead us not into temptation' is interpreted as 'Lead us not into Thames Station': the corrupted phrase is in each case more concrete for the child than the original unfamiliar adult concept. Similarly misunderstandings can easily arise also over adult expectations and 'rules'. Take an example from toilet training, which in our society is often given particular prominence as an indicator of 'being good' or being 'grown up', and which stereotypically appears at first to be given prominence in psychoanalytic theory. A child learns that it is good to urinate and defecate on the pot, but he or she does not understand at first why it is good to perform in one receptacle, yet not in a different place. If it is the pot that is significant for the adult, it might be (psychoanalysts suggest) that for a child it is her faeces that are more significant, and that they are precious, wherever you choose to deposit them. It may therefore be puzzling for a child to realize that not only is the pot a rather special sort of container, but to discover that when she has finished, these special offerings of hers are poured from the pot into a toilet, where they are then flushed away. Puzzlement may then become bafflement when the child is then told off for placing some other precious item (such as mother's necklace) in the toilet, which by now has become a particularly sacred place! Adults may smile at such mistakes, although sometimes it is we adults who become angry and quite unjustifiably punish a child for not knowing better. Children are then mystified, not understanding what it is they have done wrong, when they so much wished to please by doing the right thing.

It is scarcely surprising that it is difficult for a young child to comprehend in so short a time the complexities and subtleties of the rules of the adult game of life. As Lowe says, a child is sometimes 'damned if he does, damned if he doesn't' (1972: 9). It is a deeply puzzling world to be living in. Just when they feel most pleased with themselves, they may be scolded for their achievements; or what feels like an achievement at one time becomes a disaster at another. A child's energy and enthusiasm can be encouraged by being told 'there's a clever girl'; and then the same actions are suddenly curbed as being too disruptive – 'there'll only be trouble'. At other times a child may want to be more baby-like, and yet find herself forced to be active and to conform to 'being her age', just when it is that age she wishes temporarily to retreat from. So although some parents can be cruel and demanding, and crush the spirit of a growing child, it is not necessarily inadequate parenting that leads to inhibition or anxiety in the face of new tasks, new situations and new relationships. Some of the misunderstandings just described can have a similar effect.

Neither should we imagine that a child is ever only a passive recipient of adult wishes. The growing child and adolescent hopefully finds plenty of opportunity for exercising her own wishes, which sometimes leads to battles of will and, particularly in the most repressive families, to frustrations of freedom, as a child seeks to get something, or do something, that the parent will not allow. If confidence and autonomy can be facilitated, encouraged and rewarded in many families, in most it also has to some extent to be won.

Chapter 7 takes this set of issues further, demonstrating how the exercise of control, and autonomy, and learning to live with, challenge and submit to authority figures, constitute different aspects of what is sometimes known in psychodynamic theory as the 'anal character', the principal indications of which are best summarized as: rigidity (the uptight, controlled person); anxiety (about getting it wrong, or making a mess); the opposite characteristics of being disorganized, uncontrolled, 'letting it all out' indiscriminately; the need for clear answers; unquestioning adherence to authoritative ideas or figures; gratuitous challenging and antagonizing of others, who are not necessarily oppressive; and the ability to control and manage themselves and their relationships with others. In the therapeutic relationship too, clients show various characteristics that are relevant to the themes around authority and autonomy. Some of their difficulties may need considerable working through before therapy can make any progress with the concerns brought by the client: for example, where a client views the therapist as an authoritative oracle who has all the answers, this is in itself a difficulty, whatever else the client may bring. Presenting issues can also be directly related to different manifestations of the theme as examined in this chapter and the two that follow.

Unfortunately the emphasis upon anal functions and anal eroticism in psychoanalysis has tended to minimize the significance of other aspects of muscular development in infancy, which includes walking, grasping, playing with toys, speaking, feeding oneself and so on. All these developments introduce new ways of relating for parent and child, as each learns to adapt to the consequences of the child's growing abilities. Most parents are of course delighted with their child's achievements, although there are bound to be mixed feelings: when a child learns to walk, nothing in the house is quite as safe as it was when she stayed where she had been put, and everything was safely out of reach: watchfulness and a little anxiety go hand-in-hand with pleasure at the child's first steps. Overwatchfulness on the other hand can convey overconcern, and hamper a child's confidence in moving around and exploring. When a baby begins to grasp a spoon and use it as a tool this is another important step; but her attempts at feeding will of course at first mean food goes everywhere as well as in her mouth, and the wrong reaction of the parents to the resulting mess may again inhibit the child. Parental reactions to a child's advances provide important feedback on her initiatives.

These parental attitudes were of course present when their child was a baby; and they will probably continue to be the same as other developments take place, such as the child going to school and negotiating the question of limits in adolescence. A mother may therefore go by the rule book in providing feeds when the baby is young; a father may be disturbed by toys cluttering up the floor with his 3-year-old, and by the latest fashions creating disagreement with his teenage son or daughter. Parents can show anxiety about a child's performance at school which resembles the pressure to produce faeces at the right time and place when the child was a toddler. Requirements for order and reactions to chaos, inevitable when there are children growing up, run as deep as the first theme characteristics around trust and doubt, attachment or withdrawal. A parent's attitudes to the growing child are probably influenced by what he or she learned from his or her own parents; although some parents make a determined effort to 'be different' in their own parenting, remembering the stresses caused them in their upbringing by rigid parenting on the one hand or unboundaried parenting on the other.

The kind of authority exercised by their parents is often clear from the way clients speak of their past, because they remember (in a way that they do not about infancy) parental reactions and attitudes at different points in child-hood and adolescence. It is generally easier to gain considerable insight into the way parents have exercised their authority and responded to the child's initiatives, because these reactions are often relatively consistent throughout the client's childhood and adolescence, and may even be expressed in adult-to-adult relations between the generations. Some clients may even have early memories that throw light on how their parents reacted to them at the tod-dler stage, while others glean what it must have been like in other ways:

> Gerry had great difficulty letting go of his feelings; he seemed afraid of being emotional. He could only express himself in a distant intellec-tualized fashion. He had a dramatic insight into his mother's probable attitudes to him as a baby when his sister had her first child. He visited her home at the same time as their mother had done, and he listened with amazement to his mother telling his sister off for not putting the newborn baby on the pot straightaway: 'You and your brother were put on the pot from the first day out of hospital'. Gerry was partly amused, but also partly relieved as he heard this, because he realized that it was not all his doing that he had become a person who felt compelled to have everything carefully ordered; and he was somewhat angry as he related this story to the therapist, because he recognized that his mother's need to control potty training from 'day one' might have contributed to his problem about being spontaneous.

> Henry initially came to therapy with problems of premature ejaculation. He found it very difficult to relax when making love. Although he 'let go' too soon, his tension also contributed to his difficulty. He recalled an early memory of walking in the country with his parents, and bursting to pee. He asked if he could go behind a bush, but his mother forbade it – he had to wait until he got home and do it in the right place. Not only did Henry as an adult find sex rather dirty, but he also recognized that whenever he was asked to produce results, whether in his work or in what he called his 'sexual performance', he worried inordinately in case he did not do things the right way.

Other examples of parental rigidity, not necessarily related to toilet func-tions, show similar reasons for tight self-control:

> Imogen was a quiet girl, who was very tense when trying to relate to others. She found it difficult to enjoy herself, and she particularly feared losing control when she was with a man, in case the early playful stages of the physical relationship got out of hand. She found it equally difficult to let go of her thoughts and feelings in therapy. The therapist's experience of being with Imogen was that she constantly needed to draw Imogen out: in her countertransference the therapist found it difficult to play with words and ideas in the session. Imogen always seemed to be looking for some guidance as to what to say or do. In one session she told the therapist of a memory of a time in her early adolescence, which probably typified her parents' attitudes to her. It happened when she had some cousins to stay. The youngsters were all excited, and were bouncing

up and down on the sofa, and when her parents came in they told Imogen off, but not her cousins. She felt very small and ashamed. It was a telling example to the therapist of how her parents' 'wet blanket' dampened getting too excited and letting off steam, and suggested that such attitudes probably pervaded her home, continuing to influence Imogen even when she had grown up and left it behind her.

These examples demonstrate inhibition about letting go; and in two instances spontaneity was also absent from the therapy sessions as well. Each of these clients was afraid of what would happen if they lost control, perhaps worried about what they might spill out too if they let go more in therapy. Such characteristics can also be seen in clients who are very precise and particular, planning what they want to say, perhaps with a written list of points they want to be sure to talk about; or in clients who speak in a measured way, detailing precise times and dates, as if each session is a minute-by-minute report of the last week. 'Getting it right' seems to dominate. Perhaps they too are afraid of letting something slip:

Joan was a really pessimistic woman, convinced that things would never work out for her. She really began to irritate her therapist by the way she tried to express herself. She constantly introduced so many qualifications into each sentence that the therapist almost forgot how the sentence had begun by the time she got to its end. 'I was pleased to be able to go to London – well, not exactly pleased, but to go to London – well, not to go to London, but to get away from Birmingham – it wasn't like a few years ago when I went to London ...'. After so many false starts and corrections the thread was lost. Joan seemed so afraid of making a mistake in her choice of words, that the therapist eventually put this to her, linking her dread of the things going wrong in the future to her fear that she was always getting it wrong in what she spoke of today.

Keith began every session by alluding back to the last. 'I'm sorry I said ... I didn't mean ...', and so on. After a time the therapist observed: 'You seem to leave here each time afraid that I have got you wrong'. It is also possible that in both these cases there was a lot of unexpressed anger in each of these clients, but their most obvious need was to try to make everything right in order to neutralize it.

Right and wrong, and particularly words such as 'ought', 'must' and 'should', seem to feature highly in those who are hampered in their spontaneity by their rigid self-control. It can even be a relief when such a precise person can actually come late to a session (when normally the therapist would wonder why) without having to apologize:

Lionel was a very ordered and precise individual. It therefore felt as if it was a significant step forward when, after a missed session, he returned the next week, quite gleefully saying that he had hired a car for the day; and how much he had enjoyed sitting on a hill at the time of the session feeling that he could pay for the therapist's time but he did not have to attend! It was, of course, also an unconsciously aggressive act towards the therapist, who had been left worried about what had happened to someone who was normally so regular. But in this particular context it felt like a rather healthy 'one in the eye' for the therapist, as well as a bid to be independent, without having to feel guilty about it. Lionel could at one and the same time meet his obligation (he was of course still going to pay for the session), yet he could assert his freedom of choice. In this instance the therapist too needed to be free enough to see the positive side in this otherwise rebellious acting out. Some psychoanalytic training results in rather rigid therapists who feel obliged to interpret anything that is not precisely 'by the book'.

Conscience and internalized parents

Why is it, though, that many adults, who have long left their parental home behind them, still go on acting as if their parents were around, still the controlling figures they might have been in their childhood? In looking at the first theme of trust and attachment, I discussed the way a baby takes in (or internalizes) the experience of the nurturing parent, who becomes one rather important facet of the child's self-image. The internalized parent may be a good image, or a bad one, and in most cases probably has some good features and some bad features; continued exposure to good experience in the parental relationship is likely to lead to a more confident self-image, a sense of being good enough (without becoming narcissistic or omnipotent), but inevitably there will be a few negative aspects to the internalized self-image, because no one, thank goodness, is perfect.

The child's inner world continues to act as a container for internalizing experience of the parents, including icons of the type of authority they represent. The key word here is 'represent', since the child's inexperience may make the perceived authority of a parent into something much more fearful than a parent intended. In this way internalized figures take on a life of their own, moulded by the child's perceptions. Although children are often highly intuitive, they do not have the breadth of knowledge and experience that an adult has. So, when something goes wrong for an adult, a balanced view would be to regret the mistake and to learn from it how to do better the next time. But when something goes wrong for a child, a child may exaggerate how 'bad' she has been, especially if a parent's anger at a mistake was sudden, forceful and frightening. While the parent's anger soon cools, and may even be quickly followed by a reparative hug, the outburst continues to echo in the child's mind like the echo of a warning shot across the bows. If the child is in turn angry with the parent, a parent's anger may be felt even more intensely, because the child attaches to it her own anger projected on to the parent.

A child can therefore cope with a parental rebuke in a variety of ways: she probably learns not to repeat the offending behaviour; she may copy her parents in telling off her doll or cuddly toy, or a younger sibling; she may get cross with a fantasy companion, thus disowning her own responsibility. In all these responses the critical parent is internalized, and replicated in the child's relation to other objects or of herself. This internalization or introjection gradually takes up a permanent position within a child's mind, and forms (or so Freud felt) the basis for the 'super-ego', or what might more popularly be called the 'conscience'.

To some extent this process is part of learning what is deemed right and what is deemed wrong, in the context of a particular family, in a particular subculture, and in society (or society as far as the growing child knows it). But while the formation of conscience and the superego follow a similar process, through absorbing parental injunctions as well as learning from parental responses, a distinction perhaps needs to be made between the two concepts. Conscience is more aptly used of the relatively rational, conscious, self-observing aspect of a person, which enables choices of behaviour to be made and self-control to be consciously exercised. Thomas Aquinas defined conscience as 'the mind making moral judgements'. The super-ego has a rather different meaning, and is better reserved for that aspect of reflection and evaluation, before and after actions, which is unconscious as well as conscious and which is often irrationally hostile to the self. When something goes wrong, even if the person has not themselves done wrong, that person might say, 'I feel very bad about myself, even though I know I have no reason to'. That is not at all an uncommon situation for many clients to find themselves in.

Other technical terms have been used in psychoanalytic literature to describe this kind of reaction. Fairbairn (1952), for example, prefers the terms 'internal saboteur' and 'anti-libidinal ego'. 'Internal saboteur' is a good phrase to consider using explicitly with clients: 'It is as if some part of you sabotages you'. We notice here, as in the phrases used in Chapter 3 (for example, 'I don't understand myself') how ordinary language portrays a divided self, one part of the self in relation to another part of the self. Klein's phrase 'the persecutory object' again graphically describes an internalized 'voice' (as people often hear it) which aggressively and sometimes destructively tortures the core 'I'.

> Mandy was such a tortured person, always deeply anxious about whether she was doing the right thing. She had made some progress in her therapy, and as a reward for an event that had gone well she decided to treat herself to some new clothes. But when she walked out of the shop with them, she seemed to hear this voice inside her telling her off for spending the money, and asking her what she thought she would look like, 'all dressed up like that'. When the therapist said to Mandy, 'It's almost as if one side of you is persecuting the other', she seized on the phrase: 'That's just it – that's exactly how it feels'. Her therapist then wondered whether Mandy in any way recognized the voice. Mandy did not have to think for long. She soon responded that she knew that voice anywhere: it was just what her mother would say – even the tone of the voice was just like hers.

Bettelheim (1983) points out that the translators of Freud's works into English did him and psychoanalytic terminology an injustice by choosing to use Latin terms such as 'id', 'ego' and 'super-ego'. It may have been from a mistaken notion that such terms appeared more scientifically respectable. In the original German Freud's terms are personal, and should have been translated as the 'it', the 'I' and the 'over-I', and this is reflected in many of the new translations that appear in the Penguin Classics versions of Freud's essays and books. 'Over-I' may be as ugly a phrase as 'super-ego', but the other terms make more sense. They reflect everyday speech, as in the phrases 'It wasn't me', 'It came over me', 'I don't know what took me over', 'I feel as if there's a little voice in me telling me how awful I am'. An alternative dynamic explanation is used in Transactional Analysis (Berne 1968) and provides another readily understandable terminology that can be used by psychodynamic practitioners: 'It's as if there is a critical parent inside you getting at the child in you'. A rather different image is also apt: 'It feels as if you are at war with yourself'. All these phrases (I–myself; you–yourself; parent–child) illustrate the inner dialogue, or even the inner shouting match that so easily takes place.

In identifying the different aspects that appear to constitute the self, and in using terms for these internalized figures with which a client can identify, therapists provide support for the central self, the 'ego', or the 'I':

In Norma's case the therapist was able to use images taken from Norma's own words. She was saying how restricted she felt in her digs. She could not play music late at night, because it disturbed people; but other people also disturbed her, because the walls were so thin. Her parents had been and still were protective of her, never allowing her any real freedom or independence, in case in some way or another she got hurt. What they said when she was with them continued to exert a strong influence upon her when she was living on her own. She always felt, for example, that she ought to be working. Working was her only safe activity. She found it difficult to enjoy herself, which of course made it difficult for her too when she could hear the other people in her digs enjoying themselves. Her therapist took Norma's description of her digs, and suggested that there were thin walls inside her too, and that when she wanted to enjoy herself, she heard her parents saying inside her: 'Do be careful', 'You should be working' and so on.

The internalized parental figure easily finds support in anyone who is in a position of authority. The internal saboteur finds an external ally when it needs it. Teachers, those in managerial positions, those who enforce law and order, clergy as well as therapists – any of these may be perceived as being critical and punitive even when they are not, and even when they have said or done little that could warrant such a perception. Therapists particularly need to be careful that they do not present themselves in an authoritarian way, because they will easily feed such notions; and they need to listen especially for any indication that this is the way their interventions are being understood. Even observations that are intended to be facilitative can be taken as judgmental. Confrontation or challenge, which must always be used sensitively, are doubly difficult to get right if the client sees the therapist not just as a parent figure (not unusual, and not in itself damaging), but as a critical parent.

Where this appears to be the case, therapists can look for opportunities to link the client's feeling of being criticized, or their wish for an authoritative answer, to other significant authority figures past and present. If clients appear to have to defend themselves, particularly following an intervention, the therapist might observe: 'You appear to think I'm being critical of you – as if I was like your stepfather, who always picked on you'; or 'You know, you are very hard upon yourself, and I think you see me as treating you the same way'. It is valuable in itself to lessen the severity of a client's self-criticism, or anxiety about others being judgmental, but it is essential to do this if fear of criticism makes it impossible for a client to express those private thoughts and feelings, of which the client is likely to feel guilty or ashamed.

Shame and guilt

In looking at the underside of narcissistic pride in Chapter 3, I referred to a sense of shame that may be present in the earliest months, describing this as lack of self-esteem. Nathanson (1987) refers to the basic form of shame ('primary shame'), which already manifests itself in withdrawal and down-turned head and gaze at the age of three months, when the infant's effort to approach his mother fails. Others place the beginnings of shame in the second year, and Erikson (1965) certainly locates shame as a second-stage issue related to autonomy, rather than as linked with earlier issues. This apparent difference may be related to Erikson's association of shame with the inability to perform tasks, with feelings of incompetence, with failure to reach the aspirations and expectations set by others (or even by oneself), and with a self-image of being immature. All these are different occasions for shame from the despair that might be associated with narcissistic damage and the feeling of being ashamed about one's whole self. In both instances the feeling of shame may be completely crippling: it is what occasions it that is different. A further difference is that there is more hope for a fairly rapid recovery from a single failure to perform a task than there is from that pervasive and basic lack of worth, or from a perpetual sense of not being able to do things well.

It seems sometimes that in common usage the terms 'shame' and 'guilt' are interchangeable, just as 'envy' and 'jealousy' may commonly be used as alternative expressions. In psychoanalytic terminology, however, envy and jealousy are quite distinct (see p. 79), and shame and guilt are similarly used to describe quite different types of emotion. Precisely what these differences are is not consistent in the literature. Erikson makes it appear that guilt is a feature of later development (he associates it with his third stage), following Freud, who suggested that the capacity to experience guilt is one of the results of the Oedipus complex (whether successfully negotiated or not). Shame, Erikson posits, results from failure to negotiate tasks involved in the mus-cular-anal stage of development. Therefore guilt is placed in the third stage, because it is a response more to what a person has done (Erikson places emphasis on 'initiative' as a virtue in his third age), whereas shame is related to that which the person has been unable to do.

My position throughout this book is that it is unhelpful to link any of these emotions or psychological features to any particular age. What is more useful is to be able to 'name' what the client is experiencing. Definitions and distinctions may be useful, but only as long as it is recognized that guilt may also be experienced at an early stage of development, particularly in Klein's association of guilt with oral aggression and anal aggression in infancy. Guilt may then refer to the anxiety experienced that we may have damaged the other; whereas in shame it is the self that feels damaged. Shame may arise from feelings of failure to achieve control, and from a sense of letting oneself down, or of letting others down. It is a kind of disappointment, sometimes very intense disappointment, rather than anger with oneself, the latter being more obvious at least in some expressions of guilt. Feelings of shame may be expressed in language that is reminiscent of anal imagery: 'I fouled it up ... I made a mess of it'. Indeed the anal stage provides a clear example of the distinction: a child who inadvertently messes in his pants rather than on the toilet may experience a sense of shame if he is told off – the opposite of the pleasure he feels when he does it in the right place. But if the same child *deliberately* messes his pants, perhaps as an angry protest, then when he is told off he is more likely to feel guilty. Anal terminology provides a number of good expressions of more obviously aggressive feelings, such as the wish to spoil or soil, to shit upon, as a token of angry defiance.

Ozzie gave an interesting example of the difference between shame and guilt in a rather different situation. In a nostalgic moment, he returned one dark evening with a friend to their old secondary school to see their old classroom. They both climbed over the fence, and were wandering around the outside of the building when the caretaker caught them. Ozzie felt very guilty at having been caught trespassing, but his friend simply walked up to the caretaker, and started to chat, man to man, about their reason for being there. The caretaker quietened down, and accepted what the friend had said. Ozzie, however, felt ashamed at having felt so guilty, and of not being as 'cock sure' (as he put it) as his friend had been in that situation. It is incidental perhaps, but Ozzie had regularly wetted the bed until way into his teens, and he also felt very ashamed about that.

It can be the client's tone of voice and facial expression that provides the clearest indication of these different feelings, with shame being expressed in a more depressed and despairing way. Shame is often communicated non-verbally, with the head down and gaze averted, enacting the phrase used in some cultures about shame: 'loss of face'. In such a situation a therapist's choice of language is important: 'I think you're worried that I may be disappointed in you', is more relevant to the situation than 'You may feel that I'm angry with you'.

It is an interesting question, whether people are generally more ready to acknowledge something about which they feel guilty, than something of which they feel ashamed. Shame seems to cut deeper than guilt, as in this example, where Petula described her view of the difference:

She told her therapist that she did not feel guilty if she told white lies. The therapist thought that in some way she was concerned about this, and asked what sort of lies she meant. She explained that if people asked about herself, she could never let on to them that she was really unhappy and discontented; she led them to believe that she was on top of everything, and that she got on well with others. This was not the case at all, but Petula knew that she would feel ashamed if she was seen as less than perfect in other people's eyes. She preferred to tolerate the unease of telling what she called white lies than experience the shame she would otherwise bring upon herself.

It is obviously important to help a client to talk about the trigger for his or her feelings, but this can only be done when it is clear that the therapist is not apportioning blame, or meting out criticism. Some people use denial or projection to avoid facing their feelings of shame and guilt: 'It wasn't me ... it was the drink in me'; 'I wasn't myself'; 'It was their fault'; 'It was the devil in me'; 'I blame my parents'. It is of course possible that others, such as parents, might in some way be to blame, and in some instances it is important to be able to allow feelings about that to be expressed. This is particularly valid when working with survivors of abuse of different kinds, where if anyone experiences shame it should of course be the perpetrator; but it is all too often the survivor. It is not sufficient, as some psychoanalytic practice has done, to link such experiences of shame to the fantasy wishes of the survivor. Proper attribution of responsibility is necessary when there is obvious evidence of abuse or neglect. At the same time a fully objective stance requires us to accept that those who have damaged others are often themselves damaged, and that 'the sins of the fathers are visited upon the children', generation after generation. Perhaps one of the main differences between shame and guilt is that guilt can be appropriate, whereas shame never is. Justifiable guilt involves accepting responsibility for oneself, or for a part of oneself, albeit a part a client might prefer to disown.

Conditional love and perfectionism

It is impossible to bring up a child without introducing an element of reward and punishment; when parents are pleased they reward through what they say, their tone of voice, and even by little gifts. When they are angry or disappointed, a certain degree of punishment is inevitable, again in tone of voice, but sometimes in more violent verbal or physical reactions. Do parents become more conditional in the love they express, and more ready to show displeasure as the infant grows older and becomes more active and independent? I suspect that the same type of love (which of course can be clinging, fickle, deep or shallow) applies throughout child-rearing, so that a generous parent is always so, from feeding the baby through to selfless support of the adolescent; or that a parent who shows conditional love similarly expects children to conform in order to gain their affection, as much in the early weeks as in later years. The notion of conditional love that is communicated to young children will be lived out, again through the process of internalization, in adult life. It is seen in phrases such as: 'I will only be loved if ...', or 'I will not be loved unless ...'.

Queenie showed the effects of this type of upbringing. Life was not going well, mainly, it has to be said, because her own very severe conscience (as Queenie described it) pulled her up over every little fault she detected in herself. She openly declared that there was no such thing as unconditional love – you had to work for it. She felt an inordinate need to please her parents; and from what Queenie said of her, it appeared that her mother needed her children to be successful in order to feel good enough herself as a parent. In one session Queenie declared, 'No one would really love me if they knew me – only God'. Queenie's faith was important to her, not least because God was the only one who she believed fully accepted her. But after this session she visited the parental home and told her parents that she was seeing a therapist, which up to that point she had been too ashamed to tell them. To Queenie's surprise, her mother responded by saying that she didn't mind, and that she still loved her. As the therapist observed in the following session, her mother's words still had a slight tinge of conditional love to them ('I still love you, even if you are seeing a therapist') but Queenie had found a sort of expression of unconditional love at home. What she had experienced earlier in her life in relation to her parents' love was now not quite so strong, but such a severe internalized mother image would need much more reassurance than that shown to Queenie by her mother before it would replace the more negative view she so often had of herself.

'Unconditional positive regard' is a phrase that is particularly stressed in person-centred therapy, as one of the necessary conditions for change. Perhaps it means the same as unconditional love, and as such it is a major element in any therapeutic relationship; but if it is necessary it does not always seem sufficient, even when interwoven with the other core conditions (Mearns and Thorne 2000: Chapter 5). There are other aspects of the therapeutic relationship that also need to be woven into the seamless fabric of the therapist's attitude. For example, the internalized conditional parent, who has been around in the client's conscious and unconscious mind for many years, can continue to exercise a powerful force, making it difficult for a client like Queenie to recognize, or believe in, the therapist's unconditional regard. The therapist may need time and again to help her see that it is also what she does to herself, in that her self-esteem is always conditional, as well as help her to discover where these powerful constructs may have come from.

One form of internalized 'conditional regard' can be acted out in obsessional rituals, and even more commonly in perfectionist traits. Perfectionists only feel secure and free from anxiety and at one with themselves (albeit temporarily) when what they have been doing or making has been completed 'without any blemish'; or obsessional people only feel safe from some unknown and unnamed dread when they have performed certain rituals properly. Perfectionism may involve having to make sure that a piece of writing has no obvious errors, and with the advent of the word processor some people go over and over their work, unable to complete it, afraid that errors will be found in it. Or a room must be kept in order, with nothing out of place. In the case of rituals, in order to feel blameless (sometimes in relation to God, but just as often to oneself) certain actions have to be performed, perhaps in a particular sequence, or so many times, or both. Only then does the person feel relatively calm and at peace with himself or herself. It is as though the conscience has been calmed, the super-ego assuaged, or perhaps the internalized parent satisfied. Obsessional symptoms may take the form of checking, or compulsive actions like repeated hand washing, or the repetition of certain words and phrases in the right order.

Freud (1907) observed how religious practices sometimes fall into this category: they serve the same purpose of warding off anxiety. Nevertheless some rituals serve a more positive purpose, assisting psychological change: rites of passage are perhaps the best examples. Other rituals may be used to deny experience, and to prevent change. Mitchell (1982) presents a case study where the ritual use of prayer is used as a massive denial of death:

> Valerie (as she is called in the article) was a popular high-school girl who suddenly fell ill. It was difficult to diagnose her condition, but her doctors had little hope of saving her life. In desperation they gave her drugs which had very uncomfortable side-effects. The hospital chaplain who visited Valerie found her mother and father in constant attendance, never leaving her side. The community in her home town were whipped up into a campaign of hope by friends and the local press, and her church congregation was praying for her recovery. They were convinced that if only they and she had enough faith she would come through. The pastor of her home church, despite his misgivings about the hysterical reaction, colluded with the community's wish for a vigil of prayer. Valerie's father also seemed to collude with his wife's need to maintain their watch over Valerie's bedside, while the doctors' use of drugs also seemed to be a denial, which father secretly regretted, seeing the discomfort his daughter was experiencing. It was not until the chaplain was able to visit Valerie alone (her parents being fast asleep in the room) that he was able to learn from Valerie that she felt she was having to put an act on for her parents and her community back home, and that she wished more often than she could admit that she would be left alone. Even after Valerie's death, her mother arranged a funeral that was more a celebration of resurrection than a true expression of the pain and grief that had been present throughout the whole situation, yet denied by nearly everyone.

The case is also a fascinating example of how an immature religious faith can take over a whole community. By contrast there are commendatory rituals in religious practice that give permission for the dying person to let go ('Go forth upon your journey from this world ...'). The significance of control over dying is discussed further in Chapter 8.

In the case of Valerie's parents and the community around them it is relatively straightforward to see that their anxiety is about the power of death. What might the anxiety be about in private rituals, such as those that Freud observed in his paper? It is perhaps that same persecutory anxiety that is associated with the first theme of trust and attachment, although in the context of obsessional behaviour it takes a particular form, as if actions of one sort or another can set the anxiety to rest. Sometimes the anxiety masks guilt – and it is often guilt or a similar feeling of discomfort that is experienced when the person does not perform the rituals satisfactorily. Sometimes it appears that what is being kept at bay is the expression of strong desires, such as sexual or aggressive feelings, of which the person feels scared, as well as keeping at bay the punishment that is feared for having such feelings in the first place.

Matters of religious belief are not often brought to therapists as problem areas, except where there is guilt over transgression of moral rules, failure to perform rituals at the right time, or doubt about matters of faith. There is a type of faith that has strong connections with the authority theme, seen for example in belief in a rigidly authoritarian doctrinal or political system, in inflexible moral thinking, and in the control of belief systems through dogmatism. This is often accompanied in religious belief by the expectation that as long as creeds and ethical codes are followed to the letter, then the faithful will be numbered among the elect. Such strongly authoritarian thinking also includes severe criticism of those who do not believe, or those who appear to act immorally, and that criticism is sometimes expressed in sadistic ideas about, and threats of, eternal punishment. It is far from unconditional love.

Other indications of a religion that is fixated on issues of control include ritualistic actions accompanied by obsessional thinking, mindless repetition of prayers, self-righteous discipline of the reading of holy books, compulsive attendance at services to assuage guilt, absolute and often literal authority vested in the priests and other religious leaders, and masochistic self-punishment by a sadistic super-ego. (For a fuller description of the way in which authority issues can be of value, but also inhibit the development of more inclusive and creative modes of belief, see Jacobs (2000a).)

> Roger was a devout Catholic, who intellectually put himself on the liberal wing of the church, but he could not shake himself free from the legalistic religious discipline that his schooling had imparted to him. This education probably only confirmed the right-wing authoritarian views he got at home from his mother. Despite the forgiveness he received through confession, and the reassurance he was given by priests to whom he spoke, Roger worried inordinately about minor sins, which he could see were scarcely sins at all, such as having one small drink of alcohol as a night-cap. He could not receive communion at mass following these occasions, because he felt so bad. Like other obsessional difficulties it was very difficult to shift this pattern of thinking in therapy. Roger knew he was worrying unnecessarily, but he could not get beyond listing these worries in every session. It was as if 'free association' might give rise to thoughts and feelings that he dare not express, since this would then make him feel even worse.

It has to be said that in many cases, outside as well as within unhealthy religious practices, it is very difficult to shift obsessional rituals through using the usual psychodynamic approach, unless the client is both ready to move beyond his or her preoccupation with the rituals in order to explore other experiences and other feelings and thoughts, and is able to experiment with postponing or relinquishing such rituals. It is difficult to get beneath the rituals, which are mainly successful in defending the person against ideas that they cannot contemplate: that they are only 'mainly' successful is perhaps the reason that the obsessional person seeks help; it is as if they know something is not right. But because the rituals are more than 50 per cent successful, it is still dangerous to contemplate dropping or altering them. Such clients are preoccupied with their actions, however inconvenient they find them, and their wish to give them up is accompanied by considerable reservation. For therapy or counselling to work at all, symptoms need to be experienced as alien, something a person wishes to change. Where the symptoms serve a useful purpose, it may be too hard to give them up, let alone look at what they might mean.

The same difficulty applies to working with other behaviours that have a similar repetitive, compulsive and addictive quality to them, such as alcohol and drug dependency, eating disorders and so on. (For a psychodynamic approach to addictions see Weegman and Cohen (2001).) It is difficult to ignore the symptoms, sometimes because they can carry risk of damage to the client's body or even life; but even when the behaviours are less severe, such clients set great store by them, and find it difficult to move beyond their preoccupation with them. That does not mean that a psychodynamic therapist has to give up the attempt to look at the meaning of these pre-senting issues, and at other aspects in the client's life, but it may be that it is only changes in key areas of the client's internal and external relationships that will lead to a position where it becomes possible to consider tackling and changing the more obvious presenting difficulties.

Sylvie had been seeing a therapist for a year, during which she related well to her, and had talked about many aspects of her life other than her presenting issue, which was a fastidious and obsessional concern with the number of calories she was consuming every time she ate. She was not strictly anorexic, but there were signs that her preoccupation with food might lead that way, if it was not alleviated. Therapy went well in some respects, inasmuch as Sylvie was able to reflect upon a large number of different issues past and present, although her behaviour relating to food showed no sign of shifting. What puzzled her was that whenever she went on holiday, all the worries about food completely disappeared, only to return the moment she returned home, when the internal debate about how much to eat resumed. Her husband had commented on how much she changed when she was away, almost as if she was two different people.

After one rather longer holiday than usual Sylvie started the first ses-sion back by saying how wonderful things had been, and how relieved she was by not worrying about food. She enthused about the holiday, and how lovely it was not to wear a watch (which she was not wearing either in the session); and what a contrast this was to being at home, always having to keep an eye on the time, because of this or that engagement, including returning to therapy. In her more relaxed state the therapy moved somewhat faster than usual and food no longer dominated the session. Instead the therapist followed up a remark Sylvie had made about what life was like when she was a child, with her mother constantly carping about tidiness, and the children always having to be ready for meals that were served at the same time every day, exactly on the hour. Sylvie concluded her vivid description of an obsessional parent with the words, 'You could set your clock by my mother'. Her earlier remark about how nice it was not to wear a watch made much real sense at this point. It was as if on holiday she could shed her internalized mother, whereas at home, and at work, Sylvie got into these continuous, tiring arguments within herself, as to whether she should eat this or that, about how many calories she was permitted to take in, whether she had done this right at work, and whether she was doing what others wanted and so on. It was as if her mother's voice constantly argued with her own. It was only when she could shed all her responsibilities on holiday that she found a place where she could be herself, and enjoy being herself, doing whatever she wanted, without having to count the cost. This link was not of course a point of immediate change for Sylvie. Good interpretations are still not miracle cures! But it was a breakthrough moment when some of the reasons for her obsessional worrying began to fall into place for the therapist and for Sylvie too. Sylvie went on to describe many other ways in which her mother ordered their lives as children, of which she had never before spoken so clearly. 'I'm sure I've turned out just like my mother', she said. 'I'm not so sure', answered the therapist, 'I can see a healthy part of you that tries to argue against the mother inside you, and which on holiday really shuts her up, but at other times I can also see that it's a real battle to find yourself'.

These situations are made even more complicated because psychodynamic thinking suggests that rituals or addictive behaviours, which in many ways are defences against anxiety, sometimes express the very conflicts that the person tries to repress. Freud called it 'the return of the repressed' (Masson 1985: 164–5), and he sees rituals as the third stage of a sequence which runs from conscientiousness, through obsessional ideas to obsessional ceremonies (p. 166). Rituals can be a way of warding off and yet at the same time acting out repressed wishes. This may be another reason that obsessions cannot be easily relinquished. They perform a number of functions:

Ted had to wash his genitals very thoroughly after masturbating and he worried because his penis felt so sore that he thought he may have damaged his potency. He then had to masturbate again to see if everything was all right; and this then involved more washing, and so on. It was a dreadful vicious circle, which dominated Ted's thoughts and behaviour. Although he denied feeling guilty about masturbating, it is possible to see a parallel between masturbation and washing his genitals – both of which gave him erotic pleasure, as well as leading to fear and guilt over the way he handled himself.

This is also the case with phobias, which according to a dynamic explanation similarly often ward off sexual or aggressive feelings that cannot be admitted to consciousness. In any of the types of presentation referred to here (addictions, obsessional behaviours, phobias) a psychodynamic approach may usefully incorporate behavioural techniques to help modify the symptoms, which in some cases may be necessary before any insight therapy can become possible. Helping a client to manage their addictive, obsessional or phobic responses is often a necessary prelude to an exploration of the underlying issues, as, for example, when an agoraphobic person needs help in coming out of the house for therapy. In cases of single-symptom presentations (at least as perceived by those clients who may deny that anything else is wrong) management of the symptoms through behavioural modification may be the only treatment suitable, and some change may be achieved, even if there is no insight into causes or other personal issues:

> Umberto worried about every choice he had to make, in case he got it wrong. It was not easy to shift this obsessional pattern, although the university counsellor achieved some success with one particular symptom. Umberto needed to check all the calculations involved in his studies at least five times. The counsellor persuaded him first to check only four times; then three times; and finally to make the calculation just twice (a very reasonable check), leaving it there if the results were consistent both times. Although it may have been coincidental, this change appeared to influence other areas of Umberto's life, because having achieved this small change, he became less apprehensive about other decisions, although he still sought further appointments with the counsellor whenever there were particularly crucial choices that had to be made.

With some clients this modification of rituals can be used alongside ongoing attempts to uncover unconscious feelings and ideas, which may include the guilt and/or shame that might be attached to them. This becomes possible when the client is ready to talk more freely about other things that come to mind:

> When she was on her own Vivienne went through a ritual at bedtime, checking all the doors and drawers in her room, lest there was a man hiding there. It seemed an intractable symptom, and there was no shifting of it even through behavioural modification. Vivienne was easy with the therapist, and spoke freely about herself and her relationships. She had been able to tell the therapist of an incestuous suggestion made by her father when her mother was away. But talking about this, and understanding the link to looking for a man in her room, made no difference to her bedtime ritual. The therapist was not too concerned about the lack of movement on the issues, since the focus in therapy was more on the difficulty Vivienne experienced in giving up a boyfriend, whom she was 'forced', she said, to share with other women. This arrangement appeared linked to a situation arising at home with her father and temporarily absent mother, and not to the ritual itself. In fact

the checking ceased soon after Vivienne was able to break her relationship with the boyfriend, who was sleeping around with the other women. Nevertheless the therapist was far from sure that the ritual would not return (since therapy had to stop about the same time) if Vivienne were to form another relationship that had similar (Oedipal) complications.

Perfectionism, or even as Freud suggested, conscientiousness, are milder forms of obsessive behaviour. Perfectionism is a more common presentation, and one that is accessible to a psychodynamic approach, without the need for such active intervention as may be necessary with obsessional-compulsive disorders or phobic states. Although checking may be involved in perfectionism, the obsessional element is not expressed so clearly in a definite ritual. Perfectionists similarly need to feel blameless, and although often anxious about the judgement of others, they are normally their own most severe critic. The following example demonstrates perfectionism where it is often found, in the work setting; and at the same time it illustrates anal characteristics, which appear to be related to a number of these presenting issues:

Wallace was a young doctor who had failed a professional membership examination, when a recent separation from his wife had interfered with his studies. It soon emerged that one of the reasons she had left him was that he constantly complained about her untidiness about the home.

Many other features emerged in therapy. Wallace had himself become (as he put it) quite 'lazy' in his work. He had lost the capacity for 'hard slog' which had seen him through his training, and he felt guilty about that. He found himself irritated by one of his medical partners whom he described as a perfectionist; so he condemned perfectionism in his work partner, as well as its opposite in his marital partner. As he described his background it appeared that both his parents had felt failures compared to their own siblings, and that they had put all their aspirations into their son, expecting him to be brilliant. Wallace's father was continuously afraid of 'doom striking', particularly lest he fall ill and could not keep the family. This must also have communicated itself to his son, perhaps contributing to his wish to become someone who cures illness. His father worked in quality control and hated his job, but he was doing a job that perhaps expressed some of his own desires for perfection. The father went to the toilet at least five times a day to empty his bowels, and at the age of 11 Wallace was admitted to hospital with severe constipation. He still felt very angry at the humiliation of the enemas and other treatment: he thought he should at that time have seen a child psychotherapist, and not a physician. In some ways he hated the medical profession, but he had as it were identified with his aggressors and had become a doctor (if you can't beat them, join them!). During his training Wallace realized how much he feared illness in himself, just as his father did, and how depressed he became when the patients did not respond to treatment. He felt that the life of a physician was 'purgatory' and he recognized himself how close this term was to his being 'purged' when in hospital as a child. He was constantly struggling with a lifetime's identification with 'perfection' against anxiety, and had lately reacted against this.

Parental attitudes to what is right and proper, as well as the characteristics of parental habits and authority, are internalized by a child, and form the basis for the growing child and later adult to monitor and judge thinking, feelings, and behaviours. This is an extension of the internalization of the parent–infant relationship. The formation of this critical parent inside each person is obviously of importance in making decisions, and conforming to the principles of the family and society in which the child grows up. Self-control is a necessary part of the socialization process, although sometimes the attitudes that accompany it are inhibiting for the individual, and aspects of being controlled and being controlling affect the way a person relates to authority and exercises authority as an adult. These issues of control are discussed further in Chapter 7.

AUTHORITY AND AUTONOMY: A MATTER OF CONTROL

A common expectation on the client's part in the early stages of therapy is that the therapist will not only understand the reasons underlying the client's psychological state, but will also recommend courses of action or thinking to the client. In itself such an expectation does not suggest a client is necessarily a passive person, expecting to be acted upon rather than acting, since this is a common attitude to the expert, whether a lawyer, a doctor, or a teacher. It is also a measure of the client's distress, which is accompanied by a wish for someone to make things better. Most psychotherapeutic approaches of course, while wishing to relieve distress, do not give instructions. Clients learn that the particular expertise of the therapist involves a very different approach both to factual knowledge and to advice and guidance.

But some clients with these initial expectations about the expertise of the therapist also have a passive streak to their character, conducting their lives by what others say, so that for them pleasing others is high on their agenda. They are constantly seeking advice and approval. They continue to want the therapist to tell them what to do, to answer their questions for them, and to show them the way ahead. Therapists can collude with such expectations upon them if they themselves have a streak of authoritarianism in them.

Passive clients may well be anxious, afraid of what they will feel or what others will say about them should anything go wrong. They prefer the security of hiding their own initiative under a bushel, or of someone else being thought to carry the can. It is as if even the normal uncertainties of life and ordinary levels of risk are too dangerous.

Yuri visited the family planning clinic and asked the counsellor a series of questions about the effectiveness of the contraceptive pill. He had chosen a subject upon which an almost 100 per cent guarantee could be given, as long as the pill is taken as prescribed. This led Yuri to ask another series of questions about abortion. The counsellor at first answered these questions, since giving guidance was natural in this setting; but she then realized that there was something else behind them; and instead of answering them she asked Yuri whether these questions were important to him because of the new relationship he was in. Yuri nodded, and went on to describe two areas of his life where he felt uncertain: first he was unsure whether he and his girlfriend were right for each other; and second he did not know whether he was making the right choice over a change of job. The counsellor observed that in his initial question Yuri wanted 100 per cent guarantees. He agreed and replied, 'But life's not like that, is it?' This led on to other worries, including his anxiety about engaging in a sexual relationship, and in turn to feelings of failure to meet the high expectations he always felt his father had for him.

A therapist may be tempted to collude with the passive client by providing too many answers, or even too many interpretations, taking over the initiative and control of the session. Beginning counsellors and trainee therapists can feel particularly anxious about the welfare of their clients, as if they had the ultimate responsibility for them. Like growing children and adventurous adults clients must be allowed to make the mistakes, some of which are inevitable, and most of which are far from disastrous. Clients can sometimes be protected from a contemplated action by helping them consider the possible consequences, without giving them either a green or red light. Therapists need of course to be alert to potential actions that might be damaging to the client or others, and on some occasions where there is a serious risk need to intervene in a more managerial way. Such occasions call for ethical decisions to be made, and best made, when there is time, with the assistance of supervision or consultancy. But most counsellors and therapists only see clients once a week, and they cannot watch over them during the six days between sessions. Like the toddler who moves away from the parent, but only as far as he or she feels safe, before running back to check all is well, clients need to be able to put some distance between themselves and the counsellor. The days between sessions provide the space to try out new initiatives, to continue reflecting upon themselves, to experience containing strong emotional responses, and to test out different ways of being before the next session, where they can review what has been happening to them and within them. Unlike the early days of psychoanalysis, when analysts advised their patients not to take important decisions while in therapy, clients have to make choices, many of them small, but sometimes major, and therapy involves assisting them in exercising their autonomy through the judicious use of the therapist's authoritative position.

Zena was still a student, and her parents gave her everything that she wanted. Nevertheless she still experienced a lack of trust on their part. Instead of allowing her to have her own money and to budget for herself, they had told her just to ask whenever she needed more. She experienced her parents as being too possessive, and she used the phrase that she felt 'tied to their apron strings'. She felt much more independent when she was able to negotiate with them to be paid a lump sum at the beginning of term, which was no greater than her fellow students had. She was determined to try to live within that budget. Likewise in her therapy she eventually asked for appointments once a fortnight, and then once a month. This seemed a reasonable request, since she wanted to test out her independence there too, if only gradually. With all clients, but particularly with passive clients and the young, therapists need to recognize their need to be independent, and weigh this against any advantages there may be in encouraging them to stay in therapy.

It is relevant here to distinguish between the dependent client and the passive client, because there are some similarities. A client who is extremely distressed, and unable to think, may need the security of reassurance or gentle management – this relates more to the theme of trust and attachment, and to the therapist as a nurturing figure in the transference. Such a psychological state need not be the same as the passive, anxious client, who dare not try out his or her autonomy, and who in the transference looks upon the therapist as the authoritative or authoritarian parent. The therapist in this next example was acutely aware of the dilemma, which occurred some years ago when the issue of sexual orientation was a much more secretive one:

Alan was in a real panic. He had recently, and rather suddenly, had doubts about his sexuality, and was afraid that he might be gay. He wanted the therapist to tell him that he wasn't. These appeared to be anxieties that had come out of the blue, with no precedence – in other respects it would not have occurred to Alan to doubt his heterosexual orientation. As he related recent events, it turned out that the previous weekend Alan had had a stand-up row with his father over the way his father had treated his mother. Grievances nursed over the years were unleashed. Father was taken aback. This challenge to the principal authority figure in Alan's life appeared to have brought on anxieties about retaliation from the father, and becoming submissive to another man. Much of this was related to themes about competition, but it also raised feelings of neglect that Alan had experienced from father's distant manner. Alan also thought his mother had suffered from the same neglect, and an Oedipal protection of her was another feature. But the first step was to think about the authority issue, since the male therapist could have given reassurance to Alan about his sexual orientation, since it appeared that Alan was usually clear about his heterosexuality. But the therapist thought that if he were to provide reassurance he would be putting himself in an authoritarian and superior position, and that Alan might later feel similar anxiety that he had needed a man to tell him what he knew for himself, or even that he needed a man to 'comfort' him. As the therapist thought about how to resolve his own dilemma he decided it would be better to share it openly with Alan: 'I could tell you that you are not gay, and that might reassure you, but I think you might then feel anxious about me becoming a man who tells you what to do. You do want a man, you want your father, and you want him to be closer to you. I think that makes you draw the conclusion that you must be gay'.

The way in which authority is exercised in many organizations and institutions in society can encourage the passive character. It is easy, for example, for someone in a strongly hierarchical organization to become a cog in the machine, to receive orders, and to do as he or she is told. Alternatively, lack of stimulation may also lead to passivity, such as in the person who is made redundant, and in whom all self-confidence evaporates. The passivity that sometimes accompanies being in work or even out of work may tempt the therapist to assume the role of the 'manager'. When there have been tight controls on such clients, or when their sense of security within a tight structure or ordered life is replaced by the anxiety of having few or no parameters, therapy can provide containment, without at the same time becoming a replacement for the limiting authority figures the client has relied upon in the past.

The passive person also finds it difficult to exercise legitimate authority over others or to stand up for himself or herself against people who like to be dominant:

> Brian, a trainee teacher, found it impossible to control his classes, so much so that near-riots were taking place. As he told this to the university counsellor, Brian was laughing and clearly covering up his own anxiety about the situation. But it also felt as if he was getting some pleasure from seeing the children play up, something he would never himself have dared do with his teachers or with his parents. He had decided that teaching wasn't for him, although his father had felt it a good and safe job, and he did not wish to let his father down. Since Brian was religious, he said he had prayed about it all to God, and God had said, 'Go ahead, do a different job'. In fact this seemed to the counsellor to be rather a sensible decision, but it was obvious Brian had needed to refer to his God's authority to carry it out, since it was only his God who could overrule his father! When the counsellor observed the different ways in which the problems about authority figures were causing difficulty, Brian asked the counsellor, 'Could you repeat all that? I'd like to be able to write that down!' It may have been that the counsellor had said it too obscurely, but it seemed more likely that Brian wanted to put the counsellor's authority on record, rather than use what had been said to make something of it for himself. 'Tablets of stone', thought the counsellor.

In this example, Brian's control of the children was made more difficult because there was a part of him that identified with, and wished to express, through them, his own repressed high spirits. In the next example, the anxiety about exerting control seemed related to some fear of damaging others:

> Colin was the manager of a large office, who had achieved his position through his efficiency and his ability to charm those who worked for him, as well as by his gentle nature and example. But he had problems with the occasional employee who took advantage of his quiet manner. In those cases Colin could not bring himself to administer a rebuke or a

warning. He told his therapist that he was afraid of hurting people. He related this anxiety at what he called having to play 'the heavy father' to an earlier time in his life when he had felt extremely worried. His best friend had died as a result of a heart attack when they were playing a rough adolescent game of football, around the same time that his father suffered considerable ill health following a series of heart attacks. Here issues about exercising authority and control seem to be connected with themes I will consider in later chapters around rivalry and competition.

The way in which people exercise authority over others is often influenced by the way in which they were themselves controlled and managed when they were young, in the family, and/or at school. Some of those who have been held back and put down by authoritarian regimes at home or elsewhere continue to be passive: others, of course, identify with past or present authority figures and become controlling, authoritarian, rigid people themselves, who cannot allow their hold over others to be relaxed. There are others who are also aggressive, but who show it in a subtle and disarming, 'passive-aggressive' way.

The passive-aggressive person

Another common presentation in therapy is the 'passive-aggressive' client – a term that does not mean swinging between passivity and aggression, but rather someone who expresses his or her aggression passively. The passive-aggressive person is encountered in a number of ways. Two of the most common presentations are the 'yes ... but' character; and the person who seems very passive and submissive and yet provokes considerable anger in other people but has a disarming way of appearing quite 'innocent', wondering why there is all this fuss. It is as if the angry feelings in the passive person have been projected onto others, who then find themselves more and more irritated and unable to 'pin' their irritation anywhere. In psychoanalytic terms this is an example of projective identification: the anger is 'put into' the other person, who becomes aggressive, while the passive one remains calm:

Darryl was asked to go to the university counselling service because he was not handing in work as requested. His tutor described Darryl in his phone call to the service as pleasant enough, but told the counsellor that he could never get anything out of him either by way of work or by way of explanation. He added that Darryl insisted upon standing up all the way through any interview, making the tutor feel that Darryl was a rather submissive character. When the counsellor met him, Darryl had no hesitation about sitting down, and she formed a quite different impression of him: of a confident young man, who took perverse pride in boasting how little work he did, and who obviously led an active life in all other respects at university. He mentioned himself how he had refused to sit down when seeing his tutor, as if making a point about his stance. As the session went on the counsellor suggested (in a clearly challenging way) that Darryl was actually quite angry with the tutor for expecting him to work, and that he enjoyed standing up, watching the tutor squirm in his chair. He seemed to want to impress people by turning on its head the idea that you earn praise for working hard. He got admiration from his friends for getting away with it. Darryl seemed to appreciate the way the counsellor had spoken so frankly, and he felt the counsellor had hit the nail on the head. He opened up considerably about his parents' aspirations for him, but also about his feeling that he would never be as well respected as his father was in his career. He also agreed to a short course of counselling. Within a few weeks he was working so hard that the tutor jokingly said to the counsellor, 'What did you say to him that I didn't?'

There may have been some splitting here, between male tutor and female counsellor, and beneath the humour this tutor may have been left with some feelings of failure where the counsellor had been successful. Father–mother–son dynamics may have been played out in the two helpers – this again highlights the way these different sets of themes interweave, with cooperation and competition overlapping in certain respects with authority and autonomy. Passive-aggressive clients can split authority figures, turning one against the other, getting them to do their dirty work for them and act out their anger for them, while they stand on the touch line and watch them fight. In the same way a child learns how useful it can be to run to one parent with a complaint about the other. Handling such potential splits between caring and welfare agencies, particularly when a client questions the usefulness or the authority of another helper, means that the 'good parent' helper has to be careful not be drawn into an alliance against the other 'bad parent' helper. Such splitting differs from more primitive splitting because in this situation the passive-aggressive client uses one authority figure to get at another, with whom he or she feels angry, but where the client is unable to express this directly to the person concerned.

Another expression of passive-aggression is seen in 'withholding', not through shame or fear of letting go (see below), but to convey discontent: in everyday situations this might be referred to as 'sulking', although withholding is not necessarily as obvious. A client who misses a session, or who comes late, or who unusually has nothing to say, might be holding back angry feelings towards the counsellor for something that occurred in a previous session.

Emma came very late two sessions running. On the first occasion and late on in the session she told of an incident where a man had exposed himself to her at a party. In talking of this incident, she got very upset, and the therapist, because he had a cancelled session following, let her session go on for longer. He hoped (or at least this was his conscious motive) that by helping her express her feelings, this might help make the incident less upsetting for her. Emma arrived late the next week too, and this time she was reluctant to say anything. The therapist suggested to her that she might not want to talk about the things that were so upsetting to her the previous week. His remark had some truth in it, but he did not fully realize what he was saying, nor that this interpretation applied as much in the previous session as well. After a long and difficult time Emma eventually said that she was very angry with the therapist for giving her more time the previous week. It was then that she hadn't wanted to say any more about the incident. Instead the therapist had been somewhat like a voyeur, encouraging her to expose feelings when she had deliberately wanted to keep to the minimum. She had come late the previous session, because she felt ashamed, and wanted to flee as soon as she had mentioned the incident. She had got her timing all worked out. But she had come late to the next session because she felt so angry.

Then there is the 'yes ... but' client, easily recognizable through the frustration experienced in the therapist's countertransference, as each successive intervention (or in desperation even each suggestion) is greeted with the response, 'Yes ..., but on the other hand ...', and is therefore effectively rubbished by the client. Tempting though it may be to indulge in argument with the passive-aggressive client, the client will continue to see argument as an attack and will probably continue to defend themselves in the same way. An empathic response is to be preferred: 'You sound as if there really is no way out ... that must be pretty frustrating'; or, 'My ineffective suggestions might make you feel rather angry with me'. But while the 'yes ... but' can indicate a client who is unable to express anger and frustration in any other way (so it is the therapist who feels it instead), there may of course be other reasons for such a response. The obsessional person may find it impossible to commit to any view or action, in case they make the wrong choice ('shall I, shan't I'); or there may be anxiety about any commitment that leads to situations that they fear. Again here the empathic response is better than trying in desperation to impose a solution upon a client.

The rebel

The rebellious type of person, who always seems to get into scrapes with authority, and who may even be in other relationships that are strained and hostile, is not typical of the average therapist's clientele, unless he or she is referred as part of a disciplinary process. Counselling, which in the public eye may yet have different connotations, may be seen by those who manage an institution as a means of exerting some sort of control on the difficult employee, or student, or law-breaker; and counselling will probably in such circumstances, at least initially, also be experienced as a means of social control by the reluctant client.

While always bearing in mind that today's rebel may tomorrow be recognized as yesterday's innovator, some wilful acting out may be the necessary result of earlier unconscious repression, or of family or societal suppression. Giant statements (in words or in action) may have to be made in order to gain a little freedom:

Fulton's very traditional, narrow-minded, conventional family would be very shocked when he told them that he was gay. He smiled as he said it, making it clear that it was also going to give him considerable pleasure to see how disconcerted his father would be. The 'shock, horror' aspect to his wish to come out was also apparent when his college tutor rang his counsellor: 'I hear you've got something surprising to tell me about Fulton'. The counsellor refused to be drawn into the game, particularly since Fulton's gay orientation was hardly in itself significant. 'If it's what I think it is, he can tell you himself', she replied. While telling Fulton about the call and her reply when they next met, what interested her was why he had felt it necessary to dramatize this issue with his tutor.

We might expect to find some rebelliousness as a natural developmental feature, particularly in children who want to test out their own power in relation to parental wishes, as well as in adolescents, where again rebellious views and behaviour are a way of testing the limits of parental authority as well as of their own potentialities. Older clients may need their own adolescent fling, particularly if they did not experience this in their own adolescence, or where they are still seeking for someone to set limits on what has become for them a frightening loss of control. Battles of will represent a need to assert independence, and can take place at any time, from feeding at the breast to the intransigence of the older person who fights against infirmity and having to be dependent, as well as under the domination of others. Rebelliousness is a natural part of growing up and growing away. Winnicott (1965a: 79–87; 1971: 138–50) writes well about this particular period of the maturational process in two papers, particularly in terms of the parental experience during the turbulent time of their children's adolescent years:

> If you do all you can to promote personal growth in your offspring you will need to be able to deal with startling results. If your children find themselves at all they will not be contented to find anything but the whole of themselves, and that will include the aggression and destructive elements in themselves as well as the elements that can be labelled loving.
>
> (1971: 143)

Such rebelliousness is part of the young person's need to push away from parents, both as love-objects and as authority figures. A young person and his or her parents are often involved in boundary disputes: the adolescent wants independence, while the parents want to retain their sense of authority. Winnicott, using metaphor as a powerful means of describing the process, writes: 'If the child is to become an adult then this move is achieved over the dead body of an adult ... [W]here there is the challenge of the growing boy or girl, there let an adult meet the challenge. And it will not necessarily be nice' (1971: 145, 150).

Where parents are in conflict with each other (in one sense perhaps trying to kill each other off), or where one or both parents are weakened by physical or mental ill health, it may be more difficult or impossible to challenge them, for fear that the challenge will in one way or another finish them off. Indeed where adolescent rebellion coincides fortuitously with the separation or divorce of parents, or the death of a parent, this can leave indelible marks of self-blame:

> Greta had found it very hard to express any independence openly in her teens, not only because her father was strong-willed, but also because her mother had suffered a severe heart attack. Open rebellion carried with it the fear that either her own actions, or her father's reactions, might damage her mother. Her therapist wondered at one point how Greta had felt after she had criticized him, although Greta's response was more confident than the therapist expected: that it was 'OK – I pay you to take it!' Some clients, however, are very concerned lest any bid for autonomy and independence on their part may in some way damage or hurt their therapist or the good relationship they enjoy with him or her.

Winnicott stresses the importance of parents surviving: 'there will be this long tussle which you will need to survive' (1971: 143). They can help the process 'only a little: the best they can do is to survive, to survive intact, and without changing colour, without relinquishment of any important principle' (p. 145). Which principles might actually be 'important' and which might be outdated tradition he does not question. What is felt to be an inviolable principle in one culture (for example, obedience to parental plans for marriage) may be totally oppressive in another. It must be remembered, as in all the expressions of the themes related in this book, that cultural variations exist. Independence from parents is a typically Western concept, and in some societies would be regarded as a sign of extremely discourteous, if not disturbed, relationships. In a private communication Laiqa Elahi writes:

> It may be because the Western concept of gradual 'healthy' separation and autonomy from parents to live an independent self-directive life is so peculiar, not encouraged and often blocked by parents, that when separation does occur it is often in a pathological way ... One is then faced with an ultimatum, personal freedom or family belonging. If this is the price one has to pay in pursuit of personal happiness it is no wonder people comply without question or challenge, or risk the severing of all family relationships.

Western, white, middle-class values, which often inform psychotherapy and counselling, need testing against the norms of personal development and family dynamics in other cultures. It may still be true that the critical, hostile parent who does not permit any independence, or the overindulgent parent who puts no limits on the teenager's testing of the boundaries, each in their own way prevent the adolescent achieving maturity. Winnicott gets closer to the difficulty of knowing what it is right to be firm about and where to give way when he argues that a young person must be allowed to be immature, as long as adults do not abdicate responsibility (1971: 146). All this of course applies to the therapist working with the creativity and the destructiveness of the rebellious spirit (recognized across cultures in many mythical figures as representing two sides of the same coin: Shiva, Janus, and so on). It is important to question whether therapy is in its aims basically anarchic, inasmuch as it allows someone to put everything into the melting pot and find their own ways of being and doing, or whether indeed it is concerned with persuading people to conform as part of the process of socialization. In considering the authority of the profession indeed, it is necessary to ask, as certain authors have (for example, Laing 1966; Szasz 1971; Pilgrim 1997) whether the explicit and implicit values of the therapist are informed by challenge or conformity to social mores. While these challenges from within therapy to therapeutic values largely concern the labelling of serious mental disturbance, there are also important questions about how far therapy itself is able to challenge conventions that inhibit the human spirit.

see refs.

Losing control

There is a necessary distinction to be made between creative aggression, to put it in Winnicott's terms, which is part of the process of personal (and indeed of societal) development, and the pure destructiveness of vandalism and cruelty, which is more associated with hate and envy than with battles over independence. Where there is absence of love and trust then aggression can become ruthless – another of Winnicott's preferred terms. It is also important to distinguish between destructive feelings and behaviour which Winnicott associates with the 'anti-social' character, and the explosive release of feelings. The latter may on occasion also prove destructive, because they have been held back for a long time, and their release, either in prospect or in actuality, may indeed appear to be or actually be terrifying. Following tight control of the expression of anger and of other emotions, the subsequent explosion is not unlike a volcano blowing its top. Emotions are held back, like faeces have to be held back when learning self-control, and burst out when the limits of endurance and tolerance are passed.

It is ironical, of course, that those who hold back feelings for fear of the damage they may cause eventually let them go with such force that some hurt to others, or some damage to themselves, does occur. People who fear their anger tend to bottle it up, but inevitably have to let it go every now and again. Suppression is not an effective defence: it seldom works for long. Depression is sometimes caused by angry feelings being held back (perhaps knowingly, but more often unconsciously repressed) and then turned back on the self. Constant irritability frequently indicates such held-back anger. When a client can explode at or in the presence of the therapist and learns that such an outburst does not spoil the relationship between them, this is a major discovery. Therapy of course supports the client in the view that in some other situations or over certain expressions of feeling other people may not be as accepting as the therapist: indeed the client who goes on to 'let it all out' following the positive experience of release in therapy may even be acting out feelings that belong more appropriately to the transference. But the client can also learn how feelings can be expressed appropriately.

Therapy also needs to explore the factors that provoke such strong feelings, in order to look at their possible cause as well as effect. Therapy involves the combination of allowing and yet containing the force of feelings, combined with understanding something of the origin of their force, and of rehearsing ways of expression, that both honour where the client is, as well as meet his or her concern and respect for others.

Hedda was referred to a therapist in desperation by a psychiatrist who did not know what else to do. She acted out all the time, getting herself into all kinds of trouble, effectively ensuring that she got the attention of all the mental health services in the area, and making everyone very angry. At the time of this example she had been through many ups and downs with her therapist, but fortunately the therapist remained a constant figure for Hedda throughout. Much of the work to date had been around issues of trust. There was still clearly a long way to go, but there were signs of a potential breakthrough to a different way of acting when Hedda began to express her seething anger towards the therapist. She blamed the therapist for changing her, so that she no longer acted impulsively, but instead found herself thinking first about any wish to create mayhem. The result of thinking was that the moment passed, but she was still left feeling frustrated; and because she was seen by those around her as behaving better, she got far less of their attention. Hedda spoke her mind in no uncertain terms. At the very end of the session Hedda said, 'I think I may have hurt you by saying all that'. The therapist's reply was a good one: 'Well, you shocked me by saying it, but I'm perfectly all right, and I'll see you next week'. Referring to the shock (which it had been) she let Hedda know that she had made a real impact upon her: there was no way in which what Hedda said and felt was going to be ignored, as happened so often when she kept things to herself; at the same time the therapist made it clear that she was not hurt, and that what Hedda had said had not spoiled their relationship.

Dominance and submission: sadism and masochism

Sadism is a good example of how unwise it is to seek the causes of behaviour in one single stage of human development. For example, sadism is often closely associated with sex, and therefore would appear to be better located in third-stage issues. Yet Melanie Klein uses the word in connection with first-stage issues (oral-sadistic fantasies) and second-stage issues (anal-sadistic fantasies). My own reason for addressing sado-masochism here is that it is partly about issues of control: controlling another, and achieving heightened pleasure (sexual and other) by being dominant; or being controlled, and receiving heightened pleasure through being dominated.

This is a complex area which, like some other presenting problems, requires special study. (In working with alternative sexual behaviours, see for example Rosen (1979), Bancroft (1983), Lieblum and Rosen (1989), Hudson-Allez (2005).) Sado-masochism may not basically be about sex, because as Rycroft (1972) writes, it is not clear whether the pleasure obtained by the sadistic person is due to the enjoyment of the suffering of others, or to the sense of power and control over others. Alfred Adler's view (1922) was that it was power that was the basic drive, rather than sexuality as Freud posited, and that it was the inferiority complex rather than the Oedipus complex that was the determining factor in neurosis. Without repeating those old arguments, it is clearly important to recognize that while sadism may be linked to sexual pleasure, it is also a form of aggression, which varies from currently socially acceptable sado-masochistic sexual practices to the inhumane treatment of children, torture, and so on. (I recognize, of course, that S&M and other sexual variants may not be generally practised, and may raise appropriate questions about the degree of acceptable pain in sexual relationships however willingly invited; but I describe those practices as socially acceptable because in a liberal society they are not illegal and are accepted by quite a number of people who are not themselves turned on by any of them.)

Except in particular settings (such as forensic psychotherapy) therapists do not often see clients whose sadistic behaviour causes difficulty for the client: it is more likely to be others who are troubled by those who present themselves for therapy. Where there are indications of the acting out of sadistic fantasies (whether in the client or as described in others by the client), especially with minors or unwilling partners, the therapist should consult the social services child protection team in the case of child abuse, or a forensic psychiatrist or psychologist in the case of unacceptable behaviour towards other adults. Evidence of cruelty to animals (whether in the past as a child or currently as an adult), and pleasure from the idea of acting out sadistic fantasies, as well as more obvious signs of such actions, indicate that the client or others are at risk, and must be taken seriously. This does not mean a therapist should avoid talking about these issues with the client who expresses them, since closer questioning of such fantasies and of any instances of their being acted out is not only important for the assessment of risk, but also to give verbal expression to them (Prins 1975, 1995). It is the same as with suicidal threats or anxieties, where talking openly about such feelings does not encourage acting out, and may even help to prevent it.

Sadistic thoughts rather than sadistic behaviour are more likely to distress a client – thoughts that have never been acted upon, but which cause tortuous guilt or shame – as if the 'I' of the client is attacked by a sadistic super-ego. Therapists can always help relieve a client's anxiety about such thoughts by assurance that expressing such ideas is not the same as acting upon them – this is a good example of the valid use of the therapist's authoritative position; but this should not deflect from the task of relating such ideas to aspects of the present relationship in which they are experienced, or to earlier relationships.

Sadistic ideas may represent a deep wish to get back at someone who has made the client suffer (what is known as the law of talion: an eye for an eye). Revenge is in itself a powerful drive, which mirrors identifying with negative experience in the same way as caring for others mirrors identifying with nurturing experience. Yet just as aggression has, according to Winnicott, a constructive potentiality, I have argued elsewhere (Jacobs 1991), that revenge can also be constructive and does not have to perpetuate the sadistic pleasure of inflicting pain on others as a compensation for the pain inflicted upon oneself. One component of sadism may be the wish to turn the tables on past oppressors, and compensate either for intense feelings of inferiority, or for the pain of being severely hurt and punished. The compulsion in some men to attack women, for instance through indecent exposure, through denigration, through rape, in domestic abuse and so on, is probably indicative of a deep fear of women, or an indirect fear of men; each gender in its own way is experienced as a threat, not just to the masculinity of the offender, but sometimes to his very being. The object of the sadistic attack is often someone who is perceived as physically weaker, and therefore easier to control. Women who have been subjected to this type of attack may similarly need the opportunity in therapy to vent their own feelings of revenge, which could understandably take a sadistic form.

Masochism is at the other end of this particular spectrum, although it is a serious mistake to see those who are subject to undesired sadistic attacks as being 'unconsciously masochistic'. It is not unusual to find that women living with abusive partners also had abusive parents, and indeed find themselves entering a series of such abusive relationships (Walker 1990: 145–71). It is simplistic to see these patterns as indicative of a masochistic wish, and to suggest that such women simply provoke such behaviour: these types of explanation are themselves denigrating of the motives of such women in staying in such relationships. One element may be the powerful pull towards a mirror image of the father; or indeed of mother – Freud suggested that women can find partners whose most negative features mirror the negative features of their mothers: 'Many women who have chosen their husband on the model of their father ... nevertheless repeat towards him ... their bad relations with their mother' (1931: 377). It is an indication of the power of unconscious conflicts that, despite the obvious wish to repair past damage by making a relationship that can work better, the new partner is found simply to re-enact past relationships. A further aspect may be that it is the very vulnerability of such women that attracts men who need to dominate.

Masochism is seen however in the *satisfaction* that comes from being dominated; or in the perverse pleasure of some self-criticism and self-denigration – the mental equivalent of flagellation and the hair-shirt in mediaeval piety. It is not unusual to find that the 'martyr' touch has its own pay-off: the fantasy, for example, that others are being made to worry about you, a fantasy that in itself contains the sadistic flip-side of the masochistic personality.

Masochism may also be anger turned back on the self rather than expressed outwardly, held back perhaps because of guilt about the sadistic expression of anger. Sexual pleasure linked to masochism may indicate guilt about sexuality, which has to be punished at the same time as it is being enjoyed. Masochistic thinking may also be linked to the child's struggle to make sense of painful experience. If parents have been abusive towards a child, relating more obviously through physical and verbal punishment than through affection and encouragement, until the child learns otherwise this is all a child can understand about 'love', love that such parents tell the child they feel: 'I'm only saying this because I love you; I know this hurts, but I am doing this for your own good'.

We have to add to this topsy-turvy picture questions about what is culturally acceptable and what is not – questions that were raised in Chapter 2.

'Spare the rod and spoil the child' was once socially acceptable in Britain, at home, in school and in the punishment of crime. I recall an anthropologist speaking of her experiences researching Buddhism in a Japanese monastery. During meditation she found herself subjected to heavy slaps across her back. At first she thought she was being punished for doing it wrong, but she discovered that the 'beating' was a sign of encouragement and affirmation. She had to explain to the master that as a Westerner it had the opposite effect on her, and fortunately they passed her over for the rest of her stay. If, in that context, beating was a sign of the master's pleasure, it is not difficult to imagine a child (who in the early years knows no other culture) attempting to incorporate negative experiences into a more positive framework. It is not difficult to see how the once popular use of enemas, despite their uncomfortable intrusion of the body, could lead to anal masochism; or how beatings and other primitive practices in the British public school system could lead to fantasies and sado-masochistic sexual practices particularly in men in the upper echelons of society. While it is too awful to contemplate, when some children were punished or abused it may have been the only time when they have had any sort of relationship with their parents: so can the perverted expression of love become better than no love at all? And what about the child's own anger, which cannot expressed openly because of fear of retaliation by the adults? This may then be turned back upon the self, accepting another's anger as if punishment is deserved. Imber refers to Harry Stack Sullivan's notion of 'malevolent transformation':

> He observed that there were people who had learned, as children, the futility or even danger of seeking love or tenderness from their uncaring and rejecting caretakers. Rather than continue to suffer the hurt and disappointment of trying to get what was not available, such a child would instead learn to change his or her behavior from tenderness-seeking to angry rejection or mischievousness. While the need for tenderness went unmet, the malevolent transformation did protect against the pain and anxiety of being rejected or punished for seeking what was not to be had. And if the 'malevolence' was met with punishment, that at least was under one's control.
>
> (1995: 581–2)

The child, or the child in the adult, gets it all back to front. Masochistic tendencies may therefore be the result of learning about relationships 'through the looking glass'.

As with so many aspects of these major themes that illustrate the significance of past experience upon present situations, sadistic and masochistic traits are probably ubiquitous and, as Kernberg (1988) suggests, certain masochistic traits may to some extent be useful. Imber (1995: 582) instances the capacity to work hard for future benefits as adaptive masochism, or denying oneself the pleasure of certain foods 'a month before bathing-suit season'. But 'self-induced pain and suffering … can also become a pathological way of life, blocking out any possibility of experiencing happiness or deriving positive benefits. It also may be more powerful than the wish to change in therapy' (p. 582).

As this chapter has repeatedly made clear, issues of authority and autonomy are ever present in the therapeutic setting. Part of the therapeutic relationship is a working partnership, which is influenced not only by authority issues, but also by attitudes to work, and to play, which is in developmental terms partly a forerunner of work. The next chapter examines attitudes to work and play in therapy, as well as the influence of the themes currently being discussed on the wider world of work, and issues related to authority, autonomy and control in adult life.

8

AUTHORITY AND AUTONOMY: RELATED ISSUES

Work and play

Physical development in early childhood, especially muscular control, together with the psychological developments from fresh ways of relating to parents gives rise to new forms of expression, including the expression of greater autonomy and independence: there is a rapid development of mobility and dexterity, the ability to talk and express feelings more clearly, and with all this the undertaking of new different tasks, as well as pushing out the boundaries of the child's small world. Of huge significance in this period is the opportunity to play, since it is through play that children learn about objects and about people. Building and knocking down, using dolls and miniature people and animals, children create and manage a different world, a microcosm of the wider world to which they are gradually being introduced. Play is one of the first forms of learning through experience, and lays the foundations for learning through education, and for continued exploration of different areas (of place and people) in adult life. It is also a way of expressing the internal world of the child, and not surprisingly is used as a window to a child's concerns and conflicts in child therapy. Adults also play, and the relationship of play to adults in therapy is considered later.

Children who are restricted in their freedom to experiment, who are suppressed in their enthusiasm and in their curiosity by lack of trust, by parental anxiety or by threats, find it difficult to use play in this way. For them it may sometimes be that going to school provides opportunities to experiment and play, although without parental interest and encouragement it takes a determined child to make the most of the educational milieu. Even then a child who has not been able to enjoy play without innumerable cautions may inhibit the spontaneous element in learning, so that study becomes an overserious and isolating activity. In adults the repression they experienced in their childhood may show itself in rigid attitudes, an inability to give free rein to creative and expressive feelings, and a difficulty in finding any real pleasure in play or the playful. For some work becomes an obsession; for others it is hobbies, or even sport that can take on a similar mantle, so that whatever their interest, it occupies the person's whole life, excluding other ways of expression and different forms of relating. Whether it is having to order everything, or collect everything, or do everything to perfection, the fun element seems missing. 'They take themselves so seriously', we might say. Typical of such is the workaholic, the person who can never relax: like Sir Jasper in Wycherley's play *The Country Wife*, who says to his wife that he must 'go to my pleasure, which is business, while you go to your business, which is pleasure'. Where one or both partners in a relationship live for their career or interests alone, or one or both cannot relax in each other's company, but always have to be busy about the house, then such obsessional traits may interfere with the intimacy of the couple.

In some cases this can be understood in relation to an earlier theme – as if work, or a pastime, fills a void, even becoming a way of trying to pass time. For others it may be more related to the later theme of competition. In some their exaggerated single-mindedness shares the general characteristics of this theme, of being unable to let go of feelings, of being unable to tolerate imperfection or disorder, or of needing to please external or internal authority figures.

Ida initially came for counselling because of the difficulties she experienced breaking away from the influence of her parents, although it became apparent that she also had problems in her work. She was so particular about all she did that she was always behind schedule; she felt exhausted and wanted to give up her job and return to living in the parental home. Her parents had protected her when she was a child: against making mistakes; from other children by not letting her go out to play; from climbing trees in the garden; and from doing anything that could lead to her getting hurt; or (it seemed just as important) from getting her clothes muddy or torn. Through her therapy Ida became less obsessional about her work. She was able to take short-cuts, and that helped her to bring schedules up to date. She surprised herself with her accuracy, which was as great as when she had taken so much time going over her work. She was pleased for a short time, and she felt much better. But now she had time on her hands, and felt depressed and listless when she was not working. She felt guilty that she was no longer taking work back to her flat for the evening and at weekends. Her therapist began to explore what it was that made it difficult to take up other interests, to meet other people and so on in her spare time. It seemed that again she feared making mistakes, appearing foolish or getting hurt. Play and other relaxing activities also demanded the same high standards. Other people who played sports (and Ida quite liked tennis) demanded only the best. It took a long time before she was prepared to risk looking foolish, and before she found real pleasure in playing. And when she discovered some of the excitement in these other areas of her life, she appreciated aspects of her work as being even more interesting.

Therapy is of course a serious business, and it demands some quite hard work on the part of therapist and client both in terms of emotional wear-and-tear, as well as some keen thinking. Yet both client and therapist also need to relax into the work: that was one of the reasons that Freud introduced the couch for his patients, to encourage their free association, which was to be matched by the therapist's free-floating attention. And although there is much that can be hard and painful, both therapist and client need to be able to play with words, ideas, and possibilities. The imaginative and intuitive are as important as the rational and the empathic. This facility happens as clients become less anxious both about being in therapy and being with their therapist, and therapists become less anxious with them. The situations that troubled the client, or the therapeutic setting itself, become less threatening. Humour often indicates that the therapeutic relationship is relaxing, and that the client is beginning to feel more at ease: it is then that free association becomes easier, and self-reflection more wide-ranging.

At the start of therapy many clients are too weighed down by their problems, which is why they have sought help, and in no mind yet to enter into anything like therapeutic play; but there are some clients who continue to make heavy weather of their problems and who become fixated upon their symptoms. They may find it impossible to play with ideas, images and associations. The free associative method which is so important to the psychodynamic approach is a way of giving expression to different ideas and feelings apart from those that are obvious, since other avenues sometimes lead back to the initial issues, providing new angles and insights. Clients who find this difficult may be afraid of what they will reveal to themselves about themselves. Another important aspect of the psychodynamic approach therefore is being able to work with these anxious defences (Jacobs 2004b: Chapter 5).

Similarly there are therapists who are too concerned about getting everything right and are therefore unable to allow free play with their intuition, their imagination and their thinking. Yet it is playing, such as playing with words, images and ideas, together with the judicious use of hunches and shots in the dark, that is just as important a factor in good therapy as the need to use careful evidence in making interventions. Frequently it is the off-the-cuff remark that the client remembers the next week, or reports back at a later point in therapy as being significant, and not the well-thought-out and well-rounded psychoanalytic interpretation.

Therapy involves a working alliance, which includes thinking and a type of play, with the spontaneous relationship between therapist and client, which involves a type of playfulness, some of which is experienced through the transference and countertransference (Jacobs 2004b: Chapter 6). To call therapy play-acting would be to diminish the seriousness of it: but there is nonetheless a sense in which a client is encouraged to try out different ways of expression, and different ways of relating. Therapy is a stage upon which relationships can be played out, as well as tried out.

The working alliance is an example of the latency mode referred to in Chapter 1 (pp. 18–19), in which for the purpose of learning the turbulence of emotions and the irrationality of fantasies are temporarily held in check, so that a relatively cool and thoughtful look can be taken at what is being expressed and experienced in the session, and what it might reflect or might mean. It is in the latency mode that tentative explanations can be put forward for testing. Only when the transference to the therapist or internal anxieties and fantasies in therapist or client become too intense is it difficult to work in this relatively rational way. Probably the most productive therapeutic work consists of a to-and-fro movement between the expression of feeling and fantasy on the one hand, and the reflection on the other. When in a state of reflection both partners in therapy can unpack the feelings and ideas that emerge during free association, and together try to understand their significance. Work and play both have a rightful place in therapy as they do in life.

Since learning is much more difficult when a person is in a highly emotional state, there are occasions when therapists have to wait until strong feelings have been expressed and have begun to settle before they can say anything that a client is likely to hear and to use. There is rarely any mileage in making a studied interpretation when a client is distraught or furious. Empathy, warmth, acceptance, accurate reflection and sometimes even gentle management are more appropriate when the client is in full flood. Clients sometimes wish they could have seen their therapist at a time of great distress, and feel frustrated by having to wait for the next session, when their intense emotional state may have passed: 'You would understand much more if you could have seen how I was then'. Fixed regular times may then be frustrating for clients, although the reliability of the time that is reserved for them provides an incentive to contain and manage things that can be reported, perhaps expressed and certainly processed in the next session. Some clients of course hold in what they feel, and dump it all on the therapist as if the session is a toilet. Therapists need to endure being dumped on in this way, until the point comes when they can process it and invite the client to reflect. It is at these reflective times, when the ups and downs have somewhat levelled out, that the interpretation comes into its own.

There are some occasions where emotional factors are so strong that it appears to be impossible for a client to make use of therapy at all:

Jean very much wanted help, and wished to unburden herself of a number of things that were troubling her about her behaviour, but she found great difficulty in telling the therapist about them. Fortunately she was able to say that she felt very nervous before coming, that she could not sleep the night before, and that she had been physically sick on leaving for some sessions. Despite remaining calm himself, and expressing a gentle empathic acceptance the therapist appeared unable to help her feel at ease; neither did tentative interpretation of her feelings of anxious shame, or her possible fear of the therapist's reaction if she were to voice her concerns more openly. In the end, at least with Jean, it seemed it was the therapist's silent attentiveness – unhurried and unruffled – that appeared to help her to break through her reticence.

The working alliance between therapist and client depends upon being able to handle the implicit authority issues, enabling the client to become less worried about being criticized or rejected by the therapist, and therefore able to express feelings and talk freely, without censoring anything. Similarly clients need to be encouraged to take the initiative in therapy, to suggest their own understanding, and to value their own authority and expertise as being just as important as the therapist's. From their own perspective, therapists need to take account of their own countertransference feelings, particularly those that tempt them to take on the role of the dominant, knowledgeable, overordered, authoritative and judgmental parent. As Hartung (1979: 184) suggests, therapists need to have worked through all these issues themselves if they are going to be able to demonstrate the generative mode of middle adulthood, a reference to Erikson's seventh age, with its developmental tasks of generativity and creativity. Creativity depends upon many things, including trust, belief in one's own authority and autonomy issues, and freedom from competitive anxieties. The therapist, like a good teacher or parent, can provide a model that can help shift a client's inhibiting reactions:

> Ken panicked whenever he was faced with a learning task that he could not immediately grasp. He really needed time to think, but he could not relax enough to allow himself such space. Unless he was getting something down on paper, he felt anxious and began to fear that he would never complete his task on time. These work issues were reflected in his therapy, where his therapist also felt under pressure from Ken, who would, for example, drop hints that he was wondering when the therapist was going to make a helpful suggestion. The therapist shared how she felt this sense of urgency with Ken, but in a calm and unhurried manner, trying to indicate through her tone as well as her words that she and he both needed time free from anxious pressure if they were ever going to be able to produce results.

Another aspect of therapy which is related to this is the provision of freedom for clients to develop in their own way. As discussed in Chapter 2, models of development and psychological maturity are inevitably subjective and culturally determined. Therapies too have their own models of healthy relating and living, even if they tend to concentrate upon psychopathology. In the search for assurance and certainty these models may have acquired an authority of their own. Parents, teachers, and other authority figures including therapists are constantly presented with the temptation to set standards, to mould the child or point the adult in a certain direction. In the middle of the 20th century Truby King, and the strict notion of four-hourly feeds, whatever the baby's needs or demands, was one example of the way in which rigid ideas entered into childcare. The danger of books on childcare, or indeed books on developmental psychology, is their tendency to lay down what is right and wrong in child-rearing and personality development. This again is not necessarily what their authors intend, but parents who want to do their job well, and students who want to pass their exams, tend to take what they read as gospel. In therapy this can happen through trying to mould the client. Therapists respond in particular ways, encouraging certain insights and attitudes, and questioning others, sometimes restricting the unique direction in which any one individual wants to move by implicitly promoting a particular set of values. This is especially so when therapists are hampered by the need to produce results, and to show their effectiveness in response to targets set by their employing or funding authorities. Therapists who are too keen to conform to the image of the successful parent or productive worker risk turning out clones, instead of allowing individuals the opportunity to create or recreate themselves. A therapist's solutions are not necessarily a client's solutions. The relatively comfortable, white, middle-class counsellor or therapist (and there are a good many of them) particularly needs to learn from those who do not easily fit into stereotypical societal norms and assumptions. Those who write about therapy frequently thank their clients for what they have taught them: such a sentiment applies just as much to those who learn about therapy.

Winnicott stresses the importance of a mother providing the environment in which a baby does her own growing. He also underlines the need for someone to be there while children play: 'Responsible persons must be available when children play; but this does not mean that the responsible person need enter into the children's playing' (1971: 50); or, to pursue the parallel, this does not mean that therapists need to tell the client what to play or the aim of their play. Parents who are always trying to help their children to make or do things that are useful, or insist on play according to certain rules, not only act unnecessarily (since children soon develop their own system of rules for games which can be more exact than an adult's) – they also risk stifling initiative and growth.

Different attitudes to work and play can therefore inhibit or promote autonomy, and with it the virtues Erikson assigns to the seventh age, creativity and generativity. These are, however, desirable features at all ages, as indeed authority and autonomy issues can be seen in many other points of life.

Autonomy and letting go through the life cycle

The major theme of authority and autonomy involves issues of control, of rigidity in oneself or towards others (authoritarianism), of perfectionism, the expression of anger and loss of control with emotions generally, obsessional behaviours and attitudes, conditional love, internalized authority figures (conscience or super-ego) and so on. In developmental terms there is a movement outwards, like the ripples in a pond, from a relatively confident sense of an inner central self that enables exploring the potentiality, the power and pleasure not only of the body and emotions, but of the interaction with others, including those who are authority figures. In this process a child-cum-adult becomes more independent and autonomous, and at the same time creative and generative.

This is a movement that takes place from birth onward, with the physical and the somatic sometimes leading the process. Although modern medicine prefers it otherwise, the process of natural birth is one where mother and baby have little control over timing, and there are many more such occasions in the course of life, when the body leads: daily, and periodically, and in those particular times of bodily change (such as at puberty, and in aging). Despite beauty products, fitness centres and even plastic surgery, it is impossible to control the march of time, and those who are control freaks may find themselves fighting a losing battle against their bodies, raising perhaps some of the narcissistic issues discussed in Chapter 3 (pp. 66–7). There is a sense in which death is a psychosomatic event, but ultimately we have no control over death itself. This aspect of having little or no control may be masked by medical advances, but should not blind us to the ultimate futility of that authoritarian illusion that we are masters of ourselves.

Yet even where we imagine there is no control, for the infant for example, a baby possesses considerable power to bring the responsive mother to her beck and call. Parents find their lives taken over by a baby, particularly their first child; and they need to learn to accept the chaos that is temporarily caused to diaries and social plans: they will have difficulty if they find it hard to reconcile themselves to letting go of their ordered lifestyle. In the toddler stage, children learn about frustration and accommodating themselves to the other members of the family. This adjustment has to be matched by parents, since the child's play and need to experiment requires parental attitudes relaxed enough to accept a floor littered with toys, the bathroom being soaked at bath time, and advances made by their child at the cost of other inconveniences. There are, as in adolescence, challenges to parental control, and the way these are handled helps define limits for the child, about what is and is not possible, and how living with others involves restrictions as well as opportunities. Patience in answering all the child's questions encourages initiative and exploration as the child grows through school and into the adult world. The manner in which the rules of family and community life are explained and enforced also lays the foundation for a belief that parents, others and the wider world are (as Erikson says of one outcome of the second stage) basically fair and just. Parents also need to learn how to encourage without pressurizing the child to achieve beyond what he or she is capable of and wants to do:

> Lucy was an only child who had had to work very hard at school in order to satisfy her parents. She was in her opinion 'not all that clever', but she had been able to make up for the disappointment about her progress by working equally hard in her spare time to help her parents with their corner shop business. When she married and had children of her own she was determined not to put them through what she herself had experienced: her children were indeed her pride, and they grew up as well-adjusted, healthy, normal teenagers. When they left home Lucy became very depressed. She might have expected to be pleased that she had brought them up so free from the pressures she had had on herself when she was young. But she had not recognized until this point that in doing so much for her children she had also been totally occupied in 'working hard' to achieve this end. With their going she no longer had anyone to work hard for: this had become for her, over the years of their childhood and adolescence, the only way she knew of feeling that she was acceptable.

The inter-relationship which I prefer of the different stages in Erikson's model suggests that one of the virtues of the eighth stage – renunciation – has an alignment with the development of autonomy in children and young adults. Parenthood has this element of renunciation in it, albeit over an extended period, since it involves letting go of the child at different developmental opportunities. Letting go means renunciation of the wish to control, in tune with what a child and adolescent wants or needs, as well as what the child or adolescent can manage. There is a subtle balance necessary in the exercise of authority, whether by parents or others, between relinquishing control and abdicating responsibility. Winnicott (1971: 146) warns against the false maturity that comes when adults veer too much towards abdication. At the same time, in relation to infancy, he acknowledges the importance of a mother in 'providing the simplified bit of the world which the infant, through her, comes to know' (1975: 153) – and while Winnicott often warns about the effect of unmanageable impingements upon the infant, there is an argument for suggesting that what parents do in gradually relinquishing control and protection is gradually to allow the world to impinge upon the child. A mother who has met the dependent needs of her baby has to be ready to let the child take the first steps (literally) towards autonomy; parents who have a sense of the right balance between allowing freedom and exercising necessary restraint will be more confident in allowing their adolescent son or daughter to test out their own limits in relation to the opportunities facing them.

When children first go to a nursery or school, this is a further step towards autonomy, although it also involves meeting a new set of authority issues, with new 'parental figures' and expectations. Whether learning through play, or learning through being taught, the achievements of a child are immense: verbal, literary and numeracy skills, as well as physical, manual and technical skills. For some children, their evident success through education opens up new horizons, and this in some cases may separate them from their family or their culture, especially when they come from families of poor educational background, or from closed religious or ethnic backgrounds. Others, who for one reason or another fail to succeed, may be left with a different form of low self-esteem than that which is a legacy of the earliest years. Where there has been early failure in the infant's environment this can result in little or no faith in oneself. Relative failure in later childhood, particularly in education, may lead to loss of confidence in certain areas of knowledge or skills, without undermining capabilities in other areas. Learning, whether in childhood, adolescence or adult life, needs to be relatively untroubled by issues of authority and control. Psychological difficulties can diminish the capacity to learn – such as disturbed current object relations, feelings of guilt, shame and embarrassment, fear of being found out, of punishment or of disapproval (Jacobs, 2004a). And while it is obviously essential that those who teach possess authority in their subject, and skill in their communication, they, like parents, need to be able to provide confidence in those who learn that it is all right to make mistakes; that it is important to order information, as well as to play with ideas; and that it is productive to give free rein to thought and imagination. Authority problems and lack of confidence in their developing autonomy may lead to learners finding it impossible to start a piece of work, or unable to complete it and submit it for assessment, because assessment evokes memories and fear of failure. Some students think they have to get every fact and word correct. This type of perfectionism tries to obviate all criticism. Some adolescent and adult learners even fear to ask their tutors for guidance, thinking they will show themselves up as ignorant. How different such inhibition is from that early thirst for understanding that children show when asking the many questions that come from their engagement with the wider world:

> Mary approached the university counselling team as a desperate last measure since she was about to fail her exams. She had not worked for almost a year. Although initially there had been some adolescent acting out at university of rebellion against her strict home and school, which had led to non-attendance at lectures, the situation had got out of hand because she was afraid to approach her tutors to ask for help in catching up. She feared that they would tell her she was lazy, just like her father had told her in the past. Her counsellor pointed out that if she wanted to repeat the year, she would have to see her tutor – was it still fear of her tutor's criticism that prevented her from asking? Had she felt afraid of coming to see the counsellor too in case she also told her she was being lazy? Mary decided she had to see her tutor, and returned the following week to say that in fact her tutor had been most understanding! But now she had to tell her parents. Her counsellor wondered whether Mary really carried an outdated view of her father's criticism within her, and whether even he would be as severe as she imagined. Perhaps she had even fostered his criticism by presenting herself as a naughty child who expected punishment, rather than as a young adult who had a mind of her own?

Problem solving where there is a rigid sense of the need for order, may suffice at the simpler stages of learning, but sooner or later (particularly in higher education) such self-imposed expectations become impossible to meet. The person who sees everything in black-and-white terms, or who has to be certain before passing an opinion, often fails to see other dimensions, or is afraid to express any opinion at all. Caution likewise prevents the imaginative leap that often lies at the heart of intellectual and even scientific discoveries. The student cannot see the wood for the trees. At later stages of learning it is necessary to learn to tolerate confusion, particularly about the interpretation of facts. The wish for certainty can sometimes foreclose the search for more information and further thinking, which may ultimately bring about a more comprehensive solution.

School phobia may also be the result of such fears: children may try to opt out of the situation if they are afraid of putting up a weak performance; or that their teacher will shame them by criticism or punishment; or when they feel that they are not as good as their peers. Some may have experienced critical or even sadistic teachers (particularly those in the older generation), but students like Mary in the last example can feel this concern, even when their teachers and tutors have always shown themselves tolerant of mistakes and understanding of difficulties. Other children or older students may wish to please their teacher, and parents too, so that working hard becomes an end in itself and not a means to an end. While there are some who learn in order to appease authority figures, there are others who reject learning, thereby expressing their reaction against the authority of the teacher or of the institution. This may also be a rebellion against parents who have sent them to school when they did not wish to leave home, or against parents who are felt to be pressurizing them to go on to further or higher education when they wish to get a job and become more independent. Others may use opportunities for conflict with authority as a way of testing out boundaries in the institution, which they have been unable to test out at home, where discipline has either been overlax or repressive:

Naomi had got behind with her work, and saw her school counsellor when she thought that she was going to fail her first set of public exams. It soon became clear that Naomi was terrified of her father, and that she had chosen to specialize in certain subjects because he insisted. Her elder brother, who had been at the school before her, had been a rebel and a constant source of worry to her parents and to his teachers. She could not bring herself to ask her teachers for more help, saying she had wanted to do it all for herself. Her counsellor was not sure at first whether Naomi was sabotaging her chances as a passive rebellion against her father. She was obviously trying to achieve some measure of independence, by doing things herself, although it was an inappropriate time to choose to do this. The counsellor felt confirmed in this view because after a few sessions in which Naomi initially kept asking the counsellor to provide answers, to ring her father, and so on, she then seemed in a hurry to leave sessions early. This may have shown Naomi's need to feel independent of an adult, who even if she was caring was nonetheless still an authority figure; or it may have been because her counsellor was unable to give her the clear-cut answers she had come to expect from a father who always knew his own mind.

Teachers (including those who teach or supervise counselling and psychotherapy) need to have mastered their own authority problems in order to be both firm and yet flexible, including in the way they maintain boundaries. Some teachers, and some institutions, reinforce their authority through psychological rigidity and punishment, rather than through persuasion and encouragement. Even where a child's home has provided a good-enough facilitating environment, the sadistic or overcritical teacher, who inevitably becomes a parent substitute, can equally plant a strong negativism in the child, and reinforce the super-ego, often prejudicing a child's view of anything associated with education and learning. Where both parents and teachers are cold or critical, the task of achieving confidence and self-esteem becomes doubly difficult. In drawing attention to this I do not forget that there are many teachers both at school and in continuing adult education who provide a different model of the accepting and caring parent figure, and who can modify the harshness of the child's experience, and encourage the adult learner to return to education.

The adult learner's efforts may have been devalued or derided in the family or at school, so that learning has become associated with demoralization, and dismissed as irrelevant or impossible. Retraining or the learning of new skills in adult life may be thought of as like going back to school, and the new opportunities associated with previous unhappy or unsuccessful experiences. Retraining cannot be considered positively, since it is linked too much with parent or teacher expectation; or with lack of interest from parents; or with feelings of inferiority towards those peers or siblings who learned more rapidly. Anything that smacks of education might therefore be resisted, or taken up only half-heartedly, when it might be that retraining or learning about new areas of life is not just essential, but positively rewarding. In working with adult learners, a therapist may want to look into attitudes formed by previous learning:

> Omar's father was a semi-skilled mechanic who took great pride in the academic success at university of Omar's two elder brothers. As neither of them showed much manual dexterity, and Omar did, Omar became the son who shared his father's interest in rebuilding cars and other practical tasks. There was no reason to think Omar was not also bright, but his father had often said to him, 'Of course you're like me, you won't go as far as they have, but you'll be good at my sort of work'. This identification with his father was very satisfying at the time, since like most children he enjoyed being close to his father; but it also overshadowed Omar in later life, when he discovered his own intellectual ability, and went to university by way of a further education college. Exams terrified him, because he could not get it out of his head that he was treading on territory that had been reserved for his brothers.

But it is not just adults who can be authoritarian. In distinguishing types of adolescence Marcia (1975) describes what he calls the 'foreclosed adolescent'. This type of adolescent also tends to be authoritarian, less able to evaluate critically, and can easily lose identity both in the crowd and to the crowd. Such a young person's identity is determined by parents or by peers. He or she does things because someone else says so, or because others do. Black-and-white attitudes predominate. Religious faith may also be used to foreclose the real questioning of values and beliefs that might be expected in adolescents:

> Paul was actively searching for 'the meaning of life', but when he came to see a therapist he was caught between the wish to belong to a dogmatic Christian group on the one hand, and to be 'one of the boys' who had a good time on the other. His parents were very protective: they did not let him stay out at night, and had always refused him a bicycle in case he hurt himself. Seeking help might have given him the chance to work through the wish to overidentify with a group whether of the religious or the hedonistic type, but Paul wanted the therapist to tell him what to do, and appeared unable to use the space offered to him to work things out for himself.

Paul could not allow himself even to experience immaturity, as he might have found with 'the boys'. Winnicott describes immaturity in adolescence as healthy: 'Immaturity is an essential element of health at adolescence ... in this is constrained the most exciting features of creative thought, new and fresh feeling, ideas for new living' (1971: 146). Young people can be anxious about needing an adult's help, and reluctant to accept it for any longer than is immediately necessary. 'I want to solve this myself' in a young person is a good sign, indicating a healthy wish to be independent. Acknowledging this wish for independence, as long as there is no indication of a serious disturbance, is appropriate with younger or older clients, although with older clients the wish to go it alone can mask an anxiety about forming a closer attachment to the therapist, which can be more readily discounted in the young client. Young people are on the whole more adaptable, and often find quite brief therapy sufficient for the moment, preferring to arrange 'to come back if I need to' – a safety net, seldom needed, but like the toddler's parent, within reach to run back to if necessary.

An important aspect of achieving personal autonomy includes the need for economic independence, which is one of the motives for being in work. The workplace itself provides a focus for many of the issues related to this theme, some of which have already been referred to in this chapter. But these issues also apply to the experience of unemployment, redundancy and early retirement. Those who are made redundant and are unsuccessful in seeking new work have good reason to see the world as unfair and unjust. Having little to do (and 'doing' is as important as 'being'), those without work can perceive themselves as incompetent, and as criticized at home for failing to provide for the family, or by society at large which is always ready to blame the unemployed rather than the system. It may be difficult to meet others, particularly those who are still in work, because of feelings of inferiority and 'loss of face'. Deprived of the opportunity to be productive, and to take pride in their work, it is little wonder that the unemployed and even some people who are retired can feel inferior. Those who adapt better are those who develop ways of expressing their need to be creative and productive outside work, or through alternatives to paid work. The more a person has invested in their work in order to ensure their self-esteem (particularly the workaholic, or the obsessional achiever) the harder redundancy or retirement is likely to be.

On the other hand, for others to have no work, or less work, gives them the chance to learn new skills, find new interests, to play and to use time in a far from passive way. Reappraisal of their life may be particularly valuable (but perhaps also difficult) when they have been influenced by family and school to overachieve, and when work has been at the expense of 'play'. In their desire to please parents, teachers, supervisors and bosses they may have been unable to find pleasure in their own satisfaction. There may be many who look back from their new position of relative freedom to their previous full-time occupation, and see how much it depleted the rest of life; and how being an employee is to risk becoming overconformist; or, as Erikson puts it: 'a thoughtless slave of [human] technology and of those who are in a position to exploit it' (1965: 252):

Ruth feared this even before she started work. She had not made any job applications for over a year, in fact since leaving university. She became depressed because of her passivity, and her therapist was tempted to drop hints about the value of getting something to do to occupy her (as Ruth's mother was apparently saying). That would not have helped, because Ruth felt she was a disappointment to her mother, and her mother's hints only made Ruth angry. Instead the therapist took up Ruth's reluctance to seek work, which seemed based on her feeling that being in work meant becoming part of the system, and that she would only be an insignificant cog in a machine. Her father's legalistic attitude, schooling that had suppressed individual expression, and her underlying anxiety that she was not up to competing with men all combined to reinforce her inactivity. She said she preferred the freedom of not being in work, although it appeared that she was rejecting opportunities to use her own qualifications in a way that could lead to eventual seniority, and a managerial position where she could exercise authority towards others in a less restrictive way than she had herself experienced. Despite being apparently anti-authority, one of the features of the relationship between the therapist and Ruth was her constant attempt to get the therapist to give her answers, reflected in his countertransference feeling of wanting to kick her into action.

A further aspect of the world of work is the issue of mastery and control. This is put forward by Rayner, who suggests that some occupations require mastery of anxiety about the nature of the work involved, especially where that work involves coping with basic emotions. For instance, 'a dustman has to master his disgust, a spiderman vertigo, and a teacher has to master class discipline' (1986: 166). Therapists and counsellors have to master their own anxieties for the work they do (Jacobs 2001: Chapter 4), particularly about their own needs, which if not judiciously monitored can lead to abuse of the client. Two of the most difficult areas for therapists to master, which are in line with the theme of control, are first their inability to help (the need to 'do something'), and second the refusal to exercise the type of authority that the client imagines and hopes will automatically change things:

> Sue was training as a counsellor, and she was obviously anxious to do well in her practical work in order to pass her placement. In addition, like many a beginner, she took her work home with her, worrying about her clients' welfare between sessions, trying to plan ahead for all eventualities in her wish to help them in the time available to her, controlling the situation in her thoughts if unable to do this in the actual encounter. She was not helped by having parents who had expressed disappointment that she had not used her considerable intelligence and qualifications to go for a more prestigious career, but had instead chosen a course that did not hold out any easy prospect of 'success', at least in her parents' eyes. They were ambitious for her, but her own ambition was interfering with her freedom to listen and be present with her clients.

Different features about authority and autonomy can cause difficulties in intimate relationships. Living as a couple means learning to live with another person's norms, values and 'rules'. Often these are unwritten, and unexpressed, especially in the early period of establishing a relationship. Cutting across another's norms and rules, or not conforming oneself to expected patterns of behaviour learned in a partner's family of origin, can lead to resentment, open criticism, or even to one partner laying down the law to the other. In the critical-submissive partnership, ways of living and making decisions cannot be openly questioned or shared. One partner becomes (or is felt to be) the authoritarian parent, while the other initially tries hard to please and conform, until they come to the end of their tether and rebel or collapse, explode or implode. Decisions about money, about the home, about the management of children and about the expectations of wider families on both sides can all become a battleground for two people when each needs to prove to the other his or her independence or dominance. Where authority issues interfere with a relationship, conflicts and disagreements become occasions for fighting old parent–child battles about freedom and autonomy. Even minor matters can become excuses for one partner to try to impress their authority on the other.

Another aspect in the relationship may be the wish to please: one partner may always feel inadequate in the eyes of the other, sometimes because of their own expectations, not necessarily because of their partner's. They make strenuous efforts to feel good enough as a breadwinner, as a homemaker, as a lover, or even as a parent responsible for what feels like the other's children. Sex, for example, becomes both a demand and a performance, where getting results such as the partner's orgasm predominates over mutual enjoyment. Doing, again, becomes more important than being.

In concluding these chapters on authority and autonomy, with one feature being the issue of control, it is relevant to consider how this is manifested in approaches to ageing. Renunciation, or letting go, as indicated earlier, is one of the virtues of mature adulthood, alongside wisdom. Ageing and retirement (especially in prospect to those who have not reached this life stage) may appear to involve loss and limitation in terms of physical strength and stamina, a definite working role, a definite structure to the working day and week, and reduced income. But much in the end depends on attitudes and not upon these apparently all-important externals. One particular psychological type identified in old age (Lowe 1972: 248) is reminiscent of the stereotypical anal character: the old person who is fearful of old age, retirement and infirmity, and who defensively remains or becomes compulsively active, rigidly self-sufficient and overcontrolled.

Yet such a bleak picture does not include the advantages and new opportunities that ageing can bring to those who can accept the limitations, and who can enjoy the new freedom that retirement presents, as long as they have the financial means and the physical health to take advantage of them. Such people show perhaps the greatest development of personal autonomy. It can also be rewarding for those who are now senior workers and senior members of the family to watch younger people, whom they have trained and guided, taking over their responsibilities. Where older people are respected for their experience, wisdom and judgement, there can be satisfaction at being in the background in a 'consultative' capacity, knowing that their experience of life and work is valued by the generations that follow them.

Restructuring of time enables old and new interests to be pursued, and for the mind to be kept active – memory, for instance, appears to function better when there is continuing mental activity. Tolerance is frequently a quality that is acquired in old age, with older people often feeling less threatened by the young than the middle-aged 'parental' generation are. Aware too of the shortness of remaining life, it probably makes more sense to enjoy relationships while they last, and to let go of some of the rigidities and certainties of the past.

A final example of the way in which control and letting go again feature is at the very end of a life, in the way in which in some instances it appears that those who are dying almost appear to choose the point at which they die. This is what I meant earlier when I referred to death as an event over which we have no ultimate control, but which is also a psychosomatic process. A person who still has needs to be met sometimes appears to control their failing body sufficiently long enough to fulfil their dying wish; or on the other hand may abandon hope where others see it, and rapidly decline. Dying is so much harder when there is still unfinished business, or when there are open wounds, unrealized hopes, and memories needing to be relived and reworked:

> Teresa had an advanced cancer, and the doctors told her, when she asked them, that she had only a few months at most to live. Despite being confined to her bed, Teresa worked from home to help other cancer victims whom she heard or read about, writing them letters of comfort. She herself received great support from her husband. Her one regret was that her eldest son would not visit her. He lived some distance away, but she knew that the real reason for his not visiting her was that he could not face seeing her in this condition. Despite requests from others in the family he did not appear. Teresa was still alive, though much less active, a year after the last date that her doctors had given her for her survival. At last her son came to see her, and he stayed a few hours. Within a week she had died. It appeared that she had waited until then, when she had been able to say her good-bye, and was then able to let herself go.

With the confidence in the core self that comes from working through issues of trust to a place of secure attachment, and the confidence in one's abilities that can come from working through issues related to authority and autonomy, the growing child, adolescent and adult is better equipped to engage with the third major set of issues. The next set of themes cluster around aspects of competition and cooperation, and concern different kinds of relating, from intimate partnerships to wider social networks. While these relationships, as already seen in the examples in this and earlier chapters, involve different aspects of trust and authority, there are further important elements to their dynamics which the next three chapters address.

COOPERATION AND COMPETITION: GENDER, SEXUALITY AND SEXUAL RELATIONS

The foundations of relatedness are trust and attachment (Chapters 3–5). The way power and will are exercised in relationships are shaped by attitudes towards authority and autonomy (Chapters 6–8). These issues profoundly influence the way relationships are expressed in the family, in intimate partnerships, in friendships, as well as at work or in other social and societal groups, and in particular in those aspects of the theme of cooperation and competitiveness which are discussed in this and the following two chapters. If the first theme developed into different types of attachment, and the second into different degrees of independence, the third is essentially about mutuality and interdependence, and appropriate forms of intimacy. Too clear a division between these themes would be artificial, and it has been my argument throughout that the themes run into each other and through each other. Thus the intimacy of the first theme clearly relates to intimacy in this theme, and power relationships in the second theme are played out in healthy or unhealthy ways in matters of cooperation and competition.

This third theme takes its cue from psychoanalytic writing about three-person relationships (triads) rather than the two-person relationships (dyads) which are more typical of mother and baby or parent and child with the key issues about attachment and authority. While the relationship in the first theme can be described as partly about symbiosis, and the relationship in the second as partly about separateness, the third is more about complementarity: about togetherness with the acceptance of difference, or separateness and relatedness as twin poles in any relationship, sometimes with one aspect predominating and sometimes the other, sometimes with movement between the two, sometimes with rigidity. While it is more common for psychoanalytic concepts to describe psychopathology rather than health, taken together these three themes represent a potentiality for wholeness in relationships in which we see others as complete persons. They are therefore not simply providers of care on the one hand or of rules on the other; instead the other is one who has her or his own needs, to whom we may give, from whom we may receive, and with whom we may share, in acts of love, of friendship and of social cooperation.

Relationship problems in adult clients that relate to this theme are probably the most commonly presented ones, at least initially, with issues about internalized authority figures and difficulties about being more autonomous running a close second. Yet modern psychoanalytic writing has tended to concentrate on the first year of life and the problems related to it, although it was with many of the issues with which this chapter deals that Freud's initial investigations began. Those who write extensively about the earliest period of life acknowledge that what this chapter addresses as Oedipal issues cannot be bypassed, even when deeper disturbances are clearly present. Guntrip (1968: 278–9) writes that 'the first few years of analysis' will be concerned with the Oedipal period! If that is the case in a perfect world, it is clear that, in the more limited help that short-term or once-weekly therapy can usually offer, this theme is also going to predominate.

Psychoanalytic theory particularly highlights sexual anxieties as central to this theme. In developmental terms this chapter reflects the way adult clients might re-experience questions, anxieties and pleasures that first arose for them as children, as they encountered physical differences in gender, and as they explored birth and sex and relationships in the family. Oedipus, castration anxiety, penis envy, and the differences between men and women are all central ideas within psychoanalytic thought, about which there is plenty of disagreement and much common misunderstanding. Some of these terms may appear dated and inappropriate, but if they can be understood as representing vital issues, they are then relevant to the material clients can present.

Gender and sexual orientation

Issues about gender are of vital importance to both women and men. Indeed the more the imbalance between the genders is corrected, and the greater the challenge to patriarchal dominance in politics, at work and in the home and family, the more personal issues about being a man or being a woman, in society, at work and in intimate relations become. Western society has undergone a revolution in gender expectations which is bound to have a major impact on women and men and upon sexual relations.

At a basic level sexual difference fascinates, repels and attracts. With the possible exception of the colour of a person's skin, identification by gender is probably the initial reaction to any meeting between people – whether of strangers passing in the street, or introductions to a family or the workplace. Perhaps the most frequently asked question in a pregnancy or at a birth is 'Is it a boy, or a girl?' In some cultures the gender of the newborn child is of crucial economic importance (girls are seen as a greater financial burden and boys as future additions to labour, for example, in some economies), but such attitudes are not confined, as might be thought, to Oriental or African societies:

Ursula was one of two girls, who were rejected by their father because he wanted boys. As far as he was concerned, they could be left to their own devices after he separated from their mother, and he largely ignored them in their growing up. When Ursula herself had two boys she found her father showed more interest in her and her family, as if she had provided him with the sons his former wife had failed to. Although this came both as a surprise and a reward to Ursula, it was quite clear from the way she described herself that bearing two boys was about the only really positive thing she had done. In much of the rest of her life she felt a failure. Some of this might be attributed to her mother's 'perfect' example of motherhood, with which Ursula felt she could not possibly compete. But it was also to do with her deep-seated feelings from childhood that she and her sister were never good enough for her father. In psychoanalytic terms, indeed, one might almost say that (for her father) she was born imperfect, lacking what she needed to be her father's son.

A psychodynamic view values post-Freudian psychoanalytic theory since it extends the nature of human relatedness beyond Freud's drive-based model. Those who followed him took up particular aspects of his work, about relating to objects, so that in object-relations theory it is the wish to relate that is stressed over the need to discharge instinctual drives. Nevertheless sexual and reproductive drives remain powerful in the human species, however much the veneer of civilization may have curbed and directed sexual energies in other directions. (It was Freud's contention that much of civilized culture was an expression of sublimated sexual libido.) The physical differences that distinguish boys and girls are significant to children, and remain significant to adult men and women even if their relations (in childhood and adulthood) have many other facets. Initial reactions to sexual similarity or difference generally make way for meeting the other as a whole person, and not just as a sex object, but that the other is of the same or other sex continues to influence any interaction. For some people same-sex relating can evoke rivalrous, or homophobic/homosexual feelings; or opposite-sex relating seductiveness, anxiety or power struggles. As I shall discuss further in Chapter 9 (pp. 205–7), such reactions may also mean that the gender of the therapist is an important factor in how the client relates in therapy.

Gender difference and sexuality are signalled (or hidden) by the way men and women dress. The wish to appear attractive should not be mistaken as a seductive ploy, but the way in which people present themselves certainly signals their body image. There is of course more to being male and female than physical difference although it is important to distinguish between the terms 'male and female', which describe primary genital and other secondary physical characteristics with which we are born, and the terms 'masculine and feminine', which describe what are commonly supposed to be distinct psychological characteristics and gender roles. Then there is a further distinction about sexual orientation, which may be heterosexual, bisexual or homosexual. Thus a male client may present with sexual difficulties within a heterosexual partnership, in which anxieties about being stereotypically 'feminine' seem to play a part:

Vernon suffered from secondary impotence (i.e. he was occasionally impotent in sexual intercourse with his female partner). At college he had been laughed at by a particularly 'macho' group of friends, who played a lot of sport, and thought that Vernon's love of poetry and the theatre meant that he was effeminate. For a time Vernon decided to try to join these so-called friends by becoming a member of their sports club, and going for long training sessions with them. In fact his anxieties around sex were related much more to unexpressed anger with his partner, and when he began to express these and recovered his confidence in his sexuality, he felt able to give up his attempts to be a tough rugby player, realizing that this was not at all his scene. His sense of being a male became rooted both in sexual confidence, and in a conviction that love of the arts need not in the least be regarded as either feminine or masculine.

More recent signs of the recognition of the diversity of sexual relationships are a welcome return to an attitude in Freud towards sexuality which was less hide-bound than in many of his followers. His attitude to homosexuality, for example, was that while it might be a variation from normal sexual orientation, it was not psychologically abnormal. For Freud bisexuality is the common path of development until the Oedipal stage, and it is only then that the developmental process splits into different paths for boys and girls, with different consequences in terms of the eventual sexual object. Freud clearly labels homosexual love as an inversion, and not a perversion, the latter label being attached more freely by him to certain sexual practices such as exhibitionism and voyeurism. Inversion is the only distinguishing mark of the homosexual, who in other respects need not be psychologically impaired, and may even be 'distinguished by specially high intellectual development and ethical culture' (Freud 1905: 49). In other words, a person's sexual orientation, whether gay, lesbian, bisexual or straight, is not in itself an indication of his or her psychological health: therapists have gay and straight clients who present a whole range of issues. Gay relationships may sometimes be presented as problematic, but this does not mean that all gay relationships are; and of course there are plenty of heterosexual relationships that are equally difficult. It is also important to recognize important distinctions between, as well as different issues for, gay men and lesbians. Simon observes that much liberal heterosexual thinking assumes that a gay or lesbian couple will function as a heterosexual couple. This they may do, but 'a gay couple's description of their behaviours which might not fit with the therapist's ideals may provoke discomfort, impatience and disapproval in the therapist and a retreat to more stereotypical beliefs about lesbian, gay and bisexual "psychology"' (1996: 106).

Simon goes on to suggest the importance of contextualizing a gay or lesbian couple within the experience of their own gay or lesbian community. We also have to recognize that where a society's, or a community's, or an organization's attitudes to gay men and lesbians (or indeed to any particular section of the society, such as black people or those with disability) is antipathetic, this causes distress. Gay and lesbian groups have rightly rejected the type of classification of their difficulties in psychiatry, behavioural therapy and psychoanalysis which has in the past labelled homosexuals as psychologically damaged. But in psychoanalytic circles, particularly in some of the more conservative societies, there still appear to be difficulties about accepting gay or lesbian candidates for training, as if in some way they are deficient in their psychological development. Psychoanalytic writing is as yet thin on the affirmation of homosexuality as a valid sexual orientation. Ratigan (1996), writing from a psychodynamic perspective, cites some positive approaches, including Lewes (1988) on male homosexuality and O'Connor and Ryan (1993) on lesbianism and psychoanalysis. Davies and Neal (1996) have assembled a collection of essays from a variety of theoretical perspectives that challenge the views of all therapists on gay and lesbian issues, with two further volumes extending the subject (Davies and Neal 2000; Neal and Davies 2000; see also Shelley 1998).

With the changing climate of opinion, clinical presentations about gay or lesbian identity *per se* are far less common than they once were. These issues are sometimes a concern, and may continue to be seen where older clients face up to a sexual orientation that they have perhaps suppressed from earlier in their life, when it was unacceptable for them to adopt any other path than the socially dictated one of heterosexual marriage.

In terms of the development of sexual aims (the persons to whom we wish to express our sexual feelings) we need constantly to remember that Freud's view was that bisexuality is part of normal development, and that indeed homosexual attachment is a normal part of the development of the mother–daughter, father–son relation. Homosexual expression of sexuality may even be a fairly normal feature in childhood and early adolescence, without it in any way dictating eventual sexual object choice. Loving, idealizing and sexual feelings are often directed initially to peers of the same gender (known in old magazines and books about school life as a 'crush'). These feelings are sometimes acted out in early adolescence. It is often helpful to reassure the anxious teenager on this point, without in any way dictating their sexual preference. A young person is free (external and internal psychological pressures notwithstanding) to develop as he or she wishes:

> Alex (now a young man) recalled that at his single-sex school he and other boys in their early teens had played fantasy games of who was going to marry whom amongst the other boys. Like other boys of that age, they would also compare the size of their penis and growth of their pubic hair. None of this was felt to be either abnormal or necessarily homosexual at the time, nor did it worry Alex now, despite more recent anxieties about his sexuality. At that time he had felt fine.

When there were more single-sex schools than now, same-sex relationships not only acted as a mirror to a developing young person, but also represented a rather better known, and therefore safer way of relating sexually. Co-education in most schools has changed much of the anxiety about relating to the opposite sex. There are still attractions, of course, to same-gender as well as opposite-gender peers, and to older students and staff: some things do not change. Attraction to older adolescents or adults of the same gender sometimes takes the form of admiration of someone who represents the man, or the woman, whom the young person wants to be like, this person often demonstrating physical or personal characteristics that the younger or less confident person would like to possess. We also need to remember that sexual identity – like other aspects of identity – is still plastic throughout adolescence, especially when there has been little or no sexual experience. It is often only by asking sensitively about the fantasies that people use when they masturbate, or when they get sexually excited, that a therapist gets a sense of where the client's dominant sexual orientation appears to lie:

> Barry, a student at university who had not yet had any sexual experience, found himself gazing at other young men who were well-built, good looking, and 'macho' in their relationships with others. The more he looked at these men, the more he feared that he was gay, although the thought of sex with a man turned him right off, and when asked about his fantasies when masturbating they were obviously only about women. In the course of counselling, these sexual anxieties were relatively quickly settled as Barry went on to look at other aspects of himself. He described how he swung between thinking himself 'top dog' (as he had been at home and at his school) and a 'right little shit' (which he had sometimes felt at home, but more often felt now he was at university). In comparing himself with the men he looked at, he felt the 'bottom dog' – a passive, somewhat anal image, and in the animal world a female position. So he felt cowed by these men whom he admired. There was a sense in which he wished he was inside them, or they inside him – which of course might have given rise to his homosexual anxiety. There was another element, because Barry also wished to be hugged by some of the men he admired, which might have been a way of latching on to some of their strength, and perhaps an indication of a wish to make up for a less than adequate relationship with his father. Given that in some cultures, such as the British, hugging by men can be considered threatening, it was little wonder that Barry felt confused about what his different feelings meant.

The false dichotomy between masculine and feminine has already been mentioned. This dichotomy is just as false when applied to sexual orientation, and the sexual positions that people adopt, despite the populist stereotypes of gay men as camp, and lesbians as butch. Therapists need to be especially aware that they do not get caught up in such stereotypical reactions or attitudes. It is often other factors, which are described throughout these major themes, that are relevant in helping a person reflect both on their sexual orientation, and the expression of their sexuality in relationships. Trust and attachment issues, questions of power and authority, autonomy and independence, parental attitudes, and societal pressures, personal experiences and private fantasies – all these contribute to the way any one individual works out his or her sexuality. Sometimes overconcentration upon sexuality itself masks the essential issues that actually make a person feel inadequate:

Clive had visited many gay clubs in search of a permanent relationship. When he came for counselling he was depressed and disillusioned, since his experience over the last year had consisted of one date after another, in which he had been picked up for a night, and then dropped. In therapy Clive began to recognize how submissive he was in these relationships, but he also realized that this submissiveness, as well as his difficulty in taking initiatives, applied just as much to his relationships with women, to whom he had been unable to relate, for that very reason. What was at issue were these interpersonal difficulties, and not his sexual orientation.

Despite over 100 years passing since Freud realized the importance of sexuality in the issues presented to a therapist, sex in both its heterosexual and homosexual expression is only just beginning to emerge from the closet. With the lid of repression and oppression in society lifted, psychodynamic therapists increasingly have to re-examine their attitudes, knowing that in following Freud they are seeking to understand one of the most basic forces in human relationships. Heterosexual relationships are complex enough, but in gay and lesbian communities there is a wide variety of lifestyles, as if in throwing off the yoke of heterosexuality, gays, lesbians and bisexuals have found an opportunity to experiment with restructuring sexual relationships. We need further research and experience in these matters: but bearing in mind the dangers of impressionistic judgements made from the narrow sample represented by client groups, it is possible that in some respects gay men have more in common with heterosexual men (that is to say, men tend to be more promiscuous than women) than they have with lesbians: lesbian relationships, for example, generally seem more stable, as heterosexual women are more stable than men in theirs.

Freud twice quoted a phrase of Napoleon's: 'Anatomy is destiny'. It is a quotation that has sometimes been turned against him by others who have questioned his views about men and women. Yet what we find in Freud about gender difference is an inevitable contradiction, to be expected when he wrote so much over so long a time and concerning such a wide range of topics. On the one hand he makes it clear that psychologically there is no reason to identify any differences between men and women. To equate men with being active, aggressive and independent, for example, and women with being passive, intuitive and sensitive, has no real basis in psychology, only in social convention. We see Freud touching here, as he does elsewhere, on the social construction of gender: 'all human individuals, as a result of their bisexual disposition and of cross-inheritance, combine in themselves both masculine and feminine characteristics, so that pure masculinity and femininity remain theoretical constructions of uncertain content' (1925b: 342). Freud also recognized the way social customs can force women into passive situations (1933/2003: 105). On the other hand Freud also argues that psychological development in boys and girls, while in common through the first two stages (oral and anal), divides at the phallic stage, because boys and girls engage with the Oedipus complex in different ways. Freud suggests that this leads to psychological differences in adult men and women, and he observes that women are not as harsh in their moral judgements as men. This is a rather accurate observation (at least in the society with which he was familiar), and is to some extent confirmed by Gilligan in her criticism and development of Kohlberg's study of moral development (see pp. 11–12). Freud's reasoning that women have not developed as strong a super-ego as men because they have never really left the Oedipal stage behind them may be questionable; but the point is well made, that there may be some psychological differences related to gender. However, we also have to consider that some of these differences may be due to the way society assigns certain roles to men and women, expecting women perhaps to respond in a different way to men.

Freud's understanding of male and female sexuality, and much of his writing upon the psychological development of women, has of course come under attack, partly from feminist writers. Feminist thought is not monolithic, and there are, as in any intellectual discourse, various opinions about how far Freud got it right or got it wrong. Popular feminist thought has moved from at one time wishing to emphasize how men and women are the same, to identifying the possibility of different ways of being and relating. I have already made some reference to these differences in Chapter 2. We have to be very careful therefore about sweeping generalizations, such as those found in Lowe (1972: 92), that boys are intrusive and girls inclusive. However, those who write from the feminist psychoanalytic perspective posit significant differences not just in society's views of men and women, but in the different way in which mothers relate to their sons and their daughters. They suggest that there may be something distinctive about the female psyche that, for example, 'while the basic feminine sense of self is connected to the world, the basic masculine self is separate' (Chodorow 1978: 162).

We need also to note there have been some important differences in the way male and female writers have approached these matters. I alluded in Chapter 2 to the criticism by feminist psychologists of the way in which many male writers, including Freud, seem to have taken male development as the norm, and anything different in female development as a deviation from the norm. These critics have attached greater force to the way in which society has contributed to gender roles, and argued that differences are neither innate nor unchangeable. Values and attitudes in Western society changed so rapidly through the 20th century that it is impossible to predict what directions the debate about psychological differences between men and women will take in the present century. What is clear is that therapists need to recognize the false dichotomy between masculine and feminine that is prevalent generally in society, and therefore in the attitudes of some of their clients, seen either in their mindset or in the attitudes to which those clients were subject when growing up. How might their parents have viewed and modelled gender relations? Clients (and therapists too) have been presented in the home, in the media, at school, and where relevant in their religion, with images and models of men and women, which will have influenced their view of themselves and others.

Working with men and women in therapy may involve helping them to develop other ways of being; for example, to help women caught in submissive or intertwined relationships to develop separateness; or for example, to enable men who fear closeness or homosexual feelings to develop their capacity for relatedness with other men as well as with women. Jung (1953) expresses similar ideas to those found in Freud, that there is a type of psychological as well as physical bisexuality, although Jung uses different terms: men need to acknowledge and find greater expression for the 'anima' (the female principle) that is part of their personality, and women for the 'animus' (the male principle). Jung's ideas are perhaps open to criticism, as equating masculine and feminine qualities with animus and anima, although his intention is far from that. Whichever way we look at these complex issues, in summary it is clear that therapists need to recognize that all the qualities that constitute the full emotional and interpersonal life are capable of being developed in both men and women clients. Each client, irrespective of gender, ideally needs to find the capacity as it is appropriate to be active and passive, rational and intuitive, assertive and sensitive, and to be able to be close to and separate from others of his or her own and the opposite gender. These are not rival qualities, but complementary.

In considering relationships between people as equals, it is essential to recognize and honour difference. Psychoanalytic thought has often appeared to equate difference with deviance from the norm. But we have to question what normality is, and whether what psychoanalysis has done (although it is common to psychology generally) is to devote so much attention to deviations from the norm, that it has not stopped long enough to study the norm, or to question whether there is a norm at all. Chodorow observes, for example, that in looking at the possible reasons for homosexual development, psychoanalysis has never given a satisfactory explanation of heterosexual development, and why that should be the way it is:

> ... heterosexuality has been assumed, its origins and vicissitudes have not been described: psychoanalysis does not have a developmental account of 'normal' heterosexuality (which is, of course a wide variety of heterosexualities) that compares in richness and specificity to accounts we have of the development of the various homosexualities and what are called perversions.
>
> (1994: 34)

No wonder gay therapists have asked the same questions of heterosexuals, as have been asked of them: 'When did you first realize you were heterosexual?' and so on. These are serious questions for those who study psychosexual development to address, not just questions that highlight bias and prejudice.

It can indeed be said of much psychoanalytic theory around sexuality, sexual orientation and about gender relations, that it is contentious. What we often find is that Freud's observations are perceptive, but that the explanations of those observations are not as complete as they could be; and sometimes they have been understood (at least by those less familiar with them) as dogmatic, literal statements. Freud (1925b: 332) can be self-effacing about his lack of understanding and the need for confirmation of his ideas before they can be considered of any value, but at other times he can be forceful in his descriptions, as in this example from the same paper, where he describes what he thinks a girl feels when she realizes she has not got a penis: 'She makes her judgement and her decision in a flash. She has seen it and knows that she is without it and wants to have it' (p. 336)!

One of the difficulties of using psychodynamic theory is that its terms are sometimes used literally, sometimes symbolically, and sometimes in a rather confusing mixture of both ways. Thus when Freud writes about the fear of castration in a man (or a little boy) or penis envy in a woman (or a little girl), he adduces these ideas partly from symbolic communications from his patients. At times he translates them into what may appear to be very narrow concepts, unless we in turn translate those terms back into their symbolical meaning. Freud also takes as his raw material both the events that his patients report, and their fantasies and dreams. Again this leads to confusion (especially so over reports of childhood abuse, another contentious subject that I take up in the next chapter), which is reflected in the contemporary debates that take place about these vital matters.

The question of genital difference is a case in point. Children are clearly interested in their bodies, in their parents' bodies, and in the bodies of their siblings and peers. Children ask questions, such as where babies come from and how they are born; and if they have some strange ideas about that, involving the stomach and food, and the rectum as the birth channel, these ideas are not so strange when parents speak of a new baby as being in mother's tummy, and when defecation is a major form of expulsion of matter from the body. Children are equally interested in and puzzled by sexual differences, and we might imagine how a little boy (without the knowledge that an older child has) might react to discovering that his mother, his sister or girl friend does not like him have a penis; or how a little girl reacts to seeing her father's, or her brother's, or a boy's penis. Indeed, we do not even have to imagine this, because children tell us, especially when they are not made to feel ashamed of interest in their bodies. The following comments were made in a child observation report by a trainee therapist learning about child development. He was observing a girl, who was at the time nearly 3 years old:

> She had watched her father in the toilet, and now wants a willy of her own. When taken to the doctor she asked him if he had a willy, and was greatly reassured to hear that he had. She expressed a desire to urinate standing up, like father does.
>
> A boy, a friend of the same age came to see her. 'He has a willy', she told her mother, and she wanted one also. She was only cheered up when mother told her that when she was grown up she would have breasts, which he would not have.
>
> A week later the little girl wanted to see the male observer's big toe. 'She pulled up her sweater to show me her stomach in an effort to get me to show her my big toe'. Later that day there was an episode when the little girl encouraged a friend who is a boy to 'shoot people with his gun'.

The first two paragraphs are clear – there is no symbolism there: she certainly wants a penis at that point of time. Freud may even be thought to be right at this stage: 'she has seen it and wants to have it'. But what is the third paragraph about? Is it purely about big toes and guns? Or is this a symbolic communication? In either of the incidents with the big toe and the gun, or both, is it possible to say that the little girl's actions are connected with her fascination with the penis? Some readers may feel it is right to make the connection. Others might only prefer to accept the evidence of what is obvious, being less impressed by the possibility of symbolic communication, although it has to be said that symbolic communication is a very important element in psychodynamic therapy. It does, however, need to be used judiciously.

If we wish to extrapolate from the little girl's interest we enter the field of speculation, although there may be other evidence in the trainee's observation which could support Freudian ideas. Might, for example, this child go on to ask the question 'Why?': 'Why has he got a penis? Why have I not got one?' Other observations through a psychoanalytic lens suggest these questions are asked, and psychoanalytic theory suggests some answers. One explanation (for the girl) is that she once had a penis, but that it has been taken away; and one possible fantasy (for the boy) is that if she has lost hers, then he might lose his too. Alternatively, such explanation or fantasies may arise not so much from within the child, as from the threats used by parents: we may wonder, for example, what the effect was on her son when a mother noticed him handling his penis and said: 'Do that again and I'll call the doctor to cut it off'. Whether or not she meant that as a symbolic message, she said it, and it must have sounded a horrifying possibility. If this seems an isolated incident, I recall a group of young mothers discussing this very example in an adult education class, and recognizing a parallel in a local expression several of them playfully used with both their sons and daughters: 'If you're naughty I'll cut your tail off'. It was an expression that had been used by their mothers to them, and which they used with their children without thinking that it might cause them any anxiety. We do not know, of course, how their children understood such words, or whether different children might have reacted differently. But it is possible that the only tail the children could identify was a boy's penis.

The symbolic significance of genital differences should not be underestimated, but for the moment it is useful to stay with more literal interpretations. While it is unlikely that every child has thoughts similar to those quoted earlier, it is equally possible that other children may have different explanations, some of them equally bizarre, about the reasons for genital differences. In adults too we find both literal and symbolic statements. Some clients show clear evidence of penis envy, as described in psychoanalytic theory. The two examples that follow show this in a man and in a woman. Literal penis envy is probably more obvious in boys and men (centring round the size or length of the penis) than it is in women; and if at times symbols appear to relate to the penis, sometimes the penis itself has symbolic significance, as I shortly explain:

Winston greatly admired his father, whom he described as a 'big man' in his business. His father was looked upon fondly by everyone, but was frequently denigrated by Winston's mother as not being assertive enough of his own rights. Winston wanted to be like his father and rise to the top of the same profession, but he could never follow through the opportunities that might have led to this. The only time he had ever criticized his father was when his father had given him a wallet, because it was a plastic one, and not like the large leather one his father possessed. Winston threw it through a closed window in his temper. It seemed to symbolize his own feeling of inferiority. Winston treated his wife as inferior too, as if she embodied the inferior side of himself. He constantly drew attention to her mistakes, denigrating her (as mother had done father). He was deferential to his male therapist, although he spoke of relations to other authority figures as often fraught: he was frequently angry at their power over him. He usually made such situations worse by lashing out at them in a manner that reminded the counsellor of the way a child can hit out at an adult – ferociously but ineffectively.

In his dreams Winston would sometimes see himself as a woman in the presence of others whom he would identify as gay men, whom he had met socially, and who at the time of his therapy were also looked down upon in the circles in which he moved. The therapist drew upon the implication of this imagery to illustrate how Winston felt inferior (like a woman in society), and that he felt weak and powerless in his transactions with other men. In his dreams he 'castrated' himself, becoming a woman and submitting to other men. Winston was thrilled one day when he was able to stand up to the driver of a huge lorry who had forced him off his pedal bike, even though inside himself he felt like running away.

The imagery used throughout this example (lorry/bike, man/woman, leather/plastic wallet) appears to link symbolically to the terms 'penis envy', or 'penis inferiority'. This thought occurred to the therapist, although he did not put it into words. But it appeared to be confirmed when the therapist drew Winston's attention to his envy of his father's wallet. Winston responded with his own association to this, that he remembered once seeing his father's penis, and thinking how big it was compared to his own.

> Yvonne had come for counselling because she was unable to enjoy sexual intercourse with her husband. Much that she said pointed to her wish to be a man, although she did not use so open an expression. She said that she liked 'to wear the trousers', and did not permit her husband to take the initiative in sex. She was very excited by pin-ups of women, and could only allow penetration if she was on top of her husband. She preferred watching him masturbate, or bringing herself to a climax with a vibrator (her own penis). She was turned on by reading letters in male magazines about men's erections. Furthermore, she enjoyed rifle-shooting, and she once cornered an instructor at the shooting range and told him what a 'lovely cock' he had, although having excited him she would not let him have sex with her. Although Yvonne never acknowledged that she envied the penis, she often expressed envy of her brother, who was very successful in his career, and who she felt was her parents'

favourite. She also envied men all the privileges they had; but what was interesting was that she was as opposed to the feminist movement as if she had been the most chauvinist type of man.

We do of course live in a culture that has absorbed much Freudian thinking and mythology: 'He is no more a person now but a whole climate of opinion', Auden (1976) wrote of Freud. We must always make an allowance for some clients using these Freudian images and terms, either because they have learned them from their milieu, or because that is what they think a therapist expects to hear. Even if this is the case, the symbolism can become an effective way of reflecting upon the wider context of a client's relationships; and on occasion the imagery may even need to be taken rather more literally.

As we pursue this symbolic path, we come to realize that in other ways Freud's thinking was too narrow. For example, while he has much to say about the significance of the penis envy in women and castration anxiety in men for the psychosexual development of men and women, he says nothing comparable about the significance of the womb, or breasts for both women and men. Karen Horney observes that there are young boys who express the wish to have breasts or who wish they could bear children (Rubins 1978: 149). There are also suggestions in later psychoanalytic ideas that each gender wishes to rediscover early feelings of completeness and unity, and that this is represented by the desire to possess the opposite sex, of which the breast or the penis is a part-object symbolization (for example, the French psychoanalyst Lacan; see Benvenuto and Kennedy 1986).

Another expression that is used in current psychoanalytic discourse is 'phallus', which originally meant the penis as an organ, but is used in a new way to mean the penis as a symbol of power. Thus it is possible to speak of a 'phallic woman' or the 'phallic mother', as a woman or as a mother who exercises power over the child, a power that the child wishes to possess, and of which the child feels envy. The equation of breast and penis in Kleinian theory similarly uses both part-objects as symbolic of each other, but also as symbolic of the powerful mother, who can give and can destroy. A man's fear of a woman's vagina, that she may use it to cut off his penis (vagina dentata – with teeth!) may then be a 'spill over' (as Segal (1992: 45) puts it) from fears of the damage that could be done by the mother, or a projection of the fear of damaging the mother by biting the nipple.

In classical times the phallus represented both the erect penis and the ruling power. We may therefore consider the appropriateness of the term 'penis envy' if it is translated not just into individual symbolism (the baby and the phallic mother) but into the way in which women, in particular in society and in the family, rightly seek equality with men. Men have dominated women through the patriarchal organization and assumptions of society and its institutions, even to the extent of calling women 'the second sex'. In working with individual clients, therapists need to be aware of the actual oppression of the engines of society, as well as the real economic and political issues that may have bearing on the client, currently as well as in any past oppression suffered by the family. Freud clearly recognized these pressures, and even if some of his assumptions about women are limited by the political and cultural climate in which he lived, he breaks sufficiently free of the mores of his time to assert that marriage, for example, as practised in his society, was damaging to a woman's mental health. Freud (1908/2002: 98–9) is especially critical of the double standards that allow men a different sexual morality.

The external world, which includes politics and society, is as important in its effect on the psyche as internal processes. Some writers, such as Winnicott, see engagement with the wider world as the ultimate in personal maturity, where the adult is able 'to identify with the environment, and take part in the establishment, maintenance and alteration of the environment' (1965a: 102). Samuels observes that Jung too appears to have thought that those who had become individuated through analysis would have a decisive effect on the world scene. Combining Jungian, Freudian and Kleinian ideas about maturity in a composite definition, Samuels appears to question whether by itself analysis achieves this object: 'The person who, via analysis conforms to the reality principle, has achieved ego mastery, become genital, or reached the depressive position, is often represented as belonging to an elite that is . . . less susceptible to the group psychological pressures of the social and political world that they inhabit' (1993: 55). Samuels himself believes particular attention has to be paid to political development of the individual, although until the individual has acquired a sufficient sense of personal power, those wider issues are not capable of being contemplated.

The individualism of much therapy and counselling, and the introspective nature of many therapists, does not give much hope of their taking on political issues as a necessary adjunct to their work with individuals. There are some signs that this is happening, but changing the system is a daunting task. As Seidler writes, 'the connections between the inner and the outer world are more direct but also more difficult'; therapy can 'help us to treasure individuality while keeping sight of the importance of transforming relations of power and subordination'. He observes that therapy has the potential to deepen our sense of injustice but at the same time 'it limits our sense of politics as we learn to expect less from political changes', and 'take responsibility for our emotional lives' (1991: 191).

Oedipus myth and Oedipus complex

The personal and the political themes feature in Sophocles' drama of *Oedipus Rex*, and are a clear reminder of the way in which the fate of the individual is reflected in society at large. But it is generally for other reasons that the Oedipus myth assumes importance in psychoanalytic therapy. Freud made it clear there are four cornerstones to psychoanalytic theory: unconscious mental processes; repression and resistance; infantile sexuality; and the Oedipus complex. These four concepts are equally important to a contemporary psychodynamic approach, although they need translating into the ordinary language of the consulting room.

The Oedipus complex takes its cue from Sophocles' tragedy, which Freud recognized initially as relevant to his own experience:

A single idea of general value dawned on me. I have found, in my own case too, [the phenomenon of] being in love with the mother and jealous of my father, and now I now consider it a universal event in early childhood ... If this is so, we can understand the gripping power of *Oedipus Rex*, in spite of all the objections that reason raises against the presupposition of fate ... the Greek legend seizes upon a compulsion which everyone recognizes because he senses its existence within himself. Everyone in the audience was once a budding Oedipus in fantasy, and each recoils in horror from the dream fulfilment here transplanted into reality, with the full quantity of repression which separates his infantile state from his present one.

(Masson 1985: 272).

In the rest of this chapter I will concentrate upon the Oedipus myth and the Oedipus complex as they are played out in relationships. In the next chapter I will look further at examples of the significance of Oedipal relationships of one kind or another. There we shall see how actual abuse or abusive attitudes affect adult survivors, and how abuse can be perpetrated by members of a child's family, by grandparents, parents or siblings, as well as by teachers, clergy, care staff, or even (but much more rarely) strangers. What goes wrong in some families is reflected in the Oedipus story. Relationships will always contain some elements that are symbolized in the Oedipus myth, but in healthy families the extremes of that story do not occur. The Oedipus complex certainly lives up to its name, because it contains many possibilities of resolution. It includes normal development (even if there is wide variety in what is considered 'normal').

The Oedipus complex has itself acquired something of the status of a myth. It is understood mistakenly as about sons literally wanting to murder their father and marry their mother, or girls wishing to murder their mother and marry their father, with the erroneous term 'Electra complex' being coined, even though it is not part of psychoanalysis. But what Freud writes about is a fantasy – a dream – which in the play itself gets played out in reality, and becomes therefore shocking to those who witness the play. A dream: indeed Jocasta uses that word – 'many a man has dreamt as much. Such things must be forgotten if life is to be endured'. Freud is not saying that the conscious wish is there to murder one parent and have sex with the other, but that there is a fantasy which in his opinion everyone shares. His is in fact a somewhat paler version of the Oedipus story – which in his own case is described more as love of mother and jealousy of father than anything necessarily stronger. We know he was horrified when he once saw his mother naked – and in Freud's view even witnessing parental sex is horrifying because it rouses the unconscious wishes which we normally keep well out of sight.

Oedipus certainly killed his father and married his mother, and then blinded himself when he discovered what he had done. But the original story is much richer than that. Laius and Jocasta, the rulers of the city-state of Thebes, were expecting their first child, but were told by the oracle at Delphi that their son would grow up to murder his father and marry his mother. Because they feared both incest and patricide (they too wanted to avoid what they knew to be wrong), Laius ordered a servant to take the baby to a mountainside and leave him to be devoured by wild animals. Bettelheim observes the significance of this abandonment: 'Oedipus acted as he did because his parents completely rejected him as an infant' (1983: 22–3). But fate was not to be thwarted, because the servant instead softened and gave the baby to a shepherd from a neighbouring state. The shepherd took the baby to Corinth, where the rulers Polybus and Merope were childless. They adopted the child as their own son and Oedipus grew up believing Polybus and Merope were his real parents.

A chance remark at court sent Oedipus to the oracle at Delphi to question his origins, and the oracle informed him too that he was destined to kill his father and marry his mother. Believing Polybus and Merope to be his real parents, Oedipus vowed not to return to Corinth, because he also wished to avoid such heinous crimes, unaware of course that he was much safer in Corinth than anywhere else. On his travels he got involved in a brawl with a nobleman and killed him, not knowing either that it was Laius or that Laius was his father. Further on his travels he came upon Thebes, a city racked by plague and famine, and there he rid the city of the malign influence of the sphinx by solving its riddle: what is it that in the beginning of life goes on four legs, in midlife on two and at the end on three? The answer was 'man'. As a reward Oedipus was offered the widowed Jocasta in marriage, and he became the ruler of Thebes.

A few years passed, and another plague overwhelmed the city: the oracle suggested that it was because the death of Laius had gone unavenged. Oedipus resolved to find the murderer, and set about calling witnesses who might help him get at the truth. Sophocles' drama resembles a piece of early Freudian psychoanalysis (or perhaps analysis resembles the play) as Oedipus pursues the truth, but cannot see it when it is staring him in the eyes. He finds relief when he learns that Polybus has died a natural death, but is soon again in anguish when the same messenger tells him that he is not Polybus's natural son. Jocasta recognizes the truth first, that she has married and borne children by her long-forgotten son. When Oedipus discovers her body, where in remorse she has hanged herself, he blinds himself with the pins of her brooches. Bettelheim observes that he does this as much for failing in knowledge (not seeing) as for the crimes themselves: 'Oedipus acted out his metaphorical blindness – his blindness to what the oracle had meant, based on his lack of knowledge of himself – by depriving himself of his eyesight' (1983: 23).

There are many different levels upon which any myth can be interpreted. Bettelheim observes how much rejection and lack of knowledge lie at the centre of the Oedipus story. It also deals with fate, or as it might be expressed, the question of determinism and free will. Oedipus certainly had the fates stacked against him. What Freud found telling in the myth is the idea that in every child there is a desire for closeness with the first love object, a desire that at first is met in the intimacy of the mother–baby relationship. As the child grows older mother and child have to separate, a complex process in which both child and parent need to find the right balance between love and intimacy, without becoming over-close, sexual, or incestuous. As I will show in the next chapter, Oedipus's fate may be repeated when either or both parents reject the child's love and sexuality, or when either emotionally or sexually overstimulates the child. In successful resolution of this stage children learn that their love and their innocent sexuality are accepted. Through a positive relationship to both parents they identify with them both, and form a good enough but not over-close relationship with them both. A child can then begin the process of growing away from parental ties, so that later in adult life he or she can form intimate relationships of her or his own outside the family, based upon identification with the parents and with their relationship with each other. Such identification often includes negative as well as positive features.

Early psychoanalytic writing placed the Oedipus complex at the age of about four or five. That timing was based on the idea that in the oral and anal stages of development a child's relationships are essentially dyadic. The themes of trust and attachment concentrate upon the maternal side of the parent–child interplay (even if other women, and fathers, may play a part in the mothering), a one-to-one dyadic relationship. The theme of authority has much that is paternal about it, even though mothers as well as fathers are authority figures – Samuels (1993: 133–5), for example, writes about 'the father of whatever sex'. Fathers are traditionally seen as authoritarian figures, although it is often mothers who carry the bulk of the responsibility, sometimes invoking the name of the father as a threat. These may be called one-by-one relationships, still in essence dyadic. In both these stages (so more traditional theory runs) it is felt that the child relates to mother or to father, but not to mother and father as a couple.

By the time the third stage is reached one-to-one and one-by-one relationships broaden out, to recognition that the parents have their own relationship. Similarly siblings are related to more fully. In play, within and outside the home, children begin to interact properly with each other, not just playing singly in each other's company, or using each other as objects to be manipulated as part of their play. Three-person relationships have now become significant, and with the recognition of three persons there are new conflicts about who goes with whom, and who gets left out. Two's company, three's a crowd.

So runs a typical Freudian interpretation. It goes on to suggest that children have *fantasies* of killing off the parent of the same gender, and having the other parent all to themselves. Such ideas are present in dreams and nightmares, as well as in innocent expressions of affection, like the 6-year-old boy who said, 'If anything happens to Daddy, I'll marry you, Mummy'; or the 8-year-old girl who said to her mother, 'I'll never find anyone as good as Daddy to marry'. There are inevitably rages when a child wishes one of the parents dead, but such thoughts are normally soothed by bedtime. There are bound to be times when a child feels jealous of the parents' relationship, and comes into their bed, not just to share their closeness as before, but also to separate them, so that the child can have either of them to themselves. Children and adults are not normally conscious of any wish for sex with their parents, although as Jocasta says in the play, 'many a man hath dreamt as much'. They learn that their wish for intimacy has limits set on it by both parents; they recognize their parents' own intimacy; and, encouraged by social factors such as going to school and so beginning to leave the home, children take further steps towards separating from mother and father.

Later Freudian thinking (aided by Kleinian theory which places the Oedipus complex in the first year, not the fourth or fifth year) is broader. The three-person relationship can be used as both a literal and metaphorical idea, as, for example, when we acknowledge the presence of the father in the early months of life, acting as a natural force against the baby's intense wish for mother: 'fathers are also felt to come between the baby and the breast, separating them and destroying phantasies of fusion with an internal and external mother/breast' (Segal 1992: 49); or in the way in which a mother, in weaning her child, comes between her child and her breast, the mother acting as a third force. Three-person, or three-object situations arise throughout life: such as the parent who comes between a child and her faeces, taking them away from her; or in the struggle implicit in Freud's model of personality structure between ego, id and super-ego (the latter perhaps coming between the first two). Nor are Oedipal anxieties confined to infancy. At adolescence sons, daughters and parents often do not quite know how to manage intimate feelings which previously had been expressed naturally, such as a hug or a kiss, since each is in some way conscious of the sexuality of the other. In adult life, triangular relationships are a common feature, as the next chapter demonstrates.

A further aspect of Oedipal issues relates to the earlier discussion about gender and sexual orientation. The traditional Freudian view about the development of infantile sexuality is that boys and girls follow a common path of psychological development up to the Oedipal stage, but that they then negotiate the Oedipus complex in quite distinct ways. Both boys and girls start life literally attached, and after birth emotionally attached, to mother. It is probably with her that they relate most closely in their early years, and it is probably with her that they mostly wish to share their love. Boys have to make a transition from directing their love towards mother in childhood, to sexual intimacy with other women from adolescence onwards. The woman to whom the young man is later attracted often has some psychological resemblance to his mother. Father plays a significant role, because in the Oedipal stage he represents the barrier to a close relationship with mother. He is also a model for the boy of what he would like to be. Freud believed that boys wish for a close relationship with father too, and in that case mother comes between son and husband. In this triangular situation a boy wishes to push mother away, and get closer to father, and in order to do so identifies with mother. He identifies too with his father, as well as (Freud believes) fears father's punishment for his desire for mother. It can be seen that this is all more complicated than the simple 'kill father, marry mother' formula as it has been popularly understood.

Oedipal resolution is not a smooth path for boys, even if at first it appears relatively straightforward given that (for many of them) their love object in adult life is the same gender as mother. It is generally supposed that it is an even harder path for girls, and it can be seen why. Their first love object, their mother, is a homosexual attachment, and they (in most instances) move from this to heterosexual love. That means separating from mother. But father is a temporary love object, because girls have to make yet another shift away from father towards other men. Such a double shift may appear to carry with it a greater risk of problems than a single shift of object. It is suggested by Freud that this leads to a different resolution of the Oedipus complex: the significance of fathers for boys is that they drive boys out of the Oedipus complex; but in the case of girls, fathers take them into it, and they never completely leave it.

Yet these differences in Oedipal paths occur earlier than the standard idea of an Oedipal stage. A number of feminist writers who are also psychotherapists (for example, Belotti 1975) have described, as Freud himself suggested, how mothers tend to nurture their daughters less generously than their sons. However, they also observe how mothers identify more with their baby daughters than their sons (Chodorow 1989: 47–50). If there is truth in these observations, it may mean that it is less easy for a girl to detach herself from mother from whom she still wants more. Men often fail to recognize that women want mothering as much as men do; there are often problems because a man takes a woman's wish for comfort as her wanting sexual contact whereas it often is an expression of the wish for comfort alone. In the following example, the young woman was still attached to a mother-substitute, not yet ready to integrate the sexual into her relationship with her partner:

> Zoë did not know how to cope with her partner's wish for sex. As long as he was caring, did things for her, bought her presents, and was kind towards her, the relationship went well. But when he wanted to sleep with her, not only did she feel anxious and refuse him, but she turned to her close girl friend for sex. As long as her partner was maternal Zoë appeared to be happy; as soon as he wanted to be 'male', she was driven back to a homosexual love object, and to her need for a mother figure alone.

It is the greater difficulty of detachment for a girl from the same gender as mother that helps us to understand what is in some instances a greater tempestuousness in adolescence in a mother–daughter relationship than we are likely to find in mother–son or father–daughter relations. Since a heterosexual young woman has to make such a major change, from a female to a male love object, and not just a change of person in her object choice, she needs more assertiveness if her wish for separateness is to overcome her wish to remain attached. Even then many mother–daughter relationships remain very close. Chodorow confidently comments from 'near-universal clinical observations' on how 'a woman is pre-occupied with her mother as an internal image and object and that this intrapsychic pre-occupation helps shape her love relationships (and much else about her intrapsychic and interpersonal life)' (1994: 83).

The more deeply the Oedipal situation is examined in the literature, the less straightforward it is to suggest that one or other gender has an easier or more difficult time of it. It used to be thought that successful resolution of the Oedipus complex led to heterosexual object choice; and that homosexuality represents the negative Oedipus complex, where love for the parent of the opposite gender has not occurred as it 'should' have: a boy, for example, has overidentified with his mother, or has to be literally submissive to father in the Oedipal struggle; or that a girl has not been able to separate from her original homoerotic love for her mother. Such views in psychodynamic thinking are now reckoned to be simplistic, partly because the gay and lesbian community has rightly challenged straight psychologists and psychoanalysts on such questions, and partly because the variations in development are now given fuller recognition. Chodorow refers to the work of Kenneth Lewes, in which he takes classical theory apart, especially for boys. She observes the complication that even in heterosexual development a boy's identification with his father can only take place if father is also a love object:

> Lewes suggests that the origins of normal heterosexuality in the Oedipus complex are much more complicated than Freud and those that follow him believed. He describes twelve different possible oedipal constellations for the boy: depending upon whether his attachment is anaclitic [someone unlike self] or narcissistic [someone like self], whether he takes himself or his father or his mother as object, whether this mother is phallic or castrated, whether he identifies with father or (phallic or castrated) mother, and whether his own sexual stance is passive or active. Six of these constellations are heterosexual but only one ... is 'normal'.
>
> (1994: 43)

This passage illustrates what variations we need as therapists to recognize in the negotiation of Oedipal issues. The need to leave parents to their own relationship, and to form intimate, sexual partnerships of one's own is a common task for many people, although we also have to acknowledge that some choose to remain single. Each person undergoes their own Oedipus complex, so that as Chodorow urges at the conclusion of her short book re-examining these matters: 'We must investigate individually how any person's sexual orientation and organization, erotic fantasy, and practices arise from anatomy, from cultural valuation and construction, from intrapsychic solutions to conflict, from family experience and from gender identity. All these will enter the individual case of how any woman or man loves' (p. 91).

Difficulties arise when the issues around sexuality and the limits of its expression are made more obvious, less natural, and more bewildering than they already are, through the action of parents and others acting them out: when a child or young person feels that one parent's attention takes precedence over feelings for the other parent; when the parents' relationship is so bad that the child is terrified of the wish to split them; when sexual feelings for the child are expressed or acted upon directly or indirectly by the parent; when death or separation takes one parent away; or when a child experiences her or his love and sexuality as being rejected. At those times elements of the Oedipus myth are repeated, inevitably affecting intimate relationships later in adult life. As Chodorow writes: 'How women and men love will be heavily influenced, though not determined, by their navigation through the relationships and fantasies of early childhood, and this is the terrain that we think of as more typically psychoanalytic' (p. 82). The next chapter shows the different forms that the Oedipus complex can take.

COOPERATION AND COMPETITION: OEDIPAL CONFIGURATIONS

Francis Grier writes, in his introduction to *Oedipus and the Couple*:

> In the myth of Oedipus we are confronted with a number of couples. First, there is the couple of Laius and Jocasta, the king and queen of Thebes. They are immediately presented to us as a couple who cannot cope with a threesome relationship. As soon as their first child is born they feel under deadly threat; their equilibrium is fatally undermined.
>
> (2004: 1–2)

Grier observes that one of the reasons that this couple might not be able to cope with a threesome relationship is that the prophecy that their son will grow up to murder the father and marry the mother is perhaps a projection of their own feelings towards the child – the strong emotions both of hatred of the rival which perhaps was Laius's reaction to the birth, or the strong desires of the mother for her baby, the projection of Jocasta's emotions. But they cannot, Grier observes, contain those emotions, 'to allow the more difficult and complex relationship to develop emotional maturity in response to its demands' (p. 2).

A two-person relationship becomes a threesome when the first child is born. This is the most obvious way of interpreting the Oedipus myth, and indeed this is what lies behind Freud placing the Oedipus complex as a developmental task that engages the threesome of child, father and mother. In his view this occurs at a point where the child is engaging more fully in three-person relationships, recognizing that his parents are a couple and have a prior claim on each other. If the child cannot accept the threesome as he or she develops, as much as if one or both the parents cannot accept the threesome when the child is born, then this can have negative consequences for later relationships in adulthood.

The Oedipus complex therefore focuses on the impact of a third person, and how the intrusion of a third person alters for good or for ill a couple relationship, whether that couple be mother and baby, parent and child, or two adults in a close relationship. If we think in terms of a triangle, there are then a variety of triangular situations where the Oedipus metaphor throws light upon them. Far from this being purely negative, however, there is a definite sense in which working through the situation, or as psychoanalysis terms it, the resolution of the Oedipus complex, leads to more wholesome relationships.

Triangular situations

The Oedipus myth highlights the consequences of rejection of a child who threatens the marriage of a couple. While the birth of a child is often an occasion for the renewal and deepening of a couple's relationship as they find a new role together as parents, it can also be the trigger for a couple's relationship taking a downturn (see Figure 10.1).

baby

mother   partner

Figure 10.1 The triangle of mother–baby–partner.

A common example, according to Grier (2005: 5), is when a couple feel that the biological clock is ticking away, and that they should have children, although each partner is still wedded to enjoying his or her own individual life – where there are no children to hold him or her back from doing what they wish – and are enmeshed in each other. The child interferes with this, threatens independence, and may be feared as taking love away from them, as if love is a finite quantity that will be depleted in being shared.

As the child grows, this fear of exclusion may grow: for instance, one partner, fearing that he or she is going to be excluded from the partner's love by the child, or perhaps experiencing a change in the other partner ('not the person you were', another example of a third element) may foster instead the love of the child, creating a relationship that feeds that person's needs through the child, and then indeed does exclude the other partner. Morgan (2005: 19–20) gives an example of a husband who became very involved in a new business he was developing, and the wife who was very involved with their baby, and each sought to escape from this painful couple situation through work and the baby respectively. And we know from the people we see in the consulting room, those who as children saw their parents splitting apart, whether or not they stayed in the relationship, can feel that they are themselves responsible for the split. John Le Carré wrote of what a child can feel in his novel *Tinker, Tailor, Soldier, Spy* and in a later interview confirmed that he drew upon his own experience: 'Most of all he blamed himself for the break-up of his parents' marriage' (1974: 15). A variation on this might be seen in a different example, where a child expressed concern lest the parents' rows meant that they would split up. Yet the rows often occurred because the father, who was absent most of the week on business, returned to his wife and son, who had developed a very close relationship – the son almost taking the emotional place of the father when he was absent from the home (see Figure 10.2). The child appeared to resent the father returning, as the father resented the way his son appeared to get the mother's attention more than he did; so the son's fear was also about his wish that father would go for good – a thought too difficult to admit, hence anxiety lest the fantasy became reality.

returning father

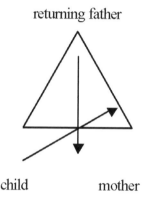

child   mother

Figure 10.2 The triangle of child–returning father–mother

As Grier points out, the third party may not be a person. One or both partners will probably in one way or another change over the years – they may take up an interest which was not important at the start of the couple relationship; one or other is quite likely to change in some way in their personality, so that the new interest or the change that takes place in the partner becomes something like the child, meaning that the couple need to adapt to take account of this third element.

The intrusion of a third element may be that of a person, or of an aspect of that person (see Figure 10.3). Another obvious third element is the person whom we indeed call 'the third party' involved in one or other partner's affair outside the marital or marital-equivalent relationship. But this third person may well reflect an element of the primary relationship which from the beginning was not present, and was therefore sought outside the marriage, or which has become impossible to fully access within the marriage and is therefore split off outside it.

For example, Martin had been married for 22 years, and his partner appeared in many ways to have been a good mother to their children, and an

partner B as s/he is now

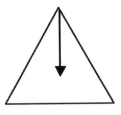

partner A   partner B as s/he was then

Figure 10.3 The triangle of partner A–partner B as s/he is now–partner B as
s/he was then

aspiring partner in relation to their ambition as a couple – her drive meant
that he had been encouraged, to put it positively, or pushed, to put it more
negatively, to do well in his career to ensure that they were provided with an
ideal home. But his wife was much too much like his father in that respect,
ambitious, and critical, and their sexual relationship had never been satisfactory, partly because her energetic drive made him impotent with her.
Martin had a series of mistresses who enjoyed his love-making and com-
plemented him upon it. In this type of Oedipal situation he could not bring
together his energies as a home provider and his energies as a lover into the
one relationship. So we have a triangle which may partly have arisen because
of his wife's dominance of the partnership, but partly as a result of his own
failure to stand up to his wife in more ways than one (see Figure 10.4).

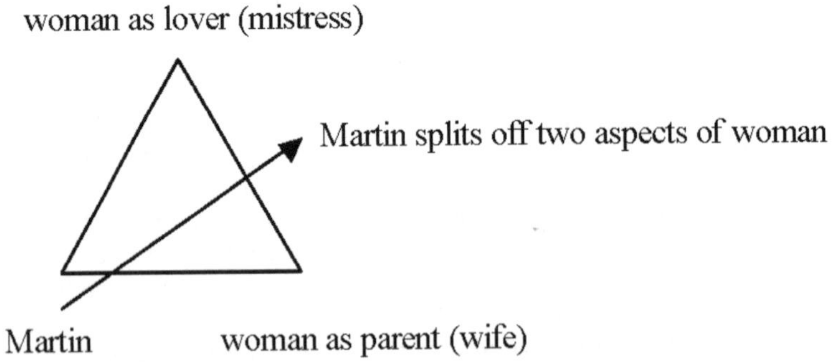

woman as lover (mistress)

Martin splits off two aspects of woman

Martin   woman as parent (wife)

Figure 10.4 Martin's triangle

These triangles are obviously all slightly different but what unites them is
that there are three clear elements, and one or more occupants of the points
of the triangle feels left out by the relationship between the other two.
Martin's triangle is not so capable of being resolved as the others could be,
where all three elements relate equally well together. In his case he splits his
attachments between two people, because he cannot unite them in one

person. The better triangle here would be if his wife and he could relate both as home builders/parents and as lovers.

In fact the same dynamic is present in all four triangles (Figures 10.1–10.4): the resolution of the Oedipus complex is not that one element in the triangle must be rejected, but that there is acceptance of both separateness and relatedness, or as Morgan calls it 'the experience of being included and excluded' (2005: 12). In other words the partner need not feel pushed out by the baby but recognizes that there are different types of relationship – mother and baby, partner and baby, mother and partner – each of which is valid in its own right, but each of which in some respects cannot intrude upon the other relationships. Oedipal resolution also means being able to relate separate aspects in one relationship, without feeling that one element will dominate or occlude the other. Separateness and relatedness is a good shorthand phrase for a satisfactory model of mature relationships

Martin's case illustrates another Oedipal situation, where the partner has been unconsciously chosen because he or she reflects father or mother, or where the relationship is such that the partner is always treated as if she or he were like one or both of the parents. Martin's father intruded upon Martin's relationship with his wife, because he carried a picture of his father inside him, which he projected onto his wife, reacting to much that she said as if she were just like his father. Lanman (2005: 156) gives another example of an Italian woman who was naturally expressive. But her mother had always lived in the shadow of her father, and indeed had had a breakdown, perhaps for that reason. When the daughter met her partner, she was an unconventional and colourful person, and yet may have been drawn to her partner because he was an apparently solid and strong person – perhaps someone *unlike* her mother. So here is one aspect of her choice. But once they got together she seemed to submit herself to her partner as much as her mother had done to her father. Her partner had his own history, having been sent to live with relatives when his parents went abroad to work. His mother had been grief stricken by this separation, so perhaps he was drawn to his wife's freedom and exuberance. But then he found himself trying to cut down that exuberance just as his own had been when he had been separated from his mother.

Here the relationship has to cope with the intrusion of figures from the past – not literally present, but present at an unconscious level in the way one or both partners relate to each other, so that they play out past relationships with their parents, or between their parents, in their own relationship (see Figure 10.5).

The intrusive element can of course be a relationship with a parent that is just as strong in the present, or feared by the other to be as strong in the present, as any past relationship may have been. As Morgan writes: 'Couples psychotherapists frequently see couples in which one or both partners are still too enmeshed in a relationship with a parent' (2005: 13), and where there is a lack of emotional investment in their partner. There has not been a sufficient break of the tie – sometimes of course called 'mother's apron strings' – so that emotional energy can be more fully invested in the new relationship. Morgan also observes that children can be drawn in as a supporter or confidant of mother or father, causing problems for the child's own Oedipal development,

internalized parental relationships

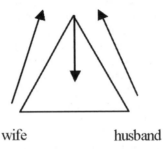

wife   husband

Figure 10.5 The triangle of wife–internalized parent–husband

which crucially involves both separateness and relatedness with *both* parents (p. 13).

Grier (2005: 204–8) provides an example of a couple who had a row because his wife was furious that her partner wanted to celebrate his birthday by having his mother to stay. While they both saw the matter of the invitation to his mother as a separate issue from their presenting problem of having no sex after the birth of their second child, there was a sense in which his wife was right to be jealous, since he had never properly separated from his depressed mother and did not want to lose the special closeness he had with her. He would sometimes telephone his mother secretly, as if he felt there was something not right about the relationship between him and his partner and his mother. If we bring into this equation part of his wife's history, that her own father appears to have preferred her to her mother, we can see how she might not only have denigrated her husband as never being as good as her father whom she idealized, but also how she perhaps feared being excluded by the relationship between him and his mother, just as her own mother might have feared exclusion by the relationship between her and her father (see Figure 10.6).

There is yet another way of looking at the triangle as a model for understanding couple relationships. The starting point is that we know that genetically it is good for a species to reproduce through mixing the gene pool – that is one reason on a biological level that incestuous sexual relationships

husband's mother

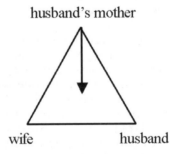

wife   husband

Figure 10.6 The triangle of wife–husband's mother–husband

are risky, leading sometimes through inbreeding to weaknesses or deformities in the offspring. The same desirability of mixing is perhaps equally true of psychological relationships – perhaps it even lies behind Plato's mythical idea of human beings needing to meet their other half – woman and man complementing one another psychologically as well as physically. Rosenthall observes: 'The partners in a couple must have relating styles that are complementary to each other's, although what we often see is a more complex picture with each partner changing positions at different points' (2005: 182).

There will perhaps always be a debate about whether like attracts like, or whether opposites are attracted to each other. There is an exercise in Skynner and Cleese's *Families: And How to Survive Them* (1983) where strangers in a large group are asked to pick out a partner in the room who either reminds them of a member of their own family of origin, or who would fill a gap in their family of origin. Their choice may therefore be the same or different from their family of origin. This pairing then chooses another pair on the same grounds, and the four compare notes about their families of origin. This is an exercise I have conducted many times, and it is remarkable indeed, as Skynner and Cleese observe, how many similarities there are in the families of origin in each group of four, which are not necessarily replicated in the other groups. It seems as if even without knowing people we are drawn like to like.

However, there is evidence from some casework that where couples come together sharing the same characteristics in their family of origin, this can make for difficulty – there is not sufficient variety in their personality differences, and they seem to be drawn to someone who narcissistically mirrors themselves. While it may be felt to be very cosy and comfortable to begin with, this can obviously lead to difficulties as each person grows – or finds that apart from shared positives, there are also shared negatives. The seeking out of someone who shares the same background – so that the relationship is not able to engage with the 'otherness' of the other as well – is a collusive choice, which may spell trouble, since neither partner is strong enough to help the other if both share the same character weakness over a particular matter of concern. When the chips are down each needs the other in precisely the same way, and neither is strong enough to provide the support and understanding that is necessary. Grier (2005: 211–13) gives an example, where on the face of it the two partners came from very different families, but in their families of origin neither of them could voice feelings about not getting individual attention, and both felt their upbringing was marked by a real sense of psychological deprivation. They each brought into their marriage a grievance towards their parents. Their resentment took the form of guilty, passive aggression. It is easy to see how destructive this would have been of their relationship when trying to work through negative feelings towards each other. We might imagine that there could be sullen silences in their relationship, without really being able to voice and work through any difficulties they had with each other, particularly over matters of the attention of the one to the other's needs. So here we may have yet another version of the triangle, but without the separating factor that is so valuable in the richness of a relationship, because it has flattened out making more for a one-dimensional than a two-dimensional relationship (see Figure 10.7).

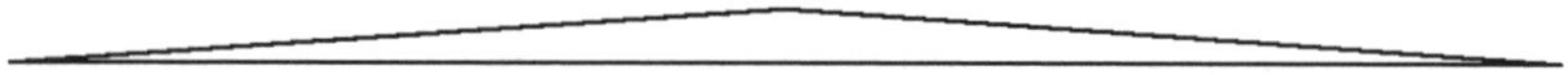

partner A   partner B

Figure 10.7 The one-dimensional relationship

The third element, as shown in some of the earlier triangles, can cause problems, because it is felt to be a threat, intruding upon the couple, taking the attention of one partner away from the other, evoking jealousies and other negative feelings. But here there is sameness in the couple's backgrounds, and where there is not the variety that is introduced by the third element, such as character differences as well as similarities, then the couple relationship loses richness, complementarity and so the potentiality for growth, both as individuals and as a couple.

This applies equally to the way in which couples view each other. If one partner only wishes the other to demonstrate certain qualities, which are to the partner's liking and fulfil his or her needs, but does not wish the other to demonstrate qualities that are less to his or her liking, and which may even frustrate his or her needs, then there are likely to be considerable difficulties in the relationship. Just as one partner may enjoy the attention of their spouse, but resent the attention given by the spouse to their child when that partner is wanting attention, so that partner can also resent it when their spouse, instead of being attentive to their needs, is concerned for their own needs, or is perhaps angry about something that has happened and is therefore not in the mood to give the required attention.

I begin here to give examples that move away from the classic Freudian Oedipal situation, which is concerned with three-person relationships, but with two-person, three-element relationships, more along the lines that Melanie Klein and the Kleinian school have interpreted the Oedipus complex. I do not want to get into the contentious area of whether the baby has knowledge of the father's penis, or whether the part-objects of the breast and the penis are an early version of the Oedipus complex. Some of that theorizing is of little practical use in the consulting room, in my opinion, since it is far removed from the client's experience and comprehension. But there is a more useful line to follow in Kleinian theory that there is a third element that interferes with the intimate and comfortable couple relationship of mother and baby, and that is the bad mother, or the bad breast. In other words a baby has a relationship to a mother who both meets her needs and also at times frustrates those needs – when, for example, she responds or fails to respond quickly enough to the baby's cry. Klein's concept is that a baby splits this experience into a good breast and a bad breast, or a good mother and a bad mother. This is indeed a sort of reality: these *are* two very different experiences. But the baby comes to know that it is the same breast that is available or not available, the same mother who gives attention or makes the baby wait. So in time, as the baby comes to recognize that there is the whole person, we see the healthy development that comes from integrating the two experiences, the two breasts, the two mothers, a first understanding of ambivalence and of reality. This concept of ambivalence is very important for healthy relationships.

In other words, if we are to see this in triangular terms, the early experience of mother contains two elements, the good and the bad, and part of healthy development is to recognize that this is inevitable in any relationship (see Figure 10.8).

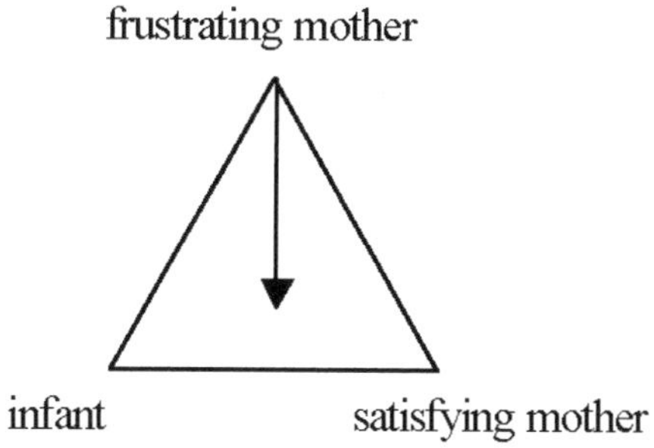

frustrating mother

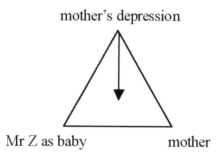

infant   satisfying mother

Figure 10.8 The triangle of infant–good mother–bad mother

Rosenthall gives an example of one of her patients, Mr Z, whose mother when he was a baby was preoccupied with depression, 'almost as if the depression constituted a third object in its own right' (2005: 199), so that in Mr Z's case the triangle would look like the one in Figure 10.9.

mother's depression

Mr Z as baby   mother

Figure 10.9 Mr Z's triangle

This early splitting is a natural defence against the need to retain a good maternal image, in order to overcome despair. As Britton puts it: 'The idea of a good maternal object can only be regained by splitting off her impermeability so that now a hostile force is felt to exist, which attacks [the baby's] good link with his mother' (1989: 90). But it is not a helpful defence in mature relationships. By splitting off the bad parts of the relationship, so that they become, for example, someone else's responsibility outside the couple, or are even denied altogether, what the couple tries to do is to maintain an illusion – indeed Britton talks about an Oedipal illusion – where only the good qualities are permitted. Mature development means, as Rosenthall puts it: 'Each of us has to negotiate a journey from being a babe-in-arms, absorbed with the illusion of being our mother's only love, over a hurdle where the existence of the father and other siblings, either potential or real, is recognized and accepted' (2005: 181–2). We might want to add also needing to recognize and accept other aspects of mother as well.

It is possible that only one partner has this illusion, and this makes it very difficult for the other partner, who is only permitted to express one side of her or his character, and not the other (third element) side. But both partners may be involved in this kind of illusion, so that they have to mirror each other only in respect of one way of relating, without the all-important third element that makes for completeness, variety, and indeed the value of ambivalence in their relationship. Britton reports one patient describing this kind of relationship: 'We were to move along a single line and meet at a single point' (1989: 88): so that the flattened triangle above (Figure 10.7) between the couple with similar backgrounds becomes so distorted that it is indeed only a single one-dimensional line (see Figure 10.10).

partner A   partner B

Figure 10.10 The triangle of a couple with similar backgrounds

Morgan has called this 'projective gridlock', and provides an example:

> Rachel and Tom did everything together: studied together, had the same interests, operated as one. Tom would choose clothes for Rachel and at parties speak for her. It never occurred to her that she might have a different point of view. For a long time she had felt content with this situation, although she never enjoyed sex with Tom. Tom said that what felt awful about having sex with Rachel was that he worked out what she thought, felt and wanted to such an extent that it was like having sex with himself; he had never really known what was going on for her at all.
> (summarized from Morgan 1995: 44)

What we therefore see is how important this triangle is, and how damaging it can be when it becomes distorted. We are involved throughout life, as social beings, in multi-person relationships, not just in two-person relationships; or in multi-dimensional couple relationships, not just in one-dimensional relationships. If the triangle becomes flattened, the couple lose the third element that makes for fullness, growth, ambivalence, and all the advantages that come from continuing to have to engage with difference. If the triangle is pulled too strongly one way rather than another, then jealousies can arise which make it much more difficult to accept separateness or togetherness without feeling deprived or guilty. The Oedipal triangle is not rigid: it moves one way and the other in the way that relationships should do, so that the three persons or elements involved at any one time enjoy both separateness and relatedness.

Triangles in therapy and supervision

There are two other triangles that also need to be recognized in therapeutic practice. The first is the presence of the third person in the role of the therapist (see Figure 10.11). Every therapist working with a couple is obviously drawn into this Oedipal situation – although it is also a feature of working with an individual client where there is a significant other who is not actually present in the consulting room, but features strongly in the client's life.

therapist

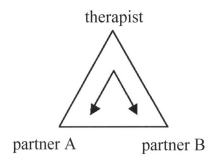

partner A   partner B

Figure 10.11 The triangle of partner A–therapist–partner B

It is not difficult to find many examples of this – where the therapist finds herself or himself being drawn towards one person's side, and against the other partner. Lanman (2005: 158) observes about one of the couples she worked with, that she could easily be drawn into attending to the husband, egged on by the wife, because the husband was the more obviously troubled. But gradually it became clear that the wife was projecting her own distress onto her husband, and actually felt ignored and taken for granted, as if she had no needs of her own, even though she had contributed to this deflection of attention. This is the most familiar Oedipal situation for the therapist, where one partner or the other gets the most attention.

But Ruszczynski (2005: 35) relates a different situation, where he as the therapist felt excluded (see Figure 10.12). He was apparently in the sessions themselves treated by his two clients as if he was a very wise sage, whose every word was profound, and each of them seems to have preferred him as a partner. But in his countertransference he sometimes found himself feeling seduced by one or other of them, and then he would suddenly be rejected by them both as they conspiratorially left the session, making him feel, by their giggling and excited whispering outside the consulting room as if he was the one excluded from their relationship. But we might also envisage the

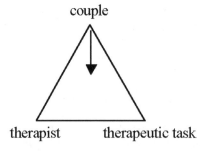

Figure 10.12 The triangle of therapist–couple–therapeutic task

resistance of the couple to change as coming between the therapist and the therapeutic task. Three-person dynamics were blatant both in and out of the consulting room.

Then there is the triangular situation of the third person in supervision (see Figure 10.13). Some writing on supervision imagines it as something like Winnicott's nuclear family, where the supervisor contains the counsellor who contains the client as in Winnicott's view the father holds the mother who holds the baby. This is a comforting and perhaps a positive expression of a type of Oedipal relationship. But it would be limiting only to see supervision through that lens. Lanman sees herself as a supervisor as the outsider who often finds herself drawing attention to the partner who is not being focused upon in the presentation of the case, or to an avoided topic or affect (2005: 154). She represents then the excluded aspect. But she goes on to say that 'at any one time, either the supervisor or the supervisee is likely to be more involved with one aspect or another' (p. 155) and she stresses the potential for movement in this dynamic. So the supervisee also has an equal part in this triangular relationship, meaning that it is not only the supervisor who can be right. Lanman refers to the danger of an 'idealized "deadly equal" triangle where everything must be even-handed all the time' (p. 155), which applies as much to other Oedipal situations as it does to supervision. The rivalry in the supervisory relationship, handled well, leads to much greater richness than cosy collusion, in the same way as the three-dimensional is so much richer than the two-dimensional.

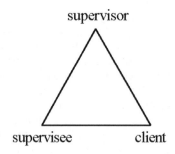

Figure 10.13 The triangle at supervision

There is one further feature of the Oedipus myth that is important to recognize, which brings in another aspect in the myth which is emphasized by various authors, and that is Oedipus's journey from not knowing, and not seeing, even when the truth of the matter is almost forced upon him, through a journey of discovery, which keeps coming up against his resistance; and the wish to retreat from what he is learning to a more comfortable solution. Bettelheim observes that when Oedipus fled Corinth he paid no attention to the inscription at the oracle at Delphi, 'Know thyself'. Because he was unaware of his innermost feelings, he fulfilled the prophecy. So Oedipus acted out of a kind of metaphorical blindness, and he punishes himself for this by depriving himself of his eyesight. Bettelheim goes on to reinforce that the guiding principle of psychoanalysis is knowing oneself, recognizing the hidden pressures that lead us to act one way or another, sometimes in ways that are apparently detrimental to ourselves and others. So Freud's concept of the Oedipus complex contains the warning that we need, as far as we are able, to become aware of our unconscious.

This emphasis on knowing is also present in the concept in psychoanalysis, initiated by Freud and reinforced by Klein, of the epistomophilic drive – the urge to know or understand, the desire for knowledge which exists along with love and hate in our relationships with ourselves and others. As Britton puts it: 'Human beings have an urge to love, to hate, to know, and a desire to be loved, a fear of being hated, and a wish to be understood' (1989: 11). But alongside the wish to know is the fear of what we will learn. That is very obvious in Oedipus's brave quest to find out the truth of the cause of the pestilence that has struck Thebes. What he learns is too shocking for him to comprehend and therefore he twists and turns what he learns until eventually the truth comes out. He cannot cope with the shocking knowledge of what he has done – of his failure of knowledge as well as his murderous and incestuous actions. Freud wrote, as noted in the previous chapter, that every member of the audience watching this play recoils in horror, and perhaps recoils from recognizing how much the story of Oedipus is, in certain respects at least, also his or hers. We would rather not know.

Finding a place for the third element, or recognizing just how strong the attachment is to the third element, is not an easy task. Clients will not want to see it – or if they see it they will not want to admit it; and therapists may even recoil in horror from what they are on the edge of seeing, and so water down their words and obscure their insight. These Oedipal situations are not necessarily easily recognized by the therapist, unless the therapist has come to terms with the struggles involved in her or his own Oedipal resolution; and they will not be readily accepted by clients and couples who are not only to own the way they are relating, but also to take on the implications for change that such knowledge highlights. They have sought understanding in coming for help, but they may also fight against learning. Knowledge, or the rather better term that Bion symbolized by the letter K – getting to know – itself may be a third element which they are reluctant to admit into their relationship as a couple. As Thorner writes: 'Side by side with the desire for knowledge there is a resistance to knowledge. Getting to know inevitably brings the individual into contact with objects that arouse displeasure' (1981: 75). There is then even a triangle here, where getting to know can either come between a therapist and the client, or can contribute to the strengthening of the therapeutic task (Figure 10.14).

getting to know

therapist   client

Figure 10.14 The 'Getting to Know' triangle

Freud links this 'getting to know' to the sexual drive. Whether or not that is so, biblical terminology equates knowing another person with sexual intercourse as well as with the seeking of truth. So getting to know is an appropriate part of a couple's relationship, meaning not only getting to know each other sexually, but also getting to know each other, and their relationship, throughout their partnership, in yet another triangle such as the one shown in Figure 10.15.

the couple

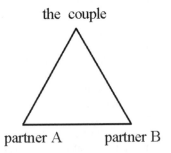

partner A   partner B

Figure 10.15 The couple getting to know their relationship

Psychoanalysis was founded on the basis of one person (the analyst) assisting in the process of enabling insight on the part of another (the patient), as well as in the process the analyst, as Casement (1985) makes clear, learning from the patient. This mutual process of knowledge is also possible for the couple. They have in each other the potentiality to go on getting to know long after therapy has ended.

Parent and child: Oedipal problem areas

In the above overview of the Oedipal triangle and how it may be worked through for the greater fulfilment of the different parties involved, there are some clear problem areas that have already been identified. Since many Oedipal difficulties in adult life go back to the parent–parent–child situation, some of the problems in those relationships merit further discussion.

It is ironic that psychoanalysis, historically so eager to identify its roots and its developments as being true to Freud, should have developed attitudes towards two important aspects of sexual behaviour that are so antithetical to Freud. Homosexuality is one such area, although attitudes to homosexual orientation as a psychopathological phenomenon are changing. The other subject that is again having to change, and look back to Freud's original findings, is that of sexual abuse. The psychoanalytic position has often been that much that is remembered by adults as sexual abuse in childhood is in fact a screen memory based on the fantasy wish of the child for a sexual relationship with the parent, combined with the experience of erotic stimulation that inevitably comes through childcare, such as in washing and powdering of the genitals. The blame for this view is sometimes laid at Freud's door, and his retraction of his theory of infantile sexual seduction (Masson 1984). I and others have argued that this is an exaggerated criticism of Freud (Jacobs 2003: 111–14). Those arguments should be considered briefly here, because this is another of those complex areas in which mistakes can so easily be made, in understanding theory as well as in therapeutic practice.

Freud's earliest explanation for the symptoms of hysterical conversion which he witnessed in many of his patients (where a limb, or one of the five senses, is numbed, paralyzed or in some way affected physically due to emotional tensions), was that they had been traumatized by parental sexual seduction. He then realized that such an explanation was too general, and could not explain every neurotic presentation. He therefore added a further explanation, that of the child's fantasy of sexual seduction. This is still too limited an explanation of neurotic symptoms, but nonetheless it is important to recognize that this was an additional explanation, not an alternative one. There is plenty of evidence to show that throughout the rest of his life and writing Freud retained his belief in the actual seduction of some patients, citing it as an important factor in a number of his cases, while the explanation of the fantasy of seduction occurs as a major factor in others.

We now know that Freud's original explanation, preferring actual abuse over the fantasy, was very close to the truth. The number of actual instances of child abuse is considerable. It is as if the repressive censorship imposed by society on the memories of individuals has been lifted and it has become possible for a large number of survivors to speak about the abuse they have suffered. They are now more widely believed, whereas for too many years followers of Freud, and other health professionals, dismissed such memories as fantasies. There are of course some who now claim that recovered memories are false memories, including some who defend themselves, despite successful legal prosecutions against them, by saying that memories have been implanted by unscrupulous therapists.

On the other hand, there are also therapists who, having recognized this issue, now see it everywhere. They prematurely suggest the possibility to clients whenever they hear of difficulties that sometimes can be linked to the experience of childhood abuse – such as eating disorders. It is as if they, like

Freud at the beginning of his career, have only one explanation. There are others who accept a client's blank memories in childhood years as incontrovertible evidence of the repression of abusive experiences. Alongside these doubtful diagnoses, there are many apparently genuine examples of memories of childhood sexual abuse, and even more examples of childhood physical and emotional abuse, which arise spontaneously without any suggestion being made to the client, and in some cases being confirmed later from external sources. Therapists can cite many examples from their adult patients, and social and family workers many examples from the children they work with, where it is not fantasy, but rather a clear memory or clear evidence of actual abuse. It no longer surprises those in the caring professions when such material is included as a presenting issue, or emerges later in therapy, when it becomes safer to recall or recount such dreadful events.

We have then today, as much as in Freud's thinking in his early years of practice, a struggle to comprehend the dimensions of these issues: to know when clients are speaking about actual events, or when they may have unconscious reasons for believing themselves to have been abused. We can no longer dismiss these accounts as examples of sexual precociousness, or label clients as sexually provocative. Those who have had their own sexual boundaries invaded as children may sometimes be deeply defended against anything erotic; or may themselves not know how to manage erotic boundaries in their own behaviour:

Doreen came for therapy after an interview for a job, in which the man interviewing had tried to date her. She had refused him, and he, in turn, declined to give her the job. The initial session gave Doreen the chance of expressing her feelings, and calmed her furious tears. In the next session Doreen said she felt better and she began to talk about her relationships with other men. She had noticed how often men tried to pick her up – in pubs and elsewhere. She felt she must be giving off some signs to them. She was sitting in her chair in the therapist's room in what might be called a provocative fashion, in a short skirt with her legs wide open – and in the presence of a male counsellor who could not help but take notice of these apparently sexual signals being made to him as well. But as Doreen went on she talked about her father's sexual advances when she was in her teens, sitting next to her and stroking her breasts while watching television. Doreen managed to control the situation by sitting in another part of the room and resisting his invitations to come and sit with him. But she deeply regretted that she had to lose out on the closeness that in her pre-adolescence years she had always enjoyed with her father. The therapist pointed out how she may well have wanted to impress the interviewer and other men, and was very upset when they inappropriately asked her out; in her interview this meant she had lost the job she wanted; just as her father's approaches were inappropriate to their relationship, and turning him down meant that she lost out there too. Her father's lack of sexual boundaries were perhaps still unconsciously being played out in her manner with men, but the therapist was not going to make such a blatant interpretation, when at this point at least Doreen did not realize how her behaviour might be one factor.

Time and again the dilemma can be seen, either of wishing for a close relationship and yet needing to stay clear of sexual implications, or getting involved promiscuously but not able to tolerate a close relationship. Later relationships go wrong, it appears, as a result of past damaging experiences:

Erica could not allow herself to get too close to men: she preferred a series of casual sexual relationships. She had once had to resist her stepfather when he made it clear that he wanted to come into her bed when her mother was away. On protesting to him she was told, 'But you're not my real daughter'. This added a deep personal wound to his sexual threat. Erica tended to get caught up in relationships where she was 'the second woman'.

Other examples could be given (though they are less frequently encountered) of men who have been seduced by a close female relation, in whom there appear similar difficulties. Women do abuse, both boys and girls, although it is possible that the taboo on mother–son sexual relations is stronger than the father–daughter one. It is more often a man who invades the boundaries, whether father, stepfather, grandfather, brother or half-brother.

Fiona's father had married a second time when she was still small and she acquired a new 'mother', as well as a stepbrother 10 years her senior. She idolized the brother (perhaps as a substitute for her rather distant father), and was content just to sit at his feet and enjoy being in his presence. When she was 12 he suddenly left home to join the army, and she was heartbroken. Two years later she received a further blow when he married. He and his wife came to stay, and when everyone was out except herself and her brother, she cuddled up to him for comfort, but the closeness led to sex. Fiona felt so guilty afterwards that she could not speak to her stepbrother, and she had not done so since. She was unable to let men near her (except on the stage, since she enjoyed amateur dramatics). She could only be friends with those men she described as 'older and married . . . on a sisterly basis'. It was ironic that these were the men with whom she felt safe, since they also represented the one man with whom a sisterly relationship had gone wrong. It was, as in so much that goes wrong in relationships, as if she was trying to find a relationship close in character to the one that had gone wrong, where she could make it alright.

The therapist working with Fiona tried to remain sensitive to her wish to end her isolation from men, but also to her fear of letting any man get too close. As a man himself he tried to demonstrate to her that he could be trusted, so that she could learn to trust in turn her sexual and loving feelings for men, without fear that her feelings would provoke an invasion of her body. She tended to see men as the ones who had designs on her, and found it difficult to acknowledge her own desires. Her anger with the stepbrother gave way to feelings of the love she still had for him. In this case therapy had to finish before it was clear whether the issues could be resolved, but the therapist felt that Fiona made some progress towards talking about intimacy, and towards the expression of her love (including her affection for the therapist) without it turning into an inappropriate sexual relationship.

There are also many examples where clients have been abused sexually even earlier in their lives than the clients reported in the examples above. Working with survivors of child sexual abuse is an area of work that requires if not specialist training at least specialist supervision, and there is a growing literature that supports the understanding of the dynamics of the different relationships and the therapeutic task, including the even more therapeutically taxing presentations of multiple personality, or dissociative identity disorder as it is technically known (Walker 1992; Davies and Frawley 1994; Jacobs 1994; Scharff and Scharff 1994; Mollon 1996; Walker and Antony-Black 1999).

With so much emphasis rightly being given to actual sexual abuse, we should not forget another section of the client population where the sexual intimacy, even if not genital, was emotionally just as seductive to the child – and just as difficult for a child to know how to respond, since it involved intimacy without the threat of physical intrusion. These are those instances where parents use their children as confidants, revealing to them the secrets of their sexual relations, or their sexual frustration or dissatisfaction with their partner; or where the parent–child relationship is emotionally overclose. In these instances a child may find the apparent level of trust and attentiveness attractive, but it may also be aware of a threat, since such a situation appears to drive out the other parent, or other siblings. These are seductive relationships too, in which the child is presented with tempting rewards, but can feel equally guilty or frightened, especially when the opportunity comes for them in adult life to make their own intimate partnerships.

Some clients have parents who have their own difficulties about sexuality and have conveyed the impression that sex is something to be ashamed of or guilty about. They do this in what they say, such as those who simultaneously stimulate and put off their children by making them their confidants about their distaste concerning sex; or by what they do, such as switching off the television whenever sexuality or nudity is shown.

Gill received such mixed messages from her home. Her mother confided to her that she found sex distasteful and painful while her father, though not physically touching her, related so closely to her that Gill herself normally avoided any young man who might present a sexual threat. Her closest friend was a young gay man, who represented for her a safe way of relating to a man without the usual sexual complications. Only when she had drunk too much at parties did Gill become aware of any sexual desire in herself for the opposite sex.

A child's fantasy wishes, which include thoughts of having the undivided attention of one or other of the parents, can get acted out when either parent gives substance to the child's fantasy, for example, by using the child as an ally against his or her partner. Where a child becomes a confidant (sometimes from an early age), perhaps being inappropriately told intimate details about the parents' relationship, he or she may feel very confused. The child may feel excited at being given such privileged information, the details of which feed the voyeuristic wishes of the child. Children and adolescents are not slow, given the opportunity, and not fully realizing the troubles it might cause, to exploit the differences between the parents, sometimes playing off one against the other, sometimes trying to achieve closeness with one to the exclusion of the other. At the same time a child may feel guilty (or even disgusted) by what they hear or in some other way witness. Freud suggested that the primal scene of the parents' bed was both fascinating and frightening to the child. Perhaps it is this voyeuristic fantasy that the tabloid newspapers also feed upon when they divulge juicy gossip about famous people, who are significant popular transference figures.

The triangular relationships that I illustrate in this chapter seldom consist of one triangle alone – the apex of each triangle can also be the apex of another. Systems theory similarly would want to look for the interconnecting threads that mean that when part of one relationship alters, other relationships are similarly affected. It is a kind of cat's cradle, a web of connections. Herbie's situation illustrates this well:

Herbie was a mild-mannered man, married to a woman who appeared by his accounts to be something of a tyrant. He was pushed around by her, always feeling unable to make his own decisions. The relationship survived for some years, as long as Herbie was willing to take on this role. Then his mother died. The death of a parent sometimes leads to a radical shake-up in the balance of the relationships in the next generation. Herbie's mother had been a fairly timid and distant person, perhaps a figure with whom he had closely identified. Now Herbie 'found himself involved' (as he put it, as though he was purely the passive recipient of the situation) with a woman who was herself engulfed by her husband. Her situation aroused anger in Herbie towards the husband. He identified how she felt as also being true of his own relationship (and perhaps of his mother's too?). They started an affair, which after a few months was discovered by her husband, who forbade his wife to see Herbie. This she refused to do, trying to draw Herbie away from his wife, yet at the same time taking fright whenever he seemed prepared to take such a step. Then, when he did leave his wife, she distanced herself from Herbie.

Herbie began to feel guilty, but also very angry with this woman, and he described in therapy how he felt just as he did when a child, with his mother being distant, and father making life hell for him. His father would express violent jealousy of mother's affection for Herbie, although Herbie himself never felt that mother had dared express her feelings towards her son. He was therefore angry with the woman's husband for being like his father; and with her for not being brave enough to follow her feelings through. He also felt angry with his wife for being so tyrannical. We see in his marriage an inverted Oedipal resolution where Herbie has identified with his mother, and married someone rather more like his father. In his affair he was attempting to set that situation right by choosing a woman more like his mother. But, as can often happen, it was a false solution, with the second woman reinforcing the negative side of his mother, and simply compounding the problem. In despair Herbie left them both, and chose a third woman who was divorced, only to discover after a few months that she was periodically going back to her former husband. History repeated itself in one variation or another at every turn.

There is a further aspect to the triangular relationship which therapy sometimes invokes. There is a type of intimacy between a therapist and client, which others in the client's life may find difficult to understand and to accept. Therapy can be particularly difficult for partners (including sometimes a therapist's partner). There are some partners, of course, who are content to let the client be identified as the one with the problem, since it lets them off the hook. They may even support the client on the one hand, while undermining progress on the other by refusing to acknowledge any part they themselves play. Other partners may be jealous of the closeness the client feels with the therapist, and wonder what is being said about them, often feeling that they are being criticized, which of course is sometimes the case. These are difficult situations for the therapist who recognizes the realities of the external world, and does not simply concentrate upon the client's inner experience in the session. There is great value in a client having space and time and separateness, all of which is supported by the privacy of the session. At the same time a partner can feel excluded, creating difficulties rather than helping resolve them, and there may be value in some instances in clients sharing some of what they discuss with their partner.

The solution does not necessarily lie in joint sessions, especially if the second partner is brought in after a long spell of the client being seen alone. The partner can feel with some justification that the therapist has already taken sides. Neither is offering to see the partner for an occasional session necessarily any more helpful. The offer might be considered in some situations for the partner to see a second therapist, possibly leading to a 'foursome' involving both therapists and both clients. Above all, therapists need to be sensitive, even more so when clients make significant progress, to the way such changes may mean the need for adjustments in the client's present relationships. Therapy sometimes leads to the splitting of partnerships; but it is regrettable when therapy so concentrates upon the client that it does not also help the client to recognize the needs of his or her partner. If the partner is given the opportunity to adapt to what is sometimes a new identity emerging in the client, the partner may also change, with the result that genuine intimacy is for the first time discovered by both.

The Oedipus complex suggests different facets in the parent–child relationship. I have referred above to the twin features of separateness and relatedness. The parent–child relationship must not become too intense, but at the same time there should be relaxed expression of the affectionate love between mother and son, father and daughter, mother and daughter and father and son, which Freud described as 'aim-inhibited' – that is, the sexual aim of love is curbed. Searles expresses it well when he writes of his own children:

> If a little girl cannot feel herself able to win the heart of her father, her own father who has known her so well and for so long . . . how can the young woman who comes later have any deep confidence in the power of her womanliness . . . ?

Then, writing of his son and his wife:

> . . . their deeply fond, openly evidenced mutual attraction is good for my son as well as enriching for my wife.
>
> (1965a: 296)

A child wishes to reach out, and to say, as it were, 'Let me give you, let me love you, let me touch you', with the emphasis here upon 'you', as distinct from the emphasis upon the 'me' which was such a feature of the earlier narcissistic years. Rejection of what a child offers takes place not only through open hostility, but also through passive distancing; and a rejecting parent so easily becomes translated into difficulties in making relationships in adult life; such a parent fosters fear of rejection, as well as inhibits the expression of love. The child's love and sexuality need to be affirmed as being good; and yet deflected gently away so that love, including sexual desire, can be offered to and accepted by another as the child becomes adult. Yet in many triangular situations there is as much frustration as there was in the original parent–child relationship. There are some men and women who always seem to be in search of the unobtainable, and who go through a succession of relationships that do not work out for them as they wish.

Isadora's father was often abroad on construction work during her childhood and adolescence. As a teenager she was not perhaps unusual in developing a crush on one of the male teachers at school, and she tried to show her love by working especially hard for him. She remembered being very disappointed when he did not remark on her special efforts. When Isadora went to university, as a mature student, she again idolized one of her male tutors. Her work again became a way of pursuing him and she felt sure that he also loved her. When, however, her tutor appeared to respond to her (although it seemed from her account only by a friendly gesture, not a sexual move) Isadora became angry with him for wanting to seduce her; and she left university at the end of her first year. She then got a job in an office, where a manager of a different department would come in and flirt with the typists. At first she thought he was 'dishy', but then began to feel he had his eyes on her. Isadora engineered a meeting with him, and confronted him, asking him just what his intentions were.

Taken aback, the man was angry and unfortunately told Isadora she had 'a screw loose'. So she left that job. When she came to the therapist she was experiencing these feelings all over again in another work situation, although by now she had recognized that she was projecting her wishes for a sexual relationship onto an unattainable father figure, and that she needed to look at the reasons for her turning down the genuine interest shown in her by other men who were available to her.

This example is a reminder of the possibility that when a child goes to school, he or she may seek in teachers the affirmation not given at home; or may wish equally to please, to give to and to emulate their teachers as much as they do their parents. Some of these feelings encourage the process of learning. Anna Freud suggests that latency relationships will include love, admiration, dislike and rejection of teachers 'not because they are men or women but because they are either helpful, appreciative, inspiring or harsh, intolerant, anxiety-arousing figures' (1973: 159). Difficulties arise where the relationship becomes more than a good working alliance: where admiration and love become highly charged, and where acceptance or rejection of the child's love becomes inseparable from acceptance or criticism of the child's work, as in this last example. Problems can also arise where teachers (as can happen with those who teach older adolescents and adults in particular) take advantage of their 'parental' role to seduce their students. The damage to some of these students can be as severe as the damage from seduction by actual parents. Teachers and those who work with the young have to master their own sexuality and Oedipal wishes in order to relate appropriately to children and adolescents.

Several writers have drawn attention to the significance of the father for the development of a girl, in her growing confidence as a woman, both in close relationships and in the workplace. Samuels points out the damage when fathers cannot affirm their daughter's attractiveness: 'The father's failure to participate in a mutual attraction and mutual painful renunciation of erotic fulfilment with his daughter deprives her of psychological enhancement ... In the absence of Eros ... the daughter loses sight of herself as a sexually viable adult, with disastrous consequences' (1985b: 31). The same is also true of the need for a boy to be loved by his mother, although in many cases the problem here is not lack of affection, but overcloseness. Not a few men are still 'mother's boy'. We may wonder how these situations might work out in single-parent families, or in gay and lesbian partnerships, where there is not the presence of two parents of opposite genders. It is of course too early to know whether these dynamics will be any different, since it is only in recent years that such families have been generally accepted as part of the normal range of relationships in Western society. On the other hand there is plenty of experience of families where a father has been absent literally or emotionally. In some cases it is clear that a grandmother in a three-generation household performed a similar task to a father figure, acting as the third force that helps to separate mother and child, and reaffirming the child in his or her value. It is possible that the principle of the third person, whether a same-gender partner, or a grandparent, or even a sibling, acts therefore in the same way as the father figure to whom psychoanalytic thought has in one way attached so much importance. (In another way psychoanalytic theory, although with a heavy emphasis on the father in Freud, has pushed fathers into relative insignificance in the emphasis given to early mothering!).

Walker provides an interesting example of the absent father, whose place was filled by a grandmother during the Second World War. Suzanne's early years were spent with mother and mother's mother, with father away in the forces. His return at the end of the war meant that grandmother had to move into a house nearby. 'Suzanne felt ill at ease with her father and missed her grandmother … A year later, when Suzanne was six, her sister was born; the baby was adored by her father. Suzanne remembered feeling lonely and isolated, and spending much of her time with her grandmother, who was in considerable conflict with her father' (1990: 1–21). In this example it is clear that the returning father displaced an important third figure, and came between child and grandmother in a way that was unhelpful for Suzanne's development as a woman.

Another client described how her father's particular form of attention to her was similarly unhelpful:

Jane was the third girl in her family, when her father had desperately wanted her to be a boy. As she grew up, her father encouraged her (but not the other girls in the family) to help him around the house; he took her to football matches; he discussed business matters with her. He did much of what some feminist writers would have fathers do, that is introduce their daughters to a particular aspect of the wider world. Jane was happy enough to go along with this, and it meant that she was very close to him. But she never felt close to her father as a woman, but rather as the son he had never had. Her relationship with her father seemed to have resulted in mother devoting herself more to her sisters than to Jane.

As an adult, Jane found it difficult to believe in herself as a woman: she was never sure of how genuine friends were when they complimented her on her clothes she wore, on her cooking, and on other sides of her which she thought of as particularly feminine. She was diffident about making love with her husband, who perhaps made it no easier for her, because sex seemed to satisfy his own needs rather than hers. She felt used by him to meet his needs as she had done by her father, meeting his needs for a son.

Many clients struggle with the ambivalence they have towards one or both parents, on the one hand needing them as love objects, and as protective figures especially during a time of emotional turmoil; on the other hand needing to be able to express their resentment towards their parents for what they have not been able to give them. It is perhaps when they have not received what they would have wished for that they become most protective of their parents when speaking of them in therapy:

Such push–pull ambivalent feelings were clearly present in Kathy, who while at home was always arguing with her father, and pouring scorn on his lack of education and his ignorant and bigoted views; but away from home at college she told her counsellor how much she adored her father. She defended him against any criticism, and even wrote letters back home to him telling him what a great father he was. Kathy found it difficult to express those hostile feelings about him to her counsellor. She very much needed the affirmation she did not really get at home. Yet she pushed her father away by looking down on him, since he had disappointed her by not matching her intellectual development.

A therapist has a vital role to play in the need for affirmation. Searles's (1965a) words cited earlier come from an article in which he explores the feelings of Oedipal love for the client which he as the therapist has in some instances felt towards the conclusion of therapy. Searles believes that countertransference feelings of the attractiveness of a client are a sign of the value of the therapeutic work, and of the need to work through the final stages of Oedipal loss in therapy. The Oedipal situation is implicit in therapy, especially although not exclusively where therapist and client are of the opposite gender. There is a fine line for the therapist, as there is for a parent, between accepting and affirming a client's attractiveness and sexuality, and being seductive, such as through encouraging the expression of sexual feelings to feed the therapist's narcissistic needs. In addition to accepting the expression of strong loving feelings by some clients, a therapist must also be prepared to accept the client's disappointment, frustration and anger at the failure of the therapist to allow the active expression of that love. Just as a therapist working with dependent clients may need to identify feelings about the therapist's failure to be a sufficient source of care and nourishment; or with passive clients they may need to observe their feelings about the therapist's failure to tell them what to do; so a therapist may need to interpret a client's feelings about his or her failure to become a sexual partner or lover. Not responding to sexualized wishes does not imply that the client is unattractive. Yet sometimes a client's expression of inadequacy or unattractiveness arises because of a therapist's emotional distance, particularly where a therapist is frightened of her or his own loving feelings for a client. This may then be related by the client to the way his or her attempts to share loving and sexual feelings towards a parent were pushed away.

Some professional relationships involve considerable intimacy: a nurse or doctor is entrusted with a person's body, and often knows the most intimate details about it. Other professionals are trusted with deeply personal material; and some therapists suggest that psychotherapy of any depth or length is on a par with the closest of human relationships. Psychotherapy and counselling in fact involve a curiously one-sided relationship (Lowe 1972: 220–1), and it is important to draw a distinction between the different types of intimacy present in a helping relationship. It is a unique situation, stemming from a client probably being more open to a therapist than he or she is to anyone else. It does not follow that this inevitably involves the wish for an intimate physical relationship, although this can certainly be experienced in the transference and countertransference feelings of client and therapist. Although there is something illusory about this desire for the therapist (as Freud defined illusion, as a wish-fulfilment), it also represents a deep need, which is difficult to express, and can be difficult to get right.

Lorna was an attractive woman, and her male therapist was aware of this, as she described her feelings for him. In the first six months of counselling his positive countertransference feelings appeared to match hers. He was therefore cautious about taking up what she said, lest he should be encouraging her for his own ends. But when Lorna talked of her need to make men admire her and pay her compliments he had a stronger sense of what was happening to him. What he was experiencing with her was not simply his own wish to be found attractive to her, but the sort of flattery that Lorna sought in the compliments she so much needed from others.

The therapist was then less worried about Lorna talking about her feelings for him; and he helped her begin to realize that she was valued, without having to dress herself up either literally or metaphorically in everything she said; she did not have to put herself in the best light. Lorna found herself relating to the therapist as a more ordinary man, no longer idealizing him; and outside therapy she began a relationship that went better than usual for her. She did not ruin it by fishing for compliments in a narcissistic way. It was as if the therapist's ease with issues around what was indeed a mutual attraction had released Lorna to think more highly of herself.

One feature in nearly every session was that Lorna found it difficult to stay until the end: she wanted to leave about ten minutes before the end, acknowledging at one point that if the therapist called a halt to the session, this felt like a rejection of her as someone dull and uninteresting. Towards the end of the therapeutic contract she brought a complex dream, in which a leopard gently got hold of her arm but would not let her go; and in which there was a tussle over a coffin between herself and someone who reminded her of her therapist. The leopard was reluctant to let her go and she was reluctant to let the coffin go. The therapist interpreted this feature of the dream as a possible indication of her feelings about ending. There was a part of her that wanted to leave and get away, but there was also a part of her that wanted to stay. It was something like the premature end of each session which she had also described as a tussle: she wanted to leave, while he tried to help her to stay.

Lorna agreed that this was a possibility, but said that she did not experience the therapist as trying to hang on to her. At that point the session had to end, for it was indeed time for her to go. But as she tried to open the door, she found that the latch on the door was down and she could not get out of the room! The therapist, looking for a hidden meaning to this 'accident', did not believe in sheer coincidence, and wondered whether he had 'inadvertently' slipped the catch when he had closed the door when she first came in. In his countertransference he seemed to be struggling with the same issues about ending as her.

There is yet another response by parents to children that affects the way in which children negotiate those issues identified in the Oedipus complex, and has repercussion for the way they regard themselves in adult life. It is related to the issues of critical or destructive authority that have already appeared in earlier themes. A parent who cannot trust a child's exploration of his or her sexuality, or who regards anything sexual as messy or dirty, is liable to encourage shame or guilt, and so symbolically castrate the child (boy or girl) when it comes to the expression of genital love. When the early 'masturba-tory' gestures in the child are smacked down or harshly rebuked, this is likely to lead to inhibition or guilt about more intentional masturbation in ado-lescence, as well as about the expression of sexual feelings in relationships. Menstruation or wet dreams might similarly become associated with shame, as an uncontrollable bodily emission that is thought of as 'disgusting'. Mas-turbation may be a matter of choice, but sexual excitement can be sponta-neous: erections or vaginal moistening can be embarrassing when involuntary. These are issues of control which are carried over into this theme of competition, where a parent may feel in some way threatened by the developing sexuality of the child.

Where sex has been frowned on in the parental home, such an attitude can be internalized in the adolescent and adult. Sexual games in childhood might similarly be greeted with parental horror, conveying all the wrong messages to the child:

As a grown man Matthew was terrified by the fantasy (since it had never occurred in reality) that if ever he got close to a child he would want to touch him or her sexually, and that he would then be imprisoned for this. He told an illuminating story of his mother's reaction when she dis-covered that a slightly older boy had persuaded Matthew to compare the size of their penises. Although Matthew was only five at the time, he remembered his mother threatening to call the police, and himself hiding under the table in fear of their arrival, because he felt he would also be arrested. Mother's concern, perhaps wanting to punish the older boy, led Matthew to think he had himself committed the crime. She did not realize that sexual games and homosexual activity at this age (and even later) are quite normal precursors to heterosexual development, and do not necessarily indicate either perversion or corruption (see Freud 1973: 159).

In addition to the rejection and criticism of a boy's or girl's sexuality, therapists notice plenty of examples, illustrative of issues about masculinity and femininity discussed in Chapter 9, where clients recall the scorn poured on them as children at attitudes or behaviours that were not felt to be con-sonant with 'being a boy' or 'being a girl'. Boys (and men) do cry, and girls and women do like to get muddy, climb trees and so on. Criticism, particularly by the parent of the same gender, may lead in fact to doubts not just about the self, but also about wanting to identify with him or her, pushing the child towards greater identification with the parent of the opposite gender.

These Oedipal relations are therefore of crucial importance in the devel-opment of a child's confidence in self, as someone who has sexual feelings, who can express love, who can enjoy the love others offer, and who is able to be loving to others without having to sexualize all such relationships, making them too exciting or too threatening. These are major issues for adult rela-tionships, although, as the next chapter examines, the themes of cooperation and competition, and their relation to gender and sexuality, have other dimensions to them as well.

COOPERATION AND COMPETITION: RELATED ISSUES

Sexual and gender relationships

Preceding chapters have shown what can damage or threaten the growing identity of the child. In the previous chapter it was seen how abuse, rejection, hostility, criticism or seduction may lead to difficulties relating more completely to others, not just in terms of self-esteem, but also in terms of sexuality. One way in which such difficulties were demonstrated is in the splitting of the different aspects of a single loving relationship onto different people. Love is of course an elusive concept, involving many different features dependent to some extent upon cultural context. Nevertheless for many people an intimate relationship involves sexuality, companionship and mutual caring. Some can only relate relatively free from anxiety as long as the nurturing, the sexual and the companionable aspects of an intimate relationship are split between two or three different people. Someone who cannot integrate the different aspects of love in a single relationship may then split off friendship and sexuality, or sexuality and care. The marital partner may therefore become the parental figure who is there to nurture and protect, while a sexual partner is sought outside the relationship. Some can only relate to another person closely as long as there is no obvious sexual attraction; presented with a sexually exciting person they clam up and do not know how to conduct themselves. In these instances it is as if sexuality has to be inhibited before there can be any form of relatedness. Some people can only be sexually active with a person to whom they are otherwise uncommitted. There are others – less likely to seek therapy until they begin to recognize the shallowness of their relationships – who seem unable to achieve the aim-inhibited development of their sexuality, and who relate to people only in sexual terms, actually or in fantasy treating them only as sexual objects. This balance between the ability to integrate sexual desire appropriately into some relationships, and the ability to inhibit it appropriately in others, might be one of the signs of mature relating.

There are other ways in which the threat presented by sex is acted out. Freud (1905: 62) described variations in normal infantile sexuality as 'polymorphous perversions', defining them as activities that extend beyond the parts of the body usually related to sex (such as foot fetishism) or that linger over aspects of relating sexually which normally are only one part of the total sexual act – touching, or looking, or being seen, for example, which can become exaggerated in voyeurism or exhibitionism. Young people in their first love objects outside the family sometimes fasten upon isolated physical features in the person whom they idealize – their hair, breasts, ankles, eyes and so on. I have suggested in an earlier chapter that some sexualized behaviours such as sadism and masochism might be located more appropriately under the theme of control and power (pp. 137–40). It is necessary to distinguish of course between sexual perversions as abusive and intrusive acts towards others, and sexual choices made in private adult consenting relationships where it is a case of *chacun à son goût*. Freud felt that exhibitionism and voyeurism are related to castration anxiety, and since it is mainly men who enjoy voyeurism, or who offend through exhibitionist behaviour, we might indeed wonder whether they are threatened in some way by women, and have in turn to threaten, in fantasy or in fact, the gender that threatens them. Attacks on homosexuals would seem to indicate similar fears in the perpetrators about their own sexuality. An abusive act may be more than an extension of sexual pleasure, being more an attempt to exercise power and domination. The women upon whom the voyeur or exhibitionist preys represent the woman such men feel has emasculated them or will damage them. The phallus, symbolic of power, as well as the actual penis, and anxiety about castration combine in one abusive act. By interpreting the penis and the vagina symbolically as well as literally, we may relate these acts to the fear of being swallowed up by a woman, not just genitally, but existentially. According to one feminist source it is because 'the hand that rocks the cradle' is female that men

> fear the will of women and the helplessness of infancy, and employ such strategies to avoid facing their fears as the segregation of men and women at work, in religious activities, in legal and social restrictions on women's rights, and the separation of physical and emotional love to avoid the 'melting' experience of intense intimacy.
>
> (Dinnerstein 1978: 236)

Therapy with sex offenders is a specialized area, but these anxieties may be present less dramatically in other men. Their primitive fears also appear to be projected onto their female victims, who can themselves be rendered powerless and fearful by their partner or by other men, not just because of what has actually happened in their relationships, but also because their experience reflects the position women often feel more generally in society. No therapist can overlook the reality of this total experience. When past and present experience or present fears are paralyzing a woman's capacity to relate equally with men, therapists not only need to give space for past experiences to be talked through, but also to distinguish the symbolic 'man' from men who as individuals do not act offensively and oppressively.

In a paper on feminism Winnicott used the concept of WOMAN (his capitalization to emphasize that every single person 'was *absolutely* dependent on a woman, and then relatively dependent' (1986: 191, original emphasis)). Similarly we might therefore need to distinguish MAN from man, so that individual men are not stereotyped. Some women deny the possibility of trusting men at all. In this respect – in their fear of the opposite sex – male perverts, chauvinists and some separatist feminists appear, for different reasons, to have one thing in common: a symbolic and perhaps also an actual perception of the other gender that is filled with hostility and fear.

Nora's feminism was based on a serious and convincing analysis of sexual politics. Nevertheless it contained a hostility to men in general which led to a wish to humiliate them intellectually and socially. It was not just her political analysis, but also the extreme terror and humiliation that she experienced when she was raped at the age of 18, that had led her to this position. Such an event cannot but have made an indelible impression upon her. Nora imagined that every man she passed as she walked along the street had a gun in his pocket. The fantasy was an obvious reference to her horrifying experience. It happened that Nora first saw a male therapist for her assessment session, and having been able to broach her fear to him, decided to continue seeing him. He enabled her in her own time to talk about the rape, which up to then she had shared with no one, not even her women friends. He helped her too by understanding her wish to exact revenge. Through the influence of their therapeutic relationship Nora began to enjoy the company of men, although she remained cautious about getting too close.

She also began to develop a critique of the sexism that she perceived in some of her feminist friends, which she felt was as damaging to good relationships as the sexism present more generally in society.

In these matters in particular, but perhaps more generally, the gender of the therapist can be very significant to a client; because of this many agencies try to offer a choice to clients of working with a male or a female therapist. Experience suggests that where gender choice is important to a client, it is more often a female therapist who is sought, by both men and women, although sometimes a client will deliberately choose the gender that they know has caused them difficulty in the past, as a conscious way of trying to face up to their anxiety. It may, however, be too threatening for a woman to work with a man, or vice versa, when it is a man or a woman who has been seen as responsible for the damage that the client feels has been done to him or her. On the other hand working with a therapist who represents the feared person, and who does not repeat the trauma or abuse, can be a major step towards a new perspective. Clients who specifically ask to see a man or a woman counsellor or therapist are making an important choice, which where possible should be respected, even if in making such a choice these clients are already saying something about themselves which it will in time be useful to explore. When it comes to matters concerning sex and sexual orientation, the gender of the therapist is more obviously significant.

It is often suggested in psychoanalytic writing that it matters little what gender the therapist is, since a client will 'transfer' on to the therapist different attitudes, wishes and fears related either to mother or to father. It is indeed so that a maternal and paternal transference is equally possible towards therapists of either gender. ('Maternal' and 'paternal' are used here for convenience, although I recognize this implies some stereotyping of the characteristics of mothers and fathers.) Furthermore, therapists may adopt a maternal or paternal stance towards a client: Mohamed and Smith (1997: 107–9) make some apposite observations on this in relation to time-limited psychodynamic therapy. On the other hand, Freud (1931: 373) doubted whether he as a man received the same transferences as a woman analyst, and I myself wonder whether gender blindness, as we might call it, is necessarily common. It is true that where there are early issues of trust and attachment, the maternal side of the therapist, whether a man or a woman, is paramount, but there are trust and attachment issues in relation to actual men in a person's life as much as to the mother. Similarly we have already seen in the second theme that to equate authority with the father promotes a mistaken notion of family roles. Some clients fear a woman counsellor more than a man not because she is paternal, but because she represents the mother who has been the critical force in the family, especially where the father has taken a passive role.

If a particular gender match in the therapeutic relationship works well, this can have a ripple effect upon other relationships. There may be some areas in which it is more difficult for a man to empathize with a woman (and vice versa), but this may be compensated for by the experience of working with a therapist of the opposite gender who listens respectfully, is not intrusive, and who makes an effort to understand. Some feminist therapists have challenged the separatist position that only women can work with women, although it is interesting that while the separatist argument can also be applied to the transcultural counselling, it is rarely expressed that only male counsellors should see men. The following example illustrates how helpful cross-gender pairing might be:

> An American woman hospital chaplain was visiting a very weakened man in intensive care. Mario had collapsed after a violent argument with his wife, who had become an active member of a women's group. On one of the chaplain's visits, Mario had unleashed a flood of anger and resentment, pouring out his feelings about his wife. 'He was one of the angriest and most violent personalities I have ever encountered', writes Chaplain Haines (1978). 'We were two enemies with reason to be suspicious and hostile toward one another. I am a liberated woman; Mario is a machismo man. And still we met on common ground. Each of us represented, to the other, someone who had done something unspeakable to us'.

It is important to bear in mind that clients who have anxieties about closeness to their own gender may need careful allocation if a choice can be offered. The therapeutic relationship is an intimate one, and initial anxieties in clients need to be respected:

Olivia initially saw a woman therapist for an assessment, and the therapist picked up some anxiety in Olivia, although she had nothing upon which to base this sense. Olivia did not ask for a male therapist, but the assessor referred her to a male colleague. Her intuition was confirmed in the first session that her colleague had with Olivia. She told him that there were things she had been unable to tell the woman she had first seen; and that she never went to women doctors. She had once been involved in a lesbian relationship which continued to upset her, and she obviously feared the re-emergence of such feelings if she saw a woman doctor or therapist.

Interwoven themes

The interplay between the major themes, which has already been alluded to in relation to sadism and masochism, is also illustrated in examples about anxiety of being in the spotlight – a reaction perhaps against a form of exhibitionism; or even in the need to be on show, although it appears in a non-sexual way. There is something more narcissistic about enjoying being on show, although it can be socially acceptable narcissism, such as in professional acting. There are other factors involved in being on show, because the stage or screen is a place where different roles can be taken on temporarily and acted out, by actors for themselves, and on the audience's behalf. This type of exhibitionism and narcissism (which I am not portraying as pathological) can be seen in other forms of work and play where people hope to bask in admiration and applause. Sometimes these people (and this often applies to public figures as well) may also be quite distant in their relationships 'off stage', as if they have a more fragile sense of identity in private. There are therefore plenty of metaphorical stages where people take on roles, and hide behind masks. In this example both aspects are obvious:

> Pat had never felt affirmed as a girl by her father, who spent his spare time fishing, away from the home. She was also unable to allow herself any sexual relationship, and was even afraid of being touched. She had been sexually abused by a much older brother. As someone involved in amateur dramatics she not only received some sense of value from the audience's applause, but she was also able to play the sexual woman on stage. But if one of her fellow actors ever asked her out, she always refused, even steering clear of post-production parties.

The need to put oneself forward, and to sell oneself, is often a key factor in career and academic success. Ambition involves being comfortable with competitiveness and with showing oneself off. Indeed, it is something with which a child needs to feel comfortable when starting out in the world: success at school depends to some extent on the child's capacity to demonstrate her or his abilities. In a home where there is a repressive attitude to 'showing off', a child may be reluctant to stand out in a class. Certain topics, such as creative writing, require not only imagination, but a certain amount of positive exhibitionism in order to reveal one's ideas, and other sides of oneself. Conversely, it is possible to find examples where clients' shyness or inhibition are linked to a conflict in themselves about their wish to be 'on show' and 'out in front':

Rachel arrived for counselling with a beautiful smile and a striking red beret – these were the first impressions the college counsellor had of her. She had recently started at college as a mature student, but could not go into lectures, because she felt faint in the crowded room. She was able to identify the first occasion of this feeling as the third week of term in one particular lecture.

During the initial session she related how she had once wanted to go to college to study drama, but she had had at that time to go out to work to keep herself. She had been able to enjoy her interest in drama through amateur societies. She was fine, even now, in crowded rooms, when she felt she was 'the life and soul of the party'. She could not understand what had made her feel so bad in the lecture room. She said she did not want to faint and 'make an exhibition of myself'.

While she was talking her counsellor registered a number of these phrases, put them together in his thinking, and tested out an inter- pretation: that although Rachel did not want to make an exhibition of herself, she might also feel frustrated at having to sit still and listen when she liked to be up front entertaining. Her eyes lit up, and she capped his explanation with a forceful condemnation of the lecturer who was teaching at the time when she first felt faint. He was dreadfully boring; he did not allow anyone else the chance to speak, or to ask questions, or make a contribution themselves. It was as if she needed to 'protest' in some way (by fainting or walking out because she felt she might faint) both at the boredom of the lecture, and also at her inability to 'show off' herself, since she could be much more entertaining than him.

Showing ability at certain academic subjects may also be related to the ease with which a child at school or an older student feels comfortable with themselves and their body: biology, sport, dance and drama all involve interest and pleasure in the body as well as in the total self; or certain subject areas may be associated with being a stereotypical man or woman, and some subjects may be seen as too 'cissyish' or 'only for boys'. There is greater freedom and opportunity to learn where sexuality and sexual identity are not pressing issues that intrude upon other activities. One of the major problems for learning in adolescence, when so much depends upon being able to secure academic or technical qualifications, is that some of the learning evokes the very emotions to which adolescence is so open. Some young people find it too difficult to hold together their studies of certain areas with their emotional volatility, and they either push away their studies, or repress their feelings by using an intellectual defence and becoming over-immersed in their books.

There is a particular form of exhibitionism that is seen in the client who shows off sexually, traditionally called the 'hysteric', although the term has largely become a pejorative label which provides little in the way of under- standing of such men and women. These people sometimes flaunt their sexuality, but quickly cut and run if a relationship gets too close. In this example, the therapist appeared to get beneath the obvious presentation:

Steve talked for a number of sessions about his relationships with women and his fantasies about them, and led the therapist to think Steve saw women only as sexual playthings. Eventually the therapist chanced a remark about all this sexual talk being something of a red herring, and Steve broke down and cried. He began to speak about feeling unloved, unwanted and useless, particularly in relation to his mother. For the first time the therapist felt she had touched a more genuine side of Steve than the previous bravado had ever allowed her to see.

Although hysterics have commonly been identified as women who taunt and tease, there are plenty of men who do the same, seen perhaps in this last example, and certainly in the Don Juan character. Yet in classical psychoanalytical literature it is difficult to find the term 'hysteric' being used of this type of person. In Fenichel's encyclopaedic work *The Psychoanalytic Theory of Neurosis* (1946), the term does not appear in the comprehensive index. The closest to it is a section on character disorders; and elsewhere when Fenichel describes the histrionic person and the schizoid character we find parallels to the stereotypical 'hysteric'.

We have in these histrionic presentations another example of the way in which the major themes interweave, and how what a client presents may be understood in a number of different ways, depending upon which perspective we take: the theme of trust and attachment, for example, might just as well help us understand this type of presentation of sexuality as the theme of competition and cooperation. To be sure, there is a certain metaphorical 'castrating' by such people of those who try to get close to them. But therapists trying to work with such clients, if they can help them to stay in therapy, find problems that run deeper than sexuality, such as a deep hunger for love, and yet a terror of rejection. It is important not be seduced by the excitement of the sexual presentation or to be repelled by distaste of it. It will in time be necessary to interpret deeper levels than the sexual, and those who work short term may want to refer such clients for longer-term therapy. Fenichel suggests that there are pre-Oedipal factors at work in these presentations. Sex is used as a substitute for a more primitive need, such as the wish to be reunited with mother; and the sexual greed that is often apparent is a substitute for infantile needs of love. The flight of such people indicates their ambivalence about closeness.

Jenny was very perceptive about her feelings, and could see what was happening in her regular seduction and dropping of men. She experienced three clear gains each time, although she felt some regret afterwards. First, she wanted to give a man such a good time that he was left with a memory of her as someone really special. Second, she chose men who thought they were macho, and she so dominated them in sex that they felt weak and inferior. She compounded this by never speaking to them again, just nodding at them in a condescending way if they met. She admitted she got great pleasure from seeing such 'fine' examples of manhood become so submissive. Third, Jenny enjoyed other women admiring the way she could pick up men and be so disparaging of them afterwards.

There seemed to be a link between her present behaviour and her childhood. For years she had been her father's special favourite, but she was suddenly pushed out of favour when he remarried: his new wife came between them. She hated her father for this. At the same time, while some of this material was obviously linked to Oedipal problems, Jenny described her need to treat men the way she did as 'like a drug', with the possibility that the loss of her mother early in her life had led to this deep hunger for revenge.

Cooperation and competition as a lifelong process

Apart from the rivalries involved in the Oedipal triangle, three-person and other competitive situations arise throughout life. For example, apart from parent–parent–child rivalry, there is of course sibling rivalry, with older children having to make way for new members of the family, and younger children born into a shared environment of care. Order in the family, the gap between births, and many other factors need to be taken into account in assessing the impact of new siblings, but when a sibling is born before the older child has become relatively independent of mother, there may be stronger rivalry:

> Una was apparently devoted to her younger sister, born when she was 18-months old. Yet there were signs that beneath the devotion there was much jealousy. Una had been told by her mother that she used to hug her little sister so tightly as a baby that her mother thought she was going to strangle her – although Una thought it was because she loved her so much. In her dreams Una would sometimes scratch her sister, even doing this once when sleep-walking. Una was a member of an anti-abortion group, and as a teenager she had sorely tested a close friendship when she told her pregnant girlfriend that she was a whore. Both these factors made the therapist wonder what Una made of her mother's pregnancy when her sister was expected. She was very competitive in nearly everything she did, jealous about anyone else doing well, even when another's success cost her nothing. Over a long period of therapy Una saw how she had felt pushed out by her sister. It may have been significant that she stopped campaigning against abortion, and became much more understanding of the dilemmas facing women. It may have been that her fanaticism was a reaction against her own wish to kill her young rival while still in the womb.

Where there is a miscarriage or still-birth, or the death of a sibling, a child's fantasy of getting rid of the new arrival and rival (often expressed in the apparently innocent phrase 'Can we send baby back now, Mummy?') might cause a child to think their wish has brought this about, in turn leading to a sense of guilt. We have already seen in Chapter 10 how rivalry may also be felt in a more obvious way in pregnancy and at the birth of a child by the father, who not only feels pleased, but may also feel excluded. Sex may of course be more difficult during his partner's pregnancy, and the baby may feel like a rival for her care and attention. A few men develop physical symptoms which seem to indicate a sympathetic pregnancy of their own; others turn away from their partner and engage in an affair.

Nursery groups, play groups and school provide for the social development of the child, and for some their first taste of cooperative and competitive situations. Children can benefit from learning that they and their peers have varying abilities in different areas. These experiences also encourage cooperative play and learning. 'Mutual play is a keystone in social development', writes Rayner (1986: 108), observing the way in which play requires a child to sympathize with others as having their own needs. In their play children make and break alliances, and forge and forget friendships. Erikson calls this period 'the infantile politics of nursery school, street corner and barnyard' (quoted by Lowe 1972: 91). Children's games and make-believe give them opportunities to fight and make it up, to share power and leadership, as part of the preparation for living as adults in a wider society. Cooperative work in pairs and in groups might be preferable to the subordination of learning to competitive tests and examinations, although this seems far from the spirit of what governments and the inevitably competitive business world wants. What is perhaps frightening, as Erikson writes in *Toys and Reasons* (1978), is not that children should play such games, but that adults (particularly politicians) do not appear to have grown beyond them.

A certain degree of competitiveness is essential for success in life, sometimes in love, often in work. Lack of confidence, low self-esteem or anxiety about losing in competition may cause all kinds of difficulty. Behind the unwillingness of some people to engage in competitive situations, even those where it really does not matter who wins or loses, we may find shame at lack of success in the past. Other non-participants sometimes appear to react against their unconscious wish to triumph over others.

Some people can become overcompetitive, fanatical over their support for a team, as if the team carries their need to triumph over others. Rivalry with others can become so intense that healthy competition (the wish to achieve what others achieve) disappears, and aggressive competition takes its place. The pressure from some parents for academic success for their child (as if the child is as much a status symbol for them as their car, their house and the latest gadget) may serve a child well in the examination system, but can cause great difficulties later in their education or their career. Alternatively, inhibition of the ability to work may arise from unfavourable comparison with others. A combination of factors is seen in this example:

Victor had lost his father a few months before he was due to go up to university. He initially deferred his place for a year in order to help his mother to cope. University was at first an easy enough place for him, and a relief from the sadness at home. But by his third year Victor explained to the university counsellor that some of his difficulty in working academically was because his mother had invested so much hope in his success. He felt he was being asked to work hard to give her the same sort of pleasure she had gained from her husband's success and popularity. Victor felt he had slipped too far into his father's shoes, and that not studying was one way of trying to get out of the predicament.

Depending upon the levels of unemployment at a given time in society, seeking work may mean intense competition. Application forms, interviews, and rejections are almost inevitable, for young and old alike; and getting a particularly sought-after job may involve some guilt at succeeding at the cost of others who have not. Professional sportsmen and women often require what is called the 'killer instinct' – the ability to drive the winning stroke home. By contrast some people are concerned at meeting other applicants at interview, because their success will mean another's failure. They find it difficult to present themselves well:

Will (although not a serious sportsman) described his difficulty over winning at tennis. He felt he gave up trying just at the point at which he could win a match, particularly when he was playing his father, even though Will was the better player. This seemed to be the case in interviews too: he felt so bad about outdoing the others waiting with him that he fluffed every interview, until he attended an interview that did not involve meeting the other candidates. This time he was able to secure the position.

The impact of second marriages and of step-families provides another potential place for fierce rivalry between step-parent and child, or the siblings in a reconstituted family:

Yolande's mother died when she was 12. Her father remarried a year later. Yolande was very angry, because she thought her mother had been forgotten; but she was also resentful for herself, since she was pushed out from the special closeness she had with her father in their shared grief. As soon as she was old enough, she left home to live with a man who was old enough to be her father. She continued to be what she described as 'insanely jealous' of other women, and would not permit her partner to go out for a drink with his friends. She would cause scenes on many mornings when he was leaving for work. To compound the picture, her partner's mother was also very jealous of Yolande, as indeed she had felt about her son's previous girlfriends. Yolande's greatest fear was that her man would look at other women and lose interest in her. Her partner, who came with her for joint counselling, may not have realized how significant the phrase was, when he described her relationship to himself as 'almost incestuous'.

There is a different sort of rivalry apparent in adolescence between parents and their growing children. At the same time as young people are finding work and making their first close relationships, their parents may be conscious of imminent or present changes in themselves. A mother may be anticipating the menopause as the daughter has her first periods. A father may be aware of his spreading midriff and lack of muscular tone as his son is reaching the peak of physical fitness. It would be surprising if parents did not in some way feel jealous of their teenage children, aware of their own past youth, and sometimes envious of the freedoms and opportunities that were less openly available to them when they were young. Winnicott describes it well, sympathizing with the problems of being a parent:

> Your rewards come in the richness that may gradually appear in the personal potential of this or that boy or girl. And if you succeed you must be prepared to be jealous of your children who are getting better opportunities for personal development than you had yourselves. You will feel rewarded if one day your daughter asks you to do some baby-sitting for her, indicating thereby that she thinks you may be able to do this satisfactorily; or if your son wants to be like you in some way, or falls in love with a girl you would have liked yourself had you been younger.
>
> (1971: 168)

There may be rivalries as the young adult sets up in a relationship with a partner, who is obviously someone from outside the family and its values, who also brings different dimensions to a person's experience. Conflicts with in-laws may indicate an unwillingness to let go of child and/or parental roles. A person's parents (in his or her internal world) may intrude upon their own close relationship. Freud once wrote that there are four other people present in the bedroom, including the parents of the opposite sex in phantasy: in one extreme instance a client told how he found it difficult making love to his wife because he kept thinking she had turned into his mother. The parent–child relationship is inevitably carried over into the husband–wife relationship, with all the positive and negative features of the original relationship enhancing or impeding the present one, again as has been illustrated in Chapter 10. In some instances these rivalries are made more difficult because of living arrangements, such as early in a relationship, where a young couple has of necessity to live for a time with one set of parents; or later in a relationship where a widowed parent is brought into the family home. These are not easy situations, but they are even harder when Oedipal ties interfere.

Rivalries can of course exist between the two partners in a couple. Competitive anxieties about gender and role can lead to tensions:

> Adam had always been the major bread-winner in the family. When he was made redundant it was natural that he should have felt depressed. But his depression was made worse through having no income of his own and becoming dependent upon his wife's salary. He became increasingly angry with her and women generally. In his therapy (paid for by his wife) it was a long time before the therapist (a woman) was able to create a sense of equal partnership, because Adam also resented her having an occupation. There was something of a breakthrough when he was eventually able to tell her that he was also depressed because his situation had made him almost totally sexually impotent; it appeared that he no longer feared so much that such an admission would put him in a totally inferior position.

Winnicott's recognition of the pleasure that accompanies some rivalry, pleasure for the success of the child or another loved person, takes an interesting twist in old age. No doubt the same issues of rivalry can be directed towards the younger generation, but there is a particular pleasure which Hanns Sachs (1948) refers to, that of reading the obituary columns and forgiving old acquaintances for those things in them which have irritated us, because with each death we have triumphed over them by outliving them!

Rivalry and competition are also present in the relationship with the therapist, either in its own right as in Adam's case above, or in relation to other clients whom the therapist sees. Some clients wonder how important they are in comparison with the others.

> Bob arrived for his session after a three-week break. In fact the break had been intended to be two weeks, but the day that he should have met his therapist again, she was ill and had to cancel. When the two of them met, Bob asked her whether she had seen her other clients that week – he imagined he was the only one she didn't want to see.
>
> He went on to say that he felt his mother was more interested in his sister and her children than in him; and how distant he felt from his wife, who was expecting their first child. These references all clearly linked to show the struggle he had with rivalrous situations.

A therapist's presumed outside relationships may also be the subject of interest, or occasions for jealousy:

> Calum had always felt inferior to his brother, and Calum's wife, before he had met her, had been his brother's girlfriend. One night Calum dreamed of anger and jealousy towards a dark-haired man. When he associated to this dream in therapy, he realized that the dream had occurred the night after seeing his therapist at a concert with her dark-haired husband.

A further aspect of rivalry accords with Winnicott's view of parents and their growing children. Therapists need to come to terms with their own Oedipal issues, so that they can rise above issues of rivalry with their clients. Hartung (1979) particularly relates this issue to supervision, and the need for teaching to be 'done in order that students finally surpass the teacher'. There are also interesting issues of competition in supervision which Searles (1965b: 601) raises; but in the context of therapy, therapists need to be careful not to cling to their status as authority figures, and should always be working with the aim of clients becoming equal, or better, at the business of understanding themselves. Whatever jealousy and envy may arise in the transference, there is no place for rivalry in a good working alliance (Greenson 1967: 190–216).

The single person

Much space has been given over in this theme to intimate relationships, which tends to assume that such relationships are representations of maturity. It is obviously true that in one way couple relationships are the norm in many societies, although even here there are variations in marital arrangements that mark a divide between cultures. I have stressed in a number of places how definitions of psychological maturity, whether intra-psychically, or in relation to others, are culturally determined. Furthermore, although Freud's famous definition of maturity was 'to love and to work', how a society understands both love and work at any one period of time is also a changing concept. People work, even if they are not in employment. People are in loving relationships even if they choose to stay single. Much that can be defined as healthy depends perhaps more upon an inner state of mind, and upon self-perception, than upon external appearances.

We have therefore to be cautious in promulgating psychological and societal norms. Erikson (1965), for example, in his scheme of the Eight Ages, believes that before the stage of intimacy a young person must achieve a sense of personal identity; that before coming together with another, there must be a securely based sense of self. Rayner (1986: 192, 196–7) argues that women's comparatively greater discontent with long-term partnerships, which is well documented, might be related partly to their losing much of their identity (characteristically, losing their surname in legal marriage). Nevertheless feminist critics have rightly observed that Erikson's model is male-centred, since it is men who fear losing their identity in closeness more than women. Intimacy and self-identity are issues that run throughout life, not being confined to a particular stage of young adulthood.

Societal expectations for early marriage and child-bearing are less obvious in Western society, although they are still prevalent in some communities and in other societies. In addition to these pressures, there are those who find it impossible to contemplate living alone or being alone, and seek a parent substitute in an early partnership. Some young men look for an immediate replacement for mother, so they never really leave home, particularly in teenage marriage where adolescence is foreshortened. For some young women early pregnancy may also be a way of avoiding being alone, projecting their dependency needs onto their child. Similarly early pregnancy in a new partnership may be a way of avoiding intimacy in just being a couple.

David's 18-month-old relationship had just broken up. He was, of course, very upset, but perhaps as much because he was losing the promise of the home they were going to set up, as because his partner had left him. They had lived together all that time and were creating a secure place in which he enjoyed doing things around the house. He was 18. He also spoke in the first session of his parents' separation, when his mother had walked out on him and his father. He went into great detail about the domestic arrangements at that time. His therapist observed that the present break was all the more painful because he and his partner had been recreating what he had lost when he was 11. David agreed, but hastened to add, rather defensively it felt, that his girlfriend was not a mother substitute. A few weeks later he had moved in with an older separated woman.

Ellen became pregnant when she was 17 outside the context of a steady relationship. She had been the apple of her family's eye as a baby when she was the only child. When she was 2, her brother was born and her mother told her how her princess-like behaviour changed to constant tantrums. Ellen herself said she had been depressed 'as long as I can remember'. She recalled dreams since early childhood, still occurring now, with images of being locked out, left out, left behind, pushed out and so on. She described herself as 'like a leech' although she also appeared so independent now that it suggested a fear of what might happen if she allowed herself to become attached. Her baby appeared to be an attempt to recreate the intense relationship with her mother from which she had experienced her brother's birth as separating her.

A very high proportion of adults live relatively alone in Western society, some of them as single parents with children, some perhaps in community accommodation, such as the elderly. The number of single people appears to be rising, so that despite concerns about the importance of the family, the traditional nuclear family is nowhere near the norm. Adults living alone are therefore as much part of a therapist's clientele as those in committed sexual relationships. Some are alone by choice, and others by circumstance, such as the widowed, those whose partners have left, or those who have spent their life looking after parents. Being single may be a problem, but it also may not. There are, for example, distinct advantages in being single, such as the opportunity to withdraw and (as one person put it) 'shut the front door on other people'. A single person need not be without close companions and deep friendships, yet have the bonus of being more free to move, change jobs, make decisions, without the ties of partner and children. Care for others, as well as the generativity and creativity that Erikson associates closely with mid-adulthood, may be expressed in a person's work and interests rather than in partnership and family.

The single status has its own kind of difficulties. Single parents, for example, frequently have to combine two functions, which we might call maternal and paternal, without allocating a specific gender to either role. They generally experience less freedom and greater financial problems than two-parent families. A single parent may have chosen this extra strain instead of the tensions of being in a destructive relationship, but others may have been deserted by their partner:

> Fran described what it had been like bringing up her two children single-handedly for five years, contrasting that period with the time since she had remarried. She said how difficult it had been to be both mother and father. It wasn't all sweetness now because 'Daddy is the good guy and I'm seen as the bad guy when he comes home from work, but that is far better than being the bad guy, and having no one to share your feelings with, or to discuss how to handle the kids'.

Single people can experience being felt as a threat to couples. A single woman, perhaps divorced or a relatively young widow, can be viewed with suspicion by some women who are in a partnership. Such feelings of rivalry, although not the single person's issue, can be hard to endure. A single person whose life has been intimately bound up with their work, and has found their principal companions through work, may find retirement or redundancy even harder to manage, although of course some marriages are equally put under enormous strain when in such circumstances the partners are forced more closely together:

> Gabby had never married and she had no family responsibilities, so she chose to leave her job when she was offered the opportunity of early retirement. She was able to indulge herself in the reading and thinking that she had always wanted to enjoy. In many respects she seemed to have adjusted well to this way of life; but she had an egocentricity about her which was not the same as the self-contentment often found in an older person. She did not show the same interest that older people often do in those who are younger than themselves. To those who knew her, there seemed a hollow ring to Gabby's constant recommendation: 'You just get out of the rat race. It's the best thing I've ever done'.

In summary, the issues that trouble a single person need be no different from those that concern those in intimate relationships. There are specific areas of concern to each, but being single need not be seen as a failure to relate. Indeed the capacity to be alone has already been seen as a vital developmental achievement, which I discussed as part of the first theme. The avoidance of being alone can be understood as a difficulty. Rayner writes that 'to find one's identity it seems centrally important to be *able to be alone* ... *alone with one's conscience*' (1986: 192, original emphasis). Actual aloneness is also very much part of life: becoming single will be a common experience, as people adjust to being alone at various points such as separation, divorce, the death of a partner, redundancy and retirement. And in any relationship too there needs to be this ebb and flow between closeness and solitude, or as I have expressed it earlier, relatedness and separateness. Couples who are too closely bound up in each other appear to be afraid of separating out. Each individual in a partnership needs space to work through his or her particular concerns, alone as well as together.

There are of course instances where a therapist wonders whether the single person has difficulties about initiating and maintaining relationships, either of an intimate or a companionable kind. The type of non-sexual relationships, or even the type of sexual relationships (such as the promiscuous), may provide indications as to how genuine is the psychological health of a particular single person. There may be difficulties breaking the parent–child bond sufficiently to engage freely with others, where the 'child in the adult' cannot leave the actual or internalized parent in order to make other relationships. Living alone may indicate a defence against intimate relationships, which, as long as it works, need not of course be of concern. Fear of closeness may indicate schizoid characteristics (see p. 62), but there are plenty of people with schizoid traits who enter into apparently close relationships, and are far more lonely than single people are.

Towards integration

Freud's original ideas consider the release of tension as a constant aim, without appearing to take fully into account the relationships that enable this release to take place. Later he stressed the need to live by the principle of reality, rather than the principle of pleasure. He also portrays the reality principle as consisting of the need for the central ego to balance the demands of the id, the super-ego and the external world. Klein describes the state of relative equilibrium as the depressive position, one that is able to contain love and hate, and other contradictory emotions, as well as one that shows concern for others as well as self. But the paranoid position is always lurking round the corner, even when things are going relatively well! Erikson elaborates a scheme in which the different strengths of each developmental age come together in the eighth age of ego integrity. Jung wrote of progress, particularly in the second half of life, towards individuation, which is more than a sense of individual identity. It also involves integration of the unconscious, the collective unconscious, and a sense of one's place in the wider scheme of things.

Most of these models of mature development describe an inner world in which different 'parts' or 'objects' need to relate together – a kind of integration. In the external world mature relationships suggest that people are able to relate closely, socially, in work, politically and internationally, as well as acknowledge the importance of the environment in which they live, and from which they draw different resources. Following Winnicott we might also see life as a perpetual adaptation to the environment, immediate as well as the wider world; or following Erikson as a continuous process of finding identity. Identity is, however, particularly in a fast-changing world, a fluid concept, stressing perhaps how vital the early experiences of the child are for adaptation throughout life. What we might hope for is a sufficiently secure sense of self, or ego, or individuality (call it what you will), to meet and work with the inevitable changes that growing up and growing older bring. In the psychological typology of adolescence referred to in Chapter 8 (p. 152), there is a very different character to that of the foreclosed adolescent. This is the questioning, identity-seeking adolescent, who, when asked to describe himself or herself, tends to reply, 'I am searching, I am wondering, I am curious' (Marcia 1975). Such a description fits well the adult who is open to adaptation. It also indicates a desirable quality in those who seek help through counselling and psychotherapy.

The process of change involves introspection, imagination, a capacity to look back as well as look forward, an empathic concern for the impact of personal change upon others, as well as healthy narcissistic concern for oneself. The major points of life for the majority of the population involve having to handle changing relationships and changes in relationships, with their inevitable issues about trust, authority and cooperation. For example, Rayner emphasizes that when a couple become parents:

> as a child grows, so it is necessary for a parent to change in sympathetic responsiveness to his/her child. This entails not only being intuitively

aware of himself at equivalent ages to the child, but also being aware of his own life and his child's life as separate and with differing present-day problems.

(1986: 203)

So relationships do not remain static, and in addition to changes in parent and child, each partner is almost bound to change to some extent. In the early years of a committed partnership there are likely to be changes of home and of jobs. Some career changes bring different identities with them for one or other partner. There may be geographical relocations which involve making new friendships, more easily made when there are children at home, or other social interests that take people outside the home. If in becoming parents a couple changes, this happens just as much when grown children leave home. Some couples take a 'second honeymoon' at such times, but it is noticeable that divorce rates are at their highest at significant points like this: in the first two years (when it is discovered that intimacy does not work); after seven to eleven years (when the children are at their most demanding); after twenty or so years (when the children have left home); and at retirement age.

The work setting, as we have seen in previous chapters, raises aspects of the various themes including cooperation and competition. There is a growing literature on the dynamics of the work setting (Obholzer 1994), and on counselling at work (Carroll 1996; Carroll and Watton 1997; Coles 2003). Part of the satisfaction of work in the past has been a sense of belonging, of having taught younger people the skills of a job, and upon retirement handing over responsibility, knowing that one has helped others to take over. In a society where jobs are not for life, and where it is rare to work for a single institution or company in one place for more than 10 years, the continuity of past employment practices and its attendant psychological rewards have largely passed. Change is frequent in work as well.

Many people at retirement now have 10 or 20 years of life ahead of them, with opportunities for them to develop, although this is dependent upon their attitude to retirement and old age, as well as upon finance. One feature of ageing is the way in which the presenting past comes alive in a new way. Ageing provides time for life as a whole to be reviewed. Memory can play tricks, although sometimes memories of the more distant past are clearer than those of more recent events. Perhaps the unconscious need not be feared so much; perhaps the super-ego, those internalized parents, ceases to exert so strong a hold; perhaps what has been repressed comes through in a fine balance of positive and negative experiences – hardship in childhood, for instance, can be remembered for what it was, but its positive qualities are recalled as well. Rayner (1986: 255) describes old people as living historians to society, but their history is just as important to themselves. Older people enjoy telling their history, and in this telling of old stories there is a reworking of their life, which Lowe (1972: 225) lists as features of the eight Erikson ages: (a) whom one has learned to trust; (b) what to hold on to and what to let go; (c) initiatives taken; (d) practical and social skills; (e) confirmation of identity; (f) marriage; (g) and work.

Change, long before old age, also means coming to terms with loss, as certain relationships, old patterns, and tangible objects and occupations have to be let go of. Involved in all loss, but more obviously following the death of a parent, child or partner, a significant process of change involves the internalization of the person who has gone. C. S. Lewis (1971) describes such a process in the diary written after the death of his wife, a story now familiar through the play and film *Shadowland*:

Something quite unexpected has happened. It came this morning early. For various reasons, not in themselves at all mysterious, my heart was lighter than it had been for many weeks. For one thing I suppose I am recovering from a good deal of mere exhaustion, and after ten days of low hung grey skies and motionless warm dampness, the sun was shining and there was a light breeze. And suddenly, at the very moment when so far, I mourned H. least, I remembered her best. Indeed it was something almost better than memory: an instantaneous unanswerable impression. To say it was like a meeting would go too far. Yet there was that in it which tempts one to use those words. It was as if the lifting of the sorrow removed a barrier. Why has no one told me these things? How easily I might have misjudged another man in the same situation. I might have said, 'He's got over it. He's forgotten his wife', when the truth was, 'He remembers her better because he has partly got over it.'

The ability to carry on living, with confidence in oneself, after such a loss, depends upon a number of factors. Where a relationship has been brief and only touched the surface, separation is likely to be felt as a simple memory: good, bad or indifferent. Where the relationship has been more extensive and has reached into deeper feelings, the situation is more complex. One that has caused hurt and damage leaves a particular memory, together with pain and caution about relating on the same level again. But most relationships of any depth contain good and bad feelings. Perhaps what is important is how we perceive the feelings towards us of the person we have lost. Yet even that perception may be influenced by our view of ourselves, especially if we have underlying uncertainties about ourselves carried over from early experience. We may feel the other did not care, when in fact he or she did. Any anger we then feel, however unjustified, makes the process of internalization difficult.

Where the relationship has been felt overall to be a good, caring and loving one, then of course that person will be greatly missed; but in time sadness will be combined with the pleasure that comes from recalling positive memories, and from the internalized figure bringing sustenance and strength to the self. There will be no need to cling, no need to rail. Instead there is quiet contentment, a feeling of good fortune, a deep sense of having been added to; and we can say with conviction, 'I'm glad we knew each other'. Recalling the phrase cited in the list of stages of grief on pages 4–5, 'The loved object is not gone, for now I carry it within myself and can never lose it' (Abraham 1927).

For some people, and in some societies, religious beliefs, images, symbols and rituals assist the process of change, enable coming to terms with loss, and promote psychological integration. A person's faith can be repressive, or can reflect some of their psychological problems. As referred to in earlier themes, religious belief can be used or misused as a support of a defence (pp. 71–2,

120–1). I examine different expressions of belief and knowledge elsewhere (Jacobs 2000a), finding myself particularly drawn to that expression of belief that is to my mind more integrative, drawing upon different resources in terms of the unconscious as well as poetry, art, and other spiritual belief systems. There can develop a faith position that is essentially coherent without being rigid, and which in the end acknowledges just how much we do not know and do not understand; and yet in certain respects comes full circle, so that we know old things in new ways.

Full circle? There is certainly a circularity about personal development, which the three major themes in this book have illustrated, a process that is never completed, but is repeated in many forms and at different ages: in forming bonds of trust and attachment, in moving from dependency to independence, in becoming more autonomous and in managing one's own authority as well as the authority of others; in letting go of aspirations about certain aspects of the relationship with parents, yet identifying with what is best in them and in the right measure then leaving them behind; in learning and in training, in work and in play. These patterns recur through adolescence, in first and subsequent relationships outside the family, in becoming a parent and grandparent, at retirement, through bereavement and in approaching death. It is a process not only of relating to others, but of internalizing them in the building up of the self. The continually developing self relates anew to others and becomes, in turn, internalized in part in them. The mirroring of mother and baby in the nursing couple takes place in all kinds of relationships throughout life.

Counselling and psychotherapy have become recognized as legitimate ways of helping people deal with crises in this development. In the psychodynamic orientation this takes place by reviewing and reliving both the present and the past, with the therapeutic relationship itself becoming a means of doing this. That relationship also presents the possibility of modelling new ways to meet the future. The major themes in these chapters are just as significant in the therapeutic relationship, and it is these aspects of trust and attachment, authority and autonomy, and cooperation and competition that the final chapter roots in that vital interaction.

THE MAJOR THEMES IN
THE THERAPEUTIC
RELATIONSHIP

While the presenting past lies at the heart of psychodynamic therapy, it is certainly not the past that is at the centre of the work. It is rather the way the past presents itself currently, that is, in the here-and-now of the therapeutic relationship. The impression given by those who criticize psychodynamic therapy, that it is overconcerned with the client's history, is erroneous. The past is only relevant in as much as it is present, still in the thoughts, feelings and behaviours of the client. What is really at the centre of the work is that therapy can be a living example – a better phrase than the more usual 'living laboratory' – of the client's internal and external world, through which therapists are presented with opportunities to re-experience with their clients certain aspects of the presenting past. The therapeutic relationship is a medium in which the effects of the past can be reviewed; and through which (the effects to a varying extent can be adapted to the present and the future.)

I have in Chapter 1 questioned the usefulness of a stage model in relation to personality development, at the same time acknowledging the significance of certain clear events – single events such as birth and death, and continuous events such as childhood, adolescence, and ageing. All of the issues arising in the major themes may be present at any of these occasions or during these periods of time. We similarly need to question whether a stage model can be applied to the process of therapy, even though there(it clearly has a begin-ning, a middle and an end.)All of the major themes can be present at any of these points: so that the trust that is so important in the beginning of therapy has also to be present at the end, as the client sets out without any further assistance from the therapist. The trust at that point is in oneself; and that whatever the future holds it can be met without formal therapy. Similarly loss occurs not just upon leaving therapy but, as Wolff's (1977) perceptive article describes, upon entering it as well. He cites, for example, the loss to a person's self-image, that they need the help of another.

I hesitate therefore to describe the therapeutic relationship as a series of stages of therapy, although I cannot avoid discussing its beginning, middle (of varying lengths) and end. Yet the major themes set out in earlier chapters bear some relationship to a progression through therapy. Trust issues are most significant at or towards the beginning of therapy, and issues of letting go are more significant towards its end. Nevertheless the reader will by now be used to the principle that this scheme is one of convenience, and that the major themes may appear at different times. Rarely is anything as clearly sequential as it is in books! The order of the appearance of the themes may then be different from the order set out here. The different themes may be present at the same time, running alongside each other, so that the emphasis given to one theme rather than to another becomes a matter of careful choice on the part of the therapist in deciding in what way to make an intervention. Furthermore, allowance always has to be made for regression, so that therapist and client may have to rework earlier issues at a point of crisis, when they may be understood more profoundly than they were at the beginning; for example, if one party in the therapeutic relationship lets the other down, the relationship may temporarily go back to issues about trust and dependability. Yet if an attachment has been formed, such disturbances to the relationship are more readily endured.

There is a danger, when a useful model is developed, of forcing everything into particular patterns. My description of the way in which the therapeutic relationship reflects the themes of this book came originally not from a deliberate effort to fit the different stages of the therapeutic process into this thematic model. It was rather that as I analysed more carefully the typical course of therapy, I saw how closely the themes related to the therapeutic relationship as well. This is, of course, scarcely surprising: a psychodynamic approach, as I have already emphasized, suggests that anything to do with past and present relationships is likely to be reflected in the therapeutic relationship. All relationships are different, but it is interesting to see the way the therapeutic relationship, which likewise is different from other types of relationship, can resemble at various points the parent–child, the intimate, the working or the friendship relationship. I shall observe these various parallels in the following sections below.

Preparations

There is some similarity between the initial stages of therapy, and pregnancy and the immediate days after birth. As in a pregnancy, therapy starts before the client and the therapist meet face to face. It probably starts for a client before it does for the therapist (just as a foetus is developing before a woman knows she is pregnant), since either the client makes a decision to seek help, or another person suggests it, before the therapist can be contacted. This apparently practical business of making arrangements for therapy involves more than is usually recognized by the therapist, and may indeed influence the start of the therapy itself.

Concentrating for the moment upon what this preparatory period means for a client, there is initially a period of thinking about whether or not to ask for help, and whom to ask. A client may enter therapy voluntarily, or may have the first meeting arranged for them. In the former case, this involves the client in making enquiries, arranging an appointment and waiting for it. Initial contact, before or after assessment, is often with an intermediary – a receptionist perhaps, or someone else other than the therapist.

This intermediary person may be seen as in some way indicative of what to expect from a therapist as well. In many agencies clients have an assessment with one person, before meeting the actual person with whom they are going to work. Before the first meeting, a client's attitude is probably ambivalent, with some hope but also with some anxiety. There may be relief at having made an appointment, since it represents taking a first step in a new direction, and to some extent therefore represents trying to take control of the situation. The hope and the anxiety probably include some concern about the therapist, what he or she will be like, or even look like. There are no doubt heightened expectations about the therapist's knowledge and expertise.

Much of this can be called pre-transference, since it is based on little factual information, and a lot of fantasy and imagination. How the therapist and therapy are anticipated may be influenced by past experiences of important figures – whether they could be trusted, what sort of authority they had and how they used it. The setting for the therapy may also enter this imaginary picture: what the place itself will be like. There are also the arrangements that must be made for getting there.

This preparatory phase involves the therapist as well as the client, and if a client needs a therapist, it is just as valid to say that a therapist also needs a client, since this is the therapist's work, and probably her or his means of earning a living. A therapist (albeit relatively passively) may be looking for clients, as much as clients are seeking therapy. Once a client has rung, or the therapist has received a letter of referral, the therapist also has fantasies about the client. There may be previous notes, a referral letter, or information from an assessment, or even the brief conversation making arrangements for the initial session, any of which can provide tentative ideas about the client. A therapist may also wonder what the client will be like, whether he or she will be able to help this client, and how he or she will feel as a therapist when they first meet. There is therefore a 'pre-countertransference', which may or may not match the client's pre-transference. There is surely anxiety and hope on this side as well which will go on throughout the therapy, however experienced the therapist is. These early feelings may be heightened when the therapist accepts a referral from a third party, in that the therapist may also wonder whether he or she can fulfil the expectations of that person as well.

At this preparatory stage either person may be rejected by the other. A therapist or counsellor may have no spaces; or the initial arrangements may prove abortive if the client gets cold feet and decides to withdraw. Rejection is less likely on the therapist's side once the initial stages have been satisfactorily negotiated, but for the moment nothing is fixed.

Beginnings

Winnicott uses an interesting phrase in describing the initial relationship between the baby and the breast: he writes about 'the theoretical first feed' as 'also an actual first feed, except that in real experience it is not so much a matter of a single happening as a build-up of memories of events' (1988b: 100). He is describing the phenomenon whereby a baby wishes for the breast, and the breast appears, so that it seems to the baby that she has created the breast. He suggests that this does not necessarily happen only at the literal first feed, but over a series of early feeding experiences.

A similar phrase might be used of the beginning of therapy, using the term 'theoretical first session' to cover what occurs in the actual first session, but probably more accurately includes what may occur over a series of sessions right at the start. This theoretical first session (or series of sessions) is distinct from the first major theme of trust and attachment in therapy, even though it probably runs concurrently with it.

Whether or not the first session is the initial assessment of the client, or the first appointment with a therapist after another has conducted the assessment, the theoretical first session involves a mutual assessment process on the part of client and therapist. Each is sussing the other out, trying to get a feel of the other, so that both parties are wondering whether they want to get to know each other, and whether they will be able to work together. It is something like a job interview, although, like some job interviews, a client may be so desperate for help that the ability to assess the viability of the therapist is hampered by the urgency and nervousness of the situation.

In a theoretical first session it is possible that a client has much to say and express, but there are also many facts and feelings that cannot yet be shared. A client will present certain problems, but these may well mask others, which the client does not yet see as relevant. Indeed, this theoretical first session may have a feeling of being predominantly problem-centred, as a client explains his or her difficulties, and the therapist tries to understand their nature and their triggers, making (often silently) some tentative hypotheses. At this stage both the client and the therapist only present their most obvious aspect to each other, although each also has first impressions of the other. It is an interesting question of whether or not such initial impressions are significant. Many therapists have learned by experience that first impressions turn out to have considerable substance in the light of later events, even if for a time the first impression is temporarily overridden by the desire not to prejudge.

On the therapist's part, the theoretical first session consists of building up an initial picture of the client, mainly through receiving the preliminary information the client wants to share, with perhaps some judicious questioning. Taking a full history of the client is rare, although it is a little more common in some forms of psychotherapy – in psychodynamic as well as other approaches. Given the significance attached to the past, it is scarcely surprising that a psychodynamic therapist begins the task of piecing the client's history together from the start, although the pieces are like those in a jigsaw, falling into place throughout the therapy, but always with some or even many pieces missing. A psychodynamic therapist is particularly looking for pointers that might link presenting issues with past experience. In the first session, he or she may ask about earlier occurrences in order to get a wider picture – perhaps to find the edge pieces of the jigsaw. A psychodynamic approach also involves testing a client's capacity to acknowledge or make such links, because for this approach to work well, a client needs to relate his or her history, both as a narrative in its own right, as well as a story that connects with the present. Where they are very distressed, clients may not yet be in a position to engage in this type of thinking, and building a history may come later, as a client begins to see the significance of their past.

It is also possible that in this theoretical first session clients are interested in the therapist's history. I mean by this not simply their wish to know about a therapist's own past or their connections outside therapy – this type of interest may come later. I mean rather that there may be some concern for their history as a therapist: where they have trained, how long they have been working, what their orientation is and so on. Where this information is important to a client, and where it concerns professional background, it should be shared. Good therapists have no reason to hide their training or their way of working. They want clients to find the right person as much as clients do. When other relationships are first formed, they similarly often include finding out sufficient information about the other to identify whether they have enough about them that might encourage the relationship to develop. I suggest that this happens through a mixture of explicit information and implicit clues in the early meeting of client and therapist. At the same time there is much that is not known and not shared. On the client's part, this includes the greater part of their history, and probably the client's perception of the therapist; on the therapist's part this includes preliminary ideas about the client and the presenting issues as well as personal information.

This initial exploration, being to some extent a mutual one, also involves finding a common language. The client is the one who provides the impetus for this; the therapist follows, trying to understand her or his images, metaphors and symbols, as well as the actual way in which the client uses words. Clients vary in the way they use the first session: sometimes they wish to offload, and they care little whether they are being understood – they simply need to spill it out. The therapist may experience this as being 'dumped on', but this is an important part of the start of the therapeutic process. The therapist receives what is said, holds it and contains it, so that later in therapy, or towards its conclusion, much of it can be handed back in a reprocessed form. Therapeutic listening is not waste-disposal, but the first stage of recycling.

George brought a box of live cartridges to the second session. He had a licensed shot-gun, and he was afraid that he might use it against his former wife who had walked out on him. He asked the therapist whether he could look after the cartridges for him. The therapist took them from him, and in front of George he put them into the bottom of his filing cabinet, under his client files, so that the box was hidden but safely contained. They stayed there throughout a year's therapy, and when the rage and the suicidal feelings had passed, and George felt more secure within himself, at the last session he asked for return of the cartridges. In this symbolic act the therapist had contained the rage until such time as it was safe for George to receive it back.

If some clients at the start just want to let it all out, and dump it on the therapist, others are desperate to know whether what they are saying has been understood. This is especially important when they have not been believed in the past, which is a devastating experience, all too common in survivors of abuse. On her or his part too, a therapist or counsellor is also keen to know whether the language of therapy, suitably put across in words that make sense to the client, can be understood and worked with. This capacity to communicate is essential for the working alliance. One question that both parties are pondering, although it is more likely to be at the forefront of the therapist's mind, is whether they can work together. This is not the same question as whether I want to work with this client or this therapist. There may be features of the other that I like, but I still consider that therapy will not work. There may be aspects of the other that I dislike, but I do not believe these will prevent us working relatively well together.

Both parties are therefore looking for ways to make sufficient contact at this early stage to know that they have been heard. It may be a passing glimpse of something at a deeper level, but enough to signify for both the hope of going on. On the part of the therapist this is often found in the client's response to a 'trial interpretation', a rather grand term for an attempt on the therapist's part to make a link between what the client is describing, and what may be happening to the two of them in the session. If a client responds to this – either with a flash of recognition, or at least thoughtfully – this is a good sign for the use of a psychodynamic approach, which so much wishes to integrate past with present, and outside situations with what is experienced in the therapy itself.

There is another important aspect to the theoretical first session which sets the tone for much that follows, and which may arise again as it is tested out at a later stage. This consists of the practicalities, such as the contract, fee, time and frequency of meetings, and boundary issues which need to be clarified; for example, whether contact can be made outside the times of sessions. While these are in one way technical matters, each of these aspects involves setting up a boundary, which gives an indication as to the type of relationship being offered. The practical arrangements suggest how far this relationship can go; for example, contact is limited to sessions, or making contact in emergency situations is clearly fenced. The therapeutic relationship is not the same as a friendship. Arrangements about time and fees create a working contract, entered into by the two parties as adults, however much a client at other points may regress and behave in more childlike ways. Similarly the frequency of sessions sets a marker for the likely intensity of this relationship. Once-monthly meetings create a fairly distant relationship; twice-weekly sessions suggest the willingness to permit or even encourage dependency, which in turn leads to a very intimate relationship – more continuous attention to the client than anyone else in her or his adult life is likely to give them. It is interesting that once-weekly sessions in therapy and counselling appear to have become the norm (even for psychotherapists trained in greater frequency), as though this arrangement provides the right balance between intimacy and separateness, and between dependency and independence.

The psychodynamic approach is also interested in how a client responds to these practical issues, and the way boundaries are treated as the therapy or counselling progresses. I discuss this more fully later and in my chapter in Sills (2006).

Arrangements for times, frequency and places of meeting give a clear indication of the limits of the therapeutic relationship. It is interesting to note, in an article by Schwartz (1989), that research into psychiatrist–patient sexual abuse suggests that the use of first names, the extension of the length of sessions, and flexible appointment times are the first three steps on the path to full sexual relations. This does not mean that use of first names inevitably leads in that direction. It is common practice (although certainly not universal) for first names to be used when addressing clients, and when clients address therapists and counsellors. This may be indicative of a general loosening of formalities of Western culture, although it is interesting to note that GPs are encouraged not to use first names, as well as colloquial terms like 'dear'. In psychodynamic practice flexibility with appointment times is less common, and extending session times is generally not acceptable. Such variations in the original contract alter the frame of the therapy or counselling, often to the detriment of the therapy as well as the therapeutic relationship. There is a particularly strong concern for 'the frame' in the work of Langs and his followers (Smith 1991; Sullivan 1999).

Before the first session it is clients who hold most of the information, and therefore most of the power in the therapeutic relationship. During the assessment session or the theoretical first session, sharing this information, and perhaps exposing strong feelings, puts the client in a more vulnerable position, a position that is reinforced by the therapist having a much clearer sense of what therapy is about and what may happen in therapy. Since it is also the therapist's 'territory' upon which they are meeting, and it is generally the therapist who calls the tune over most of the practical arrangements, the therapist at this point will probably be seen as, and indeed have become, a very powerful figure.

Trust and attachment – the early sessions

Early sessions are not the same as the theoretical first session. There is not the same clear agenda, and not necessarily the same 'excitement' that there was in the first, when there was so much to say and so much to hear. At a first meeting a client usually has a mental list, or a diary of events that he or she wishes to relate. Therapy now needs to move away from a person's 'problems' to the less tangible aspects which up to now may not have been in the forefront of the client's mind: other significant people, other events, what a client thinks, how they relate to themselves, and how they relate with the therapist. The relevance of the therapeutic relationship may at first seem bewildering to a client, who is used to contact with other professionals being about problems 'out there', and not what is passing between them 'in here'. The trial interpretation in the theoretical first session may have given a clue to the client's willingness to shift from the immediate issue to underlying factors, and from thinking only in terms of outside relationships to including the relationship in therapy itself.

Building up trust is a life-long and a therapy-long process, but initial trust is vital. In time that trust is probably going to be tested more fully, but at this stage the client is looking for initial trust in the therapist and in the process. The therapist is looking for a sense of commitment to the process on the part of the client. This usually becomes clear after four or five sessions, which is why some practitioners like to offer an initial period with a possible review, before deciding upon a longer or open-ended contract.

Clients place enormous hope in their therapist, and sometimes even ask for confirmation that therapy will work. This is not an easy question to answer, because at this early point a client probably has little knowledge of what is involved. They know that it may take time, and (given the greater public knowledge about therapy) they probably think they will be encouraged to find their own answers. Underneath these rational thoughts, clients are often desperate for much more, expecting the therapist to be both omniscient and omnipotent, and wanting therapy to be immediately effective. How might a therapist handle these expectations and this idealization?

Winnicott (1965b: 180; 1975: 240) is helpful here with his concept of illusion, and his description of a mother as enabling her baby to have the illusion that the baby has created and governs the breast. He prefers the term 'illusion' to that of 'magical thinking'. At the beginning a mother allows her baby to hold this illusion of the baby's omnipotence; later she gradually allows the baby to experience disillusion, coming to terms with the reality that mother is also independent, outside the baby's control. I suggest that where a client appears to need it, a therapist may for a short time allow the illusion that therapy or the therapist has this omnipotence, that therapy works, and that the therapist knows: by this I do not mean claiming knowledge and power, but rather gently diverting high expectations if it is clear that the client, in desperation, needs to cling on to that kind of hope.

Therapists know, of course, that therapy does not always work, or that its results are not always as profound or extensive as the client wishes. Therapists are only too aware that while they know something, they never know enough, and that it is just as much a struggle for them to understand the client, as it is for the client to achieve self-knowledge. Openness about the nature of the therapeutic task and the limits of the therapist is not necessarily desirable at this early point. I am not here in any way supporting deception or false promises. It would be wrong for a therapist to make inflated statements about the efficacy of therapy. But it is possible to keep quiet, and to permit the illusion, when a client speaks of what they are expecting of therapy and therapist. The time for disillusion will come sooner or later, and that will need to be handled well.

Another interesting parallel to the early mother–baby relationship is seen in the way clients begin to see the therapist. This is sometimes demonstrated as clients for the first time notice pictures, or see for the first time other features of the consulting room. I once had a room in which a large poster of the Victoria Falls covered a particularly ugly feature opposite the door. It was significant how many clients, at about the third or fourth session, would enter the room and comment on 'your new poster' although it had been there all the time. This focus on the more immediate surroundings is a reflection of the client's relationship with the therapist too: it is probably a sign that the therapist has become a significant figure, and that clients are turning from their preoccupation with their initial concerns to what happens within the session as well. This might also be called the first sign of attachment: the realization that the therapist matters, and that (for the time being at least) 'I need him/her'. Indeed for some clients therapy becomes a literal lifeline, and the therapist's room a haven, a place they long to return to almost as soon as they leave the session. A therapist probably feels this close attachment too, although it is frequently masked because they immediately turn their attention to the next client and the next session. Trainees, who have only one or two clients, know how much they invest in them, and how much they too look forward to their client's return. Similarly, when clients do not turn up, the therapist's disappointment is a sign of this early attachment.

Coming together and being apart become significant, depending to some extent on the neediness of the client and the degree of dependency fostered by the frequency of meetings. The setting of boundaries in the assessment session, as stated earlier, is likely to mean that infrequent meetings deter the development of intense need for a close relationship with the therapist, while more frequent sessions often encourage it. For some clients being apart in the time between sessions is very difficult, and it is through their reactions to the gap between sessions that a therapist or counsellor may predict how a client might face breaks and holidays. Although these reactions may also suggest a difficult ending, this intense need early in therapy (or a return of such intense need if there is a crisis at a later period in the therapy) may make the absence of the therapist much worse, and more painful than it will be if therapy is able to end both successfully and at the right time.

It is perhaps an indication that this early phase has passed – even if issues of trust and attachment can continue to feature – when the therapeutic relationship itself is seen as having developed its own history and acquired a life of its own. Clients and therapists begin to recall things that were said or experienced a few weeks or months ago: 'Do you remember two weeks ago, when you said ... ?' There is a sense of continuity, that this will go on, without the ending being in focus at this stage, except in short-term work where the ending is one factor in a therapist's interventions. A client begins to share more thoughts and feelings, some of which were perhaps initially too dangerous to express. There are also memories and feelings, and thoughts about the therapeutic relationship itself that are not yet ready to be shared. The therapeutic relationship may still be idealized, although as the first signs of frustration and the hint of negative feelings appear, this may be a sign that therapy is settling down, and that issues related to the next theme are ready to come into focus.

Authority and autonomy – testing the therapeutic relationship

The middle phase of therapy and counselling is usually the longest, often consisting of working and reworking particular themes that make their appearance time and again in different guises and various situations. It is also a time of testing – testing out how much can be said, what feelings can be allowed, trying out different ideas, daring to think the unthinkable, and in some cases testing the authority of the therapist, or the validity of the initial boundaries. Clients who feel secure enough can therefore ask the question of themselves and of their therapist, 'How far can I go ... ?':

- in honesty to myself, to the therapist, and to others outside therapy?
- in depending upon and trusting the therapist?
- in the expression of negative feelings of all kinds (bearing in mind that for some clients even love is a negative feeling)?
- in using the therapist, by putting feelings and object-relationships onto her or him, that partly belong towards others (through transference and projection)?
- in challenging the therapist on points where I detect he or she is weak, perhaps by pushing at boundaries (such as the contractual arrangements made at the start of therapy)?

At the same time therapists are also faced with the question of how far they can go in honesty with their client, and in putting back to the client some of the projections and transferences that the client has placed onto them. Both client and therapist may also test out how far they can go in entering and staying with the 'chaos' of the inner world. For a client this may mean facing terrifying feelings from the past, or even the void within; for the therapist it may mean pushing at personal frontiers of knowledge, thought and experience. To do this means assessing how much the client can take, and how much the client can be allowed to express, as well as how well fitted and supported the therapist is for this task. The descent into chaos may involve regression (and all the issues of trust and attachment again), although therapists need to remember that the deliberate encouragement of regression is only for the most experienced. Winnicott, for example, experienced and highly skilled though he was, would apparently only allow one of his patients at a time to enter a deeply regressive phase. Little describes how 'he spoke of patients having to "queue up" sometimes to go into such a state [full regression], one waiting until another had worked through it and no longer needed him in that way' (1990: 47–8).

Essentially the client needs to test out what kind of relationship the therapeutic one is, and whether the therapist can accept, and even withstand, the expression of strong negative and positive feelings. In the case of boundaries the client may also test out what the therapist is prepared to tolerate, and where the therapist draws the line. I am reminded of Winnicott again, and his description of the need for parents to be responsible, while their adolescent children are permitted in their immaturity to test out aspects of relationships for themselves. But while clients may push at boundaries to test the therapist, we have to remember that rejection of the therapist's interventions, for example, is not always defensive. It is sometimes because the client is now strong enough to tell the therapist that he or she has got it wrong.

Involved in this testing is the almost inevitable occurrence that a therapist will from time to time let a client down. If nothing else he or she will fail to understand, or will make wrong interpretations. But there are other ways in which failure can be experienced. There will be breaks, or times when the therapist is late, or ill. The therapist has to disappoint the client who is looking for the therapist to become the parent, lover, friend, the magician, or even the authority that he or she so much desires. Without the client therefore pushing at boundaries, the relationship is bound to be tested in one way or another. The experience of such failures may be seen as equivalent to Winnicott's concept of disillusion, whereby a mother gradually lets the baby down, as far as the baby is able to take it, allowing more and more of the reality of the external world to impinge upon the baby. Therapeutic failure may be unplanned, accidental or the result of a mistake. Yet working through the experience of the therapist's failure, through the negative feelings in the client, and the disillusionment with the therapist and the process, are of equal importance to therapy, as is the whole psychological 'weaning' process in infancy. Kohut (1971, 1977) similarly emphasizes the need to work with empathic failure, so that with narcissistic clients, even if empathy is the principal intervention, failure to be empathic, or failing the narcissistic needs of the client, is a second major intervention (see also Siegel 1996).

Where this testing does not break the therapeutic relationship, and where both client and therapist survive these experiences, this leads the client to a realization of the 'permanence' of the relationship: that whatever happens and whatever is said, it will stay secure within the boundaries initially stated and negotiated. I am of course describing a process that may have been repeated many times before it reaches this stage. Things may go wrong on either side, but they can (eventually) be overcome, as long as both parties stand by their commitment to the process. The client knows the therapist will still be there; the therapist knows that even if the client misses one week in anger, he or she will still turn up to the following session. Disappointments and failure no doubt continue, but they can now be overcome without disastrous consequences for the therapeutic relationship. Disillusionment proves creative.

Although there is this strong sense of permanence, and confidence in the survival of the relationship, this is yet another illusion: therapy or counselling must of course end, and when it does the actual relationship will finish. For the present moment, however, even if the impermanence is head knowledge, it is not the way it feels; and it need not feel otherwise. Attachment deepens as a result; and therapist and client now deeply value the reliability, rock-like, staying qualities of the other as a foundation for all the other turbulent material that in many cases continues to emerge. At this stage there may be no thought of the therapy ever ending. It has yet to reach a point where the client is confident that 'I will survive even though these sessions have to end'. The process of working through involves recognizing patterns, some of which are rather too tightly fixed, and which need to be loosened up so that change and new development can take place. This happens within the context of the therapeutic relationship where those patterns can be repeated, and where there can be a sense (as in other relationships) of being 'stuck'. Defences have to be worked through, not attacked. These may prove to be points of potential breakthrough to new material, to things that have never been said before, or even been realized before.

Where it works well therapy and counselling begin to model how therapeutic other relationships can also be. While it is obvious that this particular relationship is perceived as unique by the client, who has probably not had a relationship quite like this one before, this is also true on the therapist's side. The client's emerging history and the particular relationship that is forged with this client makes her or him different from everyone else the therapist has seen, however much there are inevitably memories evoked of similar patterns and experiences with former clients.

Towards ending: internalization and Oedipal love

I do not wish to force the theme of cooperation and competition into this model of the therapeutic process, but there are aspects of it, particularly those to do with the negotiation of the Oedipus complex, that have particular relevance for the penultimate phase as therapy moves towards ending. Rivalry and competition issues, like the other major themes, emerge in the material and in the context of the therapeutic relationship itself long before this closing phase, as illustrated for example in the section on 'Cooperation and competition as a lifelong process' in Chapter 11 (pp. 210–14). So while these themes and stages of therapy are sure to overlap and merge, the next distinctive development for the client is the internalization of the therapist. I am sure that therapists and counsellors also internalize the clients with whom they work most intensely, in a way that is different from simply remembering them. It would be interesting to know how this affects the process of ending.

Signs of this process are seen, for example, in the way a client describes how 'I caught myself talking to myself, and then I thought "That's what you might say!"' This is a different internal process from talking more directly in fantasy with the therapist, as may happen earlier in therapy, where the client imagines what the therapist would say; it is rather that the client's ideas seem to match those of the therapist. This more developed internalization is far less conscious, and shows how both the therapist and the therapeutic method have become more part of the 'me' of the client. In time even the thought that 'This is what my therapist might have said' gives way to an unconscious internalized process in the client, joining other internalized objects past and present. On a more obvious level the therapy has become a joint venture, in which a client becomes confident of her or his own autonomy and separateness. All this resembles the way a child resolves the Oedipus complex, internalizing the parental figures, and moving forward on her or his own.

In this phase there are likely to be other signs of progress: the further withdrawal of projections and transferences; a growing realization that 'I' (the client, and not just, as in the early phase, the therapeutic relationship) am able to survive the breaks, which in turn gives hope for the ending of therapy) *does it?*

itself. On the therapist's part there may be experiences of that phenomenon that Searles describes as 'oedipal love in the counter-transference' (1965a). By this Searles means the therapist's strong feeling of the desire to be married with the client (of whatever gender), which Searles relates to the pride and pleasure that a parent has in their growing child, and their fantasy of wishing to continue in such an intimate relationship, although knowing too that this is a fantasy that cannot and should not be realized. Another parallel is the Pygmalion myth, where the sculptor falls in love with the statue into which he has breathed life. Searles believes that such feelings, that therapists should regard the client in this way, are an indication of the successful outcome of therapy. He stresses that these countertransference feelings are also a sign that the ending has to be faced, with pain and grief on both sides, because the therapist cannot hang on to the client, any more than the client can go on depending upon the therapist, or the parent can hang on to their child.

This may be one explanation for such feelings. It is true that it is sometimes at such a point that a therapist begins to like a client in a deeper way, making them realize just how far the client has come. But it is important not to confuse Searles's explanation with another different phenomenon, more sinister than Searles's obvious message about the need to let the client go. A therapist may see himself as the omnipotent white knight, who will rescue the beleaguered princess and carry her off to his castle in the sunset. Such fantasies may only be those of male therapists in relation to some vulnerable female clients, and certainly it is male therapists who are more likely to err by acting them out. The female therapist's fantasy may be a different one – of overprotectiveness and smothering, rather than a sexualized counter-transference.

In any event, these latter fantasies are different from Searles's experience, and often appear earlier rather than later in the therapy. Searles is making a particular point about countertransference feelings a long way into therapy, which are accompanied by pain and not simply by pleasure; and indicate the possibility that therapists can sense the approach of the ending by the way they feel about the prevalence of an adult-to-adult relationship with the client. Searles first saw the significance of such feelings when one of his patients rebuked him for continuing to see her as a child, and not as a grown woman. He realized how much he was resisting the therapy entering its final Oedipal phase:

> It seems to me clear enough, then, what this former child, now a neu-rotic or psychotic adult, requires from us for the successful resolution of his unresolved Oedipus complex: not such a repression of desire, acted-out seductiveness, and denial of his own worth as he met in the relationship with his parent, but rather a maximal awareness on our part of the reciprocal feelings which we develop in response to his oedipal strivings.
>
> (1965a: 303)

Endings

The setting of the end of therapy is a sign of the need to work upon the ending in the sessions that follow. In the case of short-term contracts this is recognized as something that takes place from the start. In mid-term contracts the ending may have been set at the beginning, but its advent is now imminent. One rule of thumb is to allow a further quarter of the time already spent in therapy for working through its finish. The ending is linked in its significance to earlier endings, both in therapy in respect of earlier breaks, and outside therapy in respect of the client's experiences of separation and loss. In longer-term work decisions clearly have to be made either by the client or by the therapist or agency, as to the most appropriate point to set an ending (see Murdin 1999).

Inevitably there are occasions for ending that have to be more rapid than had been anticipated, because therapy (particularly when it is short term) cannot always finish at the right time for both parties. There is also a possibility that a client, or even the therapist, may move; or other outside factors can intervene that are beyond the control of either party. In these instances there is more unfinished business than would otherwise be the case. Even when longer-term therapy finishes, there are bound to be some loose ends, or new situations yet to be faced. Prompted by his own experience with his patient, the Wolf Man, Freud wrote a famous paper on *Analysis Terminable and Interminable*, where he doubted whether there could ever be a 'perfect' analysis. Even the best results, he suggests, may only be permanent due to a patient's 'good luck in not having to face any tests that are too hard for him' (1937a/2002: 177).

Once it is decided and arranged, making sense of the experience of ending becomes the major feature of the therapy. The process that anticipates the end has obvious parallels with many of the stages of grief (described more fully on pp. 4–5). There may be disbelief ('Surely the time hasn't passed that quickly?'); anger ('You said that you would see me as long as I wished'); sadness ('I already feel how much I shall miss you'); relief ('Thank goodness I've come through this terrible period of my life'); and the recognition of unfinished business. Although ending sometimes (as in Samuel Johnson's phrase about hanging) 'concentrates the mind wonderfully', what has not yet been achieved or understood can be acknowledged.

Ending includes evaluating what has taken place during the therapy. Some therapists suggest that it is important to be more self-disclosing towards the end to assist this separation to happen, so that the transference can be dissolved in favour of a more realistic perception of the therapist or counsellor. I am not myself sure that transferences are that readily dissolved, certainly not through deliberate effort. Furthermore, self-disclosure by the therapist may occur earlier, not as a ploy to help dissolve the transference, but because the therapeutic relationship has an ease about it where the spontaneous response is less likely to be misinterpreted by the client. Therapists and clients who are fundamentally at ease with themselves (whatever else might trouble either of them) are able to relate more openly, without fear that boundaries are being traduced. This is, however, particularly true towards the end of therapy.

The process of internalization of the therapist and the therapy continues through the ending phase, with the added impetus that the client has some sense of what he or she wishes to go working on within himself or herself. At the same time it must be recognized that where therapy has really failed, especially if it has been abusive of the client, a more persecutory internalization takes place.

Then there is the finality of ending, which cannot, like the theoretical first session, be seen as an extended period. There is no theoretical last session. The end is the end. Where the relationship has been a long one, or where real contact has been made between the therapist and the client, there will no doubt be real sadness on both sides – such feelings cannot be interpreted as being transference or countertransference alone. In most cases, the ending is a kind of death, because therapist and client will probably never see each other again. Certainly a therapist must assume that this is the case, so that even if it is possible that at a future date the client may seek out the therapist again, the ending is worked with absolutely, as if there will be no further meeting. Of course, however final the ending, where the therapeutic relationship has come through these different phases and faced the issues raised by these three major themes well enough, in both parties something very deep and valued lives on.

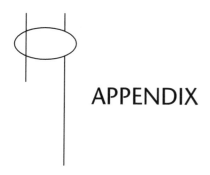

APPENDIX

Summary of the three major themes and their presentation in psychodynamic therapy

For each of the three themes the summary is divided into four parts:

(a) How difficulties relating to that theme might be presented in terms of a client's character, relationships and inner world;
(b) How such difficulties may be seen in relation to the therapist – 'in the transference';
(c) How the therapist might relate to and work with the client in order to help the client to change or progress developmentally;
(d) Ways in which more mature development might show itself in relation to the major theme – this section also indicates possible aims in therapy.

The definitions of difficulties (a) and of more mature development (d) are of course historically, culturally and socially variable, as has been emphasized throughout this book. It is hoped that these working ideas are useful not because they are definitive, but as pointers to what may be particular norms in a particular culture at a particular time.

By identifying an issue under section (a) or (b) in one or other of the major themes, a therapist may also find it helpful to look through the other issues in the same section, as a pointer to what the therapist may not yet have identified.

Trust and attachment

(a) Difficulties associated with trust and attachment:

The development of a protective false self, which is more extensive than the front most people find useful in some work or social situations (which Jung calls the 'persona').

Klein's 'paranoid-schizoid' position: experiencing the outer world, or external pressures or internalized 'objects', as persecutory, without this necessarily being as extreme as the mental disturbance known as 'paranoia'.

The narcissistic personality: overinflated concern for the self, drawing attention to self, no apparent interest in how others feel.

Idealization of significant others (including the therapist).

Splitting: idealizing some, denigrating others, problems with coping with ambivalence.

Destructive anger, especially where it is acted out, or fear of showing anger lest it proves destructive.

Anxiety or guilt over destructive wishes having severely damaged others. Envy, perhaps with destructive wishes attached.

Overdependent, clinging, possessive, demanding person.

Anxiety about the reliability of others.

Fears of being abandoned, rejected, being left alone.

Fear of being engulfed or overwhelmed by the other in intimate and sexual relationships.

Deep lack of trust and fear over invasion of personal boundaries arising from experience of childhood (perhaps even very early) sexual or physical abuse: this may sometimes also be seen in being boundary-less in relationships.

The withdrawn person, schizoid personality; unable to trust, afraid of being swallowed up by others or of draining them with demands.

Addictions: drugs, drink, food; overeating or reaction against food in anorexia (although bulimia and anorexia are also about control, related to the next theme). Acting as if limitless supplies are available: including overspending.

Problems with deferring gratification: must have it now.

Intense anger, hate, or rage as a reaction to frustration: the rage is felt as, or seen in action as very destructive: tearing apart, killing, ripping open and so on.

Difficulties accepting limits.

Guilt about making demands upon others for fear of damaging them, or of being rejected.

Ongoing anger (years on) following bereavement or loss.

A temporary loss of the sense of self or identity, particularly following a major change, or loss.

The feeling of being 'in pieces' or 'chaotic' – although note below the extreme form of this in psychotic illness.

The failure of the environment (for example, the workplace and redundancy) to provide, awakening feelings associated to earlier failures of care.

Magical beliefs and thinking, grandiose or omnipotent beliefs about oneself. The search for unitive experiences, perhaps through drugs.

The perennial search for a partner who will bring 'completeness', and rejection of each one as faults are found in them.

Making relationships in order to meet own needs, with little or no concern for others: narcissistic rather than altruistic.

The projection onto others (for example, a baby, children, clients) of one's own needs, caring for the needy side of the self through caring for others, not allowing them to be (or become) separate.

Some pregnancies (especially in adolescence) as ways of avoiding breaking dependent ties.

The self-denigrating person, unable to accept the self as having any worth. Sense of shame about the basic sense of self.

Chronic hopelessness, despair and pessimism.

Lack of faith; inability to believe anything; absence of a value system; hopeless cynicism.

Hypochondriacal (narcissistic) symptoms.

Learning difficulties arising from lack of trust.

Problems with ageing and loss of physical strength or appearance where related to narcissistic concerns.

Dependency issues relating to care of ageing parents.

Bitterness and demandingness in illness and old age; ingratitude to those who show their care.

Dissociation – being psychologically absent while in the presence of the therapist, often linked with severe trauma or abuse – a defence indicating an inability to trust their own ability to handle memories of trauma or feelings associated with these memories.

Manic-depressive swings from omnipotent feelings to self-loathing and worthlessness.

The borderline personality – on the border between reality and psychotic signs below.

Take particular care of the following signs. They may well indicate a level of psychotic disturbance beyond the capabilities of most counsellors and even many psychotherapists:

Confusion of self and not-self; confused time and spatial boundaries.

Confusion between the body and the mind.

Confused speech and imagery, thoughts or perceptions.

Cognitive disturbance, bizarre thoughts or behaviour.

Long-standing feelings of chaos, or being 'in pieces'.

Delusions or hallucinations.

Paranoid feelings from extreme self-hate to paranoid schizophrenia.

Intense prejudice, or feelings of being discriminated against without basis in reality.

Living in a fantasy world which is out of touch with reality.

Absence of 'as if' thinking: it is all too real.

(b) Trust and attachment issues in the therapeutic relationship:

Demanding, sometimes explicitly, but sometimes through incessant talking; countertransference feelings of being drained, 'sucked dry'.

Requests for more time, or greater frequency of sessions.

Reliance on the therapist as a lifeline (rather than as advice-giver in the authority/ autonomy theme).

Swallowing everything the therapist says, although not always pausing to 'taste' it.

Inability to accept anything the therapist says, as if it is poisonous, or dangerous, although not in the argumentative way seen more in the authority theme.

Use of an intellectual defence to avoid closeness.

Difficulty in forming and sustaining the relationship.

Fear of dependency on the therapist or therapy.

Suspicious, not trusting the therapist.

Fear that the therapist will reject or turn hostile.

Extreme difficulties about breaks and ends of sessions.

Idealizing or worshipping the therapist, perhaps denigrating the self as well, or running down other helpers.

The eroticized transference: it may be expressed in sexual terms, but indicates early oral needs.

Demanding more time and attention, perhaps also physical affection (the need to be held rather than sex).

The need to be special – perhaps to be the only one in the therapist's life, or the only client – and . . .

. . . the opposite: being unable to accept the time and attention offered by the therapist.

Little regard for the feelings of the therapist, who exists purely for the client.

The therapist (woman or man) is treated as a maternal figure – 'hold me', 'feed me', 'touch me' – conveyed in tone and manner even if not in words.

The client's language and images have an 'oral' quality to them: images of feeding, biting, comfort and so on.

Magical expectations of the therapist, together with difficulty accepting own responsibility for change.

Intolerance of the frustration of therapy being a long process – wanting solutions now.

Hostility to the therapist when he or she appears uncaring by setting limits, or not obviously helping.

Unable to relate to the therapist because too caught up in an inner fantasy world – bizarre thoughts and associations which are hardly responsive to the therapist's interventions (this probably indicates serious disturbance and the need for supervision and/or referral to specialist resources).

(c) The therapist's task, as related to trust and attachment issues:

Containing and holding what the client presents, until such time as it is safe enough for the client to begin to look at it, or take it back.

Providing a protective and facilitating environment, which may sometimes involve managing, or helping the client to manage, external pressures and demands.

Being reliable, dependable, and consistent; keeping to time; not acceding to demands for more except in special circumstances.

Showing care and sensitivity when setting limits.

Constant empathy when working with narcissistic clients, but owning when there has been a failure to be sufficiently empathic, and tapping the client's anger at the therapist's failure.

Holding in mind, whatever the client says or does, the depth of helplessness, emptiness or weakness in the client, even when the client does not recognize this.

Receiving the client's projections until such time as it is safe to put them back.

Permitting an illusion about therapy until such time as it is possible to be discerning about its weaknesses; and then fostering disillusion as the client is able to bear it.

Monitoring countertransference, particularly to assess how far the therapist is picking up the client's 'unwanted' feelings.

Using silence carefully, discerning a client who is learning to be alone, from a client for whom the silence is a void, leaving them deserted and lonely.

Containing one's own anxiety: not showing panic even when the therapist and/or the client feels overwhelmed.

Surviving attacks by the client (even when they hurt).

Allowing oneself to feel hatred of the client, without taking it out on the client.

Setting limits upon the acting out of anger and rage in the session.

Accepting as positive, tokens, gestures or words of reparation – remembering that this is sometimes after, but sometimes before an attack.

Encouraging expressions of concern towards others, especially those whom the client may have damaged; and of appropriate guilt.

Creating a climate of trust, where the client does not fear rejection for what they feel or say; where client does not have to fear damaging the therapist by being open about his or her demands, love or anger.

Helping clients distinguish what lies in them and what lies in others – observing projections on the one side, and negative introjections on the other.

Helping distinguish between appropriate feelings of being 'got at', or the victim of prejudice (which does occur, and has a basis in reality), and persecutory feelings involving the projection of hostility onto others.

Not colluding with the client splitting helpers – not allowing oneself to be set up as the 'good parent', while others seen as bad: or the opposite, although at times it may be important to take on the negative feelings.

Encouraging the client's ability to experience positive and negative feelings towards the same 'object'.

Encouraging the positive signs of independence – although be careful about premature independence from fear of intimacy, or fear of rejection.

Enabling clients to find self-esteem.

Linking where possible previous difficulties of trust and attachment to obvious examples of this in the therapeutic relationship.

Using failures on the part of the therapist (to understand, absences and so on) to allow the client to express frustration and anger; linking in with other failures of care which the client has experienced.

With clients showing signs of serious disturbance:

- attempting to find out about any psychiatric history, suicide attempts, and previous episodes of similar disturbance – all this will assist a supervisor to assess the risk, and plan appropriate help;
- supporting the client's positive thinking, constructive wishes or actions, and supporting all realistic perceptions of situations;
- avoiding deep interpretations, or confronting defences, unless experienced in working with this client group, and well supervised;
- short, more frequent sessions may be more appropriate than longer weekly sessions, especially at the height of a crisis;
- trying to remain a good enough figure, to help referral elsewhere to be seen as caring, not rejecting;
- encouraging a client's own wish for more specialist help.

(d) Indications of more mature development and possible aims in therapy in relation to trust and attachment:

Basic sense of trust and faith in others, the environment and the self; basic sense of the 'world' as good.

Healthy mistrust, discrimination about who or what can be trusted.

Klein's 'depressive position', with feeling of more well-being, recognition of ambivalence, and concern for others.

Recognition of positive and negative feelings towards the same person(s) without the negative destroying the positive.

Containing and working through bad experiences and feelings, without being overwhelmed by them in the long term.

Healthy self-respect and self-regard, while still able to accept one's shortcomings, own mortality, and weaknesses.

Recognition of the boundaries between self and others, self and the world.

Presence of and distinction between subjective and objective thinking and experience.

A separate identity: able to own thoughts and feelings, without continuous use of projection or introjection.

Identifying through empathy and concern for and with others.

Trust of others when learning from them, chewing over ideas, and digesting them, but also (authority theme) questioning them.

Trusting and appropriately attaching to others.

Being intimately involved with another while still retaining a core sense of self.

Caring for others and receiving care from others.

Capacity to be alone – inner harmony and self-esteem.

Putting experiences in perspective, retaining a sense of hope even in adversity.

Tolerance of frustration; ability to defer immediate gratification when necessary, or to be able to make appropriate substitutions.

Expressing appropriate anger or assertiveness when frustrated or discontented, without (the fear of) being destructive.

Creative use of fantasy and imagination, and of identification, without it becoming a substitute for real relationships or achievements.

The internalization of the positive features of others, in the course of relating to them, particularly as part of the grief process after loss or bereavement.

Authority and autonomy

(a) Difficulties associated with authority and autonomy:

Perfectionism: being overtidy and overorganized.

Wanting to overorder and overcontrol the self, events and others.

Messy or disorganized person (in terms of the way they manage things, rather than the internal disintegration more typical of trust and attachment issues).

Holding back feelings, inhibition, emotional 'constipation'.

Rigid self-control, or rigid control of others.

'Law-and-order' type (has the answer to everything!), sometimes with strict religious moralizing.

Inability to exercise legitimate authority.

Dependent upon authority figures to take decisions.

Unable to be critical of others, especially authorities.

Overreliance upon rules and orders from others.

Unthinking conformity to the peer group, society or authority figures.

Foreclosed adolescent type, unable to use adolescence to challenge conventions or to experiment with alternative ways of thinking and acting.

Unable to take acceptable risks.

Unable to resolve anything unless everything is crystal clear.

Difficulty adapting to new circumstances, because they disturb the old 'order' too much.

Cautious and overprotective of self and others.

The 'yes ... but' person; 'on the one hand ... on the other hand', without being able to make up his or her mind, or come down on one side or the other.

Lack of spontaneity.

Resentful and often passive submission to authority figures.

Passive-aggressive (making others angry, rather than being able to express hostility directly – often towards an authority figure).

Rejection of authority just because it is authority.

Highly critical internal 'voice' – often that of internalized parent(s); an overactive conscience (punitive super-ego or 'internal saboteur').

Sense of shame or low esteem over what he or she can or cannot *do* (more than over who they *are* at a core level, which is more typical of trust and attachment theme).

Compulsive behaviour – checking; or unnecessary repetition of actions, or words: obsessional rituals; guilt or anxiety, if things are not done 'properly'.

Obsessional thoughts (although the latter may indicate greater disturbance, such as paranoid thoughts – see trust and attachment theme).

Intellectualization as a way of avoiding feelings, or as a way of trying to order areas of conflict without engaging in the conflict.

Afraid of getting hands dirty (literally or metaphorically).

Overanxious need to achieve to satisfy one's own demands or what others are imagined to require.

The constant use of words like 'ought', 'should', 'must'; 'the hardening of the oughteries'.

The workaholic – inability to play, or even to relax in playing.

Inability to relax at times usually set aside for leisure; or following retirement, having to work as hard as before.

Inability to engage in work because it is seen as too conformist.

Inability to produce work (e.g. studying, or creative expression) through fear of others' criticism and consequent loss of self-esteem; or through own over-ambitious standards.

Difficulties in learning associated with perfectionism, fear of criticism, authority problems.

Parents who push their children to achieve, who overvalue children for their achievements, and critical of any failure, perhaps using their children as signals to others of their own worth.

Having to be a perfect parent (perhaps using books as providing 'rules' of child-rearing).

Experiencing love only as conditional love – having to please others to gain their love or approval.

Fear that expression of feelings will lead to lack of control, to disorder, or to spoiling or soiling situations, relationships or the self.

Explosive anger as a result of bottling it up and letting go too forcefully.

Fear of expressing anger because, having been held back, it may be explosive.

Need to 'confess' in order to feel 'clean', without any desire to look at underlying difficulties.

Uncontrolled, impulsive expression of feelings (although in some cases, especially where this is inappropriate to the situation, or where the feelings do not match the situation, this may be evidence of deeper disturbance, as summarized in the trust and attachment theme).

Domination of another through sex or pain, sadistic behaviour, sadistic attitudes and fantasies.

Satisfaction and relief through being the recipient of pain and domination (which may of course be pleasurable participation in sado-masochistic sex, but may be the only way of being able to achieve a sense of relief from guilt).

Sex seen as dirty, or soiling.

Sexual *performance* seen as more important than sexual *enjoyment*. Shame at lack of bodily control (for example, in illness or ageing).

Turning the tables on ageing parents by becoming authoritarian and dominating of them.

(b) Authority and autonomy issues in the therapeutic relationship:

Attitudes to the therapist as an authority figure:

- fear of therapist's imagined demands or criticism;
- expectation of therapist being controlling, or taking control;
- looking to therapist to provide guidance or answers;
- unable to accept what therapist says 'on principle';
- being very critical of the therapist.

The client's need to 'get it right' when telling his or her story – having to get the right word, or the correct explanation.

Holding back or holding in feelings – tears, anger, affectionate feelings, even not showing anxiety.

Difficulty revealing thoughts and feelings through shame.

Intellectualizing, being vague, or introducing a lot of detail and trivia, being very precise.

Boring and monotonous talk and delivery.

Difficulty acting upon insights, listening but unable to make decisions for fear of getting them wrong.

Shame may be seen in the bowed head, or lack of eye contact.

Shifting blame at times onto others, denying own responsibility.

'Yes ... but' responses, that might be accompanied by sullenness, or complaints about no one helping.

Hesitancy about, or fear of, the therapist taking control; not wishing to feel tied down.

A sense in the therapist that he or she and the client are getting into 'rational' arguments, each struggling to control the other.

Splitting different helpers so that one 'authority' figure is set against another, or one played off against the other.

Treating the therapist like the dominant authority figure in the family of origin: 'make me', 'tell me', 'do it for me', 'approve of my actions' and so on.

(c) The therapist's task, as related to authority and autonomy issues:

Developing the working alliance in which the client is encouraged to take as much responsibility as the therapist for thinking and reflecting upon himself or herself.

Encouraging therapy to be a place where work can be done, but also where therapist and client can 'play' with ideas, with words, with free associations.

Developing a working partnership where the therapist's expertise becomes an aid to the client, not an authoritative influence over the client.

Not acting as an authority figure – for example, avoiding laying down rules or giving advice (unless a person is very disturbed in which case such management is appropriate).

Observing the client's wish to make the therapist more authoritative or expert than he or she can be.

Observing when the client appears to be giving away own authority to the therapist.

Monitoring the client's fear of the therapist being critical, making it more difficult for some thoughts and feelings to be expressed.

Fostering spontaneity in the client (as well as being spontaneous oneself!).

While adhering to boundaries, not practising therapy in a rigid, rule-dominated way.

Being able to develop one's own way of being a therapist, not hide-bound by tradition or training.

Linking the wish for, or fear of, therapist as authority figure to the way client felt about parental authority, and the authority of quasi-parental figures in childhood and later life.

Locating client's fear of judgement or criticism, where it seems to be projected onto others as being the only critical ones, as in fact in the client's inner world.

Working to help lower defences against expression of feelings when the client is becoming monotonous and boring, or engaging only in distant intellectual talk – remembering that the client is afraid to own such feelings, and probably feels ashamed of or guilty about them.

Distinguishing between appropriate and inappropriate guilt, enabling client to express concern in cases of appropriate guilt, but looking for possible reasons for inappropriate guilt.

Where shame is expressed, showing obvious acceptance of the client, over and above the thing(s) that have gone wrong; questioning where such shame comes from (for example, over-critical parents in childhood, cultural determinants).

Helping the client to leave therapy at the right time, as a true expression of their newfound, or newly affirmed independence.

(d) Indications of more mature development and possible aims in therapy in relation to authority and autonomy:

Self-esteem and sense of competence in one's abilities: what a person can do or perform, rather than the more basic self-esteem of the trust and dependency theme.

A sense of order, justice and fairness – that the 'world' is felt to be basically fair.

Ability to be self-controlled without being overcontrolled.

Sense of personal autonomy without arrogance.

Confidence in the ability to make things happen.

Adaptable to new situations; able to create new order out of fluid situations.

Industriousness and creativity.

Ability to let go feelings in appropriate ways.

Confidence to take initiatives, including measuring any risks.

Acting independently when required to do so.

Making judgements of right and wrong, using information or even advice, but taking decisions for oneself.

Ability to challenge authority figures when necessary in a manner that encourages dialogue.

Acceptance of personal responsibility.

Balance between work, play and relaxation.

Enjoyment of physical activity and expression.

Learning from the authority of others while at the same time being able to question them.

Sense of inner order, but also capable of adaptation and change.

Tolerance of temporary disorder or uncertainty.

Acceptance and enjoyment of the whole body, especially those parts commonly seen as 'nasty' or 'dirty'.

Able to make mistakes and learn from mistakes.

Sense of coordination – being able to do things without fearing mistakes.

Ability to exercise authority fairly.

Sharing authority and decision making (in working relationships or in intimate partnerships, parenting and so on).

Ability to relinquish authority over children as they mature (without relinquishing offer of guidance and sharing of experience).

Ability to let go of positions of power and responsibility with increasing age, encouraging and enabling others to take over.

Cooperation and competition

(a) Difficulties associated with cooperation and competition:

Problems in three-person or triangular situations:

- splitting of sex/affection/care onto two or more persons;
- parent using a child as an ally against the other parent, or as a replacement for his or her partner;
- children coming between parents;
- 'the eternal triangle': one person, two partners;
- feeling left out when in threesome.

Sexual difficulties, and difficulties within sexual relationships.

Sexualizing non-sexual relationships.

Sexual inhibition.

Sexual provocativeness.

The 'Don Juan', 'tease' character, although also look for trust and attachment issues.

Gender anxieties: particularly over being 'masculine' or 'feminine' – personal qualities and gender expectations.

Undervalued as a boy or a girl by parents who wanted a child of a different gender.

Problems accepting sexual and genital differences (although there may also be legitimate difficulties caused by society's treatment of men and women).

Destructive or aggressive envy of women or men.

Anxieties about sexual orientation or sexual preferences.

Castration anxiety whether in actual or (more likely) in symbolic form.

Shame or guilt about sexuality.

Lack of confidence as an adult man or woman due to rejection or distancing by parents of the client's love and sexuality as a child.

Inhibition of sexuality through guilt or fear of rejection.

Rivalry, often as feelings of inferiority in relation to other members of own gender.

Sex experienced or contemplated as threatening because too associated with Oedipal ties.

Incestuous relationships or experiences in childhood (or adult life), acted out sexually or emotionally.

Overattachment to parents, inability to leave them psychologically in adult life.

Difficulties identifying with parent of same sex – internalizing their negative rather than their positive qualities.

Guilt about having broken parents' relationship, if they separate and/or divorce.

Rivalry or jealousy of siblings: birth of siblings; achievements of siblings; parents' relationship to siblings.

Rivalry in step-family relationships.

Rivalry in a couple relationship, over role, earnings, abilities and so on.

Guilt over the death of a sibling, or perhaps of a feared or hated parent.

Jealousy, or feelings of exclusion, upon the birth of a child (particularly experienced by the father).

Overcompetitive trait: seeing situations as competitive when they are not.

Unable to engage in competitive games or sports (this may be due to anxiety about displaying or using the body, may be to do with winning or losing).

Difficulty being 'on show', or in the limelight.

Unproductive rivalry and competitiveness in working situations, in working in a team, in measuring oneself against colleagues.

Jealousy in all types of relationship.

Inaction or lack of initiative through fear of rivalry or competition, which can take the form either of anxiety about losing or about winning.

Inhibition of curiosity, initiative and adventure, perhaps taking its cue from sexual inhibition, but seen in other areas too.

Exhibitionism or furtive sexuality (voyeurism) and implied doubts about potency and sexuality in such behaviour.

Only able to relate to opposite gender as long as they are 'safe' and unattainable – that is not sexually arousing, 'safely' married or engaged, untouchable, distant figures.

Perceiving the opposite gender generally as a personal threat.

Feelings of inadequacy as a man or woman.

Sexual relations that show need for a sexual object who is 'inferior' or submissive, who does not present too great a threat, for example paedophilia (attraction to children), or attacks on women because they represent a threat to potency.

Denigration of the opposite sex.

Denigration of the younger generation due to feelings of inadequacy and competitiveness, or envy of their opportunities.

Anxieties about own homosexual fantasies and desires, or fear of gay men and lesbians (homophobia).

Learning difficulties associated with inhibitions or competitiveness.

Learning difficulties due to sexual or loving desires towards teachers.

Difficulties with the intimate physical examinations in the medical context – this may also suggest previous sexual abuse.

(b) Cooperation and competition issues in the therapeutic relationship:

Difficulty talking about sex, not as in authority and autonomy theme because it is disgusting or dirty, but because it is too stimulating or exciting.

Using stimulating intimate talk to excite or interest the therapist: seductive behaviour, or using sex to denigrate therapist (may be used by male client towards female therapist).

Countertransference feelings of sexual excitement in the therapist – although be sure to trace where these come from – these may be the therapist's issue.

Implicit or explicit wish for therapist to be a friend or partner or lover.

Attempts to make an 'alliance' with one therapist against another helper, or against client's partner.

Jealousy of, interest in, or comparison to other clients seen by the therapist, or of other persons in the therapist's life outside work.

Wanting to be a special client: *primus inter pares* (first amongst equals), not the only one as in the trust and attachment theme.

The gender of the therapist may be particularly important where:

• there is fear of the opposite gender, perhaps because of the experience of abuse (although occasionally the therapist of the same gender may also be feared for the same reason);
• the client feels only a therapist of the same gender would understand the gender issues;
• there is homosexual anxiety.

(c) The therapist's task, as related to cooperation and competition issues:

Respecting and where possible honouring client's wish for male or female therapist; or working with these difficulties where client has no choice yet wishes to continue.

Watching for rivalry between client and therapist, especially where both of same gender.

Using the gender of the therapist as a model of good relating when working with a client who sees the gender the therapist represents as threatening.

Linking current triangular situations, or problems in sexual and other relationships, with what is known of the relationship between the parents, or the parents and client.

Avoiding being caught up in splitting, or becoming an ally for the client against another helper or member of the family.

Helping clients talk naturally about their sexuality, their sexual fantasies and their feelings towards others without being inhibited, and without titillation.

Accepting sexual or loving feelings in the therapeutic relationship (in the client or in the therapist), without deliberately encouraging them, or playing on them.

Avoiding being seductive; avoiding being unduly interested, voyeuristic or prying into the client's life; creating instead an atmosphere of trust which enables a client to show the more intimate details of their memories, thoughts and feeling when they are ready.

Looking for previous experiences in the client's life which might have led to doubt about themselves in terms of their gender, and their sexuality.

Affirming the gender, the sexuality and the sexual orientation of the client when this is appropriate, where it is genuinely felt, and where it seems helpful to the client's self-image, while not holding out the promise of a special relationship.

Observing and accepting the anger and frustration that may be expressed that the therapist cannot be a friend or a special person; linking in perhaps with the distant, unattainable or rejecting parent figure.

Remembering the partner of a client: encouraging signs of concern for the partner's difficulties, or adjustments to the relationship where the client makes significant progress through the therapy.

Considering the possibility of a client working with a therapist of the opposite gender after working with the present therapist, especially where this may help provide a corrective experience for a client now strong enough to tolerate the anxiety of the feared gender.

(d) Indications of more mature development and possible aims in therapy in relation to cooperation and competition:

Growing sense of integration, within the self, with others including people who are different, and with the external environment.

Friendships and other relationships free from sexual anxieties (aim-inhibited love).

Detachment from parents to be able to make independent choice of an intimate partner, not too influenced by the relationship with parents (especially by negative factors).

Internalization of positive qualities of parents and significant others, including the therapist.

Firm foundation for sexual identity, both in respect of predominant sexual orientation, but also the ability to accept bisexual aspects of the self.

Acceptance of physical and genital differences without fear or envy.

Comfortable with both (supposed) masculine and feminine traits within the self.

Ability, where the client wishes it, to make an intimate relationship with a partner, to bring sexual, affectionate, caring and other feelings together.

Where a client wishes to be single, to feel confident with this status, finding appropriate expression for different feelings, perhaps in sublimated form.

As parents, to be able to accept and respond appropriately to a child's sexuality and love, not crushing it, not colluding with the child against the partner.

Sharing and cooperating with others, in the family, peer group, mixed gender groups, etc.

Valuing the complementarity of the other in a relationship, as extending the capabilities of the self.

Engagement in teams or small groups at work, recognizing own and others' particular strengths and abilities.

Ability to compete in genuinely competitive situations, without guilt at succeeding or undue anger/shame/depression at not succeeding.

Growing sense of being able to integrate different experiences.

REFERENCES

Abraham, K. (1927) *Selected Papers*. London: Hogarth Press.

Abram, J. (1996) *The Language of Winnicott*. London: Karnac Books.

Adler, S. (1922) *Understanding Human Nature*. Oxford: One World.

Ainsworth, M. D. S. (1991) Attachments and other affectional bonds across the life cycle. In C. Murray Parkes, J. Stevenson-Hinde and P. Marris (eds) *Attachment Across the Life Cycle*. London: Routledge.

Alexander, F. and French, T. M. (1946) *Psychoanalytic Therapy*. New York: Ronald Press.

Alexander, R. and Jacobs, M. (2006) Rosie Alexander in discussion with Michael Jacobs. In Y. Bates (ed.) *Shouldn't I be Feeling Better by Now*. London: Palgrave Macmillan.

Allen, D. M. (1994) *A Family Systems Approach to Individual Psychotherapy*. London: Jason Aronson.

American Psychiatric Association (APA) (1994) *Diagnostic and Statistical Manual of Mental Disorders*, 4th edn. Washington, DC: APA.

Anzieu, D. (1984) *The Group and the Unconscious*. London: Routledge & Kegan Paul.

Auden, W. H. (1976) *Collected Poems* (ed. E. Mendelson). London: Faber & Faber.

Balint, M. (1968) *The Basic Fault*. London: Tavistock Publications.

Bancroft, J. (1983) *Human Sexuality and Its Problems*. Edinburgh: Churchill Livingstone.

Becker, E. (1972) *The Birth and Death of Meaning*. London: Penguin.

Becker, T. (1965) Panel reports – latency. *Journal of the American Psychoanalytic Association*, 13: 584–90.

Belotti, E. (1975) *Little Girls*. London: Writers & Readers Publishing Co-operative.

Benvenuto, B. and Kennedy, R. (1986) *The Works of Jacques Lacan: An Introduction*. London: Free Association Books.

Berne, E. (1968) *Games People Play*. London: Penguin.

Bettelheim, B. (1978) *The Uses of Enchantment: The Meaning and Importance of Fairy Tales*. London: Penguin.

Bettelheim, B. (1983) *Freud and Man's Soul*. London: Chatto & Windus/Hogarth Press.

Bowlby, J. (1947) *Child Care and the Growth of Love*. London: Penguin.

Bowlby, J. (1969, 1973, 1980) *Attachment and Loss*, vols I, II and III. London: Hogarth Press.

Bowlby, J. (1979) *The Making and Breaking of Affectional Bonds*. London: Tavistock Publications.

Breen, D. (1989) *Talking with Mothers*. London: Free Association Books.

Brinich, P. and Shelley, C. (2002) *The Self and Personality Structure*. Buckingham: Open University Press.

Brisch, K. (2002) *Treating Attachment Disorders: From Theory to Therapy*. New York: The Guilford Press.

Britton, R. (1989) The missing link: parental sexuality in the Oedipus complex. In J. Steiner (ed.) *The Oedipus Complex Today: Clinical Implications*. London: Karnac.

Broucek, E. J. (1982) Shame and its relationship to early narcissistic developments. *International Journal of Psycho-Analysis*, 63: 369–78.

Burck, C. and Speed, B. (eds) (1995) *Gender, Power and Relationships*. London: Routledge.

Burman, E. (1994) *Deconstructing Developmental Psychology*. London: Routledge.

Byatt, A. S. (1990) *Possession*. London: Chatto & Windus.

Carroll, M. (1996) *Workplace Counselling*. London: SAGE Publications.

Carroll, M. and Watton, M. (1997) *Handbook of Counselling in Organisations*. London: SAGE Publications.

Case, R. (1978) When birth is also a funeral. *Journal of Pastoral Care* (USA), 32: 1.

Casement, P. (1985) *On Learning from the Patient*. London: Tavistock.

Chessick, R. D. (1983) Mental health and the care of the soul in mid-life. *Journal of Pastoral Care* (USA), 37: 5–12.

Chodorow, N. (1978) *The Reproduction of Mothering*. London: University of California Press.

Chodorow, N. (1989) *Feminism and Psychoanalytic Theory*. New Haven, CT: Yale University Press.

Chodorow, N. (1994) *Masculinities, Feminities, Sexualities*. London: Free Association Books.

Coles, A. (2003) *Counselling in the Workplace*. Maidenhead: Open University Press.

Collick, E. (1986) *Through Grief: Bereavement Journey*. London: Darton, Longman & Todd.

Davies, D. and Bhugra, D. (2004) *Models of Psychopathology*. Buckingham: Open University Press.

Davies, D. and Neal, C. (eds) (1996) *Pink Therapy*. Buckingham: Open University Press.

Davies, D. and Neal, C. (eds) (2000) *Therapeutic Perspectives on Working with Lesbian, Gay and Bisexual Clients*. Buckingham: Open University Press.

Davies, J. M. and Frawley, M. G. (1994) *Treating the Adult Survivor of Childhood Sexual Abuse*. New York: Basic Books.

Dinnerstein, D. (1978) *The Rocking of the Cradle and the Ruling of the World*. London: Souvenir Press.

Dunne, J. S. (1979) *Time and Myth*. London: SCM Press.

Eigen, M. (1998) *The Psychoanalytic Mystic*. London: Free Association Books.

Erikson, E. (1965) *Childhood and Society*. London: Penguin.

Erikson, E. (1968) *Identity, Youth and Crisis*. London: Faber.

Erikson, E. (1978) *Toys and Reasons*. London: Marion Boyars.

Fairbairn, W. R. D. (1952) *Psychoanalytic Studies of the Personality*. London: Tavistock/Routledge.

Fenichel, O. (1946) *The Psychoanalytic Theory of Neurosis*. London: Routledge & Kegan Paul.

Flanders, S. (1993) *The Dream Discourse Today*. London: Routledge.

Fowler, J. W. (1981) *Stages of Faith: The Psychology of Human Development and the Quest for Meaning*. New York: Harper & Row.

Freud, A. (1973) *Normality and Pathology in Childhood*. London: Penguin.

Freud, S. (1900) *The Interpretation of Dreams*. Penguin Freud Library, volume 4. London: Penguin.

Freud, S. (1901/2002) *The Psychopathology of Everyday Life*. London: Penguin.

Freud, S. (1905) *Three Essays on the Theory of Sexuality*. Penguin Freud Library, volume 7. London: Penguin.

Freud, S. (1907/2004) Compulsive actions and religious exercises. In S. Freud, *Mass Psychology and Other Writings*. London: Penguin.

Freud, S. (1908/2002) Civilized sexual morality and modern nervous illness. In S. Freud, *Civilization and Its Discontents*. London: Penguin.

Freud, S. (1908/2003) The creative writer and daydreaming. In S. Freud, *The Uncanny*. London: Penguin.

Freud, S. (1911/2002) *The Schreber Case*. London: Penguin.

Freud, S. (1913/2002) On beginning the treatment. In S. Freud, *Wild Analysis*. London: Penguin.

Freud, S. (1914) *On Narcissism: An Introduction*. Penguin Freud Library, volume 11. London: Penguin.

Freud, S. (1917) *Mourning and Melancholia*. Penguin Freud Library, volume 11. London: Penguin.

Freud, S. (1920/2003) *Beyond the Pleasure Principle*. London: Penguin.

Freud, S. (1923/2003) The ego and the id. In S. Freud, *Beyond the Pleasure Principle and Other Writings*. London: Penguin.

Freud, S. (1925a) *An Autobiographical Study*. Penguin Freud Library, volume 15. London: Penguin.

Freud, S. (1925b) *Some Psychical Consequences of the Anatomical Distinction between the Sexes*. Penguin Freud Library, volume 7. London: Penguin.

Freud, S. (1927/2004) The future of an illusion. In S. Freud, *Mass Psychoology and Other Writings*. London: Penguin.

Freud, S. (1931) *Female Sexuality*. Penguin Freud Library, volume 7. London: Penguin.

Freud, S. (1933/2003) Introductory lectures on psychoanalysis: new series. In S. Freud, *An Outline of Psychoanalysis*. London: Penguin.

Freud, S. (1937a/2002) Analysis terminable and interminable. In S. Freud, *Wild Analysis*. London: Penguin.

Freud, S. (1937b/2002) Constructions in analysis. In S. Freud, *Wild Analysis*. London: Penguin.

Freud, S. and Breuer, J. (1895/2004) *Studies in Hysteria*. London: Penguin.

Gerhardt, S. (2004) *Why Love Matters*. London: Brunner-Routledge.

Gilligan, C. (1982) *In a Different Voice*. Cambridge, MA: Harvard University Press.

Golan, N. (1981) *Passing Through Transitions*. London: Collier Macmillan.

Greenson, R. R. (1967) *The Technique and Practice of Psychoanalysis*. London: Hogarth Press.

Grier, F. (ed.) (2005) *Oedipus and the Couple*. London: Karnac.

Guntrip, H. (1961) *Personality Structure and Human Interaction*. London: Hogarth Press.

Guntrip, H. (1968) *Schizoid Phenomena, Object Relations and the Self*. London: Hogarth Press.

Haines, D. G. (1978) Paths and companions. *Journal of Pastoral Care* (USA), 31: 1.

Hartung, B. (1979) The capacity to enter latency in learning pastoral psychotherapy. *Journal of Supervision and Training in Ministry* (USA), 2: 46–59.

Heimann, P. and Valenstein, A. (1972) The psychoanalytical concept of aggression: an integrated summary. *International Journal of Psycho-Analysis*, 53: 31–5.

Hudson-Allez, G. (2005) *Sex and Sexuality: Questions and Answers for Counsellors and Therapists*. London: Whurr Publishers.

Hunter, M. (1983) Personal communication.

Imber, R. R. (1995) Clinical notes on masochism. *Contemporary Psychoanalysis*, 31: 581–9.

Jacobs, J. L. (1994) *Victimized Daughters: Incest and the Development of the Female Self*. London: Routledge.

Jacobs, M. (1991) The therapist's revenge: the law of talion as a motive for caring. Contact. *Interdisciplinary Journal of Pastoral Studies*, 105: 2–11.

Jacobs, M. (1993) *Living Illusions*. London: SPCK.

Jacobs, M. (2000a) *Illusion: A Psychodynamic Interpretation of Thinking and Belief*. London: Whurr Publishers.

Jacobs, M. (2000b) *Swift to Hear* (2nd edn). London: SPCK.

Jacobs, M. (2001) *Still Small Voice* (revised 2nd edn). London: SPCK.

Jacobs, M. (2003) *Sigmund Freud* (2nd edn). London: SAGE Publications.

Jacobs, M. (2004a) The perils of latency. *Journal of Psychodynamic Practice*, 10: 500–14.

Jacobs, M. (2004b) *Psychodynamic Counselling in Action* (3rd edn). London: SAGE Publications.

Joffe, W. G. (1969) A critical review of the status of the envy concept. *International Journal of Psycho-Analysis*, 50: 533.

Jung, C. G. (1953) *Two Essays on Analytical Psychology*. London: Routledge & Kegan Paul.

Kernberg, O. (1988) Clinical dimensions of masochism. In R. Glick and D. Meyers (eds) *Masochism: Current Psychoanalytic Perspectives*. Hillsdale, NJ: The Analytic Press.

Kernberg, O. F. (1996) The analyst's authority in the psychoanalytic situation. *Psychoanalytic Quarterly*, 65: 137–57.

Kirkley-Best, E. *et al.* (1982) On stillbirth: an open letter to the clergy. *Journal of Pastoral Care* (USA), 36: 1.

Klein, J. (1987) *Our Need for Others and Its Roots in Infancy*. London: Tavistock/ Routledge.

Klein, M. (1937/1975) Love, guilt and reparation. In M. Klein, *Love, Guilt and Reparation and Other Works 1921–1945*. London: Hogarth Press.

Klein, M. (1957) *Envy and Gratitude*. London: Tavistock.

Klein, M. (1963/1975) On the sense of loneliness. In M. Klein, *Envy and Gratitude and Other Works 1946–1963*. London: Hogarth Press.

Klein, M. (1975) *Envy and Gratitude and Other Works 1946–1963*. London: Hogarth Press.

Kohlberg, L. (1981) *The Philosophy of Moral Development*. San Francisco: Harper & Row.

Kohut, H. (1971) *The Analysis of the Self*. London: Hogarth Press.

Kohut, H. (1977) *The Restoration of the Self*. International Universities Press.

Kubler-Ross, E. (1969) *On Death and Dying*. London: Tavistock Publications.

Lago, C. (1996) *Race, Culture and Counselling*. Buckingham: Open University Press.

Laing, R. D. (1966) *Self and Others*. London: Penguin.

Laing, R. D. (1967) *The Politics of Experience and the Bird of Paradise*. London: Penguin.

Lanman, M. (2005) The painful truth. In F. Grier (ed.) *Oedipus and the Couple*. London: Karnac.

Laufer, M. (1974) *Adolescent Disturbance and Breakdown*. London: Penguin.

Laufer, M. and Laufer M. E. (eds) (1989) *Developmental Breakdown and Psychoanalytic Treatment in Adolescence: Clinical Studies*. New Haven, CT: Yale University Press.

Le Carré, J. (1974) *Tinker, Tailor, Soldier, Spy*. London: Hodder & Stoughton.

Le Guin, U. (1971) *A Wizard of Earthsea*. London: Penguin.

Lechte, J. (1994) *Fifty Key Contemporary Thinkers*. London: Routledge.

Lendrum, S. and Syme, G. (2004) *Gift of Tears: A Practical Approach to Loss and Bereavement in Counselling and Psychotherapy*. London: Brunner-Routledge.

Levinson, D. J., Darrow, D. N., Klein, E. B., Levinson, M. H. and McKee, B. (1978) *The Seasons of a Man's Life*. New York: A. Knopf.

Lewes, K. (1988) *The Psychoanalytic Theory of Male Homosexuality*. New York: Simon & Schuster.

Lewis, C. S. (1971) *A Grief Observed*. London: Faber.

Lieblum, S. and Rosen, R. (1989) *Principles and Practice of Sex Therapy*. New York: Guilford Press.

Little, M. I. (1958) On delusional transference (transference psychosis). *International Journal of Psycho-Analysis*, 39: 134–8.

Little, M. I. (1986) *Transference Neurosis and Transference Psychosis*. London: Free Association Books.

Little, M. I. (1990) *Psychotic Anxieties and Containment. A Personal Record of an Analysis with Winnicott*. Northvale, NJ: Jason Aronson.

Lorenz, K. (1966) *On Aggression*. New York: Harcourt Brace.

Lowe, G. (1972) *The Growth of Personality*. London: Penguin.

Macquarrie, J. (1966) *Principles of Christian Theology*. London: SCM Press.

Maguire, M. (1995) *Men, Women, Passion and Power*. London: Routledge.

Mahler, M. S. (1958) Autism and symbiosis: two extreme disturbances of identity. *The International Journal of Psycho-analysis*, 39: 77–82.

Main, M. (1995) Recent studies in attachment: overview with selected implications for clinical work. In S. Goldberg, R. Muir and J. Kerr (eds) *Attachment Theory: Social, Developmental and Clinical Perspectives*. Hillsdale, NJ: Analytic Press.

Malan, D. H. (1979) *Individual Psychotherapy and the Science of Psychodynamics*. London: Butterworth.

Marcia, J. E. (1975) Development and validation of ego-identity status. In R.W. Muuss (ed.) *Adolescent Behavior and Society*. New York: Random House.

Masson, J. M. (1984) *The Assault on Truth: Freud's Suppression of the Seduction Theory*. London: Faber & Faber.

Masson, J. M. (ed.) (1985) *The Complete Letters of Sigmund Freud to Wilhelm Fliess*. Cambridge, MA: Belknap Press of Harvard University Press.

Mearns, D. and Thorne, B. (2000) *Person-Centred Therapy Today*. London: SAGE Publications.

Meissner, W. W. (1991) *What is Effective in Psychoanalytic Therapy: From Interpretation to Relation*. New York: Jason Aronson.

Miller, A. (1979) Depression and grandiosity as related forms of narcissistic disturbance. *International Review of Psychoanalysis*, 6: 61–76.

Mitchell, K. (1982) A death and a community. *Journal of Pastoral Care* (USA), 36: 1.

Mohamed, C. and Smith, R. (1997) Time-limited psychotherapy. In M. Lawrence and M. Maguire (eds) *Psychotherapy with Women: Feminist Perspectives*. London: Routledge.

Mollon, P. (1996) *Multiple Selves, Multiple Voices: Working with Trauma, Violation and Dissociation*. Chichester: John Wiley.

Morgan, M. (1995) The projective gridlock: a form of projective identification in couple relationships. In S. Ruszczynski and J. Fisher (eds) *Intrusiveness and Intimacy in the Couple*. London: Karnac.

Morgan M. (2005) On being able to be a couple: the importance of a 'creative couple' in psychic life. In F. Grier (ed.) *Oedipus and the Couple*. London: Karnac.

Munroe, R. L. and Munroe, R. H. (1975) *Cross-cultural Human Development*. New York: Jason Aronson.

Murdin, L. (1999) *How Much is Enough? Endings in Psychotherapy and Counselling*. London: Routledge.

Murray, L. and Cooper, P. (eds) (1997) *Postpartum Depression and Child Development*. London: The Guilford Press.

Mussen, P., Conger, J. and Kagan, J. (1969) *Child Development and Personality* (2nd edn). New York: Harper & Row.

Nathanson, D. L. (1987) A timetable for shame. In D. L. Nathanson (ed.) *The Many Faces of Shame*. New York: The Guilford Press.

Neal, C. and Davies, D. (eds) (2000) *Issues in Therapy with Lesbian, Gay, Bisexual and Transgender Clients*. Buckingham: Open University Press.

Neubauer, P B. (ed.) (1965) *Children in Collectives: Child-rearing Aims and Practices in the Kibbutz*. Springfield, IL: Charles C. Thomas.

O'Connor, N. and Ryan, J. (1993) *Wild Desires and Mistaken Identities: Lesbianism and Psychoanalysis*. London: Virago Press.

Obholzer, A. (ed.) (1994) *The Unconscious at Work: Individual and Organizational Stress in the Human*. London: Routledge.

Parkes, C. Murray (1986) *Bereavement* (2nd edn). London: Tavistock.

Parkes, C. Murray, Stevenson-Hinde, J. and Marris, P. (eds) (1991) *Attachment Across the Life Cycle*. London: Routledge.

Pedersen, P. B. (1994) *A Handbook for Developing Multicultural Awareness*. Alexandria, VA: American Counseling Association.

Piaget, J. (1950) *The Psychology of Intelligence*. London: Routledge & Kegan Paul.

Piontelli, A. (1992) *From Fetus to Child: An Observational and Psychoanalytic Study*. London: Routledge.

Pilgrim, D. (1997) *Psychotherapy and Society*. London: SAGE Publications.

Prins, H. A. (1975) A danger to themselves and others (social workers and potentially dangerous clients). *British Journal of Social Work*, 5: 297–309.

Prins, H. A. (1995) *Offenders, Deviants or Patients?* (2nd edn). London: Routledge.

Prodgers, A. (1991) On hating the patient. *British Journal of Psychotherapy*, 8: 144–54.

Quinodoz, J.-M. (1993) *The Taming of Solitude*. London: Routledge.

Raphael, B. (1984) *The Anatomy of Bereavement*. London: Hutchinson.

Ratigan, B. (1996) Working with older gay men. In D. Davies and C. Neal (eds) *Pink Therapy*. Buckingham: Open University Press.

Rayner, E. (1978) *Human Development* (2nd edn). London: George Allen & Unwin.

Rayner, E. (1986) *Human Development* (3rd edn). London: Allen & Unwin.

Reading, B. and Jacobs, M. (2003) *Addiction: Questions and Answers for Counsellors and Therapists*. London: Whurr.

Rey, J. H. (1988) Schizoid phenomena in the borderline. In E. Bott Spillius (ed.) *Melanie Klein Today. Volume 1: Mainly Theory*. London: Routledge.

Rosen, I. (1979) *Sexual Deviation*. Oxford: Oxford University Press.

Rosenfeld, H. (1978) Notes on the psychopathology and psychoanalytic treatment of some borderline patients. *International Journal of Psycho-Analysis*, 59: 215–21.

Rosenthall, J. (2005) Oedipus gets married: an investigation of a couple's shared oedipal drama. In F. Grier (ed.) *Oedipus and the Couple.* London: Karnac.

Rubins, J. L. (1978) *Karen Horney.* London: Weidenfeld & Nicolson.

Rudnytsky, P. L. (1991) *The Psychoanalytic Vocation: Rank, Winnicott and the Legacy of Freud.* London: Yale University Press.

Rushdie, S. (1990) *Haroun and the Sea of Stories.* London: Granta Books.

Ruszczynski, S. (2005) Reflective space in the intimate couple relationship: the 'marital triangle'. In F. Grier (ed.) *Oedipus and the Couple.* London: Karnac.

Rycroft, C. (1972) *A Critical Dictionary of Psychoanalysis.* London: Penguin.

Sachs, H. (1948) *Masks of Love and Life.* Cambridge, MA: Sci-Art Publishers.

Samuels, A. (1985a) *Jung and the Post-Jungians.* London: Routledge & Kegan Paul.

Samuels, A. (ed.) (1985b) *The Father: Contemporary Jungian Perspectives.* London: Free Association Books.

Samuels, A. (1993) *The Political Psyche.* London: Routledge.

Scharff, D. (1988) *The Sexual Relationship: An Object Relations View of Sex and the Family.* London: Routledge.

Scharff, D. and Scharff, J. (1994) *Object Relations Therapy of Physical and Sexual Trauma.* London: Jason Aronson.

Schwartz, R. S. (1989) A psychiatrist's view of transference and countertransference in the pastoral relationship. *Journal of Pastoral Care* (USA), 43: 41–6.

Searles, H. (1965a) Oedipal love in the countertransference. In H. Searles, *Collected Papers on Schizophrenia and Related Subjects.* London: Hogarth Press.

Searles, H. (1965b) Problems of psycho-analytic supervision. In H. Searles, *Collected Papers on Schizophrenia and Related Subjects.* London: Karnac Books.

Segal, H. (1973) *Introduction to the Work of Melanie Klein.* London: Hogarth Press.

Segal, J. (1992) *Melanie Klein.* London: SAGE Publications.

Seidler, V. (1991) *Recreating Sexual Politics.* London: Routledge.

Sendak, M. (1970) *Where the Wild Things Are.* London: Penguin.

Shelley, C. (ed.) (1998) *Contemporary Perspectives on Psychotherapy and Homosexualities.* London: Free Association Books.

Siegel, A. M. (1996) *Heinz Kohut and the Psychology of the Self.* London: Routledge.

Sills, C. (ed.) (2006) *Contracts in Counselling* (2nd edn). London: SAGE Publications.

Simon, G. (1996) Working with people in relationships. In D. Davies and C. Neal (eds) *Pink Therapy.* Buckingham: Open University Press.

Skynner, R. and Cleese, J. (1983) *Families: And How to Survive Them.* London: Methuen.

Smith, D. L. (1991) *Hidden Conversations – An Introduction to Communicative Psychoanalysis.* London: Routledge.

Speck, P. (1978) *Loss and Grief in Medicine.* London: Baillière Tindall.

Stern, D. (1985) *The Interpersonal World of the Infant. A View from Psychoanalysis and Development Psychology.* New York: Basic Books.

Storr, A. (1979) *The Art of Psychotherapy.* London: Secker & Warburg.

Storr, A. (1989) *Solitude.* Glasgow: Fontana Paperbacks.

Strachey, J. (1934) The nature of the therapeutic action of psychoanalysis. *International Journal of Psycho-Analysis*, 15: 127–59.

Sugarman, L. (1986) *Life-span Development: Concepts, Theories and Interventions.* London: Routledge.

Sullivan, E. M. (1999) *Unconscious Communication in Practice.* Buckingham: Open University Press.

Szasz, T. (1971) *The Manufacture of Madness.* London: Routledge & Kegan Paul.

Thomas, D. M. (1981) *The White Hotel.* London: Gollancz.

Thompson, F. (1973) *Lark Rise to Candleford.* London: Penguin.

Thorner, H. A. (1981) Notes on the desire for knowledge. *International Journal of Psycho-Analysis*, 62: 73–80.

Thurber, J. (1962) *The Thirteen Clocks*. London: Penguin.

Totton, N. and Jacobs, M. (2001) *Character and Personality Types*. Buckingham: Open University Press.

Walker, M. (1990) *Women in Therapy and Counselling*. Buckingham: Open University Press.

Walker, M. (1992) *Surviving Secrets: The Experience of Abuse for the Child, the Adult and the Helper*. Buckingham: Open University Press.

Walker, M. and Antony-Black, J. (eds) (1999) *Hidden Selves: An Exploration of Multiple Personality*. Buckingham: Open University Press.

Wallis, K. C. and Poulton, J. L. (2001) *Internalization*. Buckingham: Open University Press.

Weatherhead, L. (1963) *Psychology, Religion and Healing* (2nd edn). London: Hodder & Stoughton.

Weegmann, M. and Cohen, R. (eds) (2001) *The Psychodynamics of Addiction*. London: Whurr Publishers.

Winnicott, D. W. (1964) *The Child, the Family and the Outside World*. London: Penguin.

Winnicott, D. W. (1965a) *The Family and Individual Development*. London: Tavistock Publications.

Winnicott, D. W. (1965b) *The Maturational Processes and the Facilitating Environment*. London: Hogarth Press.

Winnicott, D. W. (1971) *Playing and Reality*. London: Routledge.

Winnicott, D. W. (1975) *Collected Papers: Through Paediatrics to Psychoanalysis*. London: Tavistock Publications.

Winnicott, D. W. (1984) The development of the capacity for concern. In D. W. Winnicott, *Deprivation and Delinquency*. London: Tavistock

Winnicott, D. W. (1986) *Home Is Where We Start From*. London: Penguin.

Winnicott, D. W. (1988a) *Babies and Their Mothers*. London: Free Association Books.

Winnicott, D. W. (1988b) *Human Nature*. London: Free Association Books.

Winnicott, D. W. (1989) *Holding and Interpretation: Fragment of an Analysis*. London: Karnac Books.

Wolff, H. (1977) Loss: a central theme in psychotherapy. *British Journal of Psychology*, 50: 11–19.

Worden, J. W. (1991) *Grief Counselling and Grief Therapy* (2nd edn). London: Tavistock.

Zohar, D. (1991) *The Quantum Self*. London: HarperCollins.

INDEX *incomplete*